If not the forgotten man of the Lewis and Clark expedition, William Clark is the recently neglected one. Martin Plamondon looks to correct some of that deficiency with his masterfully crafted maps of the expedition's route; he succeeds admirably. As never before, we can now see clearly the explorers' trail. The course of the Missouri River is accurately laid down with overlays of its past and current path. Campsites are precisely located, while modern and historic names are fixed for points along the way. Plamondon has the gifts of a cartographer: he brings order, precision, and art to a jumbled world of lost camps and legendary sites, of towering cliffs and tangled trails, and of waterways and wavy lines. We find our way with the Corps of Discovery because we now know exactly where they were. William Clark would love these maps.

—Gary E. Moulton, Thomas C. Sorensen Professor of
American History, University of Nebraska (Lincoln)

Mapping the West was one of the central missions of the Lewis and Clark expedition. Like the prairie dogs and plant specimens the explorers sent back to Thomas Jefferson, William Clark's maps simultaneously filled in existing blanks of knowledge and fueled even greater desire to learn more about what lay beyond the western horizon. Martin Plamondon's reconstruction of those maps helps modern-day explorers reconstruct the world that the Corps of Discovery saw with fresh eyes.

—Dayton Duncan, author of *Out West* and *Lewis and Clark:
The Journey of the Corps of Discovery*

This book will be of great value to those of us involved in the management, conservation, and stewardship of the Lewis and Clark National Historic Trail and related natural and cultural resources. We herald Martin Plamondon's important contribution to this rich Lewis and Clark legacy.

—Cynthia Orlando, former superintendent,
Fort Clatsop National Memorial

# LEWIS and CLARK Trail Maps

# LEWIS and CLARK Trail Maps

## A Cartographic Reconstruction, Volume I

**Missouri River between Camp River Dubois (Illinois) and Fort Mandan (North Dakota)—Outbound 1804; Return 1806.**

## Martin Plamondon II

WSU
PRESS

Washington State University Press
Pullman, Washington

**Washington State**
**University**

Washington State University Press
PO Box 645910
Pullman, Washington 99164-5910
Phone: 800-354-7360
Fax: 509-335-8568
E-mail: wsupress@wsu.edu
Web site: www.wsu.edu/wsupress

Library of Congress Cataloging-in-Publication Data

Plamondon, Martin.
    Lewis and Clark trail maps, a cartographic reconstruction, Volume I Missouri River
    between Camp River Dubois (Illinois) and Fort Mandan (North Dakota)—Outbound
    1804; return 1806 / by Martin Plamondon II.
        p. cm.
    Includes bibliographical references and index.
    ISBN 0-87422-232-X (hdb.)—ISBN 0-87422-233-8 (pbk.)
    1. Lewis and Clark National Historic Trail—Maps. 2. Lewis and Clark Expedition
(1804–1806)—Maps. 3. Cartography—Northwestern States—History—Maps. I. Title.

G1417.L4 P5 2000
912.78—dc21
                                                                                    00-042857

Cover art: George Catlin, *View from Floyd's Grave, 1300 Miles above St. Louis*, 1832.
Smithsonian American Art Museum, Gift of Mrs. Joseph Harrison Jr. (1985.66.398).

The WSU Press acknowledges the generous and essential assistance
provided to Martin Plamondon II by the Lewis and Clark Trail Heritage Foundation,
the Governor's Washington Lewis and Clark Trail Committee,
and two anonymous grants in the name of
the Columbia Gorge Interpretive Center, Stevenson, Washington.

# CONTENTS

# DEDICATION

## GENERAL WILLIAM CLARK

Could such a project as this be dedicated to anyone other than William Clark? Without his traverse and his journal descriptions it would have been impossible to have compiled sufficient data to create these maps. Clark poured tireless, patient, and persistent labor into completing a surveyed traverse across 7,000 miles of the West. The treasure he left his country is inestimable.

Meriwether Lewis and William Clark have become like intimate friends to me after my thirty years and literally tens of thousands of hours of research, writing, and mapping. Many were the times in the small hours of the morning, when the house was quiet and the lighting subdued, that, as I wrote or mapped, it seemed as if the two men were seated in the room with me. While I could easily identify with Lewis's temperament, style, talents, and impediments, I found Clark to be the soul on whom I truly leaned. As it is his spirit that I especially appreciate, I find it most appropriate to dedicate this atlas to General William Clark.

# ACKNOWLEDGMENTS

My greatest gratitude goes to my wife, Evelyn, who at first could not understand why I would undertake such a project, and then worried that no one else would care about a concept that drove me on year after year. She eventually became my personal cheerleader. Evelyn has been a source of solace and a font of wisdom during the difficult times. She has been patient, along with my children, when another workstation or card table covered with maps, documents, and cartographic tools showed up somewhere in a crowded house (the project often has required four or five concurrent workstations).

I also thank my mother and father, Marten and Teresa Plamondon, who always have encouraged any dream I wished to pursue. On three occasions they have advanced money allowing me to purchase equipment to continue the project.

I wish to thank all of the members of the Governor's Washington Lewis and Clark Trail Committee. If Evelyn is my cheerleader, they are nothing less than the rally squad! A few have stood out for their encouragement—such as Dick Clifton, Roy Craft, and George Tweney (all deceased), Jack Ritter, Viola Forrest, Carol Simon-Smolinski, Rex Ziak, Gary Lentz, Glen Lindeman, and Robert Carriker. Barbara Kubik, the present chair of the committee, also can be counted on for moral and administrative support at the national level for her involvement in the Lewis and Clark Trail Heritage Foundation. Sharon Tiffany, Executive Director of the Columbia Gorge Interpretive Center, and Ed Callahan probably have given more help than I will ever realize. I must also mention Hazel Bain and Archie Graber (both now deceased) and Ralph Rudeen and his wife Jackie who provided special interest, friendship, and encouragement.

In addition to the Governor's Committee, there have been many other supporters. Dr. E.G. "Frenchy" Chuinard (now deceased) sought financing nearly fifteen years ago. More recently, Joe Mussulman has led a long effort to find funds at the national, state, and corporate level. I would like to thank special supporters like Gary E. Moulton, the editor of the latest edition of *The Journals of the Lewis and Clark Expedition* and Ludd A. Trozpek and Dr. Strode Hinds (deceased) of the Lewis and Clark Trail Heritage Foundation. One cannot forget Cynthia Orlando, one of the finest superintendents ever assigned to the Fort Clatsop National Memorial, who now is in Washington, D.C., administrating National Park Service concessions. To Curt Johnson and all of the staff at Fort Clatsop, I wish to express my gratitude. Thanks also to many people at such places as St. Joseph, Missouri; Sioux City, Iowa; Bismark, North Dakota; Lolo, Montana; Chinook, Washington—anywhere and everywhere along the trail—who provided answers, ideas, and encouragement over the last thirty years. Special thanks go to Kristi K. Lee at the Mobridge, South Dakota, Chamber of Commerce for eleventh-hour information on the grave sites of Sitting Bull.

I cannot forget a good friend and avid supporter, Ruth Strong, who always was full of energy and enthusiasm. Ruth never doubted my ability to complete the *Lewis and Clark Trail Maps,* and never failed to encourage my efforts. My greatest regret is that she did not live to see *Volume I* in print.

A historical cartographic reconstruction of such a vast area demands ceaseless labor and a constant supply of funds for research materials, many hundreds of USGS and other maps, precision technical pens, mapping paper, drafting equipment, and computer supplies. In addition, there are travel, phone, and postage expenses. It is difficult to put a high priority on such expenses when the children need clothes and a roof over their heads. During the last two years, generous financial assistance has come from the Lewis and Clark Trail Heritage Foundation, the Governor's Washington Lewis and Clark Trail Committee, and two anonymous grants in the name of the Columbia Gorge Interpretive Center, Stevenson, Washington. Without this vital financial support—much of it unsolicited—the *Lewis and Clark Trail Maps* might have required another five to ten years to complete. How can one ever express enough gratitude? My thanks are everlasting to all who have helped make this dream a reality.

Martin Plamondon II
Vancouver, Washington
January 16, 2000

# INTRODUCTION

## PURPOSE OF THE *Lewis and Clark Trail Maps*

The landscape along the Lewis and Clark Expedition route has been so greatly altered by the course of nature and the hand of man that it is impossible today to view most of the trail as the Corps of Discovery saw it. On the Missouri and Columbia rivers, where the explorers in 1804-06 struggled mightily against swift currents, treacherous rapids, and shifting sandbars, there often now exist placid lakes. Twenty-four major dams along the route have created over 1,200 miles of reservoir waters. Cities, towns, railroads, highways, airports, pipelines, industrial complexes, dikes, water and sewage treatment plants, modern forestry practices, transmission lines, farms, and homes intrude on much of the trail. Several important rocky landmarks seen by Lewis and Clark have been quarried for fill. The course of the Missouri River from its mouth to mid-Montana has naturally changed hundreds of times since the Corps of Discovery fought its currents. Modern dredging and channelization has had its effects too, and the size of the Missouri has been diminished as municipalities and agriculture along its shores drain it of water.

Considering the two centuries of changes affecting the trail's terrain, a modern cartographic reconstruction offers the best medium to most accurately depict the explorers' route as it really was. This is possible today only because a detailed record of the journey was ordered by President Thomas Jefferson resulting in probably at least eight participants (and possibly one or two others) keeping journals. Two of these journals (that of Private Robert Frazer and possibly Sergeant Nathaniel Pryor) disappeared long ago, as perhaps did the journals of one or two other privates if those men had maintained journals.

Five journals survive today in their original form (i.e., the journals of Captain Meriwether Lewis, Captain William Clark, Sergeant Charles Floyd Jr., Sergeant John Ordway, and Private Joseph Whitehouse). A sixth, that of Sergeant Patrick Gass, was edited by a bookseller and published in 1807, but the original has never been found. Of the surviving accounts, only William Clark's and John Ordway's journals include entries for every single day of the journey. (Possible missing sections of Lewis's and Whitehouse's journals may come to light someday.) These accounts, particularly Clark's and Lewis's, preserve the traverse recorded by Captain Clark—a listing of directions and distances between significant geographical points and features from one end of the expedition's route to the other.

The *Lewis and Clark Trail Maps* represent a reconstruction of the vital traverse surveyed by William Clark after the Corps of Discovery left their winter encampment at Wood River (or River Dubois) and set out up the Missouri River on May 14, 1804. These maps are intended as a resource for historians and scholars to study and gain a better understanding of the Lewis and Clark Expedition. The atlas will be useful, too, for people who design interpretive projects along the trails. Hopefully, these maps will serve as teaching tools for our youth as well, in their own intellectual journeys of exploration and discovery. Persons who have poured over the hundreds of pages of the expedition's journals will find in these maps a refreshing new way to view the Lewis and Clark venture—to see, understand, and relate to the topography as it really was. For those individuals having had little exposure to the journals or other accounts of the expedition, the *Lewis and Clark Trail Maps* offer a unique way to get acquainted with the expedition, and perhaps provoke further interest in studying the journals themselves. For those who are fascinated with cartography, who can sit down with a map and lose all sense of time, may the *Lewis and Clark Trail Maps* provide enjoyment.

## CAPTAIN WILLIAM CLARK

William Clark was born in Caroline County, Virginia, on August 1, 1770, the youngest of six brothers in a family of ten siblings. The Clarks were considered members of the Virginia gentry and some of them knew the Washingtons as well as the Jeffersons. All of William's brothers served with distinction in the Revolutionary War, and several eventually became ranking officers in the military. The eldest, General George Rogers Clark, was granted authority by Governor Patrick Henry and the Virginia general assembly to secure the Illinois country for the rebelling colonies. The Virginia assembly promised to pay the expenses of the campaign, but never did. Consequently, it was the Clark family fortune that helped field the small force that conquered this vast area for the new republic. Deep in debt at the end of the war, the family moved west over the mountains to the Falls of the Ohio in Kentucky. There it was that young William learned the art of surveying land, a skill regarded with much respect in the young, expanding nation.

Beginning about 1789, William Clark served as a militiaman and eventually became a U.S. Army officer (1791) in campaigns against American Indians, including the Battle of Fallen Timbers in the Ohio country in 1794. The army utilized the brave young lieutenant's engineering talents to design and build fortifications, and Clark was sent on two missions to the lower Ohio and Mississippi to observe Spanish military operations in Louisiana. His commanding officer, General "Mad" Anthony Wayne, was so impressed by Clark's observations that Clark's reports were passed on to President Washington.

In 1796, Meriwether Lewis served in a company of riflemen under Clark's command and the two men became good friends. A few months later Clark resigned his captaincy and left the army—perhaps partly because of health reasons and his tiring of military life, but mostly at the urging of his family to help them out of their financial distress. For the next seven years, Clark maintained the family plantation. He was determined to find a way to end the constant harassment of his family by creditors. After President Jefferson took office in 1801, Clark visited the family friend, hoping that Jefferson could convince Virginia or the Federal Congress to settle the war debts owed the Clark family.

In 1803 it is possible that Jefferson, aware of the broken promises to the Clark family, may have himself proposed that Clark, who otherwise was well qualified, be invited to join the Corps of Discovery as second in command to Lewis. Jefferson's cabinet officers seemed quite pleased to have Clark added to the expedition; at least one of them had reservations about Lewis's impulsiveness. It is probable that Lewis requested that Clark, his former commanding officer, be given equal rank with himself. However, the army assigned Clark a commission as a lieutenant in the corps of artillerists, with pay equal to that of Captain Lewis. This news arrived in early May 1804, just before the newly formed expedition was preparing to set out up the Missouri. Lewis insisted that the men not be informed of Clark's true rank, that Clark be addressed as "Captain" and be treated as his own equal by the men of the Corps of Discovery.

## EXPEDITION SURVEYING

Frontier surveying, according to surveying manuals of the times, was theoretically not any different than ordinary surveying. The nature of the frontier wilderness, however, tended to hinder the preferred methods of the day. Clark faced the prospect of surveying an open-ended traverse several thousand miles long. His willingness to take on such a project says much about his determination and ability.

The accepted way to survey between two points, when measuring with a surveyor's chain was not possible, was by means of a triangle. Using a transit (a telescope on a tripod) set up on the first point, the surveyor sighted across the landscape to a distant point. A tall pole, perhaps with a ribbon tied to it, was positioned at the distant point. A crew of men may have had to clear trees and brush to allow the surveyor to establish a line of sight between the two points. A sighting compass would be used to determine the angular difference between the line and north. The surveyor then turned an angle (ninety degrees) to the left or right, depending upon which direction was more convenient. A line of sight was then cleared along the second line. A distance, convenient to the surveyor, was then carefully measured along this base line. The surveyor checked the angle between the two lines several times to assure accuracy and then

moved the transit to the other end of the base line. Then he sighted back through the telescope along the base line, known as a "back sight." The surveyor then turned the instrument until he could see through it the tall pole at the far end of his first sight line. Again, a crew of men may have had to clear a line of sight to that point. The angle between the base line and the third line of sight (the hypotenuse) was turned several times to obtain an average value of the angle, and the degrees, minutes, and seconds of the angle were carefully noted. All of this information was then recorded in the surveyor's field book, from which he could later calculate the distance between the two original points by using principles of geometry and trigonometry. From knowledge of the two base angles and the length of the base line he could determine the distance of the original sight line.

Frequently, a surveyor had difficulty seeing between two chosen points; trying to measure distances that were too great or getting a line of sight cleared in a timely fashion were typical obstacles faced by frontier surveyors. (In Clark's situation, he was faced with an exceptionally long distance—from the mouth of the Missouri River to the Pacific Ocean—and an ever twisting route. Along that route would be hundreds of features to measure and map. This could not be done with a single surveyed triangle; hundreds of triangles would be required.)

After six to twelve triangles were laid out along the chosen course the surveyor was faced with the prospect of having to lay out several more triangles in a great loop back to the start. This preferred method, called "closed traverse," allowed the surveyor to check his methods and mathematics and produce the most accurate results. If he ended at the starting point (a rare occurrence) he could move on, otherwise the error(s) had to be located and corrected before proceeding to the next loop of triangles.

For a lengthy course, the surveyor would make a list of the original sight lines for each triangle along the route, ignoring the closing triangles. He would enter the direction (bearing) and length (distance) of each line. When combined, this long list of entries would constitute the "traverse," the surveyed route across the land. From this traverse mapmakers could subsequently plot maps of the surveyed area.

It would have taken decades to survey the western two-thirds of the continent using the preferred traverse method described above, involving one to two hundred loops, each composed of as many as two dozen triangles. The original sight line of each triangle might be as short as a quarter mile or as long as seven or eight miles. Men would have had to clear thousands of miles of brush and trees. This simply was not possible within the one- to two-year time frame of the Lewis and Clark Expedition.

President Jefferson, a surveyor himself, was aware of the surveying problems his explorers might face, but he mistakenly assumed that the expedition's entire track (or at least nearly so) would be on water. He hoped for no more than a half-day portage over the dividing ridge of the Rocky Mountains. Therefore, Jefferson instructed Lewis to use the "log line" to assist in measuring the length of the lines along the rivers. He reasoned that this would eliminate the need for laying out triangles and clearing brush. The log line, devised as a means of determining the speed of a ship at sea, was simply a piece of cord of known length with a wooden object attached to one end. Jefferson envisioned that the surveyor would stand on a point of land or a downed tree trunk jutting out into the water and drop the wooden float into the current. The line would play out from its reel as the current took the float downstream. The surveyor would observe the time that it took for the current to draw out the measured length of line, thereby determining the speed of the river's current, and then factor the distance between two points along the river. Unfortunately, the log line did not work well in the large rivers of the West because of their broad, sweeping curves, debris-laden waters, and complex currents. Clark noted the shortcomings of this system in his journal on July 17, 1804.

It is apparent that the distances in the expedition's traverse were not very accurate. The discrepancies tend to correlate fairly well with the limitations of the log line. Normally, Clark was twenty-five to forty percent too long in his distances on water with the variance tending, as might be expected, to be greater in the longer distances than in the short calls.

Because of the great limitations of using a transit to survey the legs of the traverse using the triangular method described above, Clark often chose to rely on the much simpler, but somewhat less accurate, sighting compass. This instrument was large—five to six inches across—and mounted on a single leg; a swivel mount or sometimes a tripod held the sighting compass. It was with a sighting compass that Clark determined the bearings or directions of the traverse. Using the single pole mount, Clark may have taken his sights from the forward deck of the keelboat when the craft was sufficiently steady. Unfortunately, such a compass can be adversely affected by local magnetic anomalies such as large mineral deposits in nearby hills that contain enough native iron to interfere with the magnetic flux lines of the planet. The expedition also carried a number of iron objects on the boat. Storing them too close to the compass or moving them about the deck when readings were being taken could have affected the compass.

Use of the sighting compass also introduced the problem of magnetic declination. The magnetic poles, at the south and north ends of the planet, are the terminal points of the magnetic flux, or force field, that radiates in great loops around the planet. The compass needle aligns itself with these lines of flux, thereby pointing to the magnetic poles. Unfortunately, the magnetic poles are not located at the geographic north and south poles of the earth. They also tend to move over time. Because of this lack of pole alignment, a compass does not indicate "true north." It indicates "magnetic north," the direction to the magnetic pole. One has to know the "angle of declination," which is the angle of variation between the magnetic pole and the geographic pole when taking a compass reading. There is also the problem that the angle will be different moving east or west, or north and south. Consequently, as one moves across the continent to the west, the size of the angle grows from about four degrees in St. Louis to about twenty-three degrees on the Pacific Coast. These values from the second half of the twentieth century are only a little different from the early 1800s.

The phenomenon of magnetic declination was known well before Clark's time; the first reliable declination chart of the world was produced by Edmund Halley in 1702. It is obvious, when plotting Clark's traverse, that he ignored declination; the traverse constantly turns in a clockwise direction out of alignment with the landscape. Fortunately, it was not a major cartographic difficulty to adjust the traverse for the *Lewis and Clark Trail Maps*. This subject will be taken up in more detail in *Volume II,* which depicts a part of the trail were declination is a more serious issue.

Clark also employed an octant and a sextant—the standard navigational tools used to determine latitude and longitude—to position major points of the traverse into the matrix of the geophysical world. Taking a sighting from the stars with these instruments, particularly the heavy sextant, was not easy. Good sightings depended upon having substantial experience, upper body strength, and the stamina to hold the instrument steady for lengthy periods of time. A problem with longitude findings was having an accurate timepiece. The explorers possessed a good watch, but the instrument was not designed for arduous overland travel. Lewis had much difficulty with the watch. It filled with sand and dirt, stopping its operation on several occasions. It was not waterproof and ended up in the water at least once. Occasionally, Lewis forgot to wind it. Resetting the timepiece after it had stopped required a series of precise sightings over several days. The net result was that it became less accurate with each incident.

There were other complications relating to the bearings they took. It appears that Clark made most of the sightings and notations himself. However, someone assisted Clark,

## CAMP RIVER DUBOIS, WINTER ENCAMPMENT 1803–04

Camp River Dubois, December 12, 1803, to May 14, 1804, was the initial winter quarters of the Corps of Volunteers for Northwestern Discovery, informally known as the Lewis and Clark Expedition. The site, also known as Camp Wood, was located on the east side of the Mississippi River, about fifteen miles north of St. Louis. Early in 1803, it had been Captain Meriwether Lewis's intention to have the expedition spend the first winter several hundred miles up the Missouri River, but his plans suffered several delays in the summer and fall of 1803. He spent much of the summer waiting on the delayed construction of a keelboat and subsequently had to toil mile by mile down the draught-stricken Ohio River. It was October 15 by the time Lewis reached the Louisville-Clarksville area and the Falls of the Ohio River. There he spent nearly two weeks, being joined by William Clark and a number of men who would eventually become part of a group of civilian enlistees known as the Nine Young Men from Kentucky.

When they arrived in St. Louis, Spanish authorities blocked their journey up the Missouri River. Hence, the Corps spent the winter of 1803–04 at Camp River Dubois, waiting for the transfer of the newly purchased Louisiana Territory to the United States. During that winter, the size of the party increased nearly fourfold and Lewis in the St. Louis locality used army funds to buy thousands of pounds of pork, potatoes, turnips, dried apples, and anything else they thought might be useful during the expedition.

Captain William Clark spent most of his days at Camp Dubois, first supervising the construction of huts and then training new recruits. Clark drew a number of crude sketches of a fort or encampment structure, as though considering different possibilities. These sketches were drawn on a large scrap of paper on the first sheet of his Camp Wood Journal. Various notes and journal entries were written over the sketches. The drawing reproduced here represents what appears to be the only completed sketch. There is no evidence, other than its completeness, that this was the plan used for the winter encampment. It seems almost too large and complex to serve as a temporary quarters; however, Clark was an army engineer of fortifications, so it is possible. The original sketch is no more than a couple of inches in size and contains no dimensions, orientation, or indication of room uses. Neither Clark nor Lewis commented in the journals as to any specifics regarding the structures. All that is known today is that the encampment was a collection of log huts.

It is important to realize that since Lewis and Clark's time, the confluence of the Mississippi and Missouri rivers has moved about three miles southeast. In the decades following the expedition's return, the Mississippi River ate away at its eastern bank until its bed moved more than a mile east, gobbling up the bottomland claimed there by early settlers (see Map Number 1). The Mississippi has moved so far east that the global position of Camp River Dubois appears to no longer be in Illinois. Its current location is west of the river, in Missouri. The actual soil upon which the encampment stood has long since washed down to the Gulf of Mexico.

Several scholars have argued that the Lewis and Clark Expedition began in Pittsburgh, Washington, D.C., or at Monticello. Clark began his traverse, mile 0, at the mouth of the Wood River, which is where the *Lewis and Clark Trail Maps* begin.

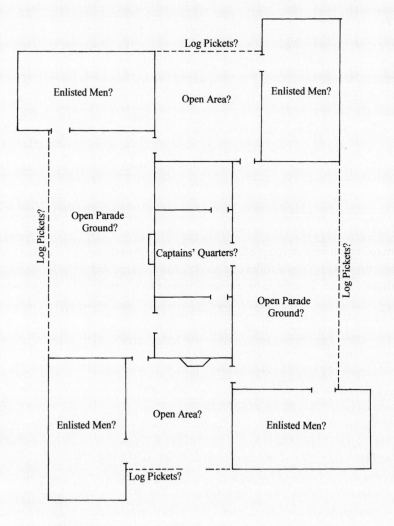

probably Private John B. Thompson, who had been a surveyor prior to joining the expedition. It appears likely that Private Joseph Whitehouse also may have helped. During the day, notations and observations were recorded on scraps of paper. In the evenings, Clark transferred the data to his deerskin-covered field book—although it appears that this was not necessarily a nightly exercise. On July 14, 1804, the survey notations for most of two days were lost when they blew overboard in a sudden storm. Later, in the evening, Clark and his journal keepers scrambled to reconstruct what they remembered regarding bearings and distances. This indicates that others beside Clark were involved in surveying the traverse, and their possible discrepancies in procedure might also account for some of the inaccuracies.

The system used to record bearings—north or south, the number of degrees, and west or east—though common, is prone to human error from reversing or mishearing a call or simply because of confusion due to fatigue or diverted attention. Sometimes errors are evident that probably occurred due to these instances. There is a strong likelihood at times that local anomalies affected compass readings; naturally, there is no way of knowing if metal objects had been moved about the boat unbeknownst to Clark.

There also were opportunities for mistakes when the data in the field book records was transferred to a journal. At a few locations along the route, when the party camped for extended periods, Clark also would remove specially protected bound volumes from lead-sealed, metal boxes. Then he would copy all entries into these bound volumes, assuring a backup record in case the originals were lost.

For whatever the reason, Clark's measurements occasionally are totally implausible; if accepted, they would have placed the men and their boats several miles out on the plains. There was little that could be done in such instances except to continue filling in the traverse to identifiable points and hope the aberrant heading would show itself.

## Clark's Mapping Efforts

U.S. Treasurer Albert Gallatin wrote to President Jefferson on March 14, 1803, noting that he had requested Nicholas King, Surveyor of the City of Washington, to draft a comprehensive map of the West. The resulting map had a longitude and latitude grid showing the lower course of the Missouri River (which had been known by fur traders for many years) as well as the Pacific Coast (which was charted by Captain George Vancouver of the Royal Navy and other European and American seaborne explorers and traders from 1778 to the 1790s). The map was incomplete, of course, because vast portions of the interior West were yet unknown to Americans and Europeans. It was intended that Lewis and Clark's discoveries would supply information to fill the conspicuous blanks in the middle of the map.

Furnished only with the longitude and latitude coordinates for the Mandan villages (recorded by the Canadian fur trader and astronomer David Thompson) and for the frontier community of St. Louis on the Mississippi River, as well as the coordinates of the Columbia River's mouth on the Pacific Coast, Clark gave it his utmost to fulfill this assignment. His cartographic efforts were remarkable, considering that he apparently took along no specially gridded mapping paper, nor even a supply of large sheets for the purpose of sketching. It appears, he had to use variously sized scraps and pieces of paper for his field maps and drawings.

It should be remembered that Clark's charge as a surveyor was to observe, measure, and record data—and later submit this information to professional cartographers for them to lay it out in detail. Despite all of the limitations, obstacles, and pressures of helping lead an expedition in the wilderness, Clark performed his duties with integrity, consistency, and unsurpassed thoroughness. In the day-to-day recording of data and creating his sketch maps, Clark's intuitive sense of geography and topography, plus his surveying skills, meshed with his ability to carefully consolidate information from various sources. First of all, he noted the data that he personally could observe and record about the terrain. Normally he was with the main party, meaning he took most of his observations from one of the boats or when they were stopped on shore. Added to this was data relayed to him by Lewis from his wanderings and observations away from the main group. Lewis, more often than Clark, made excursions to observe flora, fauna, and noteworthy topographical features in any given area. Additionally, Clark consulted with expedition members who had been sent out on hunting ventures or other assignments requiring them to travel away from the main party. It appears, as evidenced by the journal entries, that Clark showed his sketch maps to the men for verification.

Clark also queried the natives they met, carefully noting the information received from them, and he brought back a number of maps based on their perceptions. The Minnetaree of present-day North Dakota knew the upper Missouri well because of their frequent forays into that area. More useful information came from the Rocky Mountain tribes and those farther west, particularly because these peoples relied on rivers as major travel routes by canoe or on foot or horseback. They were cognizant of distances and geological and natural features along the waterways.

In the years immediately after his return to St. Louis, Clark produced an amazingly accurate overall map of the West. When a properly scaled copy of Clark's final map is placed over a modern map of the western United States, as shown in John Logan Allen's *Passage through the Garden* for example, they align closely. There is a discrepancy of only a few dozen miles across the entire breadth of the West. It seems incredible that Clark could have created such an accurate map when the distances he used in the traverse were often far off the mark. However, in Clark's day surveyors expected errors in setting bearings of a traverse despite their best efforts. Experience had shown them, however, that errors tended to be consistent.

Even though Clark appears to have had a natural bent for the discipline of mapping as an adjunct to surveying, he was by no means a master cartographer. His post-expedition map of 1810 has no decorative border, no formal title block, no fancy lettering, and no scale. The map is laid out with longitude and latitude only, as would be typical for a surveyor. The map, with its more careful lettering, is more polished than those Clark made in the field and shows his effort to consolidate his many sources of information, but the lack of artistic organization makes it obvious that his training was not in mapmaking. Clark's 1810 manuscript map was the basis, with some modification, of Samuel Lewis's finely crafted "Map of Lewis and Clark's Track, across the Western Portion of North America," which was included in the official account of the expedition in 1814.

Upon the return of the expedition, it is important to note that Clark expected scientists, naturalists, mathematicians, and cartographers to dedicate themselves to gleaning the massive amount of information in the journals concerning ethnology, natural history, geography, and topography. He expected that the recorded data provided by his survey would be utilized to produce carefully detailed, large-scale maps of the territory explored. This, amazingly, did not happen.

It is easily forgotten today that in 1806 a primary goal of the expedition had ended in failure. The Corps of Discovery had been sent to locate and report on an all-water trade route to the West Coast—a Northwest Passage providing merchants with access to the Pacific Ocean and the riches of the Orient. It had been mistakenly expected, perhaps largely due to wishful thinking, that only a short, half-day portage across the continental divide would be required to connect navigable river routes in the Missouri and Columbia watersheds. What they found instead on the outbound trip was an overland portage across 360 miles of rugged mountains, plus other difficult river portages on the Columbia River and its major tributary, as well as at the Great Falls on the Missouri River. Their report

drove the last nail into the coffin of the centuries-long quest for a practicable Northwest Passage between Atlantic waters and the Pacific Ocean. The American public of the early 1800s, with the exception of the fur seekers and some in government, lacked the vision to see anything of much value in the Trans-Mississippi West. Hence, the anticipated highly detailed professional maps were not drawn and many copies of the journals, when published in 1814, went unsold.

It appears that Clark drew more than one hundred maps covering much of the expedition's route. However, the vast majority of the the existing maps known to have been made by Clark start at the Mandan villages in North Dakota and continue to the Pacific Ocean. There also are maps done by Clark for the alternate return routes, when the Corps separated into several detachments in 1806. With the exception of data for a general overall map sent back with the keelboat in early 1805, there are no known maps by the explorer that plot the journey in 1804 from the mouth of the Missouri northwest to the Mandan villages. As Gary Moulton points out in the atlas of *The Journals of the Lewis and Clark Expedition,* there is considerable evidence that Clark drew twenty-nine detailed maps (copies of which apparently were sent downriver with the keelboat) depicting the Missouri from its mouth to the Mandan villages, but these have never been found. However, they may have a connection to seventeen maps from the Omaha, Nebraska, vicinity north to the Mandan villages that were the property of Maximilian, Prince of Wied-Neuwied. Maximilian visited Clark in St. Louis in 1833, where he is reported to have acquired copies of maps to assist him in his scientific and investigative travels up the Missouri River. Moulton believes that these may have been drawn from Clark's original maps for the lower Missouri.

This author would modify Moulton's view somewhat by suggesting that the Maximilian maps were copied, not from Clark's maps drawn during the expedition, but probably from another set that Clark updated during the years when he served in his official capacities in St. Louis. Due to his appointment as Indian agent, Clark's attention became focused on the Missouri and Yellowstone areas for which he needed accurate, detailed maps. Furthermore, there are too many inconsistencies in style between the Maximilian maps and the existing expedition maps. Whereas the surviving expedition maps are little more than sketches, the Maximilian maps appear larger in scale and show greater detail than was typical of the maps Clark drew beyond Fort Mandan. At the time of the Lewis and Clark Expedition, the Missouri from its mouth to the Mandan villages was fairly well known. Several major maps already existed for that length of the river. Perhaps, it does not make sense that

Clark would have put more time and effort into mapping this section of the Missouri than he would for the "unknown" area beyond the Mandan villages. In St. Louis as a government official, Clark probably set about the work himself of updating maps for the geographical areas most pertinent to his Indian affairs work. He would have done this by increasing the scale, adding details from his journal entries, notes, and personal knowledge gained during the expedition, and from interviewing the steady stream of Indians, fur traders, government agents, and adventurers that trekked to his St. Louis office.

## Constructing the *Lewis and Clark Trail Maps*

The *Lewis and Clark Trail Maps* are a series of over five-hundred maps, planned in three volumes, covering the entire route of the Lewis and Clark Expedition from Camp River Dubois to the Pacific Ocean and the return to St. Louis. All of the trail maps are presented in uniform detail and style. For those segments of the return journey which retraced the westbound trek, both routes are depicted on the same maps. Each map has an identifying title and number. In *Volume I,* the maps begin at the mouth of the Missouri River and continue consecutively to the Mandan villages vicinity. Expedition-era data is shown in solid lines and fonts. Modern data is indicated by dotted lines and a dot matrix font. For further details, refer to the Legend on Plate VI.

The making of these maps began with a detailed study of the Lewis and Clark journals' data and maps plus other relevant historic maps, documents, and accounts, usually of a later date. In addition, modern U.S. Geological Survey and other maps have proven to be indispensable, as have, in some cases, aerial photographs. Additional information was provided by knowledgeable individuals and agencies who generously answered inquiries.

Many of these reference materials prove more useful for the Snake and Columbia river systems, rather than the Missouri, which has constantly changed its course. Many persons have recommended the Missouri River Commission Maps as the final reference guide to the Missouri as it would have been known to Lewis and Clark. However, the commission maps were drawn up nearly ninety years after the expedition returned—in the interim, the Missouri had shifted its course and channels hundreds of times. Consequently, the commission maps had little to contribute to the cartographic reconstruction project. Local tradition also was considered, but generally was not relevant to the reconstruction of the traverse. Even Clark's own field maps served only as rough guides in the work, since the traverse could not be directly applied to them.

On the *Lewis and Clark Trail Maps,* expedition campsites and Indian burial grounds and village sites are shown at exact locations only if these places are properly protected and supervised. All other such sites are only generally located. Every effort has been made to discourage the digging for artifacts. Such action is illegal on public lands and constitutes unlawful trespass on private property without the knowledge of the property owner. In the case of Native American sites and burial grounds, disturbing or taking artifacts is a direct affront to their religious beliefs and usually against the law.

The selection of journal quotations included on the maps was based on the importance of the topic covered and the space available on the map. Clark and Ordway were favored because they were the only members of the expedition with an entry for every day of the journey, and they were faithful and meticulous in their observations. Lewis, who was intermittent in his writing, came next, and then Whitehouse and Floyd (until his death early in the expedition). Gass is also used, although his words were edited and reshaped by an editor in 1807 and his original journal is gone.

Clark was the expedition's principal journalist. During those periods when Lewis was making entries in his journal, Clark dutifully copied Lewis. Apparently, Clark soon tired of tediously copying Lewis's long descriptions and returned to his eloquently simple and descriptive spelling and syntax. Clark (and perhaps often Lewis) usually wrote entries while sitting around a campfire at night with Ordway, Gass, Whitehouse, Floyd, and others. As such, they must have discussed the entries, with the others assimilating Clark's notes in their own hand and words. Lewis's journal, however, is filled with long descriptions of the flora, fauna, and other scientific topics. Excerpts from these parts of Lewis's journal generally are not suited for placement on the *Lewis and Clark Trail Maps.*

In general, quotes on the *Lewis and Clark Trail Maps* were mainly taken from Clark, but other journalists were chosen when they better described an event or feature. Sometimes, differing journal accounts of the same event were chosen. On the maps, quotes for the outbound journey are shown with an arrow pointing to the right after the journalist's name; the return trip quotes are identified with an arrow pointing left.

On the *Lewis and Clark Trail Maps,* the journals are quoted verbatim—spelling, grammar, punctuation, etc. In the days of the Lewis and Clark Expedition, Noah Webster had yet to create his dictionary. Spelling was a relative art form and most people spelled phonetically. The spellings in all of the men's journals, except for Gass's edited journal, are anything but consistent, and at times are challenging to read. On the *Lewis and Clark Trail Maps,* the journal quotes are printed in a script font, and enclosed in quotation marks. Very short descriptive remarks—such as Strong Water or Banks Falling In—generally are not exactly as they appear in the journals. They are typed in script to show that they reflect the observations of the journalists, but have no quotation marks around them.

The name Sacagawea was spelled several different ways by the journalists, but Clark and Ordway carefully broke down the name into its phonetic parts, spelling it with a "g"—Sacagawea. Today this is the federal government's officially accepted spelling, though other spellings are still in use.

## A Brief History of the Expedition

The Corps of Volunteers for Northwestern Discovery, commonly known as the Lewis and Clark Expedition or the Corps of Discovery, was organized by the federal government in 1803. It was the successful culmination of Thomas Jefferson's long-term desire to have the far western regions of North America explored and secured for the American people. President Jefferson believed that to be a great nation, the United States needed access to both the Pacific and Atlantic oceans. He had been able to convince Congress to support the expedition, not primarily as an act of expansion and scientific inquiry, but as encouragement of the western fur trade by establishing relations with the Indians and as an effort to secure a prosperous commerce with China, which was then dominated by British merchants. Jefferson, like many others, was convinced that a "Northwest Passage" to the Orient lay up the Missouri River, with only a short crossing of the "Stony Mountains" to access rivers flowing to the Pacific.

The expedition was a military mission and the U.S. Army provided most of the supplies, weapons, materials, and men. As already mentioned, Jefferson chose his personal secretary and long-time family friend, Captain Meriwether Lewis, to lead the exploration. A second in command also was needed for the endeavor. This author believes it is possible that Jefferson, consulting with Lewis, may well have asked to invite their mutual friend, William Clark, to join the Corps of Discovery. Clark was a former army officer and had been Lewis's commander on the frontier several years before. The Jeffersons, too, had known the Clark family in Virginia.

Lewis asked that Clark, then residing in Indiana Territory, be given a captain's rank and share co-equally in the leadership. Jefferson agreed, but the army eventually rejected the request. Few officers' positions were available in the peacetime army; consequently, Clark was assigned the lesser rank of second-lieutenant although he received the same pay as Lewis. Months later, upon hearing of the army's decision, Lewis would insist that the expedition's men not be told about Clark's actual rank, and that Clark would have equal standing with Lewis before them as a "Captain."

In late 1803, the two leaders led a party of soldiers and civilians, including prospective recruits, down the Ohio River to St. Louis, which was the gateway to the upper Louisiana country. In 1800, Napoleon Bonaparte of France had diplomatically wrested ownership of Louisiana from the Spanish Empire. Louisiana extended west from the Mississippi River to the crest of the Rockies, encompassing most of the Great Plains and the entire Missouri watershed. Before a ceremonial transfer of title to France could be conducted in remote Spanish-dominated St. Louis, Napoleon already had agreed to sell this vast territory—the same which the American expedition intended to cross to reach the Pacific—to United States negotiators. This fortuitous event alleviated Jefferson's need to continue delicate consultations with foreign ambassadors to allow an American expedition seeking "geographical knowledge" to venture through land claimed by a European power.

When Lewis and Clark arrived in the St. Louis area in November 1803, however, the Spanish yet remained in control and refused to let the explorers pass. The Corps of Discovery spent the winter north of St. Louis at Camp Wood (River Dubois) at the junction of the Mississippi and Missouri rivers in Illinois Territory. Here, men were recruited and supplies and equipment were assembled for the journey. The ever-active Clark also made a map of the local region (it was sent to Jefferson in May 1804). In the spring, ownership of Louisiana Territory was ceremonially transferred from Spain, to France, and to the United States in the short span of two days, March 9–10, 1804. The door was now open and the expedition set out up the swollen spring flood of the Missouri on May 14, 1804.

Approximately forty-five men (the exact number remains unknown at this stage of the expedition) forced their way upstream in a large, flat-bottomed keelboat and two wide-bottomed pirogues or dugout canoes. They spent the entire summer pushing their way against the Missouri's flow, as Clark surveyed the traverse and the captains counseled with Indians, observed the flora, fauna, and topography, and maintained their journals along with the three sergeants and at least two of the privates. Sergeant Charles Floyd succumbed to what is believed to have been a ruptured appendix on August 20, 1804, near present-day Sioux City, Iowa. He was the only expedition member to die during the journey and the first U.S. soldier buried west of the Mississippi River.

The captains held several amicable councils with the native peoples, including the Kickapoo, Oto, Missouri, and Yankton

Sioux. However, on September 25, 1804, a battle nearly erupted with the war-like Teton Sioux near present-day Pierre, South Dakota, largely because the Indians felt the newcomers would challenge the Sioux's desire to control trade in the region. The Teton particularly wanted to deny trade goods and weapons to their rivals—the Arikara, Mandan, and Minnetaree—occupying fortified, permanent villages further upriver. Fortunately, cooler heads prevailed in the standoff and hostilities were avoided.

The first season of travel ended in late October 1804 while amongst the semi-sedentary agriculturists, the Mandan and Minnetaree, near present-day Bismarck, North Dakota. The explorers built a small fortification called Fort Mandan to shelter them through the winter. Despite a few minor alarms, it would be a calm but severely cold winter at Fort Mandan.

Some members of the expedition knew Indian sign language and spoke French, which was useful for communicating with the several French Canadian traders in the Indian villages. To further facilitate communication with the Mandan and Arikara people, however, the captains hired a local trader, Toussaint Charbonneau, and his young pregnant wife, Sacagawea, to serve as interpreters. In addition to speaking French, Charbonneau knew the local Indian dialects but he spoke little English. Sacagawea was a Shoshone from the Rocky Mountains who, in addition to her native tongue, could speak Minnetaree. When a girl, she had been captured by a raiding Minnetaree band at the Missouri headwaters and brought back to the mid-Missouri, eventually becoming one of Charbonneau's two wives. Through the winter, Lewis and Clark learned from the Indians that a short, single portage over the Rockies did not exist; rather, there were many difficult mountain ranges to overcome. Crossing them would require many days of travel and horses to haul equipment. Sacagawea's people, the Shoshone, who lived in these mountains, had many horses and knew the locations of mountain passes.

On April 7, 1805, the captains sent the keelboat back down the Missouri River with a crew of about a dozen or so men, along with specimens of newly discovered flora, fauna, and minerals to be sent to Jefferson. The expedition of thirty-three persons, including Charbonneau, Sacagawea, and their newborn infant Jean Baptiste, headed west in the two pirogues and six smaller canoes toward the "Shining Mountains" and the Pacific Ocean which lay beyond. On the upper Great Plains, the men marveled at the continuing spectacle of wildlife. They saw hundreds of thousands of roaming bison on the grass-covered plains, their dark hides turning the prairie black. Plains elk, mule deer, and antelope also grazed there. Provisioning was easy on the plains. The ultimate sporting adventure proved to

be encounters with the plains grizzly, a monster of a bear that could take a half-dozen rifle balls, even to the vitals, while pursuing desperately frightened assailants.

By July they had crossed into what is now Montana and toiled through the astonishingly beautiful Missouri River Breaks, an intricately eroded complex of gullies, buttes, and rock outcrops. Next, they had to haul their canoes and baggage eighteen miles around the impassable Great Falls of the Missouri, an especially strenuous portage that delayed their progress for a month. Continuing upriver, they entered the first ranges of the Rockies, calling a canyon passage through it the Gates of the Mountains.

Many weeks passed as they struggled up the diminishing tributaries, now pulling the canoes by hand, while looking for the elusive Shoshone. Since leaving the Fort Mandan vicinity, the explorers had traveled in solitude, not meeting with any natives. At long last, they finally encountered Sacagawea's kinspeople just where she said they would be—near the continental divide between a Missouri tributary in present-day Montana and the Salmon River country of today's Idaho. The Shoshone band proved to be the very same one that Sacagawea belonged to before her capture by roaming Minnetarees, and the chief, Cameahwait, was none other than her own brother. It was a joyous reunion for Sacagawea.

After acquiring the essential packhorses and a Shoshone guide, the expedition continued north into the Bitterroot country. There they met the Flathead tribe and proceeded on to what Lewis called "Traveler's Rest" at the junction of Lolo Creek and the Bitterroot River (near modern-day Missoula, Montana), reaching this point on September 9, 1805. After some replenishment, they turned west toward Lolo Pass and a difficult Indian track through the labyrinth of forested mountains in central Idaho. It proved to be a difficult crossing of nine days. Snow fell, there was no game, and the cold and wet men were reduced to exhaustion and near starvation. They emerged from the mountains onto Weippe Prairie in Idaho and were befriended by a band of Nez Perce who came to their aid.

Here they left their horses with the Nez Perce, built pine dugout canoes (near Orofino, Idaho), and paddled down the Clearwater and Snake river canyons, accompanied by a couple of Nez Perce chiefs to serve as guides and provide introductions to the numerous mid-Columbia River tribes residing downriver. By now the Corps had left the forests behind and entered the prairies and sagebrush lands of eastern Washington. They arrived at the Snake-Columbia confluence on October 16, 1805, where they encountered large crowds of native people coming to visit them.

Two days later they continued down the Columbia. In the days ahead, Mt. Hood became visible off to the west—an indication to the explorers that they finally were nearing their goal. The 11,235-feet volcano was known to sea captain explorers of the 1790s whose accounts had been reported on the East Coast and in Europe. Other snow-capped volcanoes in the Cascade Range likewise were seen. At Celilo Falls on October 22, they encountered the upper Chinook people. This impressive horseshoe-shaped cataract was a key salmon fishery that sustained many bands in the region. After portaging around Celilo Falls, the expedition also had to work its way through the Short Narrows and the Long Narrows at The Dalles, further serious obstacles to river travel.

Upon entering the Cascade Range, they paddled into the lengthy Columbia River gorge, a place of matchless beauty where cliffs and ramparts jut to 3,000 feet above the broad river. As they proceeded westward, they sighted spectacular waterfalls, vast forests of 200-feet high evergreen trees, massive basaltic pillars, and deeply shadowed bottomlands thick with maple trees draped in heavy moss.

There was one more significant obstacle to river travel to overcome: the Cascade Rapids of the Columbia River. Centuries before, a great earth and rock slide had temporarily dammed the water's passage at this place. When the impounded river broke free, it possibly left a natural bridge that later collapsed, filling the river with huge, house-sized boulders. For the expedition, another laborious portage was mandatory at the Cascades. Just below the Cascade Rapids, however, stood 840-feet high Beacon Rock, marking the beginning of tidewater, the signs of which the Corps observed. Had the explorers known, they were only 141 miles from the ocean!

The lands of various Chinook tribes and bands continued to the mouth of the Columbia River. Dozens of their villages consisting of large, cedar-plank longhouses were situated along that distance. Each dwelling could house about ten to twenty families, but it puzzled Clark to see how few of the longhouses were actually occupied. He never realized that Old World plagues and diseases, inadvertently brought by Spanish, American, and British explorers and traders, had decimated more than half of the native population, and nearly destroyed their culture.

After leaving the Columbia River gorge, the Corps had entered the broad "Columbia valley." Lewis said this was the most desirable place for settlement west of the Rocky Mountains, capable of sustaining thousands of souls. Lewis proved prophetic; today this is the major metropolitan area of Oregon and southwest Washington. Here, the Columbia River eventually turns north for a distance before curving west again. The expedition followed its winding course, seeking the sea.

On November 7, 1805, they arrived at a large basalt pillar standing in the river. Here, at Pillar Rock just a few miles east of Grays Bay on the north side of the Columbia, the explorers recorded their first glimpse of the Pacific Ocean. Many modern scholars and others have contested this sighting as being impossible; they claim Clark mistakenly only saw waves in the bay, and not the open ocean beyond the Columbia bar. This is, in fact, true today because massive jetty projects have extensively altered the Columbia's mouth, barring a view of the sea from here. However, at the time of the expedition, it actually was possible to see the open ocean from this point.

The party continued around the northern end of Grays Bay, pitted against storms coming in from the Pacific. They proceeded on to where heavy seas kept most of the group from rounding Point Ellice. Several men, including Lewis with a small contingent, managed to round the point. West of here, the Columbia River estuary opened up to sixteen miles wide. The main party, however, spent six cold, wet days pinned to the cliffs, camping on a mass of drift logs—some ranging up to fifteen feet in diameter at the roots—along the shore.

On November 15, the weather cleared for a short time and Clark led the rest of the party around Point Ellice, going nearly three miles west to a sandy beach where they camped. In front of them, to the southwest, was the Pacific Ocean. Today much of this view is blocked by the five-mile-long South Jetty on the Oregon side of the Columbia. Visible to the west of them was Cape Disappointment where the north shore of the Columbia terminated. Cape Disappointment was named in 1788 by Captain John Meares, a British merchant and fur trader commanding the *Felice Adventurer* on voyages between China, the Philippines, Hawaii, and the Northwest Coast. Meares mistakenly perceived the estuary to be simply a bay and not the fabled "Great River of the West," which he believed existed somewhere on the Northwest Coast. In 1792, an American trader, Captain Robert Gray in the *Columbia Rediviva,* finally sighted and entered the Columbia River.

The next few days were spent investigating the Columbia's shore, including Cape Disappointment. Clark explored northward, too, up the coast to the North Beach Peninsula, also popularly known today as the Long Beach Peninsula. On the Columbia, contact was made with Concomly, the chief of the Lower Chinook Indians. The Chinook were acquainted with white people, having traded with American and British mariners since the early 1790s. In fact, Lewis and Clark had hoped to find trade vessels on the coast, but were informed by the Chinook that the trading season was over and ships would not return until spring or summer.

On November 24, the leaders consulted with the individual members of the expedition as to where each thought it best to spend the winter. The Chinook indicated the most eligible places would be on the Columbia's south shore. Consequently, the party decided to investigate the opposite side of the Columbia for a suitable winter camp site. Returning a considerable number of miles upriver, they crossed the Columbia where it was narrower and safer, and turned west again toward its mouth, this time along the south side. Clark and the majority of the party camped on Tongue Point near present-day Astoria, Oregon, while Lewis and a detachment searched to the west looking for an adequate wintering site. Rain and wetness had constantly soaked their clothing and equipment since they left the Columbia valley. In particular, any leather clothing, the buffalo robes used for sleeping, and skin tents were rotting and becoming worthless. Food was short. In essence, their plight was desperate.

Eventually Lewis found an eligible location in a forested lowland along today's Lewis and Clark River, located a few miles southwest of Astoria. When the full party arrived, they began building two rows of log shelters. Eventually short sections of palisades blocked off each end between the two rows of quarters, enclosing a small parade ground. They moved into Fort "Clatsop" on Christmas Eve, having little more than spoiled elk meat for a holiday meal. Yet, they had a stout, dry shelter for another winter. Fort Clatsop was named after a local band of Indians. Under the leadership of Comowool, the Clatsop had arrived early to get acquainted with these newcomers who had so suddenly appeared in their homeland. Despite some misunderstandings, friendship grew between the two peoples.

On December 8, Clark had set out westward several miles to investigate the sandy beaches of the coast, where he found a suitable locality to establish a camp for making salt. Consequently, small detachments of men were assigned the task of boiling down seawater in kettles to make the precious commodity. In January, Clark also led a sizeable party, including Charbonneau, Sacagawea and their infant son, south down the coast to view a beached whale and try to buy whale blubber from the Indians to add to their provisions.

Though it was a long, dreary, and wet winter with incessant storms lashing the coast, the little fort held them secure among the tall evergreen trees. Lewis spent much of his time studying the botanical, zoological, meteorological, and ethnological information and specimens that the Corps had gathered and spent many hours writing lengthy descriptions in his journal. Clark faithfully copied this same information in his own journal. Clark, too, kept busy laying out the traverse and drawing sketch maps of the route, thus filling in blank areas on the large map provided by Nicholas King.

With the advent of spring, the elk herds that had sustained the expedition left for higher elevations in the coastal mountains.

The men, anxious to be on their way, made arrangements to leave Fort Clatsop. They left letters and maps for the local Indians to present to any traders they might encounter, turned the fort over to Comowool, and departed east on March 23, 1806. (A "note" eventually fell into the hands of an American captain and arrived in the United States after the expedition had returned to St. Louis.)

In the Columbia valley, they were informed by local Indians that game was scarce past the Columbia River gorge. On the basis of this information, the captains chose to make a camp on the north side of the river until hunters brought in enough provisions to feed the group until they reached the Nez Perce. Consequently, they remained camped from March 30 to April 5, 1806, on the Columbia's north shore, opposite to the Quicksand (Sandy) River.

On the westbound journey, Clark had been concerned because they had not found a major river in the Columbia valley flowing from the south. Geographers of the day would develop great expectations (which were later largely diminished) that a great river located here would be a key transportation route, opening up vast portions of the West. On the return, Clark still had not located such a river, and he asked the natives if it existed. On April 2, he finally found an Indian who offered to guide him to a large river. Gathering some men quickly, Clark proceeded back downstream and spent the night several miles up a river that he named the Multnomah—today's Willamette. Its junction with the Columbia had been obscured by large islands when the expedition passed by.

Little more than a week later, the expedition confronted the Cascade portage in the Columbia River gorge. After three days of strenuous effort, and losing a canoe, they were once again on the river, moving upstream. East of the Cascade Range, they acquired packhorses from the tribes and proceeded along the Columbia's north shore to the Walla Walla-Columbia junction. From there, they proceeded eastward through the rolling grasslands of southeast Washington to the Nez Perce country.

On the Clearwater River, they collected horses and equipment left among the Nez Perce in the previous autumn, and readied themselves to challenge the Bitterroots. However, they learned it was too early in the season to make a crossing; snow up to twenty feet deep on the ridges would force them back. For several weeks they stayed among the friendly Nez Perce. In late June their patience rewarded them with a passage through the mountains. They arrived at Traveler's Rest in the Bitterroot Valley on June 30, 1806.

While the group paused at Traveler's Rest, the leaders finalized plans to divide up the expedition into smaller, exploratory parties. Lewis would take a group northeast up the Clark Fork drainage and across the continental divide to the plains and the Great Falls of the Missouri River. Meanwhile, Clark set out to the south, leading the larger part of the party to where they had left their canoes just east of Lemhi Pass, nearly a year before. Taking both the horses and canoes, Clark's group then worked their way back to the Three Forks of the Missouri. There Clark divided the party again, sending Sergeant John Ordway and nine men in canoes down the Missouri to the Great Falls. Clark and his group continued east with horses over the divide to the Yellowstone River. Eventually, they descended the Yellowstone in canoes carved from cottonwood trees. In the meantime, the Crow tribe stole all of their horses.

After reaching the Great Falls, Lewis, too, divided his party, leaving Sergeant Patrick Gass and several men to wait for the Ordway party and then help portage the canoes around the falls. Lewis, with the brothers Reuben and Joseph Field, and interpreter George Drouillard, the best hunter, proceeded north on horseback to investigate the Marias River, named in honor of Lewis's cousin, Maria Wood. Lewis was following Jefferson's instructions to determine the most northerly point of the Missouri drainage. To this end, they rode up the Marias River; however, they did not accomplish the mission because the most northerly point was on another tributary, the Milk River.

Returning from the Marias, the small party encountered some Piegans, members of the Blackfeet confederation, with a sizeable herd of horses. Lewis had been warned by other Indians about the aggressive nature of these northern tribesmen. Unable to avoid them, Lewis decided to hold a council and camp that night with the warriors. In the early hours, just at dawn, the Piegans attempted to grab the contingent's rifles and steal the horses. In the confusion that followed, one Indian was stabbed to death and another probably was fatally shot (they are the only deaths, along with Sergeant Floyd, associated with the expedition). After running off their assailants and catching mounts, Lewis and his men made a forced day and night ride southeast across the plains toward the mouth of the Marias River, where they hoped to meet the portage party coming down the Missouri River with the canoes. Lewis feared that their assailants would bring the entire tribe to take revenge on the men waiting on the Missouri.

After Lewis successfully linked up with the portage party on the Missouri, they continued downstream, often paddling seventy or eighty miles a day with the current. They planned to meet Clark at the mouth of the Yellowstone River, but on arrival they found indications that Clark had already been there and left. Clark had moved the party on down the Missouri to escape swarms of mosquitoes and because game was scarce. At this juncture, Lewis decided to slow down the journey and repair the

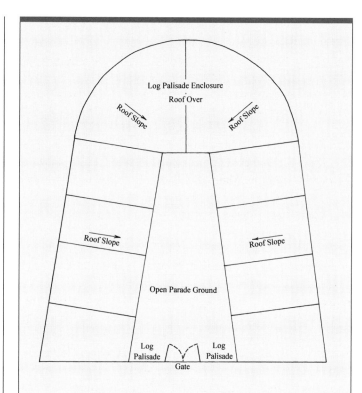

## FORT MANDAN, WINTER ENCAMPMENT 1804–05

Fort Mandan was the name given to the structure housing the expedition during the bitterly cold winter of 1804–05. Construction began on November 2 and the men moved into their quarters on November 19, followed by the leaders the next day. The external features of the structure were fairly well described in various journal entries. There are no known drawings by members of the Corps; this drawing was made from their written descriptions. The fort included a storeroom and a smokehouse, probably in the back, and sleeping quarters for the men and leaders. Firewood was cut in the open parade area, but as the cold winter advanced the operation was moved inside, along with the blacksmith work.

Clark designed the structure with the roofs sloping inward to the parade ground to allow guards to see natives who might attack from the roof. Defensive aspects were deemed more important at Fort Mandan than at the previous winter encampment at River Dubois. The Corps left Fort Mandan on April 7, 1805, and proceeded west on the upper Missouri River, soon to enter lands known only to the native peoples.

On their return in 1806, after spending several days at the Mandan villages, the expedition again headed downriver on August 17. Clark stopped at the fort briefly to look around. He reported that fire had burned all but one room of the structure. The waters of the Missouri River, in the process of claiming the fortification, reached right up to the front palisade.

By 1883 the entire encampment had been washed away.

canoes and prepare skins for raiment. His men had nearly worn out all of their clothes, and Lewis did not want them arriving at the Mandan villages appearing nearly naked. On August 11, 1806, Lewis spotted a herd of elk and entered a large willow thicket to stalk them, taking the one-eyed Pierre Cruzatte with him. This unfortunate day ended with Lewis accidentally shot in the rump and the poor-sighted Cruzatte denying that he had fired the shot wounding the captain.

The next day, Lewis's group caught up to Clark's party just before reaching the Mandan villages. Once there, Clark kept busy trying to make arrangements for any of the Mandan chiefs willing to travel to Washington, D.C., and meet the president. One chief agreed, taking his wife and child, along with a French Canadian interpreter and his family. The captains also settled accounts with Toussaint Charbonneau and Sacagawea, and Clark approved John Colter's request for an early discharge so he could accompany two fur traders as a guide into the western fur country.

The expedition set out again on the Missouri, heading for home. Clark now noted how much the river's course had changed in their absence—in some places it was almost beyond recognition. As they approached the lower stretches of the Missouri, Clark mentioned, too, how far the farms and settlements had moved upriver since they had left. They reached St. Charles on September 21, 1806, to find themselves warmly received and fêted through the night. Two days later, at about noon on September 23, the Corps of Volunteers for Northwestern Discovery arrived at St. Louis. The men were roundly celebrated, with everyone asking to hear their stories.

In early 1807, after the captains reached Washington, D.C., they were celebrated in the capital with another round of balls and parties.

Following the successful termination of the expedition, Lewis received an appointment as governor of Louisiana Territory and Clark was promoted to brigadier general in the Louisiana militia and was designated as the territorial Indian agent. Clark took his post almost immediately, but Lewis remained in Washington, D.C., to oversee the disposition of the specimens and collections. When Lewis arrived in St. Louis early in 1808, he soon found himself mired in various political difficulties, which worsened over the next one and a half years.

By 1809, the accountants of the new federal administration were rejecting Lewis's expenditure claims. Additionally, little progress was being made toward preparing the expedition's journals for publication, a project that Lewis was overseeing. Lewis, too, had taken to excessive drinking and appeared to be in a state of depression. To settle business affairs and make arrangements to publish the journals, Lewis set out for Washington, D.C., traveling by barge down the Mississippi River with the intention of taking a ship from New Orleans. It is unclear whether he sank deeper into mental depression or whether he perhaps had a relapse of malaria, but when the boat reached Chickasaw Bluffs on September 15, 1809, his mind was disordered and he had been drinking heavily. Crewmen reported they stopped him twice from killing himself. After spending several days at Fort Pickering, Lewis seemed in a better state of mind and had decided to travel the Natchez Trace overland toward Washington, D.C. Lewis made good time, despite reports of being in unsound mind.

On October 10, 1809, he stopped overnight at a farmstead that also lodged travelers. By morning of the next day, Lewis was found mortally wounded with a bullet in his side and part of his forehead shot away, exposing the brain. Whether the fatal bullets were fired by his hand, which appears most likely, or by another will never be known for certain. The last words he spoke were to his servant: "I am no coward, but I am so strong. It is so hard to die."

Clark lived a long, fulfilling life, being generally successful in administrative and Indian affairs and in business activities in St. Louis and the Missouri fur trade. His years had their joys and sorrows. He married Julia Hancock, a young woman for whom he named the Judith River in Montana. She died in 1820, having given him five children (three of which died in childhood). The following year Clark married the widow Harriet Radford, who was Judith's cousin. She died on Christmas Day in 1831. One of two children from this union lived to adulthood. Clark passed away on September 1, 1838, at sixty-eight years of age. Highly regarded by the Missouri River tribes for his wisdom and fairness, he was remembered by the American Indian as the great "Red-Headed Chief."

## Sources for the Journal Excerpts in *Lewis and Clark Trail Maps: A Cartographic Reconstruction, Volume I*

THWAITES, Reuben Gold, ed. *Original Journals of the Lewis and Clark Expedition, 1804–1806*, 8 vols. New York: Dodd, Mead, 1904–5 [reprint editions available].

This finely annotated, seven-volume set with an accompanying box containing facsimiles of William Clark's maps has served as the primary published source of the Lewis and Clark Expedition journals for both scholars and general readers. Unlike the BIDDLE and COUES volumes, THWAITES is an unabridged transcription of the journal accounts. In recent years, however, THWAITES gradually has been supplanted by MOULTON as the most complete presentation of the journals (see MOULTON, below). In the WSU Press's *L and C Trail Maps, Volume I*, quotations from the journals of Captain Meriwether Lewis, Captain William Clark, Sergeant Charles Floyd Jr., and Private Joseph Whitehouse are derived from the THWAITES volumes.

GASS, Patrick [and David McKeehan]. *A Journal of the Voyages and Travels of a Corps of Discovery, under the Command of Capt. Lewis and Capt. Clarke [sic]*. Pittsburgh: David McKeehan, 1807 [reprint editions available].

Shortly after the Corps of Discovery's return, editor David McKeehan worked out arrangements with Sergeant Patrick Gass to rewrite and publish Gass's account, which was the expedition's first journal to be released to the public. Gass's original journal subsequently was lost. The Gass quotes included in the *L and C Trail Maps, Volume I* are from this source.

QUAIFE, Milo M., ed. *The Journals of Captain Meriwether Lewis and Sergeant John Ordway, Kept on the Expedition of Western Exploration, 1803–1806*. Madison: State Historical Society of Wisconsin, 1916 [reprint editions available].

When published, Volume 22 in the Wisconsin Historical Society Collections included two recently discovered journals in the BIDDLE family papers—Meriwether Lewis's 1803 Ohio River logbook and Sergeant John Ordway's journal. The Ordway quotes in the *L and C Trail Maps, Volume I* are derived from QUAIFE.

## Other Selected Primary and Essential Sources

ALLEN, John Logan. *Passage through the Garden: Lewis and Clark and the Image of the American Northwest*. Urbana: University of Illinois Press, 1975.

This professional study of the mapping aspects of the expedition depicts the Lewis and Clark venture's visionary aspects—geopolitical, economic, and mythos—and how that vision was affected by the findings of the expedition.

[BIDDLE, Nicholas, ed.] *History of the Expedition under the Command of Captains Lewis and Clark . . .* , 2 vols. and map, Paul Allen, ed. Philadelphia: Bradford and Inskeep, 1814 [reprint editions available].

BIDDLE and Allen produced the official account of the expedition by excerpting or paraphrasing entries from the two captains' journals. Other information was provided from the Ordway and Gass journals and by the personal assistance of Private George Shannon and William Clark. This is the version of the expedition journals utilized by COUES (1893).

COOK, Warren L. *Flood Tide of Empire: Spain and the Pacific Northwest, 1543-1819*. New Haven, Connecticut: Yale University Press, 1973.

An excellent work on the role that the Spanish empire played in Louisiana Territory and the early coastal exploration of the Pacific Northwest. COOK presents the first and best source of detailed information about the several efforts of the Spanish to interdict the expedition.

COUES, Elliott, ed. *The History of the Lewis and Clark Expedition . . .* , 4 vols. New York: Francis P. Harper, 1893 [3 vol. reprint editions available].

This extensively annotated version based on BIDDLE includes a wealth of background information about the history, natural history, and geography of the West. Though COUES can be opinionated and unfair (e.g., beleaguering Toussaint Charbonneau), this work has its redeeming qualities.

CUTRIGHT, Paul Russell. *A History of the Lewis and Clark Journals*. Norman: University of Oklahoma Press, 1976.

A unique and revealing account outlining the remarkable history of the original journals over the course of 170 years.

___. *Lewis and Clark, Pioneering Naturalists*. Urbana: University of Illinois Press, 1969.

An outstanding treatment by a reliable expert regarding the expedition's contribution to natural history.

DeVOTO, Bernard, ed. *The Journals of Lewis and Clark*. Boston: Houghton Mifflin Company, 1953.

This is a single-volume, introductory work of selected journal excerpts by a gifted Western historian.

JACKSON, Donald, ed. *Letters of the Lewis and Clark Expedition: With Related Documents, 1783–1854*, 2nd ed., 2 vols. Urbana: University of Illinois Press, 1978 [1st edition, 1962].

This essential source reproduces hundreds of letters and documents relating to the origins, diplomacy, political background, logistics, and conduct of the Lewis and Clark Expedition. JACKSON's *Thomas Jefferson and the Stony Mountains: Exploring the West from Monticello* (1981) and *Among the Sleeping Giants: Occasional Pieces on Lewis and Clark* (1987) by the same publisher complements this extensive collection of letters and documents.

MISSOURI RIVER COMMISSION. *Map of the Missouri River from Its Mouth to Three Forks, Montana, in Eighty-four Sheets and Nine Index Sheets*. Washington, DC: 1892–95.

This finely detailed set of maps was completed nearly ninety years after the Lewis and Clark Expedition returned to St. Louis.

MOULTON, Gary E., ed. *The Journals of the Lewis and Clark Expedition*, 12 vols. Lincoln: University of Nebraska Press [1983 and subsequent publishing dates].

Dr. Gary E. MOULTON's edited volumes of the expedition's journals are the most comprehensive ever published and exhibit unsurpassed scholarship. The first volume is a large-format atlas of William Clark's maps and other related cartography; ten volumes include the complete accounts of the six expedition journalists whose works are yet known to exist (Lewis, Clark, Ordway, Floyd, Gass, and Whitehouse); and an additional volume is dedicated to the scientific aspects of the expedition.

OSGOOD, Ernest S., ed. *The Field Notes of Captain William Clark, 1803–1805*. New Haven, Connecticut: Yale University Press, 1964.

OSGOOD extensively annotated Clark's rough field notes which were found in a St. Paul attic in 1953. The field notes are for the period beginning December 13, 1803 (the Corps' first full day at Camp Wood), and continue to April 3, 1805 (shortly after the expedition left Fort Mandan). Clark on a frequent basis wrote down field notes as needed. He used these notes to assist him in completing his main journal entries from May 14, 1804 (the expedition's departure date up the Missouri), to April 3, 1805.

RONDA, James P. *Lewis and Clark among the Indians*. Lincoln: University of Nebraska Press, 1984.

The author focuses on the relationships and ramifications of the meetings and promises made between the explorers and the many bands of American Indians they met on the journey.

WHEELER, Olin D. *The Trail of Lewis and Clark, 1804–1904*, 2 vols. New York: G.P. Putnam's Sons, 1904.

One of the earliest and best of the many trail guides that have been published over the years focusing on the expedition's route. WHEELER was a railroad publicity writer who revisited much of the Lewis and Clark trail via horseback before the extensive changes wrought by modern America. This well-illustrated narrative complements the use of the *L and C Trail Maps*.

# INDEX MAPS AND LEGEND, VOLUME I

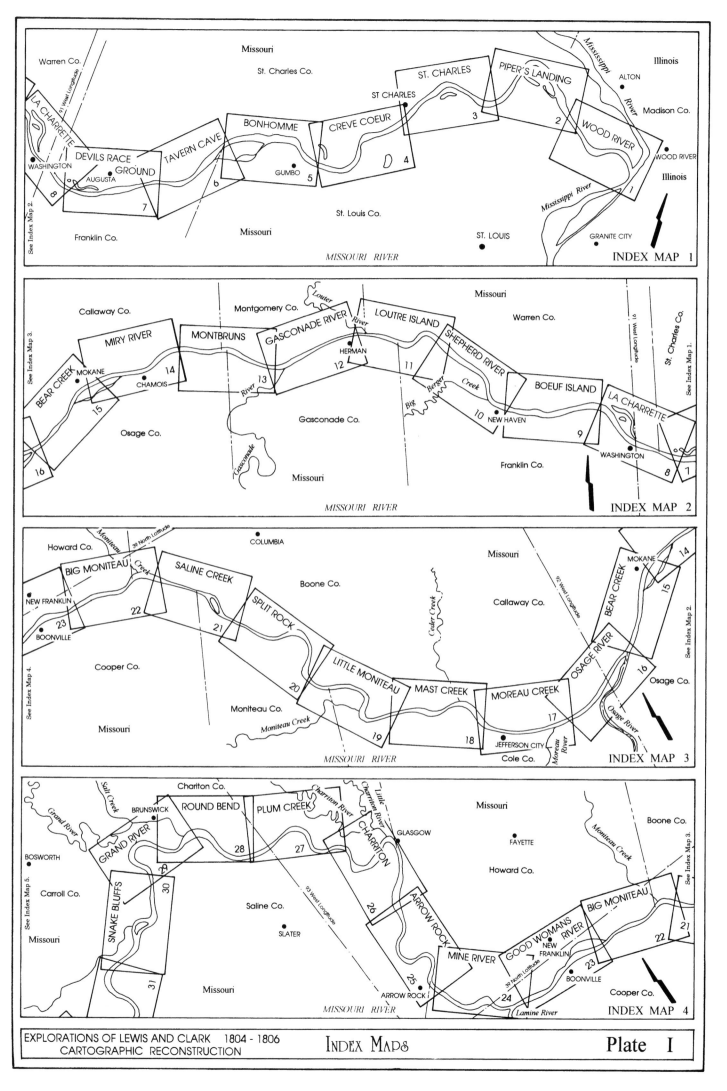

INDEX MAP 1

INDEX MAP 2

INDEX MAP 3

INDEX MAP 4

EXPLORATIONS OF LEWIS AND CLARK   1804 - 1806
CARTOGRAPHIC RECONSTRUCTION

INDEX MAPS

Plate   I

17

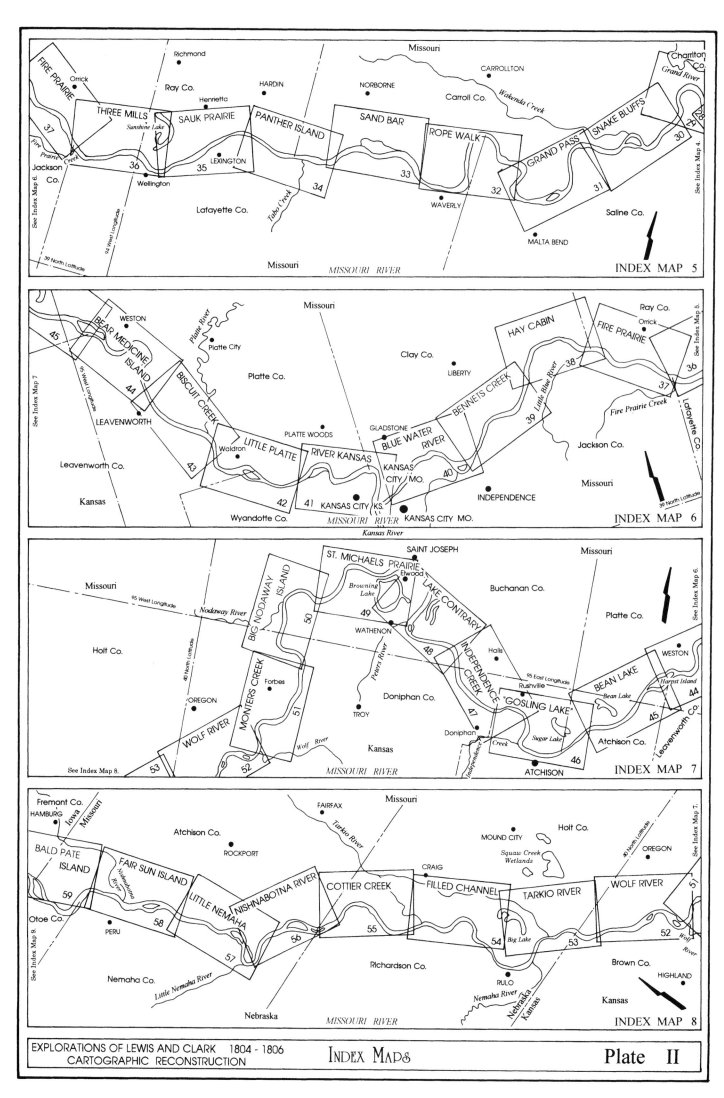

INDEX MAP 5

INDEX MAP 6

INDEX MAP 7

INDEX MAP 8

EXPLORATIONS OF LEWIS AND CLARK 1804 - 1806
CARTOGRAPHIC RECONSTRUCTION

INDEX MAPS

Plate II

18

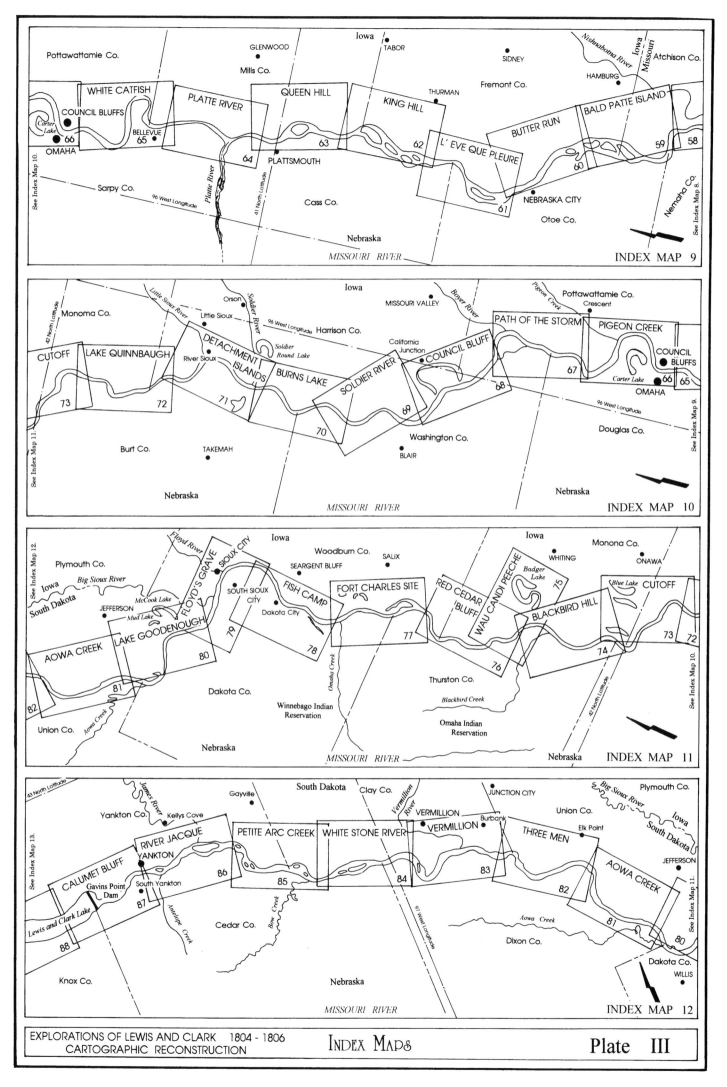

EXPLORATIONS OF LEWIS AND CLARK   1804 - 1806
CARTOGRAPHIC RECONSTRUCTION

INDEX MAPS

Plate   III

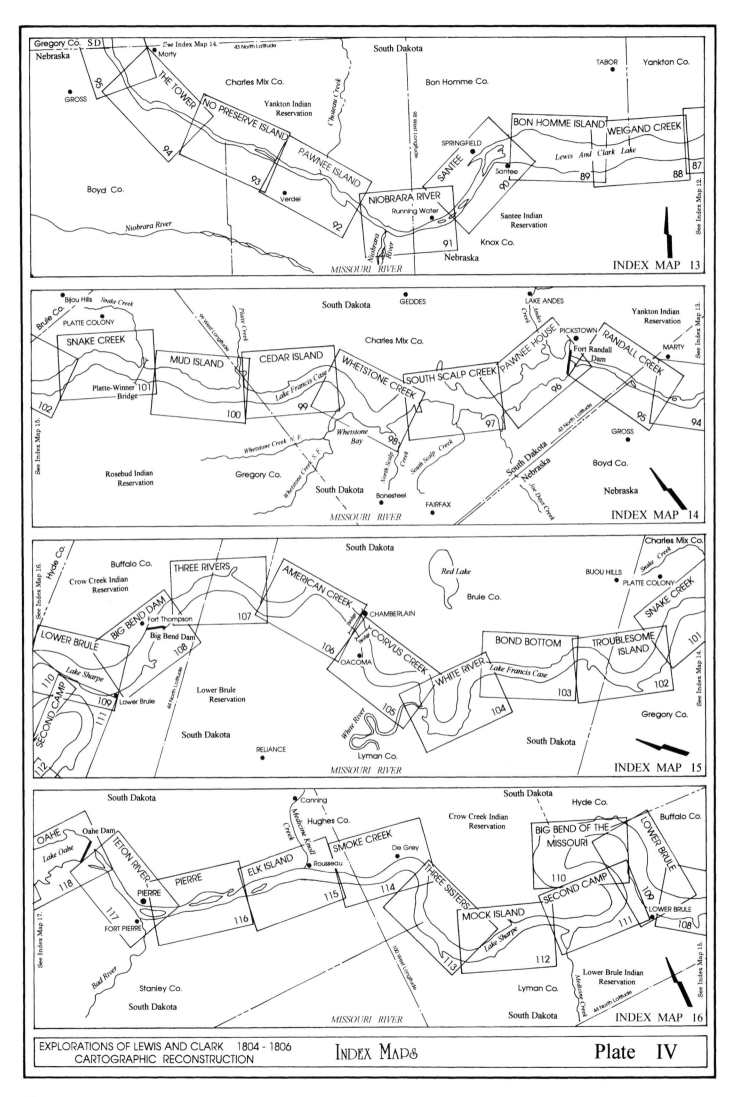

INDEX MAP 13

INDEX MAP 14

INDEX MAP 15

INDEX MAP 16

EXPLORATIONS OF LEWIS AND CLARK  1804 - 1806
CARTOGRAPHIC RECONSTRUCTION

INDEX MAPS

Plate IV

20

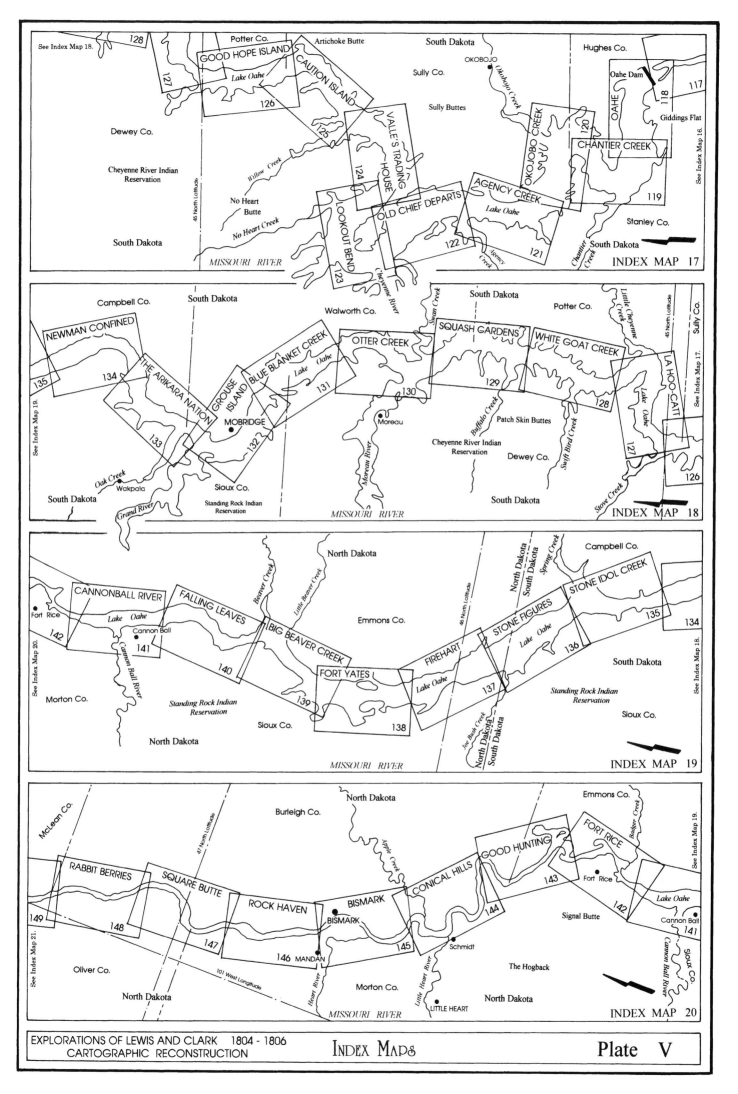

**INDEX MAP 17**

See Index Map 18.

128

127

126

125

Good Hope Island

Potter Co.

*Lake Oahe*

Caution Island

Artichoke Butte

South Dakota

Sully Co.

Sully Buttes

OKOBOJO
Okobojo Creek

Hughes Co.

Oahe Dam

OAHE

118

117

Giddings Flat

*Willow Creek*

Dewey Co.

Cheyenne River Indian
Reservation

45 North Latitude

No Heart
Butte

*No Heart Creek*

South Dakota

124

Valle's Trading
House

Lookout Bend

123

Old Chief Departs

122

Cheyenne River

OKOJOBO CREEK

120

Chantier Creek

119

Agency Creek

*Lake Oahe*

121

*Agency Creek*

*Chantier Creek*

Stanley Co.

South Dakota

Stanley Co.

See Index Map 16.

**INDEX MAP 18**

See Index Map 19.

135

134

Newman Confined

Campbell Co.

South Dakota

The Arikara Nation

133

*Oak Creek*
Wakpala

*Grand River*

South Dakota

Grouse Island

Blue Blanket Creek

132

MOBRIDGE

Sioux Co.

Standing Rock Indian
Reservation

Walworth Co.

*Lake Oahe*

131

Otter Creek

130

*Moreau River*
Moreau

MISSOURI RIVER

Swan Creek

Squash Gardens

129

*Buffalo Creek*

Cheyenne River Indian
Reservation

South Dakota

South Dakota

Potter Co.

White Goat Creek

128

Patch Skin Buttes

*Swift Bird Creek*

Dewey Co.

South Dakota

*Little Cheyenne Creek*

45 North Latitude

La Hoo Catt

127

126

*Stove Creek*

Sully Co.

See Index Map 17.

**INDEX MAP 19**

See Index Map 20.

142
Fort Rice

Cannonball River

*Lake Oahe*
Cannon Ball

*Cannon Ball River*

141

Falling Leaves

140

Morton Co.

Standing Rock Indian
Reservation

North Dakota

Sioux Co.

*Beaver Creek*

*Little Beaver Creek*

Big Beaver Creek

Fort Yates

139

138

North Dakota

Emmons Co.

North Dakota
South Dakota

*Spring Creek*

Campbell Co.

45 North Latitude

Stone Figures

Firehart

137

*Lake Oahe*

*Lake Oahe*

136

Stone Idol Creek

135

134

South Dakota

Standing Rock Indian
Reservation

Sioux Co.

*Joe Bush Creek*

North Dakota
South Dakota

See Index Map 18.

MISSOURI RIVER

**INDEX MAP 20**

See Index Map 21.

149

148

Rabbit Berries

McLean Co.

Square Butte

147

Rock Haven

146
MANDAN

Oliver Co.

North Dakota

*101 West Longitude*

47 North Latitude

Burleigh Co.

North Dakota

*Apple Creek*

Bismark
BISMARK

*Heart River*

Morton Co.

Conical Hills

145

*Little Heart River*

LITTLE HEART

Schmidt

The Hogback

North Dakota

Good Hunting

144

Signal Butte

143

Fort Rice

Fort Rice

142

141

Emmons Co.

*Badger Creek*

See Index Map 19.

*Lake Oahe*

Cannon Ball

*Cannon Ball River*

Sioux Co.

MISSOURI RIVER

EXPLORATIONS OF LEWIS AND CLARK 1804 - 1806
CARTOGRAPHIC RECONSTRUCTION

**INDEX MAPS**

**Plate V**

21

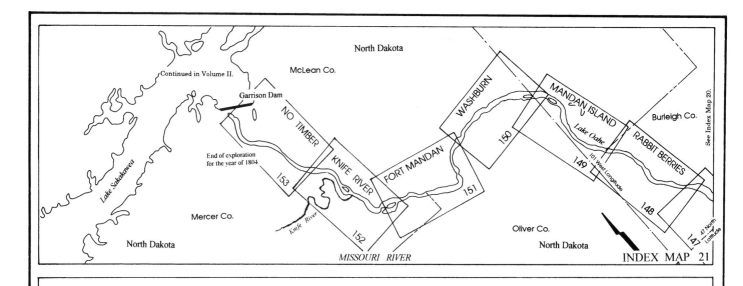

North Dakota

McLean Co.

Continued in Volume II.

Garrison Dam

*NO TIMBER*

Burleigh Co.

*WASHBURN*

*MANDAN ISLAND*

*Lake Oahe*

*RABBIT BERRIES*

150

149

*101 West Longitude*

End of exploration for the year of 1804.

153

*KNIFE RIVER*

*FORT MANDAN*

151

148

*Knife River*

Mercer Co.

152

Oliver Co.

147

*47 North Latitude*

North Dakota

North Dakota

*MISSOURI RIVER*

See Index Map 20.

INDEX MAP 21

# LEGEND

## Lines

〰️ Water boundary 1804 - 1806

Small stream 1804 - 1806

Water boundary or stream, modern

Water boundary for reservoir (normal pool elevation)

Principal parallel or meridian

State boundary line

County, reservation, or other jurisdictional boundary

Major highway, modern

Contour line (historically reconstructed)

Depression in topography

Shading lines 1804 - 1806 (water bodies only)

## Symbols

Interstate highway shield with number

Federal highway shield with number

State or local highway

Airport or landing strip

Bridge

Dam (small)

Spring

Cave

Falls

Rapid

Point of interest

**Surveyed Traverse Symbol**
End of one bearing/distance and beginning of next. Direction and distance as stated in Clark's journal. Traverse corrected for magnetic declination and adjusted to fit topography. Unusual deviation of bearing is noted.

**Universal Transverse Mercator**
Mapping grid. Grid tics are shown at 1,000 meter intervals along map border. Larger number in notation indicates thousands of meters, smaller number indicates hundreds of thousands of meters.

## Fonts

Various font styles have been used to relate certain types of information.

Century Font    *Century Font*

The Century font is used to denote feature names existing at the time of Lewis and Clark. Vertical for land features. Italicized for water features. Quotation marks about the name indicate that Lewis and Clark gave the name.

Dot Matrix Font

The Dot Matrix font is used for all notations relating to modern or post Lewis and Clark information. Notations relevant to water are italicized.

*Script Roundhand Font*

Script Roundhand font is used to convey information from the journals. Short notes that have been altered slightly to fit mapping standards do not have quotation marks. Direct quotes from the journals are enclosed in quotation marks. They are followed by the name of the journal writer and an arrow indicating whether the quote comes from the Outbound travel (⇒) or Return journey (⇐). See further explanation Maps 1 and 2.

Advance Font

The Advance font is used to denote information related to the story but not addressed adequately in the journals.

Cartographer's Note:

Generally an explanation of a mapping detail, a mapping decision, a major adjustment to the surveyed traverse, or an explanation of events as viewed by the cartographer.

All north arrows on The Trail Maps, as well as the index sheets, indicate True North.

## Campsite Notations

**Camp**
**May 6, 1805**
Outbound Camp with date of the evening camp. Corps left camp on morning following last date.

**Return Camp**
**June 23, 1806**
Home Bound Camp with date of the evening camp. Corps left camp on morning following last date.

**Camp Station**
**Nov. 18 - 22, 1805**

Named Camp. Important enough to be named by the explorers along with date of encampment.

## Notations

453    Lewis and Clark mileposts. Mileposts based on traverse distances. Distances are not scaleable. Outbound and alternate return routes only.

+398    Corrected mileposts. Outbound only.

N 23 W    2 MILES    Traverse notations. Traverse bearings (directions) based on magnetic north, 1804-1806. Notations are from Clark's journal and have been adjusted to fit topography.

VANCOUVER    City or town. Position of note indicates location of town.

American Grizzly Bear (Ursus horribilis horribilis)    Flora and fauna. New to science, first described by Lewis and Clark, or significant mention by journalist. Common name followed by scientific or Latin name in parentheses.

## Title Block Notations

| | | |
|---|---|---|
| Approximate date(s) for post Expedition data shown on map. | Visual Scale. | Dates for which the Expedition was in an area covered by a map. Outbound and return dates are shown. |
| Project Title. | Map sheet title. | Universal Transverse Mercator (UTM) zone number. |
| | | Map sheet number. |
| Map covers portions of these states. | Contour interval information. | |

EXPLORATIONS OF LEWIS AND CLARK    1804 - 1806
CARTOGRAPHIC RECONSTRUCTION

LEGEND AND INDEX MAP

Plate VI

# LEWIS AND CLARK TRAIL MAPS, VOLUME I

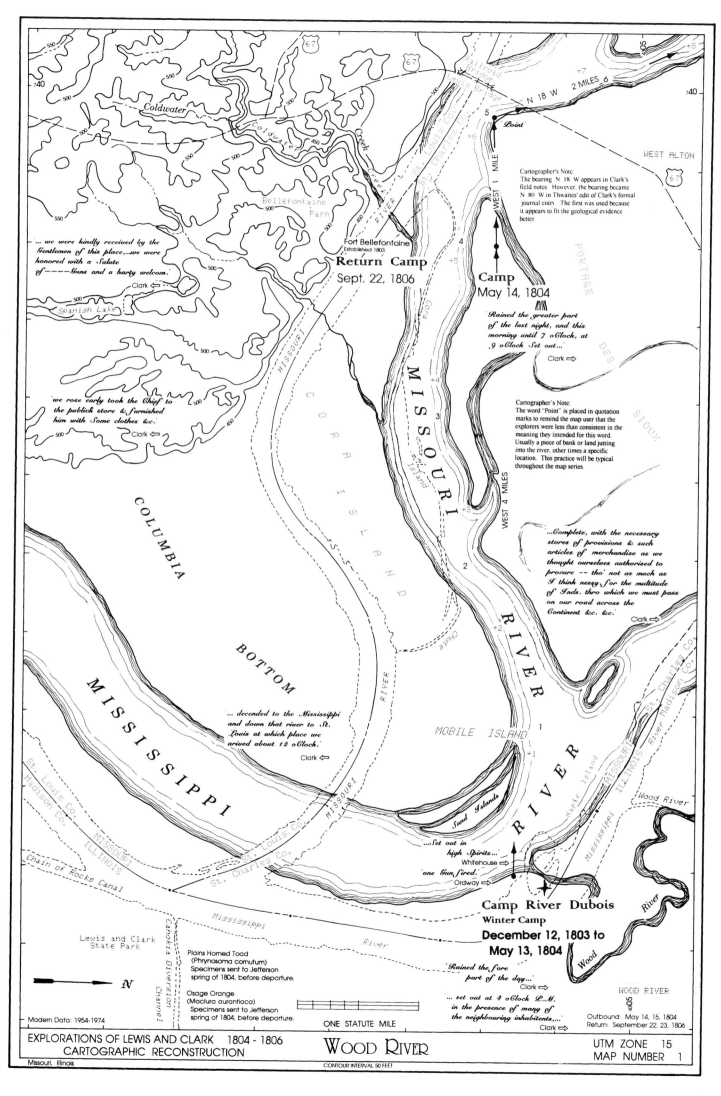

Coldwater

Coldwater Creek

740

550

550

500

450

Bellefontaine Farm

550

Fort Bellefontaine
Established 1803.

**Return Camp**
Sept. 22, 1806

*... we were kindly received by the Gentlemen of this place,...we were honored with a Salute of ———— Guns and a harty welcom.*
Clark ⇐

Spanish Lake

500

500

*we rose early took the Chief to the publick store & furnished him with Some clothes &c.*
Clark ⇐

500

MISSISSIPPI

COLUMBIA

BOTTOM

CORN ISLAND

MISSOURI

*... decended to the Mississippi and down that river to St. Louis at which place we arived about 12 oClock.*
Clark ⇐

CRANE RIVER

MISSOURI

St. Louis Co.
Madison Co.
MISSOURI
ILLINOIS

St. Charles Co.

Chain of Rocks Canal

Mississippi

River

Lewis and Clark State Park

Cahokia Diversion Channel

**N**

Modern Data: 1954-1974

Plains Horned Toad
(Phrynosoma comutum)
Specimens sent to Jefferson
spring of 1804, before departure.

Osage Orange
(Maclura aurantiaca)
Specimens sent to Jefferson
spring of 1804, before departure.

ONE STATUTE MILE

**EXPLORATIONS OF LEWIS AND CLARK   1804 - 1806**
**CARTOGRAPHIC RECONSTRUCTION**
Missouri, Illinois

**WOOD RIVER**
CONTOUR INTERVAL 50 FEET

67

67

Railroad Bridge
Route Bridge

N 18 W   2 MILES   6

5   *Point*

WEST 1 MILE

740

WEST ALTON

67

Cartographer's Note:
The bearing N 18 W appears in Clark's field notes. However, the bearing became N 80 W in Thwaites' edit of Clark's formal journal entry. The first was used because it appears to fit the geological evidence better.

4

**Camp**
May 14, 1804

*Rained the greater part of the last night, and this morning until 7 oClock, at 9 oClock Set out...*
Clark ⇒

3

PORTAGE DES SIOUX

MISSOURI Island

Cartographer's Note:
The word "Point" is placed in quotation marks to remind the map user that the explorers were less than consistent in the meaning they intended for this word. Usually a piece of bank or land jutting into the river, other times a specific location. This practice will be typical throughout the map series.

WEST 4 MILES

2

*...Complete, with the necessary stores of provisions & such articles of merchandize as we thought ourselves authorised to procure -- tho' not as much as I think nessy for the multitude of Inds. thro which we must pass on our road across the Continent &c. &c.*
Clark ⇒

MISSOURI   RIVER

1

*MOBILE ISLAND*

Maple Island

St. Charles Co.
Madison Co.
MISSOURI
ILLINOIS

ILLINOIS RIVER

Wood River

Sand Islands

*...Set out in high Spirits...*
Whitehouse ⇒
*one Gun fired.*
Ordway ⇒

**Camp River Dubois**
**Winter Camp**
**December 12, 1803 to**
**May 13, 1804**

*Rained the fore part of the day...*
Clark ⇒

*... set out at 4 oClock P.M. in the presence of many of the neighbouring inhabitents,...*
Clark ⇒

WOOD RIVER

Wood River

Outbound: May 14, 15, 1804
Return: September 22, 23, 1806

UTM ZONE   15
MAP NUMBER   1

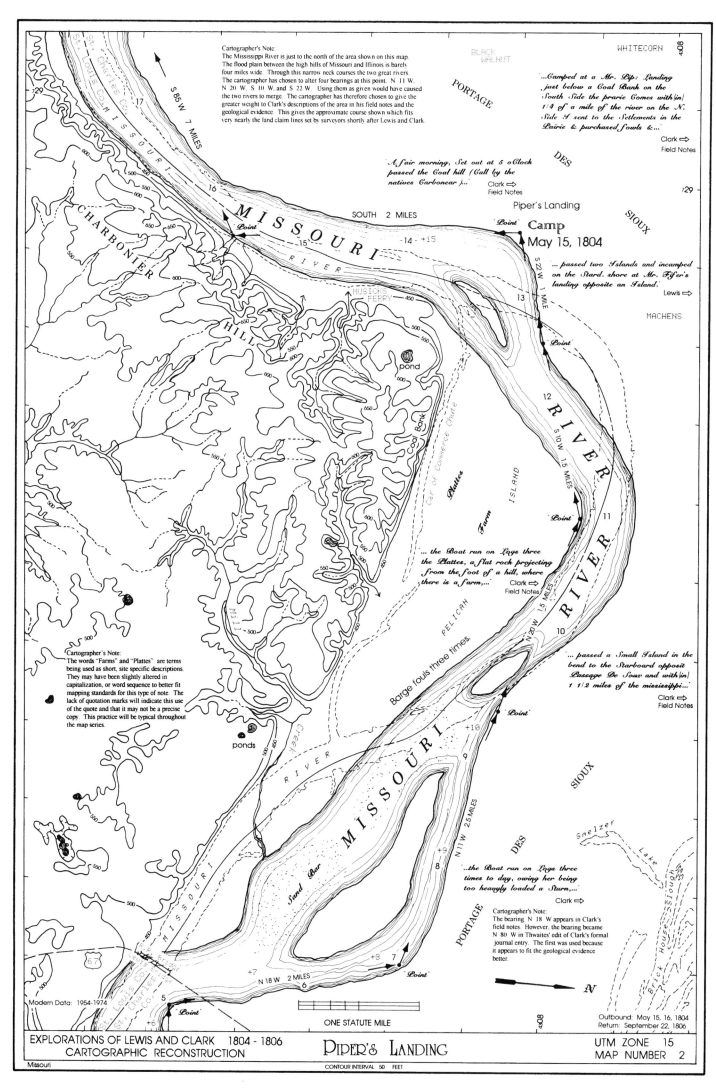

Cartographer's Note:
The Mississippi River is just to the north of the area shown on this map.
The flood plain between the high hills of Missouri and Illinois is barely
four miles wide. Through this narrow neck courses the two great rivers.
The cartographer has chosen to alter four bearings at this point, N 11 W,
N 20 W, S 10 W, and S 22 W. Using them as given would have caused
the two rivers to merge. The cartographer has therefore chosen to give the
greater weight to Clark's descriptions of the area in his field notes and the
geological evidence. This gives the approximate course shown which fits
very nearly the land claim lines set by surveyors shortly after Lewis and Clark.

BLACK
WALNUT

PORTAGE

...Camped at a Mr. Pip: Landing
just below a Coal Bank on the
South Side the prarie Comes with [in]
1/4 of a mile of the river on the N.
Side I sent to the Setlements in the
Pairie & purchased fowls &...

Clark ⇨
Field Notes

DES

A fair morning, Set out at 5 oClock
passed the Coal hill (Call by the
natives Carbonear )...    Clark ⇨
Field Notes

729

SIOUX

Piper's Landing

SOUTH 2 MILES

Point    **Camp**
**May 15, 1804**

...passed two Islands and incamped
on the Stard. shore at Mr. Fifer's
landing opposite an Island.'
Lewis ⇨

MACHENS

MUSICKS
FERRY

pond

Coal Bank

... the Boat run on Logs three
the Plattes, a flat rock projecting
from the foot of a hill, where
there is a farm,...    Clark ⇨
Field Notes

Cartographer's Note:
The words "Farms" and "Plattes" are terms
being used as short, site specific descriptions.
They may have been slightly altered in
capitalization, or word sequence to better fit
mapping standards for this type of note. The
lack of quotation marks will indicate this use
of the quote and that it may not be a precise
copy. This practice will be typical throughout
the map series.

ponds

Barge fouls three times.

PELICAN

...passed a Small Island in the
bend to the Starboard opposit
Passage De Soux and with [in]
1 1/2 miles of the mississippi...'
Clark ⇨
Field Notes

Point

+10

SIOUX

Smelzer
Lake

Sand Bar

...the Boat run on Logs three
times to day, owing her being
too heavyly loaded a Stern,...
Clark ⇨

Cartographer's Note:
The bearing N 18 W appears in Clark's
field notes. However, the bearing became
N 80 W in Thwaites' edit of Clark's formal
journal entry. The first was used because
it appears to fit the geological evidence
better.

PORTAGE

DES

Point

N 18 W 2 MILES

*N*

Modern Data: 1954-1974

Point

ONE STATUTE MILE

Outbound: May 15, 16, 1804
Return: September 22, 1806

EXPLORATIONS OF LEWIS AND CLARK    1804 - 1806
CARTOGRAPHIC RECONSTRUCTION

**PIPER'S LANDING**

UTM ZONE    15
MAP NUMBER    2

Missouri

CONTOUR INTERVAL  50  FEET

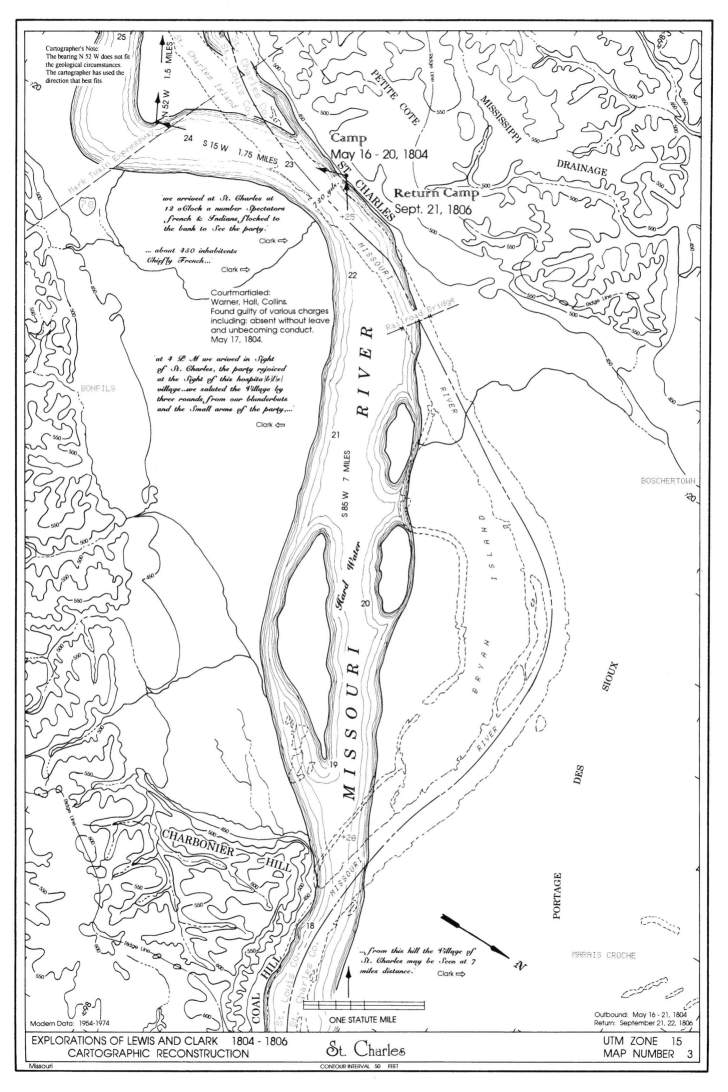

Cartographer's Note:
The bearing N 52 W does not fit
the geological circumstances.
The cartographer has used the
direction that best fits.

25

N 52 W    1.5 MILES

24    S 15 W    1.75 MILES    23

Camp
May 16 - 20, 1804

Return Camp
Sept. 21, 1806

*we arrived at St. Charles at*
*12 oCloch a number Spectators*
*french & Indians flocked to*
*the bank to See the party.*
Clark ⇒

*... about 450 inhabitents*
*Chiefly French...*
Clark ⇒

Courtmartialed:
Warner, Hall, Collins.
Found guilty of various charges
including: absent without leave
and unbecoming conduct.
May 17, 1804.

*at 4 P M we arived in Sight*
*of St. Charles, the party rejoiced*
*at the Sight of this hospita[b]l[e]*
*village...we saluted the Village by*
*three rounds from our blunderbuts*
*and the Small arms of the party,...*
Clark ⇐

BONFILS

22

21

*Hard Water*

20

19

CHARBONIER HILL

18

*...from this hill the Village of*
*St. Charles may be Seen at 7*
*miles distance.*
Clark ⇒

M I S S O U R I     R I V E R

PETITE COTE

MISSISSIPPI

DRAINAGE

Railroad Bridge

BOSCHERTOWN

BRYAN ISLAND

SIOUX

DES

PORTAGE

MARAIS CROCHE

Modern Data: 1954-1974

ONE STATUTE MILE

Outbound: May 16 - 21, 1804
Return: September 21, 22, 1806

EXPLORATIONS OF LEWIS AND CLARK   1804 - 1806
CARTOGRAPHIC RECONSTRUCTION

St. Charles

UTM ZONE  15
MAP NUMBER  3

Missouri

CONTOUR INTERVAL  50  FEET

27

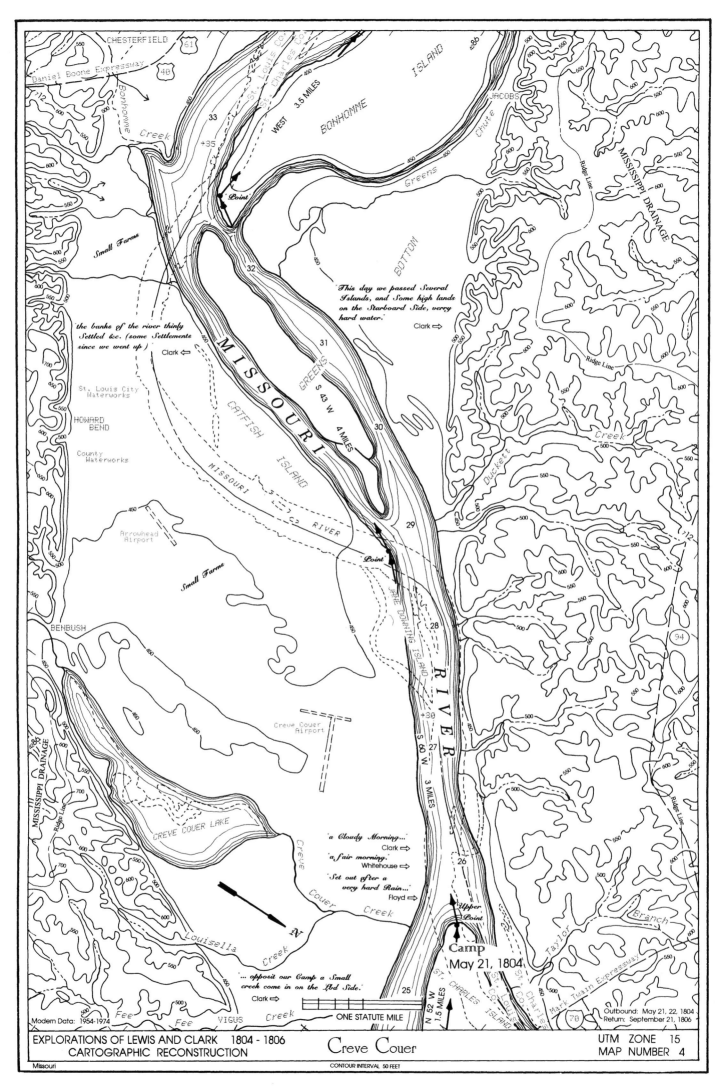

CHESTERFIELD

Daniel Boone Expressway

Bonhomme Creek

WEST 3.5 MILES

BONHOMME ISLAND

JACOBS

Greens Chute

Ridge Line

MISSISSIPPI DRAINAGE

Point

Small Farms

*This day we passed Several Islands, and Some high lands on the Starboard Side, verry hard water.*

Clark ⇒

BOTTOM

*the banks of the river thinly Settled &c. (some Settlements since we went up )*

Clark ⇐

St. Louis City Waterworks

HOWARD BEND

County Waterworks

MISSOURI

GREENS

S 43 W 4 MILES

CATFISH ISLAND

MISSOURI RIVER

Arrowhead Airport

Small Farms

Duckett Creek

Ridge Line

Point

JANE DONING ISLAND

Creve Couer Airport

+38

S 60 W 3 MILES

BENBUSH

MISSISSIPPI DRAINAGE

Ridge Line

RIVER

94

*a Cloudy Morning...*
Clark ⇒

*a fair morning.*
Whitehouse ⇒

*Set out after a very hard Rain...*
Floyd ⇒

CREVE COUER LAKE

N

Upper Point

Camp
May 21, 1804

N 52 W 1.5 MILES

Taylor Branch

Louisella Creek

Creve Couer Creek

*... opposit our Camp a Small creek coms in on the Lrd Side.*

Clark ⇒

ONE STATUTE MILE

ST CHARLES CO. ST LOUIS CO.

CHARLES ISLAND

Mark Twain Expressway

70

Fee Fee Creek

VIGUS Creek

Modern Data: 1954-1974

EXPLORATIONS OF LEWIS AND CLARK   1804 - 1806
CARTOGRAPHIC RECONSTRUCTION

Creve Couer

CONTOUR INTERVAL 50 FEET

UTM ZONE 15
MAP NUMBER 4

Missouri

Outbound: May 21, 22, 1804
Return: September 21, 1806

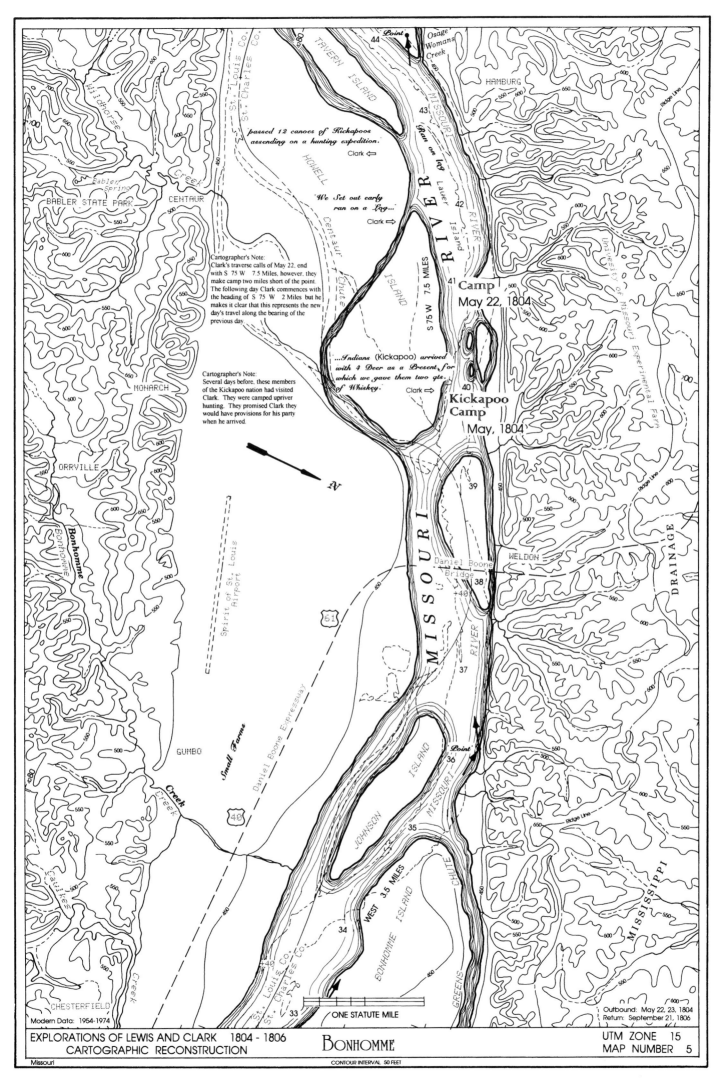

passed 12 canoes of Kickapoos
assending on a hunting expedition.
Clark ⇐

"We Set out early
ran on a Log..."
Clark ⇒

Cartographer's Note:
Clark's traverse calls of May 22, end
with S 75 W  7.5 Miles, however, they
make camp two miles short of the point.
The following day Clark commences with
the heading of  S 75 W  2 Miles but he
makes it clear that this represents the new
day's travel along the bearing of the
previous day.

Cartographer's Note:
Several days before, these members
of the Kickapoo nation had visited
Clark.  They were camped upriver
hunting.  They promised Clark they
would have provisions for his party
when he arrived.

...Indians (Kickapoo) arrived
with 4 Deer as a Present for
which we gave them two qts.
of Whiskey.
Clark ⇒

41 Camp
May 22, 1804

40 Kickapoo
Camp
May, 1804

N

OSAGE WOMANS CREEK
44 Point
43
HAMBURG
42
S 75 W  7.5 MILES
Laur Island

39
Daniel Boone
Bridge
38
+40
WELDON
DRAINAGE

37

36 Point

JOHNSON ISLAND

35

34

33

WEST 3.5 MILES

BONHOMME ISLAND

GREENS CHUTE

MISSISSIPPI

Babler
Spring
BABLER STATE PARK
CENTAUR

MONARCH

ORRVILLE

Bonhomme

GUMBO
Small Farms
Spirit of St. Louis Airport
Daniel Boone Expressway

61

40

Creek

CHESTERFIELD
Modern Data: 1954-1974

ONE STATUTE MILE

EXPLORATIONS OF LEWIS AND CLARK   1804 - 1806
CARTOGRAPHIC RECONSTRUCTION
BONHOMME
UTM ZONE   15
MAP NUMBER   5
Missouri
CONTOUR INTERVAL  50 FEET

Outbound: May 22, 23, 1804
Return: September 21, 1806

29

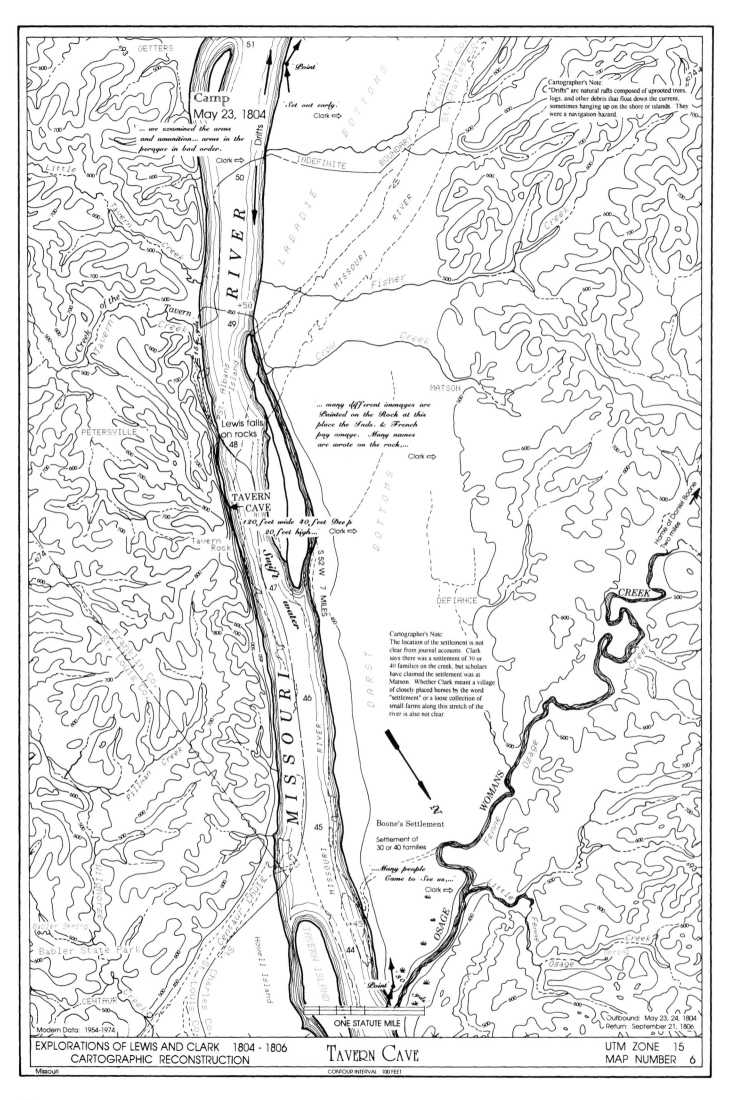

GETTERS

51

→ Point

Camp
May 23, 1804

*Set out early.*
Clark ⇨

*... we examined the arms
and amunition... arms in the
perogue in bad order.*

Clark ⇨

50

Drifts

Cartographer's Note:
"Drifts" are natural rafts composed of uprooted trees,
logs, and other debris that float down the current,
sometimes hanging up on the shore or islands. They
were a navigation hazard.

RIVER

LABODIE BOTTOMS

INDEFINITE

BOUNDARY

Franklin Co.
St. Charles Co.

MISSOURI

Fisher

RIVER

Creek

Little

Tavern Creek

600

of the

Creek

Tavern

*Tavern*

+50
450

49

Crow

Creek

Creek

MATSON

PETERSVILLE

Lewis falls
on rocks
48

St. Albans Island

*... many different immages are
Painted on the Rock at this
place the Snds. & French
pay omage. Many names
are wrote on the rock,...*

Clark ⇨

TAVERN
CAVE

*120 feet wide 40 feet Deep
20 feet high...*

Clark ⇨

Home of Daniel Boone
two miles

Tavern
Rock

Swift water

47

S 52 W
7 MILES

CREEK

BOTTOMS

DEFIANCE

Cartographer's Note:
The location of the settlement is not
clear from journal accounts. Clark
says there was a settlement of 30 or
40 families on the creek, but scholars
have claimed the settlement was at
Matson. Whether Clark meant a village
of closely placed homes by the word
"settlement" or a loose collection of
small farms along this stretch of the
river is also not clear.

MISSOURI

RIVER

46

Franklin Co.
St. Louis Co.

Pitman Creek

DARST

WOMANS

OSAGE

FEMME

Creek

45

N

Boone's Settlement

Settlement of
30 or 40 families

*...Many people
Came to See us,...*

Clark ⇨

Little
Femme

MISSOURI

Babler Spring

Babler State Park

Howell Island

1st St. Charles Co.
1st St. Louis Co.

Centaur Chute

TAVERN ISLAND

+45

44

OSAGE

Osage

Creek

Osage Spring

CENTAUR

*Point*

ONE STATUTE MILE

Outbound: May 23, 24, 1804
Return: September 21, 1806

Modern Data: 1954-1974

EXPLORATIONS OF LEWIS AND CLARK  1804 - 1806
CARTOGRAPHIC RECONSTRUCTION

TAVERN CAVE

UTM ZONE    15
MAP NUMBER   6

Missouri

CONTOUR INTERVAL   100 FEET

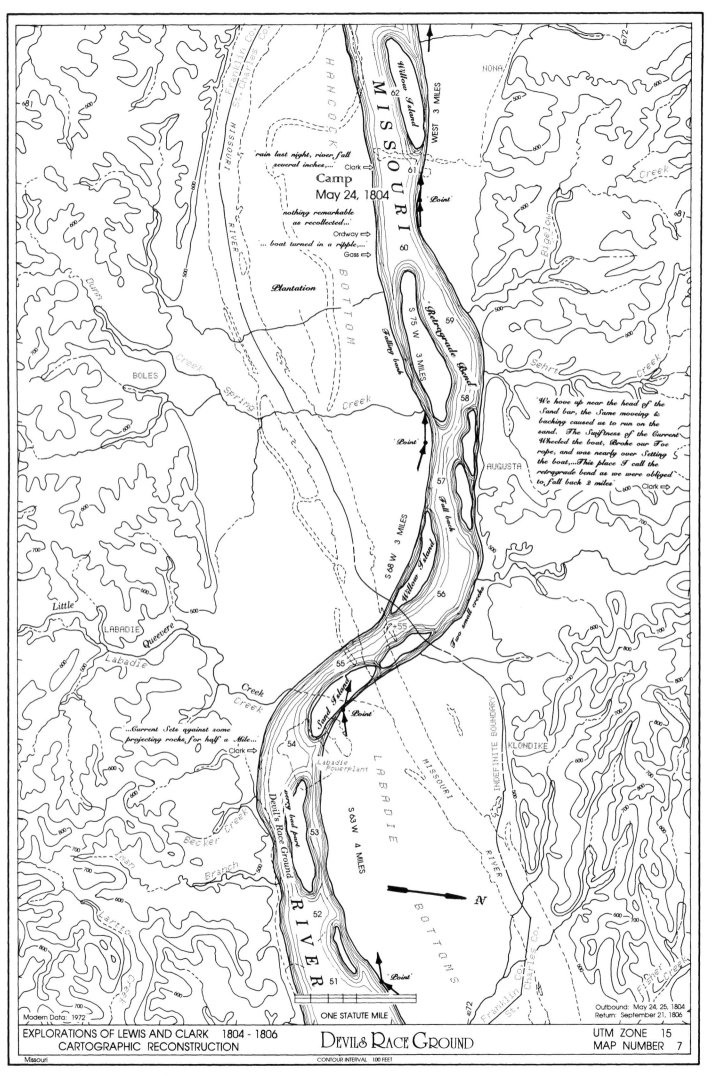

Willow Island

62

MISSOURI

NONA

HANCOCK

Bigelow Creek

681

600

72

81

WEST 3 MILES

Clark ⇒

61

rain last night, river fall
several inches,...

Point

Camp
May 24, 1804

nothing remarkable
as recollected...

Ordway ⇒

60

... boat turned in a ripple,...

Gass ⇒

Franklin Co.
St. Charles Co.

MISSOURI

RIVER

600

500

Plantation

BOTTOM

S 75 W   3 MILES

59

Sehrt Creek

"Retrograde Bend"

500

BOLES

Creek

Falling bank

58

600

Spring

Creek

600

700

Point

We hove up near the head of the
Sand bar, the Same moving &
backing caused us to run on the
sand.  The Swiftness of the Current
Wheeled the boat, Broke our Toe
rope, and was nearly over Setting
the boat,...This place I call the
retrograde bend as we were obliged
to fall back 2 miles

AUGUSTA

700

600

Clark ⇒

57

S 68 W  3 MILES

Fall back

Willow Island

56

Two small creeks

600

700

Little

LABADIE

Queevere

+55

700

Labadie

500

600

55

Sand Island

Point

MISSOURI

INDEFINITE BOUNDARY

800

700

KLONDIKE

600

800

Creek

Creek

...Current Sets against some
projecting rocks for half a Mile...

Clark ⇒

54

Labadie
Powerplant

LABADIE

600

RIVER

very bad part

Devil's Race Ground

53

S 63 W  4 MILES

N

BOTTOMS

Becker Creek

Branch

700

52

Franklin Co.
St. Charles Co.

72

600

700

Fisher Creek

800

Point

51

600

ONE STATUTE MILE

700

600

Outbound: May 24, 25, 1804
Return: September 21, 1806

Modern Data: 1972

EXPLORATIONS OF LEWIS AND CLARK   1804 - 1806
CARTOGRAPHIC RECONSTRUCTION

DEVILS RACE GROUND

UTM ZONE   15
MAP NUMBER   7

Missouri

CONTOUR INTERVAL  100 FEET

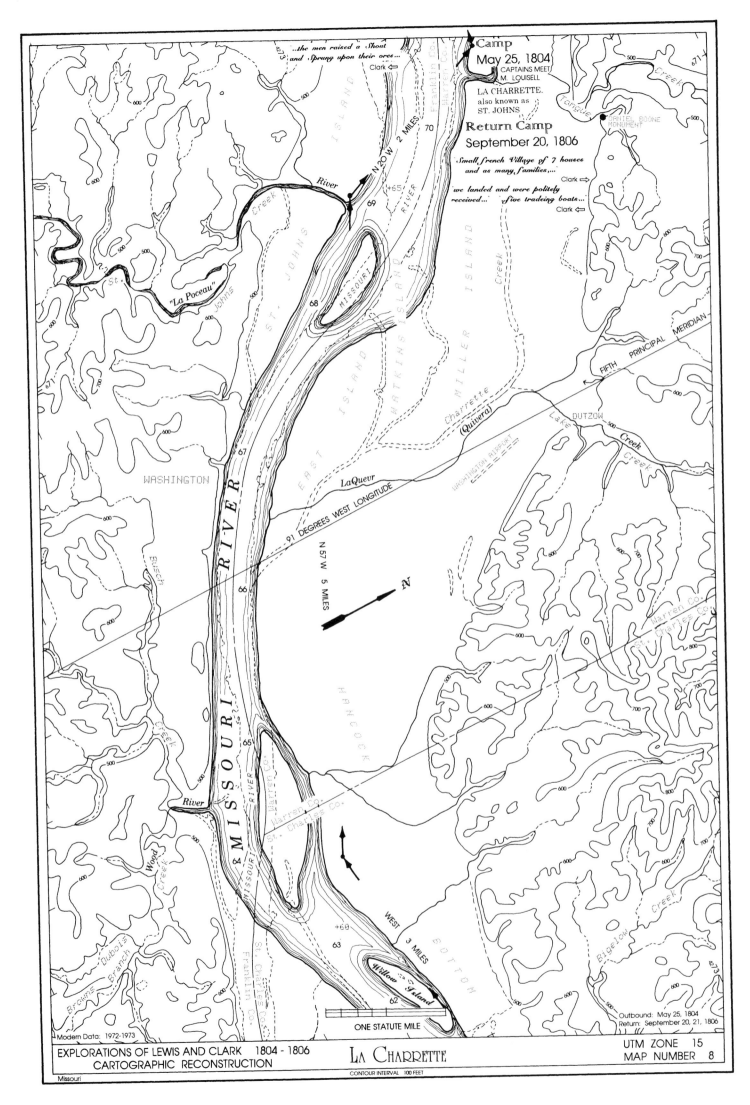

...the men raised a Shout
and Sprung upon their oars...
Clark ⇐

**Camp**
**May 25, 1804**
CAPTAINS MEET
M. LOUISELL

LA CHARRETTE.
also known as
ST. JOHNS

**Return Camp**
September 20, 1806

Small french Village of 7 houses
and as many families,...

we landed and were politely
received...  five tradeing boats...

Clark ⇒

Clark ⇐

DANIEL BOONE
MONUMENT

FIFTH PRINCIPAL MERIDIAN

DUTZOW

Creek

N 20 W 2 miles

River

"La Poceau"

ST. JOHNS

St. Johns Creek

MISSOURI RIVER

EAST ISLAND

WATKINS ISLAND

MILLER ISLAND

Charrette Creek

Charrette
(Quivera)

Lake

WASHINGTON

91 DEGREES WEST LONGITUDE

LaQuevr

WASHINGTON AIRPORT

N 57 W 5 MILES

N

HAUGHOOD BOTTOM

Busch Creek

MISSOURI RIVER

Warren Co.
St. Charles Co.

Warren Co.
St. Charles Co.

Warren Co.
St. Charles Co.

River

WEST 3 MILES

BOTTOM

Eigelow Creek

Wood Creek

Dubois Branch

Browns Branch

St. Charles Co.
Franklin Co.

+60

Willow Island

Outbound: May 25, 1804
Return: September 20, 21, 1806

Modern Data: 1972-1973

ONE STATUTE MILE

EXPLORATIONS OF LEWIS AND CLARK   1804 - 1806
CARTOGRAPHIC RECONSTRUCTION

La Charrette

UTM ZONE   15
MAP NUMBER   8

Missouri

CONTOUR INTERVAL  100 FEET

32

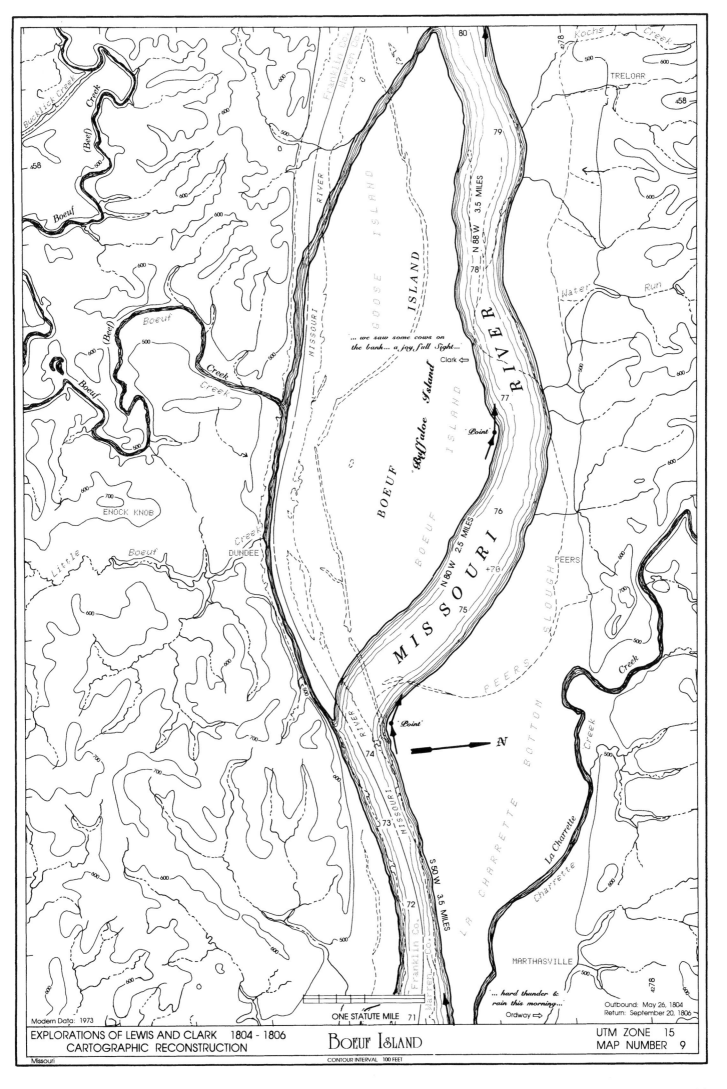

BUCKLICK Creek

Beef (Boeuf) Creek

458

Boeuf

Boeuf (Beef) Creek

Creek Creek

Boeuf

500

600

FRANKLIN CO. WARREN CO.

500

600

600

80

79

N 88 W 3.5 MILES

78

KOCHE Creek

TRELOAR

458

500

600

ENOCK KNOB

700

600

Little Boeuf

Creek

DUNDEE

MISSOURI RIVER

GOOSE ISLAND

... we saw some cows on
the bank... a joy full Sight...

Clark ⇐

"Buffaloe Island

BOEUF ISLAND

BOEUF ISLAND

77

Point

76

N 80 W 2.5 MILES

+76

75

PEERS SLOUGH

Water Run

500

600

600

PEERS

700

500

Creek

600

600

MISSOURI

700

600

700

600

600

RIVER

Point

74

N

73

MISSOURI

S 50 W 3.5 MILES

72

FRANKLIN CO. WARREN CO.

500

LA CHARRETTE BOTTOM

La Charrette

Charrette Creek

Creek

500

600

71

ONE STATUTE MILE

MARTHASVILLE

... hard thunder &
rain this morning...

Ordway ⇒

500

+78

Outbound: May 26, 1804
Return: September 20, 1806

Modern Data: 1973

EXPLORATIONS OF LEWIS AND CLARK    1804 - 1806
CARTOGRAPHIC RECONSTRUCTION

Missouri

BOEUF ISLAND

CONTOUR INTERVAL   100 FEET

UTM ZONE   15
MAP NUMBER  9

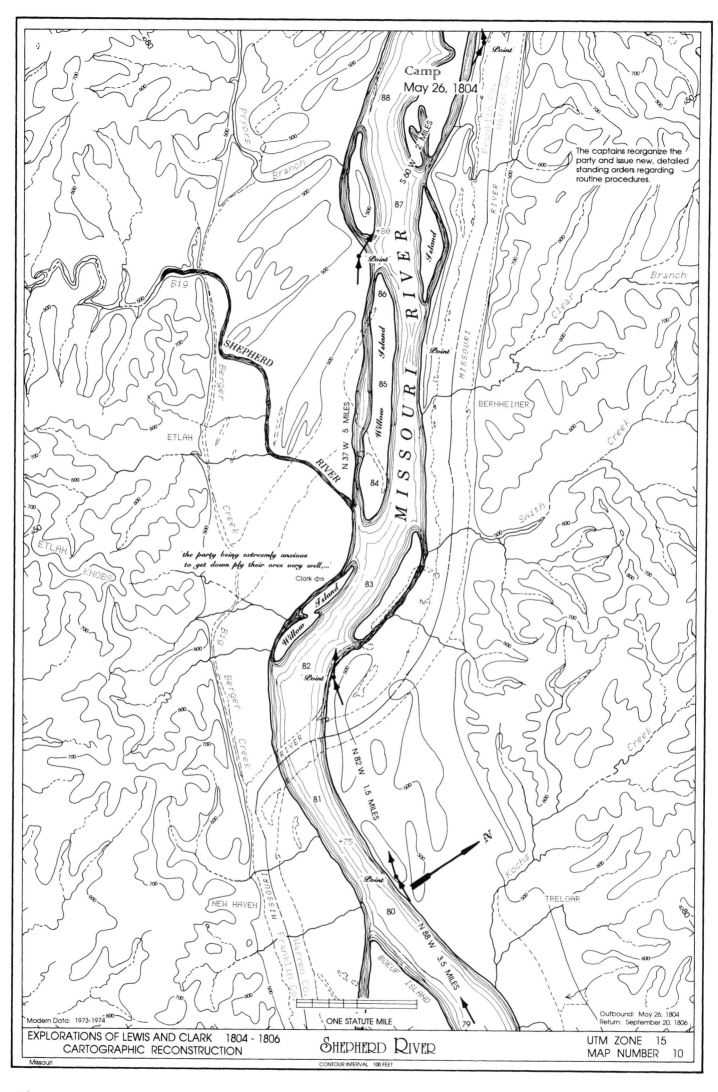

Camp
May 26, 1804

The captains reorganize the
party and issue new, detailed
standing orders regarding
routine procedures.

*the party being extreemly anxious
to get down ply their ores very well,...*

Clark ⇐

SHEPHERD

MISSOURI RIVER

ONE STATUTE MILE

Outbound: May 26, 1804
Return: September 20, 1806

EXPLORATIONS OF LEWIS AND CLARK  1804 - 1806
CARTOGRAPHIC RECONSTRUCTION

𝔖HEPHERD 𝔯IVER

UTM ZONE  15
MAP NUMBER  10

Modern Data: 1973-1974

Missouri

CONTOUR INTERVAL  100 FEET

34

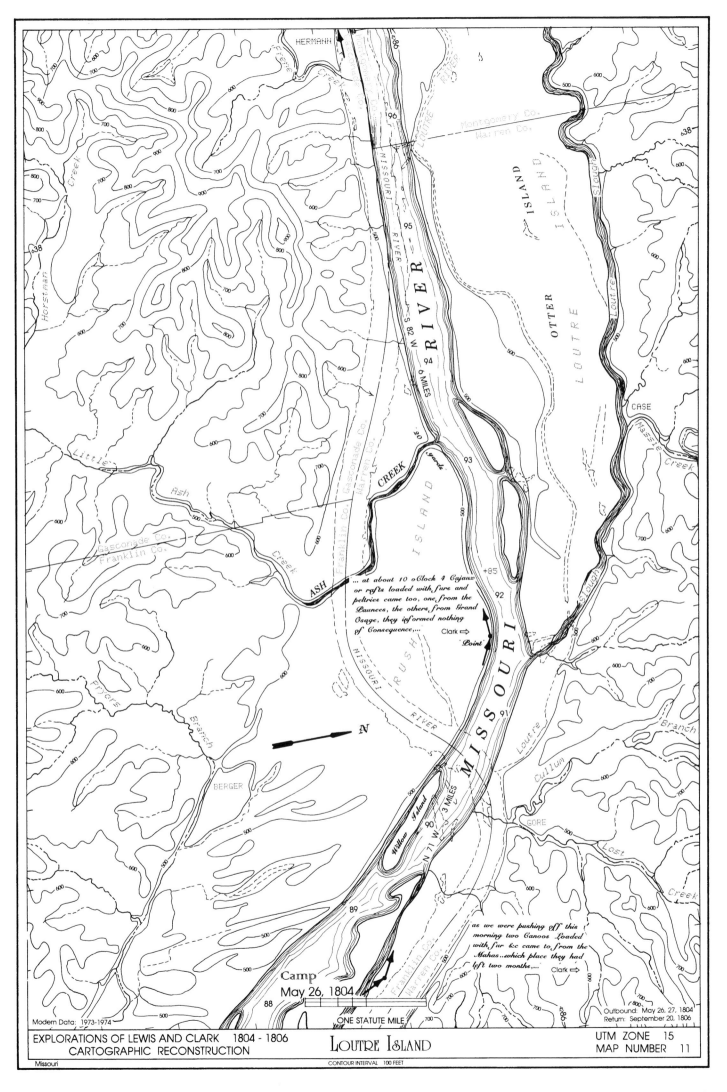

HERMANN

Montgomery Co.
Warren Co.

... at about 10 o'Clock 4 Cajaux
or rafts loaded with furs and
peltries came too, one, from the
Pawnees, the others, from Grand
Osage, they informed nothing
of Consequence,...

Clark ⇒
**Point**

N

as we were pushing off this
morning two Canoos Loaded
with fur &c came to, from the
Mahas...which place they had
left two months,...

Clark ⇒

Camp
May 26, 1804

ONE STATUTE MILE

Modern Data: 1973-1974

Outbound: May 26, 27, 1804
Return: September 20, 1806

EXPLORATIONS OF LEWIS AND CLARK   1804 - 1806
CARTOGRAPHIC RECONSTRUCTION

LOUTRE ISLAND

UTM ZONE   15
MAP NUMBER   11

Missouri

CONTOUR INTERVAL   100 FEET

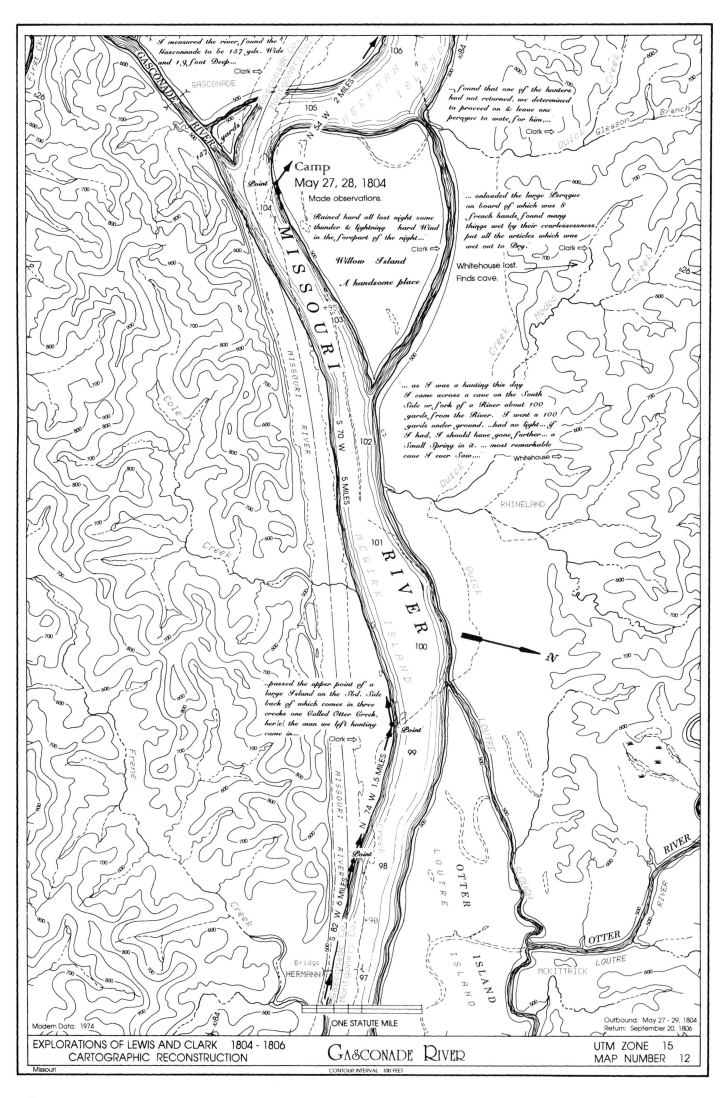

I measured the river, found the
Gasconade to be 157 yds. Wide
and 1.9 foot Deep...

Clark ⇒

GASCONADE

...found that one of the hunters
had not returned, we determined
to proceed on & leave one
peroque to wate for him,...

Clark ⇒

**Camp**
**May 27, 28, 1804**

Made observations.

Rained hard all last night some
thunder & lightning    hard Wind
in the forepart of the night...

Clark ⇒

...onloaded the large Peroque
on board of which was 8
french hands, found many
things wet by their cearlessessness,
put all the articles which was
wet out to Dry.

Clark ⇒

Willow Island

A handsome place

Whitehouse lost.
Finds cave.

...as I was a hunting this day
I came across a cave on the South
Side or fork of a River about 100
yards from the River. I went a 100
yards under ground. ..had no light... if
I had, I should have gone further... a
Small Spring in it. ... most remarkable
cave I ever Saw,...

Whitehouse ⇒

RHINELAND

N

..passed the upper point of a
large Island on the Sbd. Side
back of which comes in three
creeks one Called Otter Creek,
her/e/ the man we left hunting
came in...

Clark ⇒

Point

Bridge
HERMANN

OTTER
ISLAND

MCKITTRICK

OTTER

ONE STATUTE MILE

Modern Data: 1974
Outbound: May 27 - 29, 1804
Return: September 20, 1806

EXPLORATIONS OF LEWIS AND CLARK   1804 - 1806
CARTOGRAPHIC RECONSTRUCTION

GASCONADE RIVER

UTM ZONE   15
MAP NUMBER   12

Missouri

CONTOUR INTERVAL   100 FEET

36

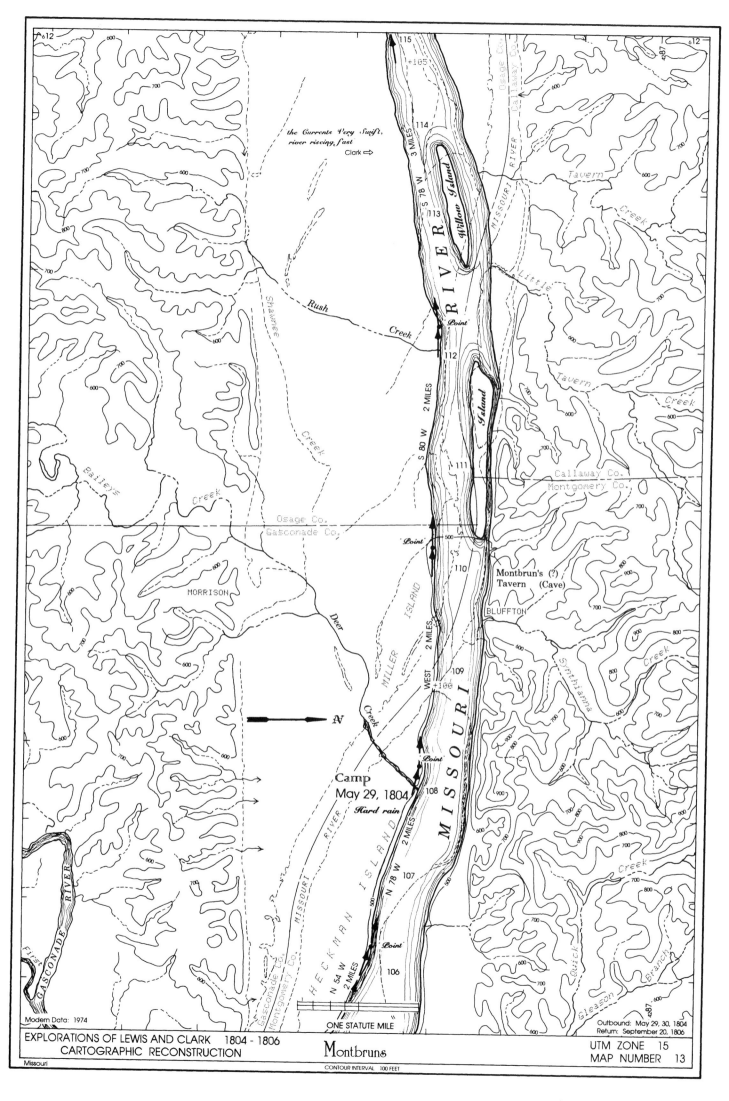

the Currents Very Swift,
river riseing fast
Clark ⟹

RIVER

115

+105

114

3 MILES

S 78 W

113

Willow Island

Point

112

S 80 W

2 MILES

Island

111

Callaway Co.
Montgomery Co.

Osage Co.
Gasconade Co.

Point

110

Montbrun's (?)
Tavern (Cave)

BLUFFTON

WEST

2 MILES

109

+100

Missouri River

Tavern

Little

Tavern

Creek

Creek

Synthiarna

Quick

Creek

Gleason

Branch

Creek

MILLER

ISLAND

MISSOURI

N 78 W

2 MILES

107

N 54 W

2 MILES

106

Point

Point

108

Camp
May 29, 1804

Hard rain

HECKMAN ISLAND

MISSOURI RIVER

GASCONADE RIVER

First

Montgomery Co.
Gasconade Co.

N

Rush

Creek

Shawnee

Creek

Baileys

Creek

MORRISON

Deer

Creek

Modern Data: 1974

ONE STATUTE MILE

Outbound: May 29, 30, 1804
Return: September 20, 1806

EXPLORATIONS OF LEWIS AND CLARK   1804 - 1806
CARTOGRAPHIC RECONSTRUCTION

Missouri

Montbruns

CONTOUR INTERVAL  100 FEET

UTM ZONE   15
MAP NUMBER   13

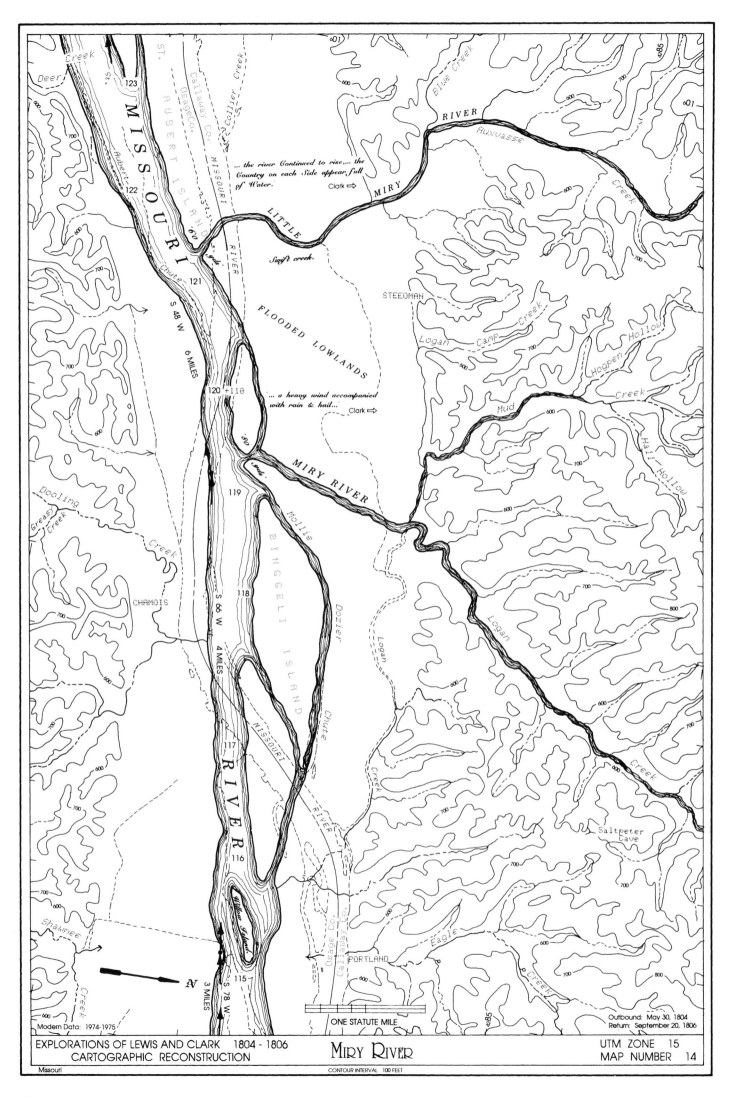

... the river Continued to rise,.... the Country on each Side appear full of Water.
Clark ⇨

... a heavy wind accompanied with rain & hail...
Clark ⇨

ONE STATUTE MILE

Modern Data: 1974-1975

Outbound: May 30, 1804
Return: September 20, 1806

EXPLORATIONS OF LEWIS AND CLARK   1804 – 1806
CARTOGRAPHIC RECONSTRUCTION

MIRY RIVER

UTM ZONE  15
MAP NUMBER  14

Missouri                                                CONTOUR INTERVAL  100 FEET

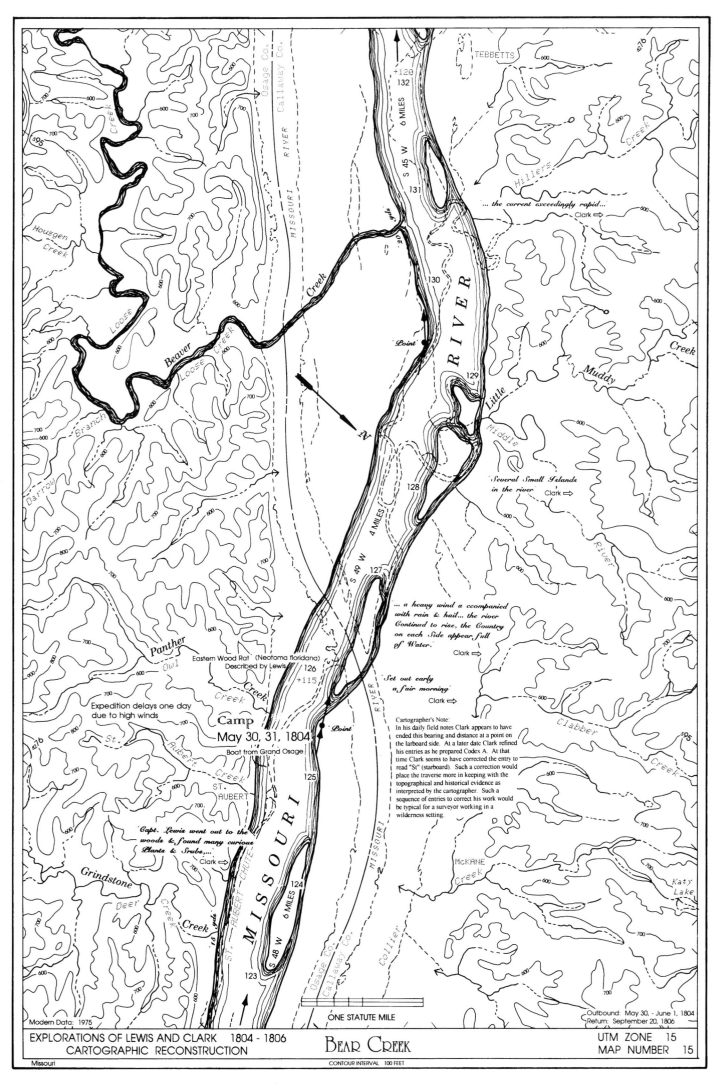

... the current exceedingly rapid ...
Clark ⇒

Several Small Islands
in the river    Clark ⇒

... a heavy wind accompanied
with rain & hail ... the river
Continued to rise, the Country
on each Side appear full
of Water.
Clark ⇒

Set out early
a fair morning
Clark ⇒

Cartographer's Note:
In his daily field notes Clark appears to have
ended this bearing and distance at a point on
the larboard side. At a later date Clark refined
his entries as he prepared Codex A. At that
time Clark seems to have corrected the entry to
read "St" (starboard). Such a correction would
place the traverse more in keeping with the
topographical and historical evidence as
interpreted by the cartographer. Such a
sequence of entries to correct his work would
be typical for a surveyor working in a
wilderness setting.

Eastern Wood Rat (Neotoma floridana)
Described by Lewis

Expedition delays one day
due to high winds

Camp
May 30, 31, 1804

Boat from Grand Osage

Capt. Lewis went out to the
woods & found many curious
Plants & Srubs ....
Clark ⇒

Expedition delays one day
due to high winds

Modern Data: 1975

ONE STATUTE MILE

Outbound: May 30, - June 1, 1804
Return: September 20, 1806

EXPLORATIONS OF LEWIS AND CLARK   1804 - 1806
CARTOGRAPHIC RECONSTRUCTION

BEAR CREEK

UTM ZONE   15
MAP NUMBER   15

Missouri

CONTOUR INTERVAL   100 FEET

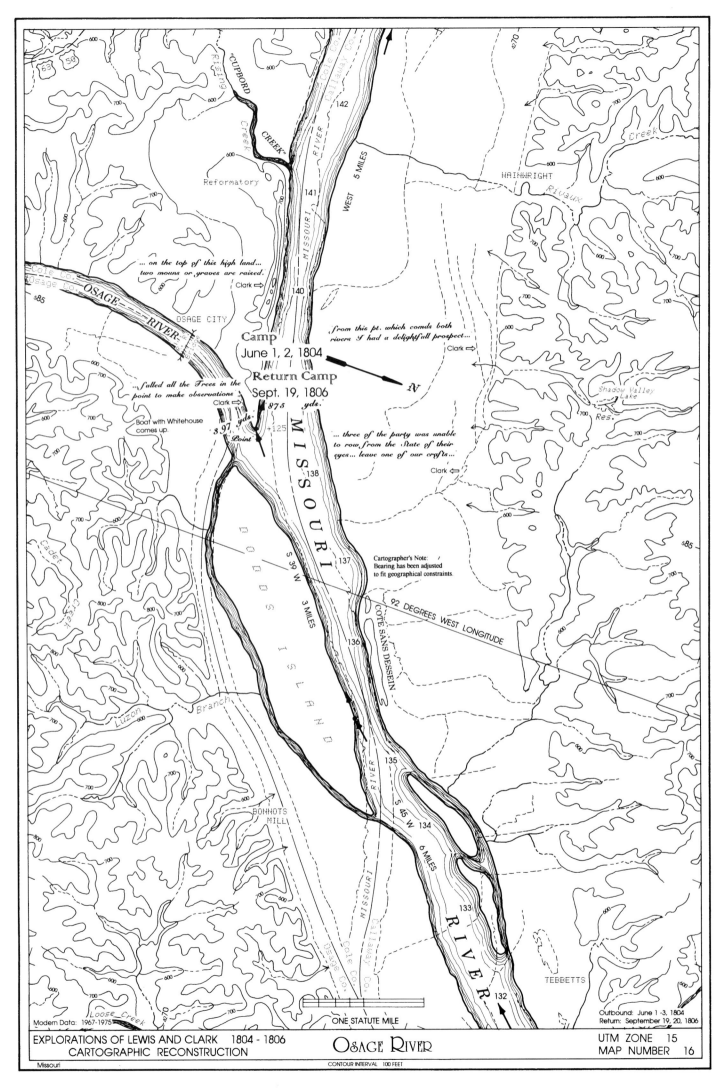

"CUPBORD CREEK"

142

Cole Co.
Callaway Co.

141

WEST 5 MILES

MISSOURI RIVER

Reformatory

Rising Creek

Cupbord Creek

63 59

600

600

600

600

700

700

600

Wainwright

Creek

600

600

700

700

670

... on the top of this high land...
two mouns or graves are raised.

Clark ⇒

140

Cole Co.
Osage Co.

OSAGE RIVER

585

OSAGE CITY

Camp
June 1, 2, 1804

Return Camp
Sept. 19, 1806

... falled all the Trees in the
point to make observations.

Clark ⇒

Boat with Whitehouse
comes up.

3.97 yds.

875 yds.

125

Point

from this pt. which comds both
rivers I had a delightfull prospect...

Clark ⇒

IV

... three of the party was unable
to row from the State of their
eyes... leave one of our crafts...

Clark ⇐

138

Shadow Valley
Lake
Res.

700

700

700

600

600

585

MISSOURI

Cadet Creek

Luzon Branch

LOOS ISLAND

S 39 W
3 MILES

137

Cartographer's Note:
Bearing has been adjusted
to fit geographical constraints.

136

COTE SANS DESSEIN

92 DEGREES WEST LONGITUDE

700

800

700

600

700

700

700

600

700

700

BONNOTS
MILL

135

MISSOURI RIVER

Cole Co.
Callaway Co.

S 45 W
6 MILES

134

133

RIVER

132

TEBBETTS

Outbound: June 1-3, 1804
Return: September 19, 20, 1806

Loose Creek

670

700

600

800

800

600

600

700

600

Modern Data: 1967-1975

ONE STATUTE MILE

EXPLORATIONS OF LEWIS AND CLARK    1804 - 1806
CARTOGRAPHIC RECONSTRUCTION

OSAGE RIVER

UTM ZONE    15
MAP NUMBER    16

Missouri

CONTOUR INTERVAL    100 FEET

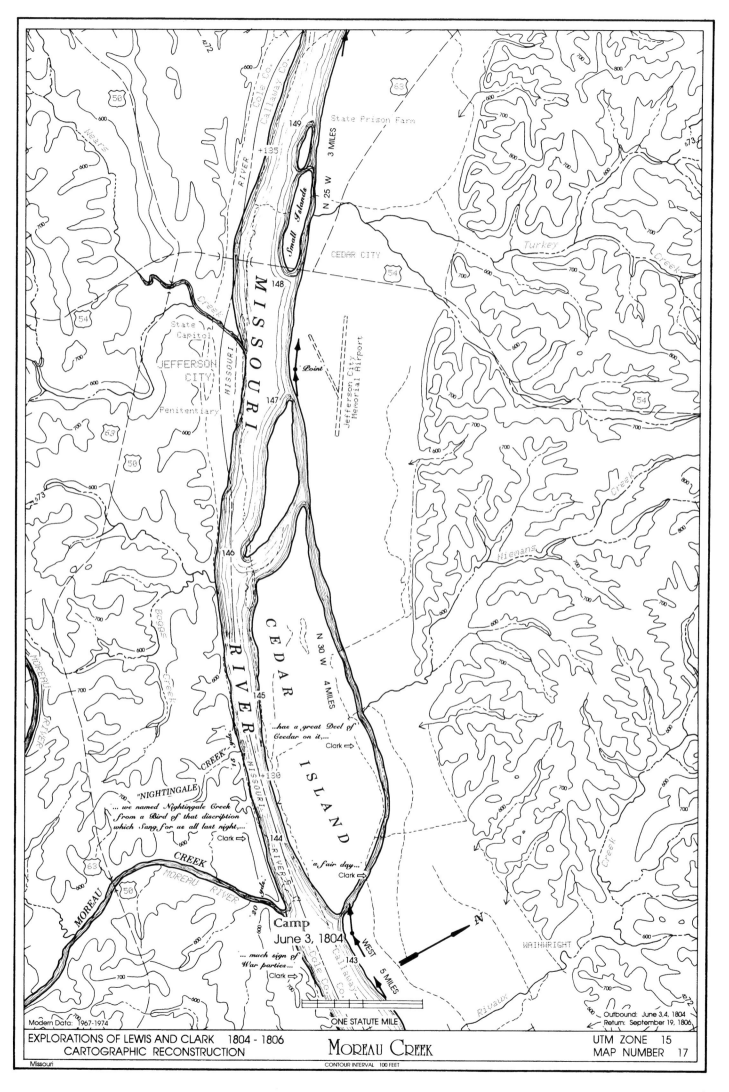

Heart's

Cole Co.
Callaway Co.
MISSOURI RIVER
State Prison Farm

3 MILES
N 25 W

Small Islands

CEDAR CITY

Turkey Creek

State Capitol
JEFFERSON CITY

MISSOURI

Point

Jefferson City
Memorial Airport

Penitentiary

Niemans

Creek

Boggs Creek

CEDAR RIVER ISLAND

N 30 W
4 MILES

MISSOURI RIVER

MOREAU RIVER

NIGHTINGALE CREEK

...has a great Deel of Ceedar on it,...
Clark ⇒

"NIGHTINGALE
... we named Nightingale Creek
from a Bird of that discription
which Sang for us all last night,...
Clark ⇒

Creek

... a fair day...
Clark ⇒

MOREAU CREEK
MOREAU RIVER

Camp
June 3, 1804

N

Cole Co.
Callaway Co.

WEST 5 MILES

... much sign of
War parties...
Clark ⇒

143

WAINWRIGHT

Rivaux

ONE STATUTE MILE

Modern Data: 1967-1974

Outbound: June 3,4, 1804
Return: September 19, 1806

EXPLORATIONS OF LEWIS AND CLARK    1804 - 1806
CARTOGRAPHIC RECONSTRUCTION

MOREAU CREEK

UTM ZONE    15
MAP NUMBER    17

Missouri

CONTOUR INTERVAL  100 FEET

41

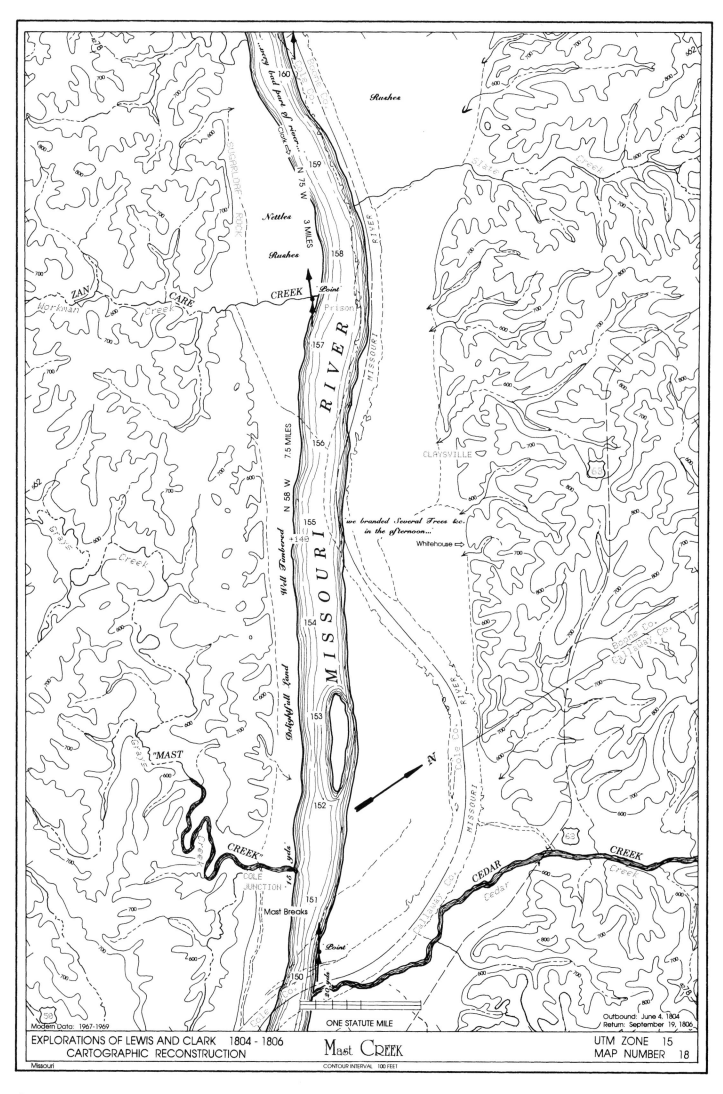

Rushes

160

159

N 75 W

Clark ⇒

...very bad part of river...

ZAN CARE CREEK

Workman    Creek

Nettles

Rushes

158

CREEK    Point

Prison

157

156

155
+140

154

153

152

151

Mast Breaks

150

Point

"MAST

CREEK"

COLE
JUNCTION

15 yds.

20 yds.

3 MILES

7.5 MILES

N 58 W

Well Timbered

Delightfull Land

MISSOURI    RIVER

Grays    Creek

SUGARLOAF ROCK

800

700

700

700

700

700

600

600

600

600

600

700

700

700

700

600

600

600

Slate    Creek

700

700

600

CLAYSVILLE

...we branded Several Trees &c.
in the afternoon...

Whitehouse ⇒

600

600

700

700

800

800

800

Boone Co.
Callaway Co.

MISSOURI RIVER    Cole Co.

Callaway Co.    Cole Co.

CEDAR    Cedar    CREEK

Cedar    Creek

600

600

600

800

700

700

700

700

800

63

63

N

ONE STATUTE MILE

Modern Data: 1967-1969

Outbound: June 4, 1804
Return: September 19, 1806

EXPLORATIONS OF LEWIS AND CLARK    1804 - 1806
CARTOGRAPHIC RECONSTRUCTION

Mast CREEK

UTM ZONE    15
MAP NUMBER    18

Missouri

CONTOUR INTERVAL    100 FEET

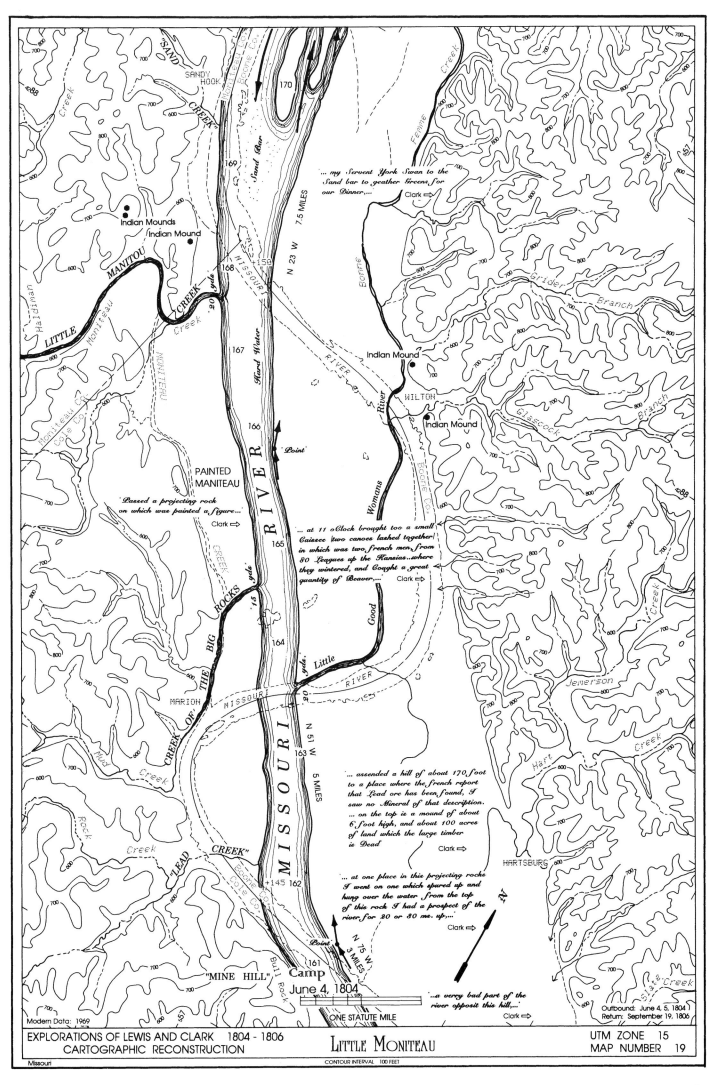

"SAND
HOOK

SAND
CREEK"

Indian Mounds
Indian Mound

MANITOU

LITTLE          CREEK

MONITEAU

Moniteau Cr.
Cole Co.

PAINTED
MANITEAU

*Passed a projecting rock
on which was painted a figure...*
Clark ⇒

MARION

CREEK OF THE BIG ROCKS

"LEAD          CREEK"

Mud          Creek

Rock          Creek

Haldiman

Manteau

Moniteau Cr.

"MINE HILL"

Modern Data: 1969

170

169

Sand Bar

168    +159

167

166

165

164

163

162    +145

161

N 23 W    7.5 MILES

MISSOURI

RIVER          Hard Water

20 yds.

15 yds.

20 yds.

Point

RIVER

MISSOURI

N 51 W    5 MILES

N 75 W    3 MILES

Point

Bull Rock

Camp
June 4, 1804

*... my Servent York Swan to the
Sand bar to geather Greens for
our Dinner,...*
Clark ⇒

Ferme          Creek

Bonne

RIVER

Indian Mound

WILTON

Indian Mound

Womans

Good

Little

RIVER

*... at 11 oClock brought too a small
Caissee (two canoes lashed together)
in which was two french men, from
80 Leagues up the Kansias...where
they wintered, and Cought a great
quantity of Beaver,...*
Clark ⇒

Grider

Branch

Glascock

Branch

Boone Co.

Cole Co.

Jemerson          Creek

Hart          Creek

*...ascended a hill of about 170 foot
to a place where the french report
that Lead ore has been found, I
saw no Mineral of that description.
... on the top is a mound of about
6 foot high, and about 100 acres
of land which the large timber
is Dead*
Clark ⇒

*... at one place in this projecting rocks
I went on one which spured up and
hung over the water from the top
of this rock I had a prospect of the
river for 20 or 30 ms. up,...*
Clark ⇒

HARTSBURG

Slate Creek

N

*...a verry bad part of the
river opposit this hill,...*
Clark ⇒

ONE STATUTE MILE

Outbound: June 4, 5, 1804
Return: September 19, 1806

EXPLORATIONS OF LEWIS AND CLARK    1804 - 1806
CARTOGRAPHIC RECONSTRUCTION

Missouri

LITTLE MONITEAU

CONTOUR INTERVAL   100 FEET

UTM ZONE    15
MAP NUMBER    19

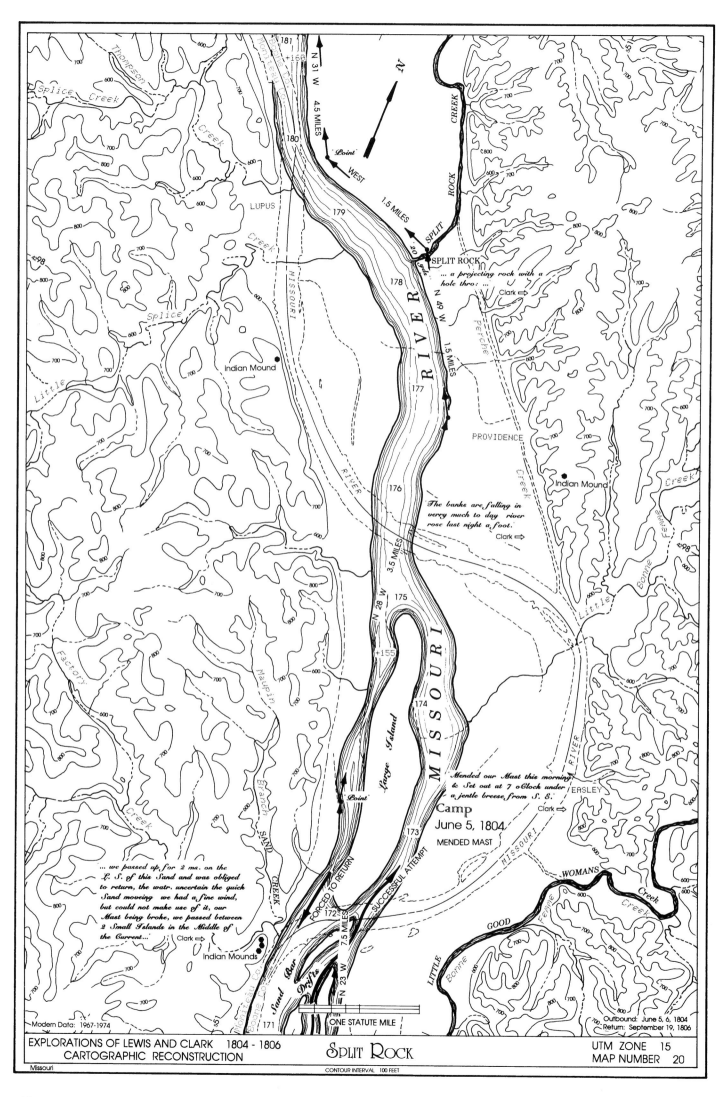

Splice Creek

Thompson Creek

Splice Creek

Little Splice

Little

Factory Creek

Montauk Creek

Maufin Creek

Maufin Branch Creek

SAND CREEK

Boone Drifts (Creek)

Sand Bar

Drifts

LUPUS

Creek

MISSOURI RIVER

RIVER

181
180
179
178
177
176
175
174
173
172
171

+160
+155

N 31 W  4.5 MILES

Point  WEST

*N*

SPLIT ROCK CREEK

1.5 MILES

30

49 N W

SPLIT ROCK
... a projecting rock with a
hole thro: ...
Clark ⇒

1.5 MILES

PERCHE Creek

PROVIDENCE

Indian Mound

Indian Mound

The banks are falling in
verry much to day  river
rose last night a foot.
Clark ⇒

N 28 W

3.5 MILES

Large Island

Point

M I S S O U R I

Little Bonne Femme Creek

4298

Little Bonne Creek

RIVER

Mended our Mast this morning
& Set out at 7 oClock under
a jentle breeze from S. E.
Camp
June 5, 1804
MENDED MAST
Clark ⇒

EASLEY

WOMANS Creek

GOOD

Little Bonne Femme

LITTLE

N 23 W

7.5 MILES

FORCED TO RETURN

SUCCESSFUL ATTEMPT

... we passed up, for 2 ms. on the
L. S. of this Sand and was obliged
to return, the watr. uncertain the quick
Sand moveing  we had a fine wind,
but could not make use of it, our
Mast being broke, we passed between
2 Small Islands in the Middle of
the Current...  Clark ⇒

Indian Mounds

4298

551

Modern Data: 1967-1974

Outbound: June 5, 6, 1804
Return: September 19, 1806

ONE STATUTE MILE

EXPLORATIONS OF LEWIS AND CLARK   1804 - 1806
CARTOGRAPHIC RECONSTRUCTION

Missouri

Split Rock

CONTOUR INTERVAL  100 FEET

UTM ZONE   15
MAP NUMBER   20

44

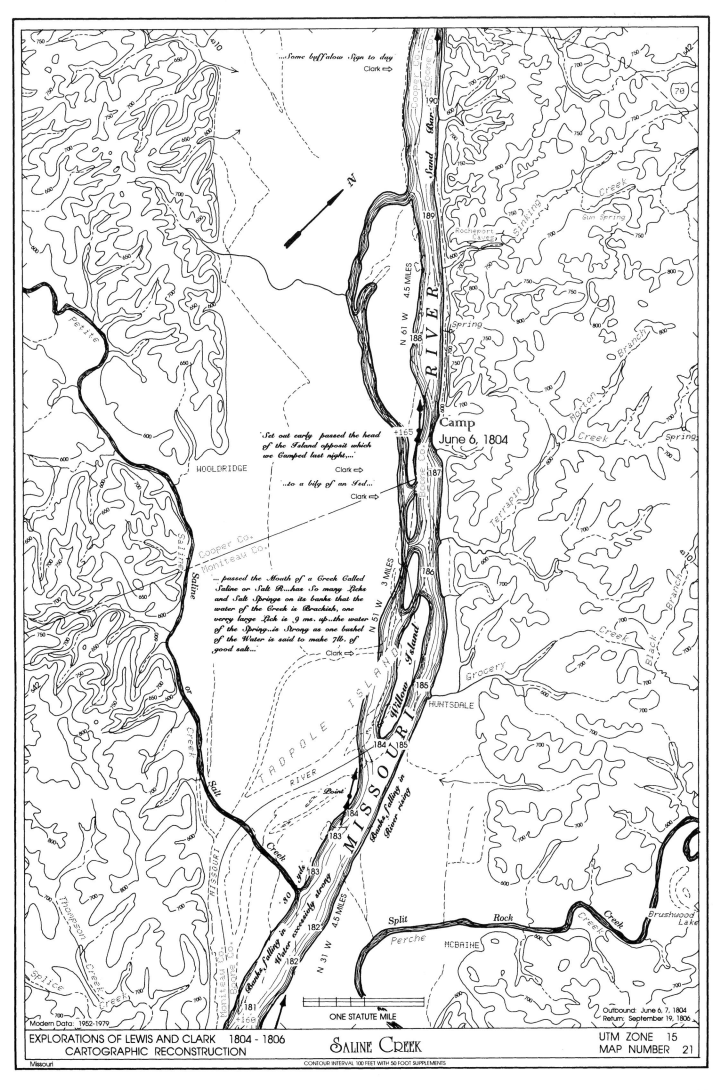

...Some buffalow Sign to day
Clark ⇒

N

Camp
June 6, 1804

Set out early passed the head
of the Island opposit which
we Camped last night,...'
Clark ⇒

..to a bilg of an Isd...
Clark ⇒

WOOLDRIDGE

Cooper Co.
Moniteau Co.

... passed the Mouth of a Creek Called
Saline or Salt R...has So many Licks
and Salt Springs on its banks that the
water of the Creek is Brackish, one
verry large Lick is 9 ms. up..the water
of the Spring..is Strong as one bushel
of the Water is said to make 7lb. of
good salt...'
Clark ⇒

Rocheport
Caves

Sinking Creek

Gum Spring

Spring

Morton Branch

Spring

Terrapin Creek

Black Branch Creek

Grocery

HUNTSDALE

Point

Banks falling in
River rising

Banks falling in
Water excessionly strong

30 yds

Split
Perche

Rock Creek

Brushwood Lake

MCBAINE

Modern Data: 1952-1979

ONE STATUTE MILE

Outbound: June 6, 7, 1804
Return: September 19, 1806

EXPLORATIONS OF LEWIS AND CLARK   1804 - 1806
CARTOGRAPHIC RECONSTRUCTION

Saline Creek

UTM ZONE    15
MAP NUMBER   21

Missouri

CONTOUR INTERVAL 100 FEET WITH 50 FOOT SUPPLEMENTS

45

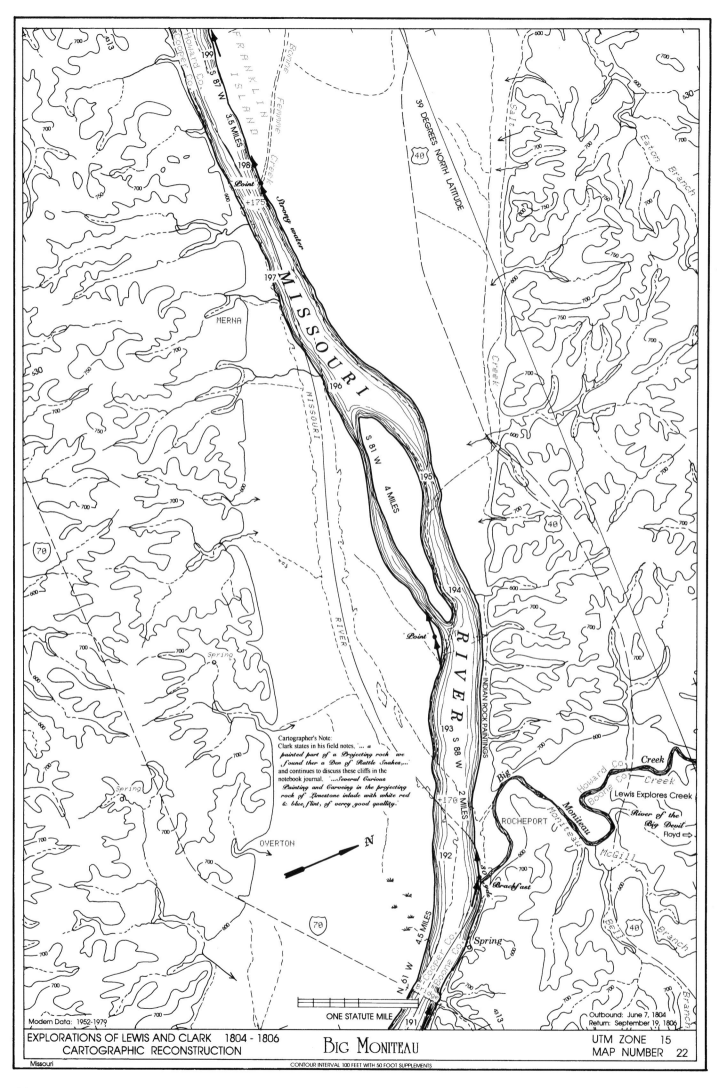

Cartographer's Note:
Clark states in his field notes, '... a painted part of a Projecting rock we found ther a Den of Rattle Snakes,... and continues to discuss these cliffs in the notebook journal. '...Several Curious Painting and Carveing in the projecting rock of Limestone inlade with white red & blue, flint, of verry good quallity.'

OVERTON

N

ONE STATUTE MILE

Modern Data: 1952-1979

Outbound: June 7, 1804
Return: September 19, 1806

EXPLORATIONS OF LEWIS AND CLARK    1804 - 1806
CARTOGRAPHIC RECONSTRUCTION

BIG MONITEAU

UTM ZONE    15
MAP NUMBER    22

Missouri

CONTOUR INTERVAL 100 FEET WITH 50 FOOT SUPPLEMENTS

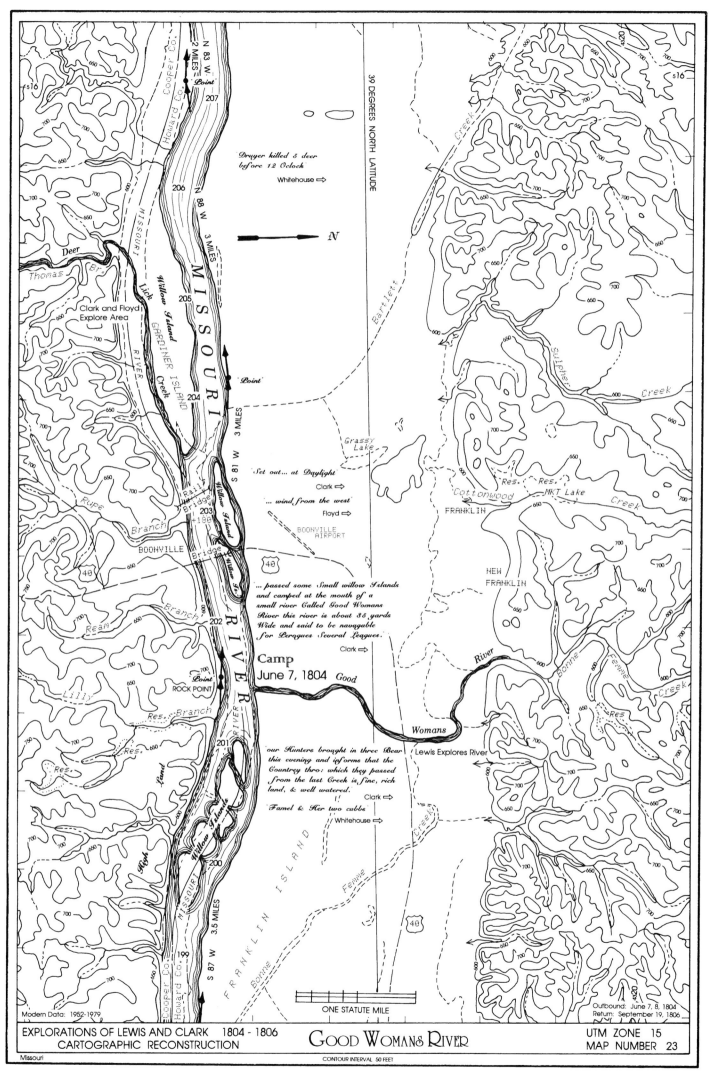

Modern Data: 1952-1979

Droyer killed 5 deer
before 12 Oclock
Whitehouse ⇨

N

Set out... at Daylight
Clark ⇨
... wind from the west
Floyd ⇨

... passed some Small willow Islands
and camped at the mouth of a
small river Called Good Womans
River this river is about 35 yards
Wide and said to be navigable
for Perogues Several Leagues.
Clark ⇨

Camp
June 7, 1804

our Hunters brought in three Bear
this evening and informs that the
Country thro: which they passed
from the last Creek is fine, rich
land, & well watered.
Clark ⇨
Famel & Her two cubbs
Whitehouse ⇨

Lewis Explores River

Clark and Floyd
Explore Area

ROCK POINT

BOONVILLE

FRANKLIN

NEW
FRANKLIN

Grassy
Lake

MKT Lake

ONE STATUTE MILE

Outbound: June 7, 8, 1804
Return: September 19, 1806

EXPLORATIONS OF LEWIS AND CLARK   1804 - 1806
CARTOGRAPHIC RECONSTRUCTION

GOOD WOMANS RIVER

UTM ZONE 15
MAP NUMBER 23

Missouri                              CONTOUR INTERVAL 50 FEET

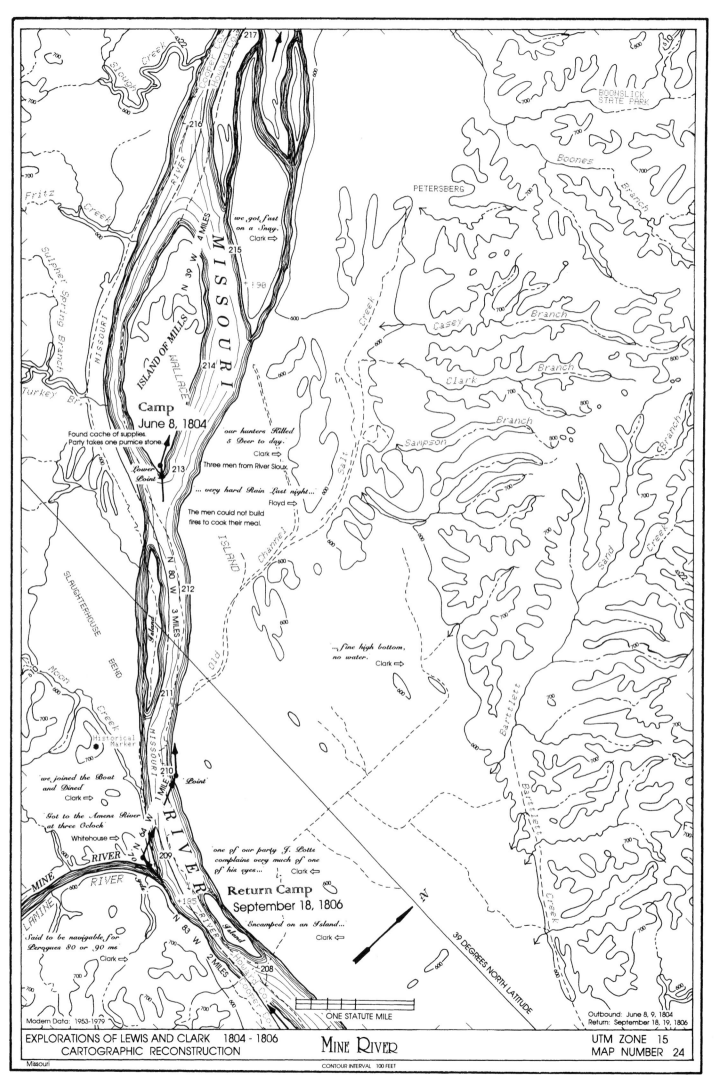

ISLAND OF MILLS

MISSOURI

MISSOURI RIVER

N 39 W    4 MILES

217

216

215

214

213

212

211

210

209

208

Cooper Co.

Howard Co.

Slough Creek

Fritz Creek

Sulpher Spring Branch

Turkey Br.

SLAUGHTERHOUSE BEND

Moon Creek

MINE RIVER

LAMINE RIVER

RIVER

Island

Lower Point

WALLACE

N 80 W    3 MILES

N 84 W    1 MILE

N 70 W

N 83 W    2 MILES

Island

OLD    ISLAND

Channel

Camp
June 8, 1804

Found cache of supplies.
Party takes one pumice stone.

*we got fast
on a Snag.*
Clark ⇨

+198

*our hunters Killed
5 Deer to day.*
Clark ⇨

Three men from River Sioux.

*... very hard Rain Last night...*
Floyd ⇨

The men could not build
fires to cook their meal.

*...fine high bottom,
no water.*
Clark ⇨

Historical
Marker

*we joined the Boat
and Dined*
Clark ⇨

*Got to the Amens River
at three Oclock*

Whitehouse ⇨

*one of our party J. Potts
complains very much of one
of his eyes...*
Clark ⇦

Return Camp
September 18, 1806

*Encamped on an Island...*
Clark ⇦

+185

*Said to be navigable for
Peroques 80 or 90 ms*
Clark ⇨

PETERSBERG

BOONSLICK
STATE PARK

Boones
Branch

Casey

Branch

Clark

Branch

Sampson

Branch

Salt

Creek

Sand    Creek

Bartlett    Branch

Bartlett    Creek

N

39 DEGREES NORTH LATITUDE

Modern Data: 1953-1979

ONE STATUTE MILE

Outbound: June 8, 9, 1804
Return: September 18, 19, 1806

EXPLORATIONS OF LEWIS AND CLARK    1804 - 1806
CARTOGRAPHIC RECONSTRUCTION

MINE RIVER

UTM ZONE    15
MAP NUMBER    24

Missouri

CONTOUR INTERVAL    100 FEET

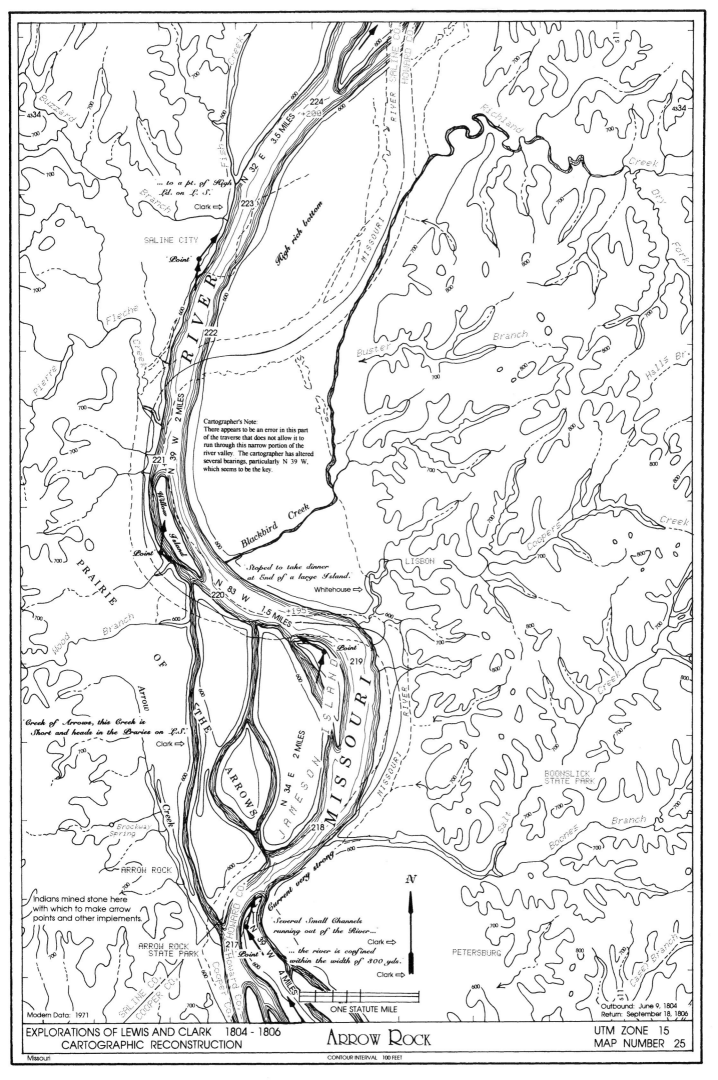

Cartographer's Note:
There appears to be an error in this part
of the traverse that does not allow it to
run through this narrow portion of the
river valley. The cartographer has altered
several bearings, particularly N 39 W,
which seems to be the key.

... to a pt. of High
Ld. on L.S.
Clark ⇒

SALINE CITY
'Point'

High rich bottom

Stoped to take dinner
at End of a large Island.
Whitehouse ⇒

LISBON

Point

Blackbird Creek

'Point'

Creek of Arrows, this Creek is
Short and heads in the Praries on L.S.
Clark ⇒

Brockway
Spring

ARROW ROCK

Indians mined stone here
with which to make arrow
points and other implements.

ARROW ROCK
STATE PARK

Point

Current very strong

Several Small Channels
running out of the River...
Clark ⇒

... the river is confined
within the width of 800 yds.
Clark ⇒

BOONSLICK
STATE PARK

PETERSBURG

N

ONE STATUTE MILE

Modern Data: 1971

Outbound: June 9, 1804
Return: September 18, 1806

EXPLORATIONS OF LEWIS AND CLARK   1804 - 1806
CARTOGRAPHIC RECONSTRUCTION

ARROW ROCK

UTM ZONE 15
MAP NUMBER 25

Missouri

CONTOUR INTERVAL   100 FEET

49

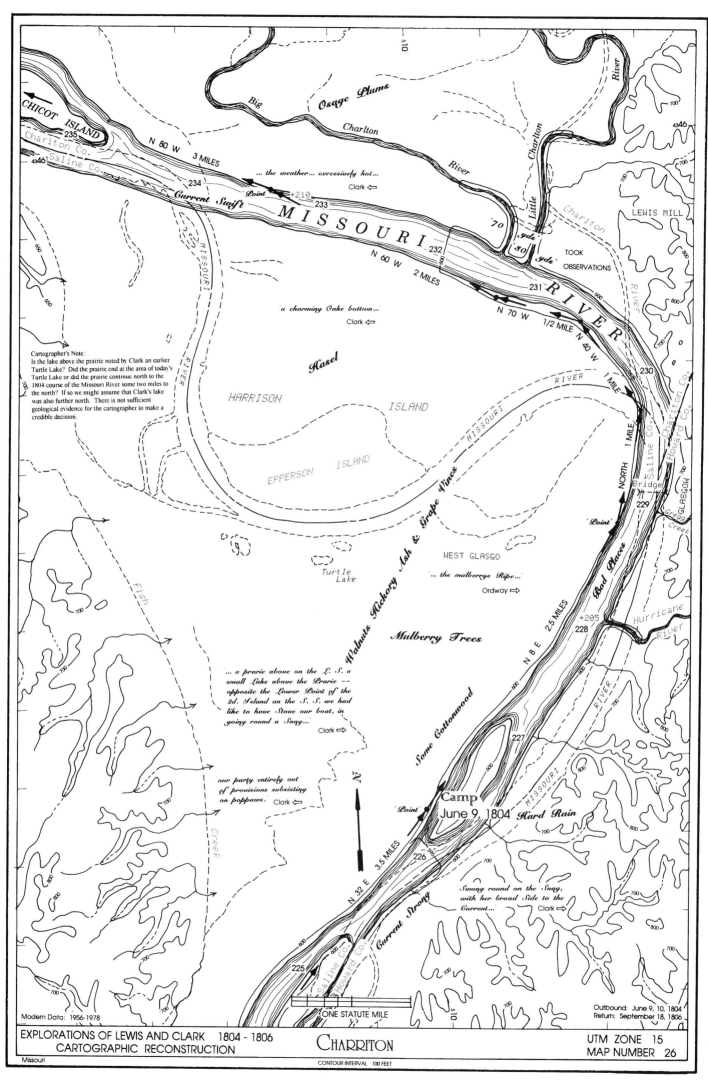

CHICOT ISLAND

235

Charlton Co.
Saline Co.

4346

N 80 W    3 MILES

234

Current Swift

Point    +210

233

Big

Osage Plums

Charlton

River

... the weather... excessively hot...
Clark ⇐

MISSOURI    232

N 60 W    2 MILES

800

N 70 W    1/2 MILE

231    RIVER

N 40 W

230

Little    Charlton    River

'70
yds.

'80
yds.

TOOK
OBSERVATIONS

LEWIS MILL

800

510

4346

700

700

800

a charming Oake bottom...
Clark ⇐

Cartographer's Note:
Is the lake above the prairie noted by Clark an earlier
Turtle Lake? Did the prairie end at the area of today's
Turtle Lake or did the prairie continue north to the
1804 course of the Missouri River some two miles to
the north? If so we might assume that Clark's lake
was also further north. There is not sufficient
geological evidence for the cartographer to make a
credible decision.

880

880

MISSOURI    RIVER

Hasel

HARRISON    ISLAND

EPPERSON    ISLAND

MISSOURI    RIVER

NORTH    1 MILE

Bridge

229

Point

Bad Places

Gregg Creek

GLASGOW

800

700

700

Fish

700

Turtle
Lake

Walnuts Hickory Ash & Grape Vines

WEST GLASGO

... the mulberrys Ripe...
Ordway ⇒

Mulberry Trees

N 8 E    2.5 MILES

+205

228

Hurricane    River

800

600

700

Creek

... a prairie above on the L. S. a
small Lake above the Prarie --
opposite the Lower Point of the
2d. Island on the S. S. we had
like to have Stove our boat, in
going round a Snag...
Clark ⇒

Some Cottonwood

227

600

800

700

700

our party entirely out
of provisions subsisting
on poppaws. Clark ⇐

N

Point

Camp
June 9, 1804    Hard Rain

MISSOURI    RIVER

700

800

N 32 E    3.5 MILES

226

600

Swung round on the Snag,
with her broad Side to the
Current... Clark ⇒

700

700

800

225

Saline Co.
Howard Co.

600

Current Strong

700

700

510

Modern Data: 1956-1978

ONE STATUTE MILE

Outbound: June 9, 10, 1804
Return: September 18, 1806

EXPLORATIONS OF LEWIS AND CLARK    1804 - 1806
CARTOGRAPHIC RECONSTRUCTION

Missouri

CHARRITON

CONTOUR INTERVAL    100 FEET

UTM ZONE    15
MAP NUMBER    26

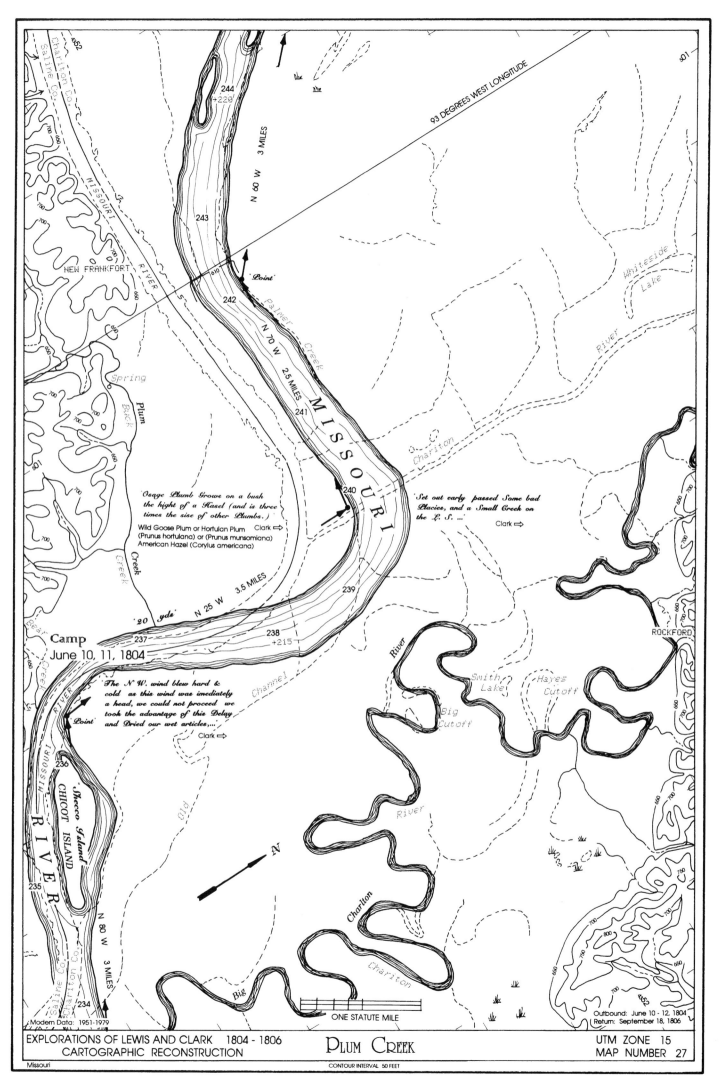

244
+228

N 60 W   3 MILES

93 DEGREES WEST LONGITUDE

243

Whiteside Lake

NEW FRANKFORT

Palmer Creek

Point

242

N 70 W   2.5 MILES

River

Spring

MISSOURI

241

Plum

Chariton

Buck

RIVER

Osage Plumb Grows on a bush
the hight of a Hasel (and is three
times the size of other Plumbs.)

240

Set out early passed Some bad
Placies, and a Small Creek on
the L. S. ...:

Clark ⇒

Wild Goose Plum or Hortulan Plum
(Prunus hortulana) or (Prunus munsomiana)
American Hazel (Corylus americana)

Creek

Clark ⇒

ROCKFORD

239

River

700

N 25 W   3.5 MILES

Smith
Lake

Hayes
Cutoff

20 yds

Camp
June 10, 11, 1804

237

238
+215

Big
Cutoff

The N. W. wind blew hard &
cold  as this wind was imediately
a head, we could not proceed  we
took the advantage of this Delay
and Dried our wet articles,...:

Channel

Point

Clark ⇒

River

Chariton

Bear Creek

236

Missouri

N

Sheoco Island
CHICOT ISLAND

Chariton Co.
Saline Co.

RIVER

235

N 80 W
3 MILES

Big

Chariton

234

Modern Data: 1951-1979

ONE STATUTE MILE

Outbound:  June 10 - 12, 1804
Return:  September 18, 1806

EXPLORATIONS OF LEWIS AND CLARK   1804 - 1806
CARTOGRAPHIC RECONSTRUCTION

PLUM CREEK

UTM ZONE  15
MAP NUMBER  27

Missouri

CONTOUR INTERVAL  50 FEET

51

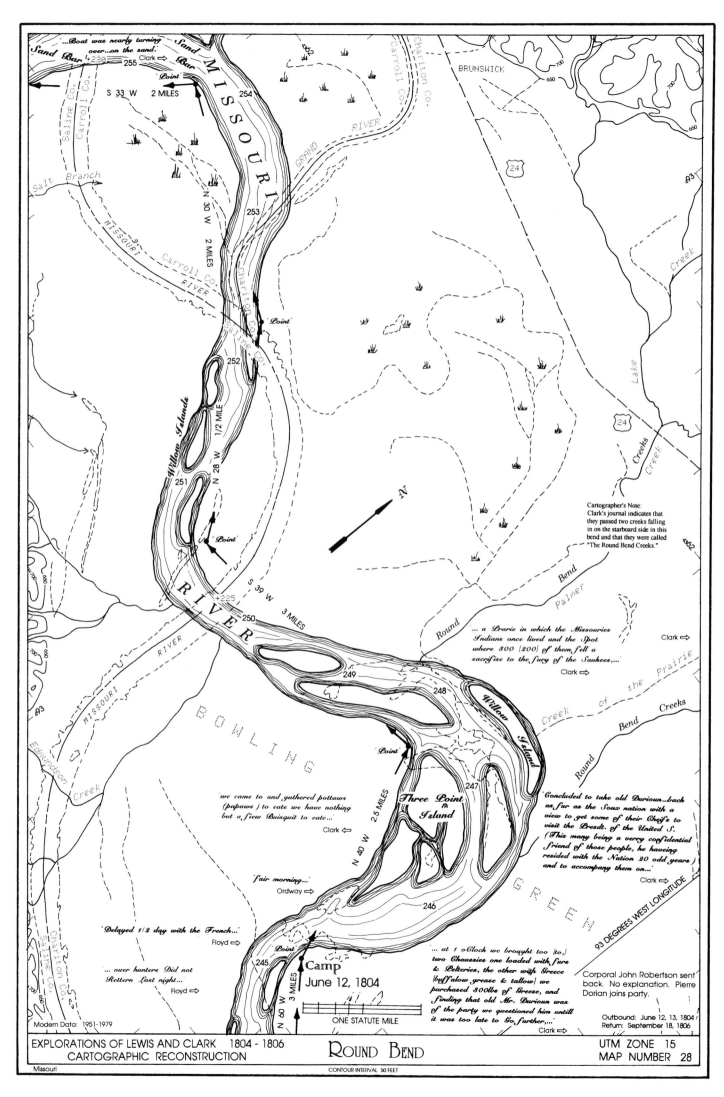

...Boat was nearly turning over...on the sand.

Sand Bar

Sand Bar

4230 255 Clark ⟹

Point

S 33 W 2 MILES

254

N 30 W 2 MILES

253

Point

252

Willow Islands

1/2 MILE

N 28 W

251

Point

S 39 W 3 MILES

+225

250

249

248

Willow Island

BOWLING

2.5 MILES

N 40 W

Three Point Island

247

246

245

N 60 W 3 MILES

Point

Point

Camp June 12, 1804

MISSOURI

RIVER

SAND

MISSOURI RIVER

Salt Branch

Missouri River

Carroll Co.

Saline Co.

Chariton Co.

Saline Co.

Chariton Co.

Salt Branch

Edmundson Creek

GRAND RIVER

BRUNSWICK

Chariton Co.

Carroll Co.

Lake Creek

24

A3

650

700

700

650

Creeks Creek

24

4562

A3

Round Bend Palmer

Round Creek of the Prairie

Round Bend Creeks

GREEN

93 DEGREES WEST LONGITUDE

Cartographer's Note:
Clark's journal indicates that they passed two creeks falling in on the starboard side in this bend and that they were called "The Round Bend Creeks."

... a Prarie in which the Missouries Indians once lived and the Spot where 800 [200] of them fell a sacrifise to the fury of the Saukees,...

Clark ⟹

Clark ⟹

Concluded to take old Durioun...back as fur as the Soux nation with a view to get some of their Cheifs to visit the Presdt. of the United S. (This many being a verry confidential friend of those people, he haveing resided with the Nation 20 odd years) and to accompany them on...

Clark ⟹

we came to and gathered pottaws (papaws) to eate we have nothing but a fiew Buisquit to eate...

Clark ⟸

fair morning...
Ordway ⟹

Delayed 1/2 day with the French...
Floyd ⟹

... ouer hunters Did not Rettern Last night...
Floyd ⟹

... at 1 oClock we brought too [to,] two Chaussies one loaded with furs & Pelteries, the other with Greece [buffalow grease & tallow] we purchased 300lbs of Greese, and finding that old Mr. Durioun was of the party we questioned him untill it was too late to Go further,...

Clark ⟹

Corporal John Robertson sent back. No explanation. Pierre Dorian joins party.

Outbound: June 12, 13, 1804
Return: September 18, 1806

Modern Data: 1951-1979

ONE STATUTE MILE

EXPLORATIONS OF LEWIS AND CLARK 1804 - 1806
CARTOGRAPHIC RECONSTRUCTION

ROUND BEND

UTM ZONE 15
MAP NUMBER 28

Missouri

CONTOUR INTERVAL 50 FEET

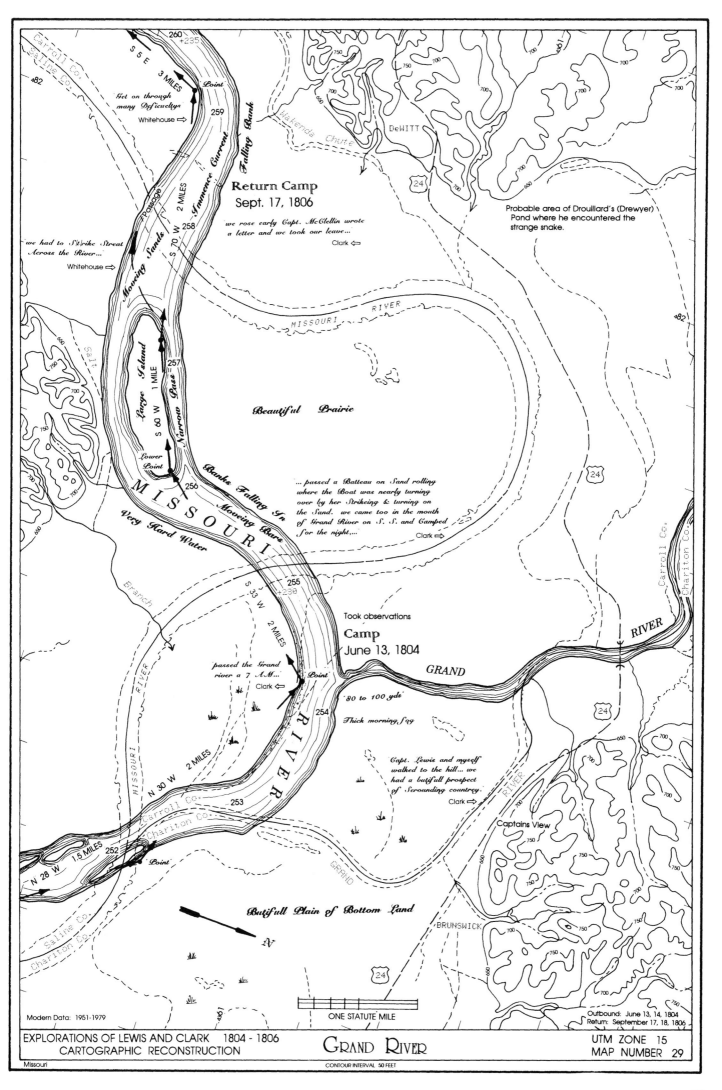

S 5 E
3 MILES
Point
+235
260
259
S 70 W
2 MILES
258
Get on through
many Deficultys
Whitehouse ⇨

Passage

Moveing Sands

**Return Camp**
Sept. 17, 1806

*we rose early Capt. McClellin wrote
a letter and we took our leave...*
Clark ⇦

*we had to Strike Streat
Across the River...*
Whitehouse ⇨

Immence Current

Falling Bank

Wakenda Chute

DeWITT

24

Probable area of Drouillard's (Drewyer)
Pond where he encountered the
strange snake.

482

Large Island
1 MILE
257
S 60 W

Narrow Pass

Lower
Point
256

Banks Falling In
Moveing Bars

MISSOURI
Very Hard Water

Branch

MISSOURI RIVER

RIVER

MISSOURI

*Beautiful Prairie*

MISSOURI RIVER

482

24

*... passed a Batteau on Sand rolling
where the Boat was nearly turning
over by her Strikeing & turning on
the Sand. we came too in the mouth
of Grand River on S. S. and Camped
for the night,...*
Clark ⇨

255
+290
S 33 W
2 MILES

Took observations

**Camp**
June 13, 1804

GRAND

RIVER

Carroll Co.
Chariton Co.

*passed the Grand
river a 7 A.M....*
Clark ⇦

Point

254

*80 to 100 yds*

*Thick morning fog*

GRAND RIVER

N 30 W
2 MILES

253

*Capt. Lewis and myself
walked to the hill... we
had a butifull prospect
of Scrounding country.*
Clark ⇨

RIVER

GRAND

Captains View

750

650

700

Carroll Co.
Chariton Co.

N 28 W
1.5 MILES
252
Point

*Butifull Plain of Bottom Land*

N

BRUNSWICK

Saline Co.
Chariton Co.

24

650

700

750

Modern Data: 1951-1979

ONE STATUTE MILE

Outbound: June 13, 14, 1804
Return: September 17, 18, 1806

EXPLORATIONS OF LEWIS AND CLARK  1804 - 1806
CARTOGRAPHIC RECONSTRUCTION

GRAND RIVER

UTM ZONE  15
MAP NUMBER  29

Missouri

CONTOUR INTERVAL 50 FEET

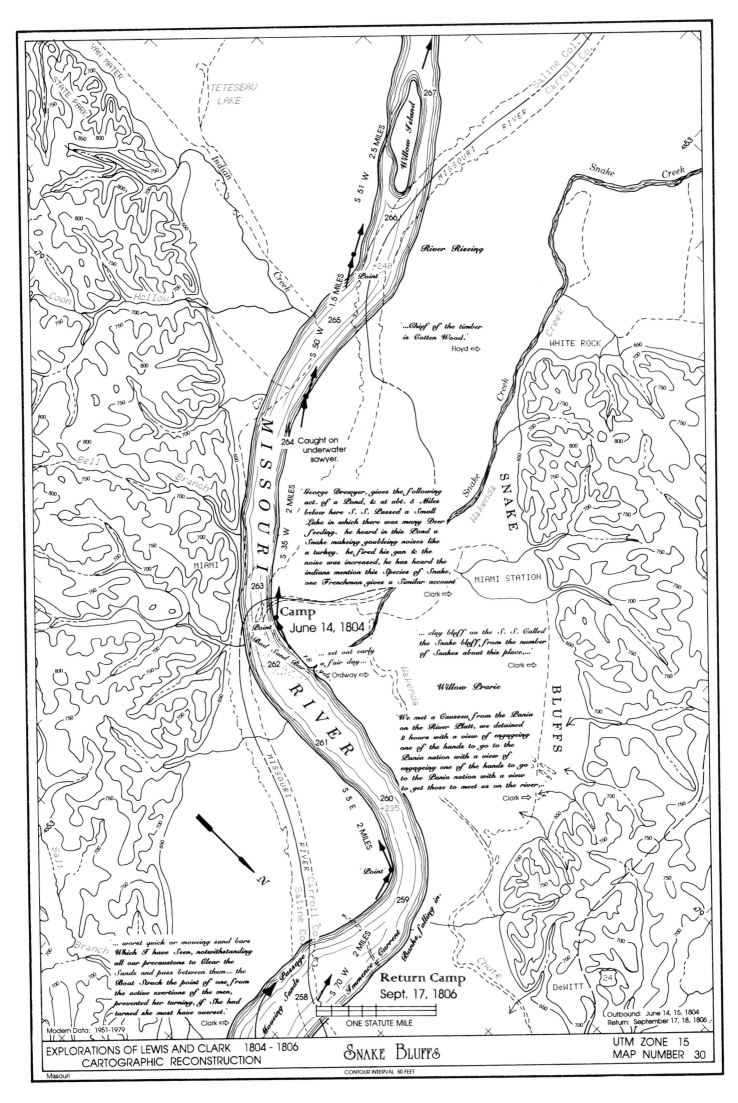

VAN MATER STATE PARK

TETESEAU LAKE

Indian Creek

Coon Hollow

Bell Branch

MIAMI

Salt Branch

MISSOURI

RIVER

S 51 W 2.5 MILES

S 50 W 1.5 MILES

S 35 W 2 MILES

S 5 E 2 MILES

S 70 W 2 MILES

Willow Island

267

266

+240 Point

265

River Riseing

*...Chief of the timber is Cotten Wood.*
Floyd ⇒

264 Caught on underwater sawyer.

*George Drewyer, gives the following acct. of a Pond, & at abt. 5 Miles below here S. S. Passed a Small Lake in which there was many Deer feeding. he heard in this Pond a Snake makeing goubleing noises like a turkey. he fired his gun & the noise was increased, he has heard the indians mention this Species of Snake, one Frenchman gives a Similar account*

263

Camp
June 14, 1804

Point

Bad Sand Bar

262

*...set out early a fair day...*
Ordway ⇒

261

260
+235

259

*... worst quick or moveing sand bars Which I have Seen, notwithetanding all our precaustons to Clear the Sands and pass between them... the Boat Struck the point of one, from the active exertions of the men, prevented her turning, if She had turned she must have overset.*
Clark ⇒

258

Moveing Sands

Passage

Immence Current

Banks falling in.

Return Camp
Sept. 17, 1806

Missouri River Carroll Co. Saline Co.

Snake Creek

Nakanda Creek

WHITE ROCK

SNAKE

MIAMI STATION
Clark ⇒

*... clay bluff on the S. S. Called the Snake bluff, from the number of Snakes about this place,...*
Clark ⇒

Willow Prarie

*We met a Causseu from the Pania on the River Platt, we detained 2 hours with a view of engageing one of the hands to go to the Pania nation with a view of engageing one of the hands to go to the Pania nation with a view to get those to meet us on the river,...*
Clark ⇒

BLUFFS

Chute

DeWITT

24

Nakanda

453

479

N

ONE STATUTE MILE

Modern Data: 1951-1979

Outbound: June 14, 15, 1804
Return: September 17, 18, 1806

EXPLORATIONS OF LEWIS AND CLARK   1804 - 1806
CARTOGRAPHIC RECONSTRUCTION

Snake Bluffs

CONTOUR INTERVAL 50 FEET

Missouri

UTM ZONE 15
MAP NUMBER 30

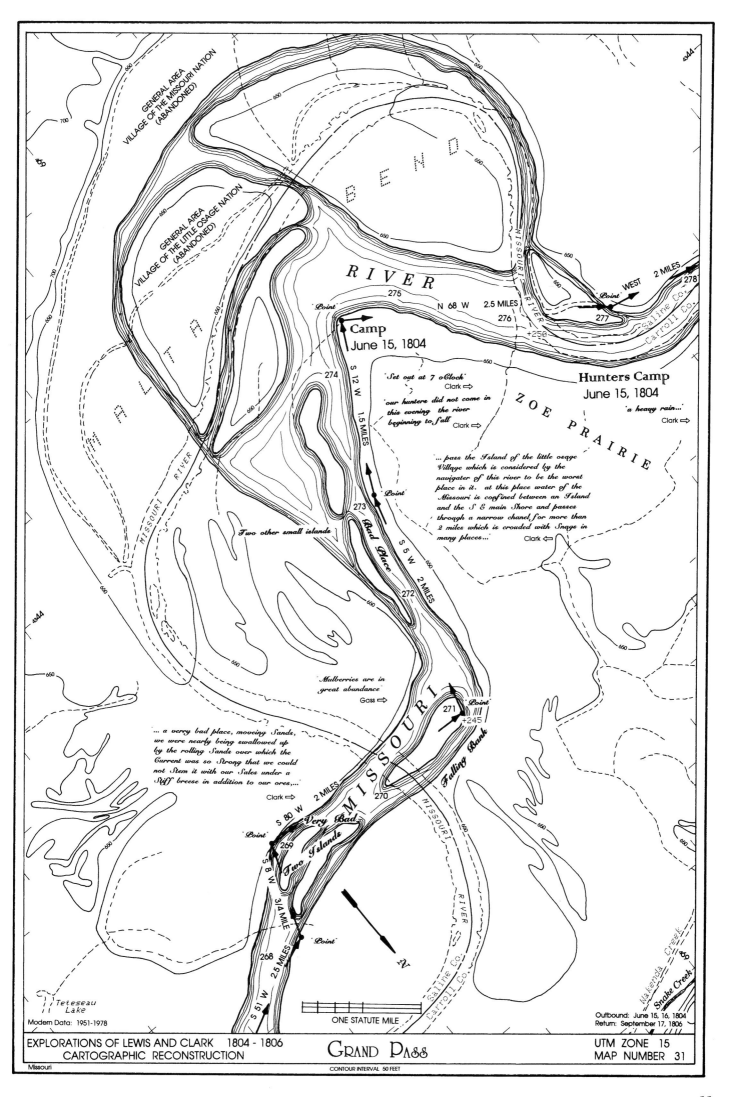

GENERAL AREA
VILLAGE OF THE MISSOURI NATION
(ABANDONED)

GENERAL AREA
THE LITTLE OSAGE NATION
(ABANDONED)

BEND

RIVER

275

N 68 W    2.5 MILES

276

+250

Point

WEST    2 MILES

278

277

*Point*
*Camp*
June 15, 1804

Hunters Camp
June 15, 1804

*Set out at 7 oClock*
Clark ⇨

*our hunters did not come in
this evening  the river
beginning to fall*
Clark ⇨

*a heavy rain...*
Clark ⇨

ZOE  PRAIRIE

274

S 12 W

1.5 MILES

Point

273

*... pass the Island of the little osage
Village which is considered by the
navigater of this river to be the worst
place in it.  at this place water of the
Missouri is confined between an Island
and the S E main Shore and passes
through a narrow chanel for more than
2 miles which is crouded with Snags in
many places...*
Clark ⇦

*Two other small islands*

Bad Place

S 5 W

2 MILES

272

*Mulberries are in
great abundance*
Gass ⇨

271    *Point*
+245

*... a verry bad place, moveing Sands,
we were nearly being swallowed up
by the rolling Sands over which the
Current was so Strong that we could
not Stem it with our Sales under a
Stiff breese in addition to our ores,...*
Clark ⇨

MISSOURI

Falling Bank

2 MILES

270

S 80 W

*Very Bad*

*Point*

269

Two Islands

S 8 W

3/4 MILE

*Point*

268

S 51 W    2.5 MILES

N

*Teteseau
Lake*

Modern Data: 1951-1978

ONE STATUTE MILE

Outbound: June 15, 16, 1804
Return: September 17, 1806

EXPLORATIONS OF LEWIS AND CLARK    1804 - 1806
CARTOGRAPHIC RECONSTRUCTION

Grand Pass

UTM ZONE  15
MAP NUMBER  31

Missouri

CONTOUR INTERVAL 50 FEET

55

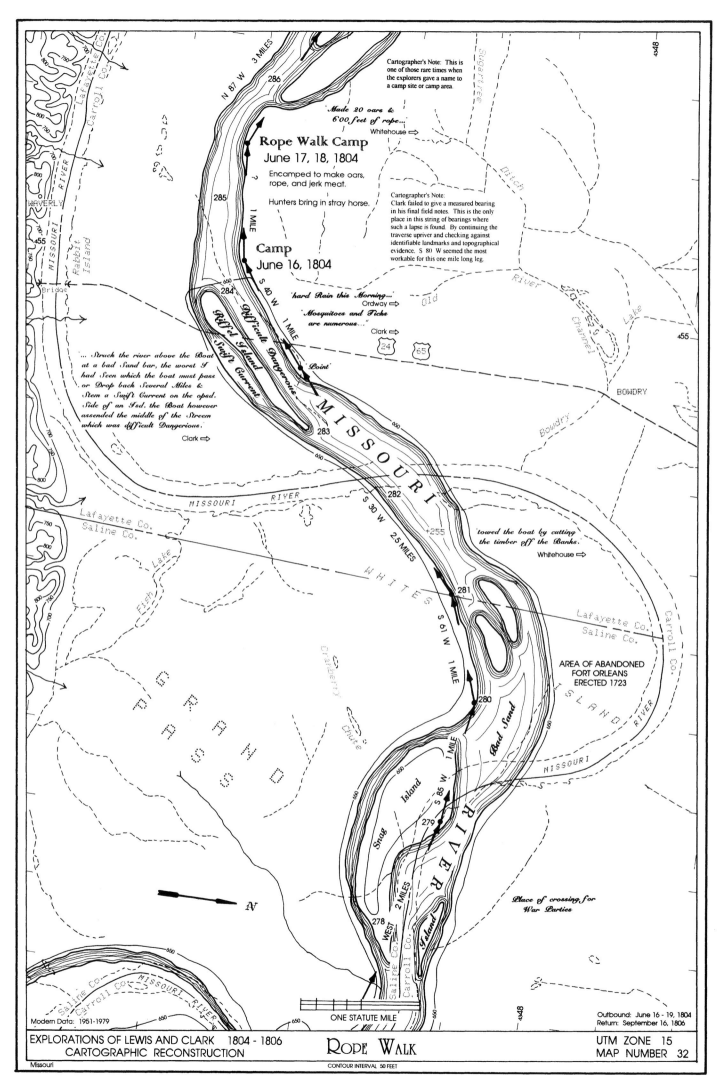

Cartographer's Note: This is one of those rare times when the explorers gave a name to a camp site or camp area.

*Made 20 oars & 600 feet of rope...*
Whitehouse ⇨

**Rope Walk Camp**
June 17, 18, 1804

Encamped to make oars, rope, and jerk meat.

Hunters bring in stray horse.

Cartographer's Note: Clark failed to give a measured bearing in his final field notes. This is the only place in this string of bearings where such a lapse is found. By continuing the traverse upriver and checking against identifiable landmarks and topographical evidence, S 80 W seemed the most workable for this one mile long leg.

**Camp**
June 16, 1804

*hard Rain this Morning...*
Ordway ⇨
*Mosquitoes and Ticks are numerous...*
Clark ⇨

*... Struck the river above the Boat at a bad Sand bar, the worst I had Seen which the boat must pass or Drop back Several Miles & Stem a Swift Current on the opsd. Side of an Isd. the Boat however assended the middle of the Streem which was difficult Dangerious.*
Clark ⇨

*towed the boat by cutting the timber off the Banks.*
Whitehouse ⇨

MISSOURI

AREA OF ABANDONED FORT ORLEANS ERECTED 1723

*Place of crossing for War Parties*

N

ONE STATUTE MILE

Modern Data: 1951-1979

Outbound: June 16 - 19, 1804
Return: September 16, 1806

EXPLORATIONS OF LEWIS AND CLARK    1804 - 1806
CARTOGRAPHIC RECONSTRUCTION

ROPE WALK

UTM ZONE   15
MAP NUMBER   32

Missouri

CONTOUR INTERVAL 50 FEET

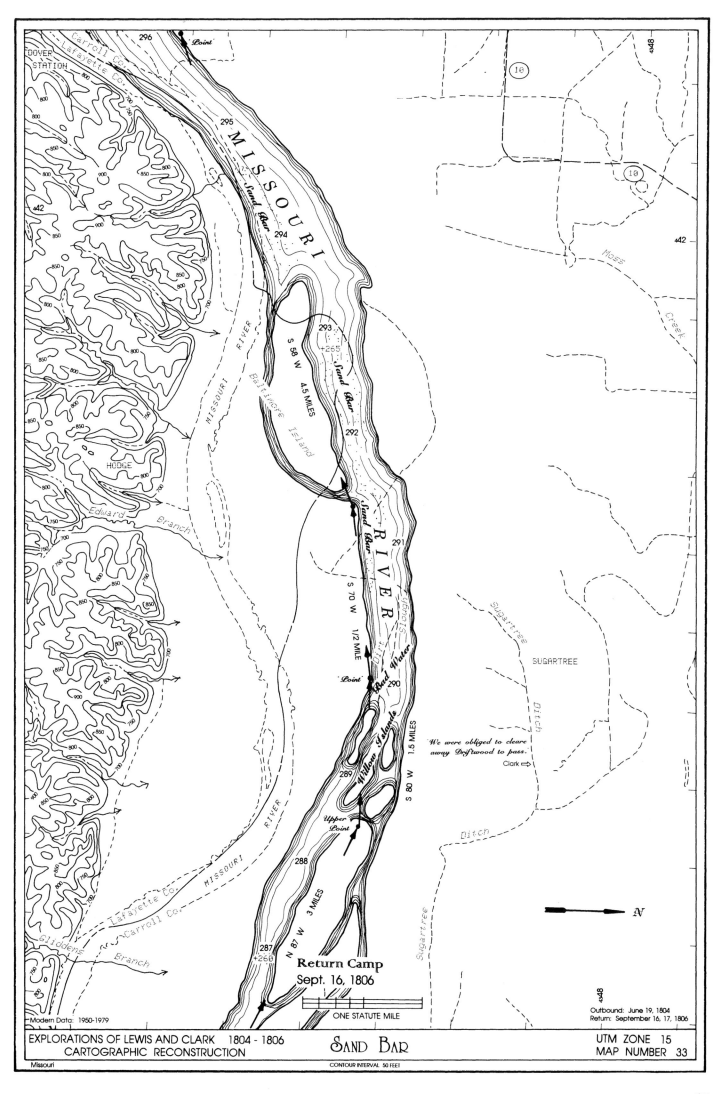

DOVER
STATION

Carroll Co.
Lafayette Co.

296

*Point*

295

M I S S O U R I

*Sand Bar*

294

*Sand Bar*

293
+265

S 58 W
4.5 MILES

*Sand Bar*

292

*Baltimore Island*

*Missouri River*

291

*Sand Bar*

R I V E R

S 70 W
1/2 MILE

*Dirt*

*Bad Water Slough*

290

*Point*

*Willow Islands*

S 80 W
1.5 MILES

289

*Upper Point*

288

N 87 W
3 MILES

287
+266

HODGE

*Edward Branch*

Glidden's Branch

Lafayette Co.
Carroll Co.

MISSOURI RIVER

**Return Camp**
**Sept. 16, 1806**

10

442

Moss Creek

442

*Sugartree*

SUGARTREE

*Ditch*

*We were obliged to cleare
away Driftwood to pass.*

Clark ⇨

*Ditch*

*Sugartree*

10

4348

4348

➡ N

Outbound: June 19, 1804
Return: September 16, 17, 1806

Modern Data: 1950-1979

EXPLORATIONS OF LEWIS AND CLARK   1804 - 1806
CARTOGRAPHIC RECONSTRUCTION

Missouri

ONE STATUTE MILE

S A N D   B A R

CONTOUR INTERVAL 50 FEET

UTM ZONE  15
MAP NUMBER  33

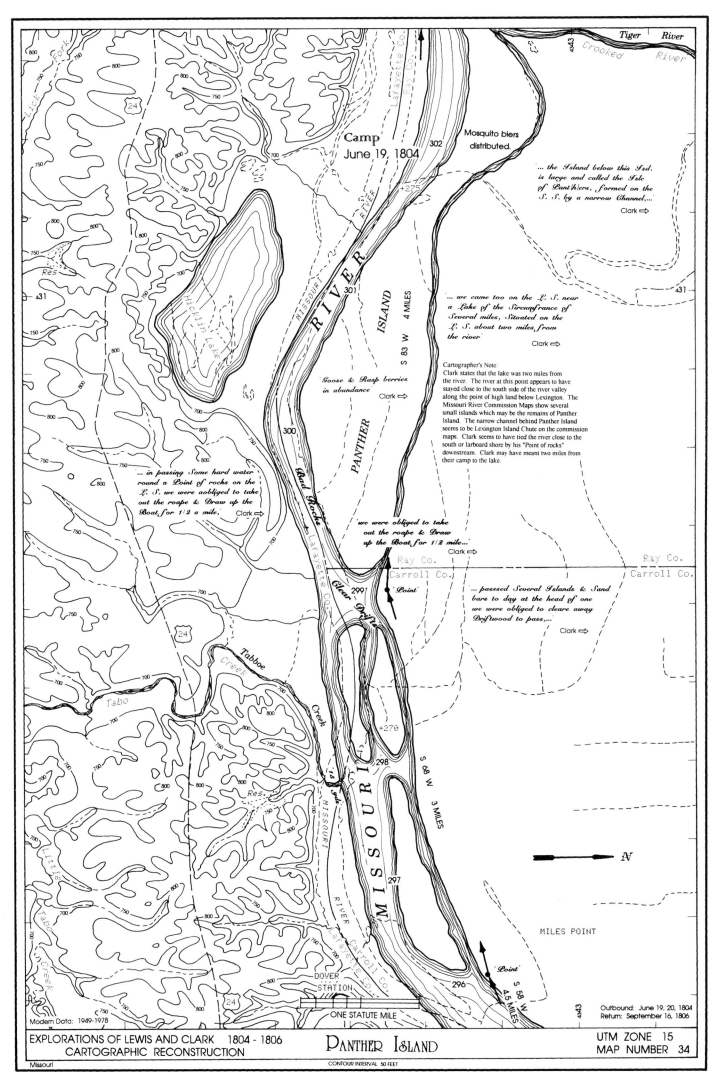

Tiger River

Crooked River

4343

Camp
June 19, 1804

Mosquito biers
distributed.

302

... the Island below this Isd.
is large and called the Isle
of Panth|lers, formed on the
S. S. by a narrow Channel,...

Clark ⇨

301

S 83 W   4 MILES

... we came too on the L. S. near
a Lake of the Sircumfrance of
Several miles, Situated on the
L. S. about two miles from
the river

Clark ⇨

Goose & Rasp berries
in abundance

Clark ⇨

300

Cartographer's Note:
Clark states that the lake was two miles from
the river. The river at this point appears to have
stayed close to the south side of the river valley
along the point of high land below Lexington. The
Missouri River Commission Maps show several
small islands which may be the remains of Panther
Island. The narrow channel behind Panther Island
seems to be Lexington Island Chute on the commission
maps. Clark seems to have tied the river close to the
south or larboard shore by his "Point of rocks"
downstream. Clark may have meant two miles from
their camp to the lake.

... in passing Some hard water
round a Point of rocks on the
L. S. we were aobliged to take
out the roape & Draw up the
Boat, for 1/2 a mile,   Clark ⇨

we were obliged to take
out the roape & Draw
up the Boat, for 1/2 mile...

Clark ⇨

Ray Co.                    Ray Co.
Carroll Co.                Carroll Co.

2991

Point

... passsed Several Islands & Sand
bars to day at the head of one
we were obliged to cleare away
Driftwood to pass,...

Clark ⇨

+270

298

S 68 W   3 MILES

N

297

MILES POINT

296

Point

S 58 W
4.5 MILES

4343

DOVER
STATION

ONE STATUTE MILE

EXPLORATIONS OF LEWIS AND CLARK   1804 - 1806
CARTOGRAPHIC RECONSTRUCTION

PANTHER ISLAND

UTM ZONE   15
MAP NUMBER   34

Missouri

CONTOUR INTERVAL 50 FEET

Outbound: June 19, 20, 1804
Return: September 16, 1806

Modern Data: 1949-1978

58

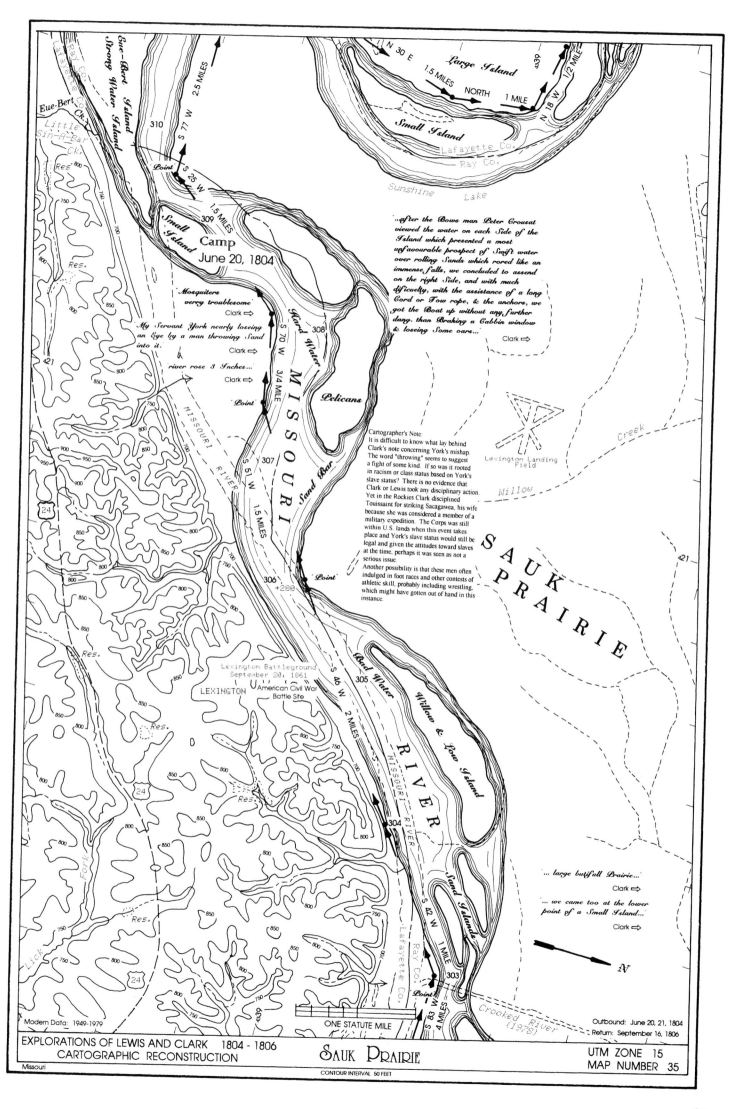

Eue-Bert Co. Ck.
Lafayette Co. Ray Co.
Little Sin-A-Bar Ck.
Ray Co.
Lafayette Co.

Eue-Bert Island
Strong Water Island

310
309
308
307
306 +280
305
304
303

310

2.5 MILES
S 77 W
Point
S 25 W
1.5 MILES

Small Island
Camp
June 20, 1804

*Mosquiters verry troublesome*
Clark ⇨

*My Servant York nearly loseing an Eye by a man throwing Sand into it.*
Clark ⇨

*river rose 3 Inches...*
Clark ⇨

Point

Hard Water
Pelicans

S 70 W 3/4 MILE
S 5 W 1.5 MILES

MISSOURI RIVER
Sand Bar

Point

N 30 E
Large Island
1.5 MILES
NORTH
1 MILE
N 18 W
1/2 MILE
439

Small Island

Sunshine Lake

*...after the Bows man Peter Crousat viewed the water on each Side of the Island which presented a most unfavourable prospect of Swift water over rolling Sands which rored like an immense falls, we concluded to assend on the right Side, and with much dificuelty, with the assistance of a long Cord or Tow rope, & the anchore, we got the Boat up without any further dang. than Braking a Cabbin window & loseing Some oars...*
Clark ⇨

Cartographer's Note:
It is difficult to know what lay behind Clark's note concerning York's mishap. The word "throwing" seems to suggest a fight of some kind. If so was it rooted in racism or class status based on York's slave status? There is no evidence that Clark or Lewis took any disciplinary action. Yet in the Rockies Clark disciplined Touissaint for striking Sacagawea, his wife because she was considered a member of a military expedition. The Corps was still within U.S. lands when this event takes place and York's slave status would still be legal and given the attitudes toward slaves at the time, perhaps it was seen as not a serious issue.
Another possibility is that these men often indulged in foot races and other contests of athletic skill, probably including wrestling, which might have gotten out of hand in this instance.

Lexington Landing Field
Willow Creek

S A U K   P R A I R I E

421

Lexington Battleground
September 20, 1861
LEXINGTON
American Civil War Battle Site

850
800
750
700
900
950

Bad Water
Willow & Low Island
S 46 W 2 MILES
S 83 W 4 MILES

MISSOURI RIVER
Sand Islands

S 42 W 1 MILE

Point

Lafayette Co. Ray Co.
Crooked River (1978)

24

Lick
Fork

Res.

*... large butifull Prairie...*
Clark ⇨

*... we came too at the lower point of a Small Island...*
Clark ⇨

N

ONE STATUTE MILE

EXPLORATIONS OF LEWIS AND CLARK   1804 - 1806
CARTOGRAPHIC RECONSTRUCTION
Missouri
SAUK PRAIRIE
CONTOUR INTERVAL 50 FEET
Modern Data: 1949-1979
Outbound: June 20, 21, 1804
Return: September 16, 1806
UTM ZONE 15
MAP NUMBER 35

59

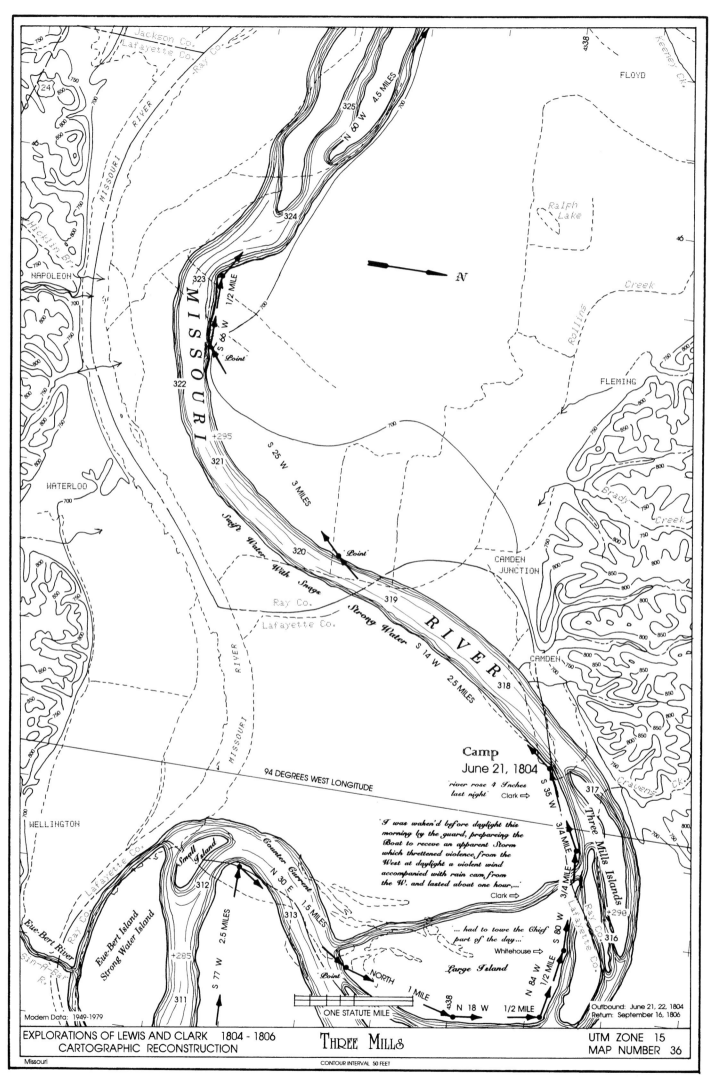

JACKSON CO.
LAFAYETTE CO.
RAY CO.

24

750

750

850

750

850

800

FLOYD

*Keeney Ck.*

438

46

*Ralph Lake*

HICKLIN CK.

NAPOLEON

700

*N*

*Creek*

MISSOURI RIVER

*Rollins*

FLEMING

325    4.5 MILES
N 50 W

324

323    1/2 MILE
S 66 W

*Point*

322

321    +295

S 25 W 3 MILES

700

700

750

850

800

850

*Brady Creek*

800

800

WATERLOO

700

*Snag'd Water With Snags*

*Point*

320

CAMDEN JUNCTION

800

850

Ray Co.

Lafayette Co.

319

R I V E R

*Strong Water* S 14 W 2.5 MILES

318

CAMDEN

700

750

850

850

800

800

*Cravens Ck.*

800

MISSOURI RIVER

94 DEGREES WEST LONGITUDE

**Camp**
**June 21, 1804**

*river rose 4 Inches last night*  Clark ⇨

S 35 W

317

700

750

*Three Mills Islands*

WELLINGTON

*Small Island*

*Counter Current*
N 30 E 1.5 MILES

*I was waken'd before daylight this morning by the guard, prepareing the Boat to receve an apparent Storm which threttened violence, from the West at daylight a violent wind accompanied with rain cam, from the W. and lasted about one hour,....*  Clark ⇨

3/4 MILE

3/4 MILE

S 80 W

+290

LAFAYETTE CO.
RAY CO.

312

*Eue-Bert Island Strong Water Island*

313

S 77 W 2.5 MILES

+285

311

*Eue-Bert River*

*Sin-A-Bar R.*

RAY CO.
LAFAYETTE CO.

*Point*

NORTH

1 MILE

438    N 18 W    1/2 MILE

*Large Island*

*... had to towe the Chief part of the day...*
Whitehouse ⇨

N 84 W 1/2 MILE

S 80 W

316

N 18 W 1/2 MILE

Outbound: June 21, 22, 1804
Return: September 16, 1806

Modern Data: 1949-1979

ONE STATUTE MILE

EXPLORATIONS OF LEWIS AND CLARK  1804 - 1806
CARTOGRAPHIC RECONSTRUCTION

THREE MILLS

UTM ZONE 15
MAP NUMBER 36

Missouri

CONTOUR INTERVAL 50 FEET

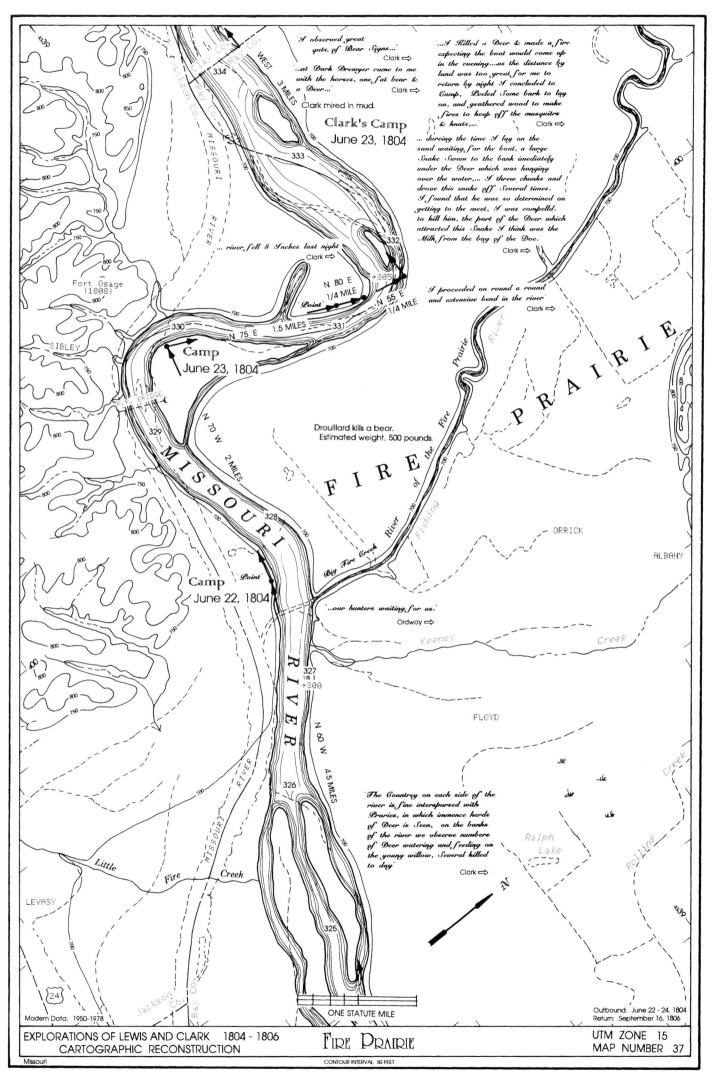

I observed great
guts, of Bear Signs...
*Clark* ⇒

...at Dark Drewyer came to me
with the horses, one fat bear &
a Deer...
*Clark* ⇒

Clark mired in mud.

## Clark's Camp
### June 23, 1804

...I Killed a Deer & made a fire
expecting the boat would come up
in the evening...as the distance by
land was too great for me to
return by night I concluded to
Camp, Peeled Some bark to lay
on, and geathered wood to make
fires to keep off the musquitrs
& knats,...
*Clark* ⇒

... dureing the time I lay on the
sand waiting for the boat, a large
Snake Swam to the bank imediately
under the Deer which was hanging
over the water,... I threw chunks and
drove this snake off Several times.
I found that he was so determined on
getting to the meet, I was compelld
to kill him, the part of the Deer which
attracted this Snake I think was the
Milk from the bag of the Doe.
*Clark* ⇒

... river, fell 8 Inches last night
*Clark* ⇒

N 80 E
1/4 MILE
*Point*
+305.0
N 55 E
1/4 MILE

I proceeded on round a round
and extensive bend in the river
*Clark* ⇒

N 75 E
1.5 MILES
331

## Camp
### June 23, 1804

N 70 W 2 MILES

Drouillard kills a bear.
Estimated weight, 500 pounds.

Fort Osage
(1808)

SIBLEY

R.R. BRIDGE

330
329
328

MISSOURI RIVER

FIRE PRAIRIE

River of the Fire Prairie
Fishing

Big Fire Creek River

ORRICK

ALBANY

## Camp
### June 22, 1804

*Point*

...our hunters waiting for us.
Ordway ⇒

Keeney          Creek

327
+300

N 60 W
4.5 MILES

FLOYD

326

The Country on each side of the
river is fine interspursed with
Praries, in which immence herds
of Deer is Seen, on the banks
of the river we observe numbers
of Deer watering and feeding on
the young willow, Several killed
to day
*Clark* ⇒

Ralph
Lake

Rollins          Creek

325

Little     Fire     Creek

LEVASY

MISSOURI  RIVER

N

ONE STATUTE MILE

Outbound:  June 22 - 24, 1804
Return:  September 16, 1806

24

Modern Data: 1950-1978

EXPLORATIONS OF LEWIS AND CLARK   1804 - 1806
CARTOGRAPHIC RECONSTRUCTION

Missouri

FIRE PRAIRIE

CONTOUR INTERVAL 50 FEET

UTM ZONE   15
MAP NUMBER  37

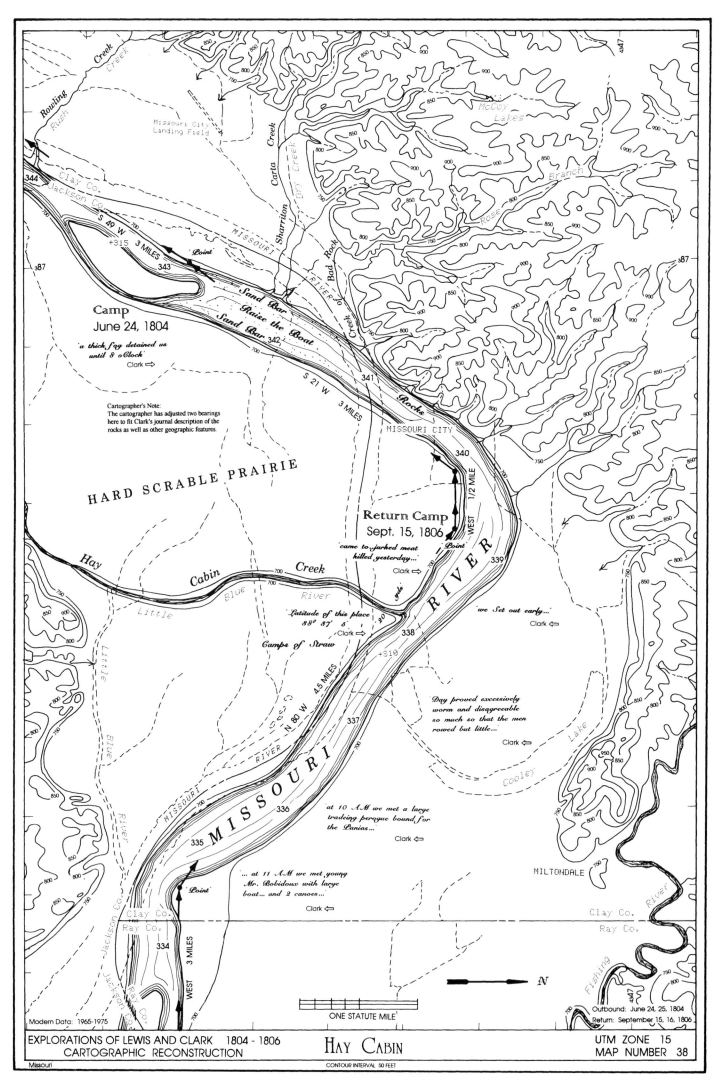

Camp
June 24, 1804

'a thick fog detained us
until 8 oClock'
Clark ⇨

Cartographer's Note:
The cartographer has adjusted two bearings
here to fit Clark's journal description of the
rocks as well as other geographic features.

HARD SCRABLE PRAIRIE

Hay          Cabin          Creek

Blue          River

Little

'Latitude of this place
88° 37' 5'
Clark ⇨

Camps of Straw

Return Camp
Sept. 15, 1806

'came to ~jurked meat
killed yesterday...'
Clark ⇨

'we Set out early...'
Clark ⇦

MISSOURI CITY

Rocks

'Day proved excessively
worm and disagreeable
so much so that the men
rowed but little...'
Clark ⇦

R I V E R

MISSOURI

'at 10 A M we met a large
tradeing perague bound for
the Panias...'
Clark ⇦

'... at 11 A M we met young
Mr. Bobidoux with large
boat... and 2 canoes...'
Clark ⇦

Point

MILTONDALE

Clay Co.
Ray Co.

Fishing          River

WEST          3 MILES

N

Outbound: June 24, 25, 1804
Return: September 15, 16, 1806

Modern Data: 1965-1975

ONE STATUTE MILE

EXPLORATIONS OF LEWIS AND CLARK   1804 - 1806
CARTOGRAPHIC RECONSTRUCTION

HAY CABIN

Missouri

CONTOUR INTERVAL 50 FEET

UTM ZONE   15
MAP NUMBER   38

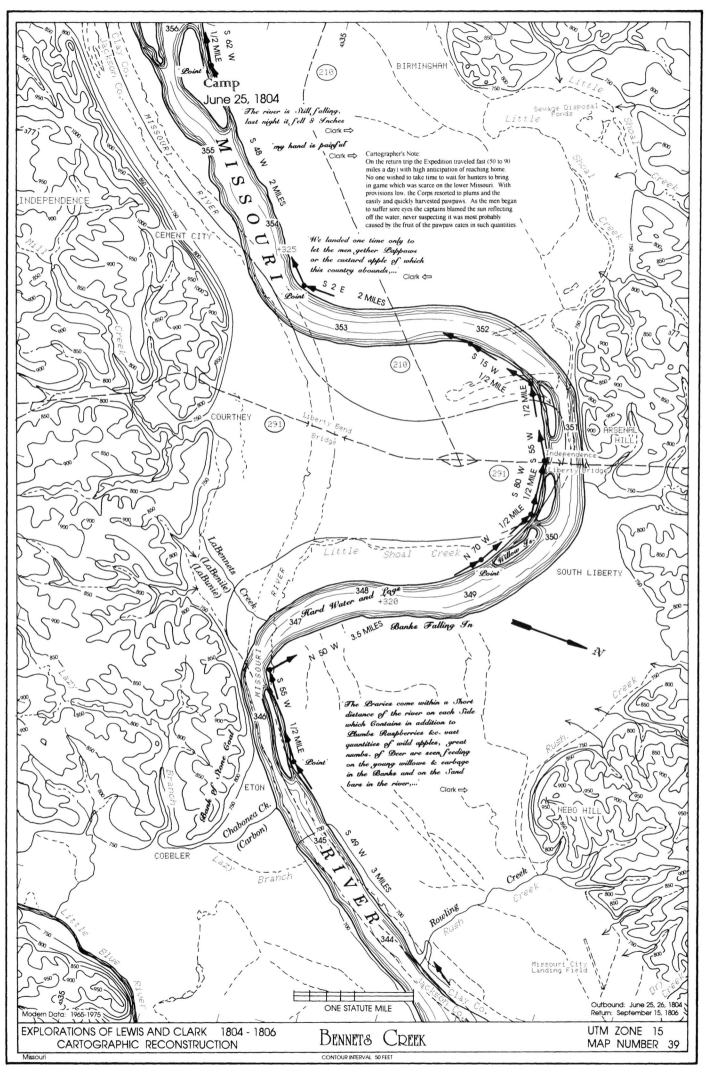

Camp
June 25, 1804

*The river is still falling,*
*last night it fell 8 Inches*
Clark ⇒

*my hand is painful*
Clark ⇒

Cartographer's Note:
On the return trip the Expedition traveled fast (50 to 90 miles a day) with high anticipation of reaching home. No one wished to take time to wait for hunters to bring in game which was scarce on the lower Missouri. With provisions low, the Corps resorted to plums and the easily and quickly harvested pawpaws. As the men began to suffer sore eyes the captains blamed the sun reflecting off the water, never suspecting it was most probably caused by the fruit of the pawpaw eaten in such quantities.

*We landed one time only to*
*let the men gether Pappaws*
*or the custard apple of which*
*this country abounds,...*
Clark ⇐

BIRMINGHAM

INDEPENDENCE

CEMENT CITY

COURTNEY

*The Praries come within a Short*
*distance of the river on each Side*
*which Contains in addition to*
*Plumbs Raspberries &c. vast*
*quantities of wild apples, great*
*numbs. of Deer are seen feeding*
*on the young willows & earbage*
*in the Banks and on the Sand*
*bars in the river,...*
Clark ⇒

ARSENAL HILL

Independence
Liberty Bridge

SOUTH LIBERTY

NEBO HILL

Missouri City
Landing Field

ETON

COBBLER

ONE STATUTE MILE

Modern Data: 1965-1975

Outbound: June 25, 26, 1804
Return: September 15, 1806

UTM ZONE 15
MAP NUMBER 39

EXPLORATIONS OF LEWIS AND CLARK 1804-1806
CARTOGRAPHIC RECONSTRUCTION

Bennets Creek

Missouri                    CONTOUR INTERVAL 50 FEET

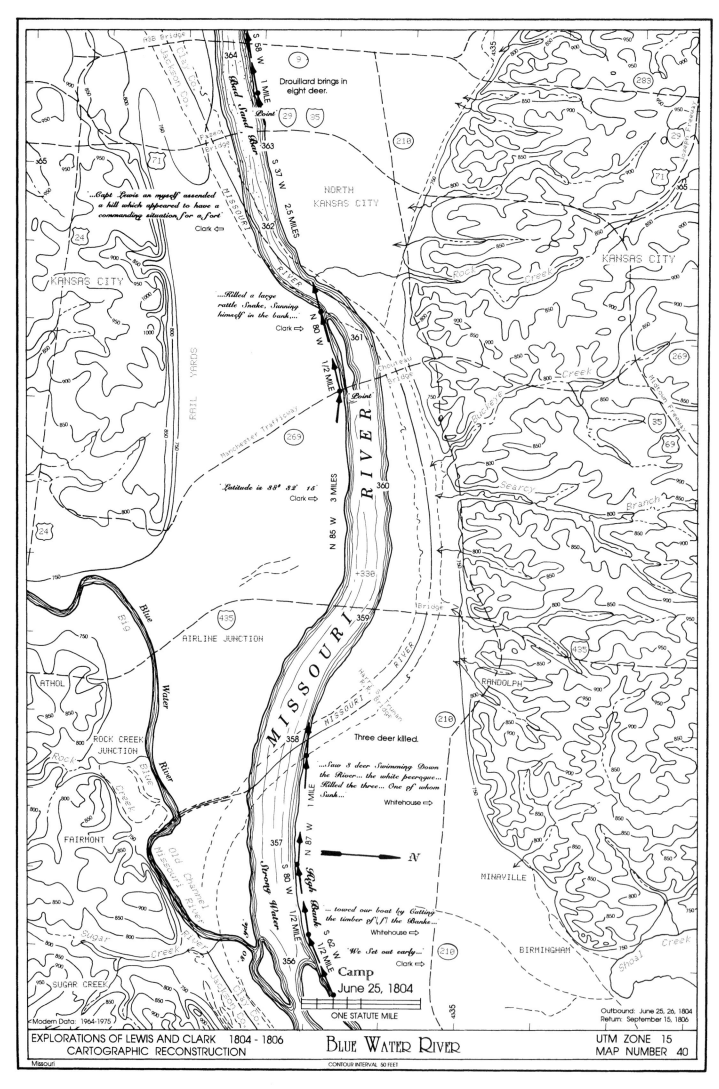

Drouillard brings in
eight deer.

...Capt Lewis an myself assended
a hill which appeared to have a
commanding situation for a fort...
Clark ⇦

...Killed a large
rattle Snake, Sunning
himself in the bank...
Clark ⇨

Latitude is 88° 32' 15'
Clark ⇨

+330

Three deer killed.

...Saw 3 deer Swimming Down
the River... the white peerogue...
Killed the three... One of whom
Sunk...
Whitehouse ⇨

N

... towed our boat by Cutting
the timber off the Banks...
Whitehouse ⇨

We Set out early...
Clark ⇨

**Camp
June 25, 1804**

ONE STATUTE MILE

Outbound: June 25, 26, 1804
Return: September 15, 1806

NORTH
KANSAS CITY

KANSAS CITY

KANSAS CITY

RAIL YARDS

MISSOURI RIVER

Big Blue Water River

ATHOL

ROCK CREEK
JUNCTION

FAIRMONT

SUGAR CREEK

Sugar Creek

AIRLINE JUNCTION

Old Channel Missouri River

Sporty Water

MISSOURI RIVER

Harry S Truman Bridge

Chouteau Bridge

Bridge

Rock Creek

Buckeye Creek

Searcy Branch

RANDOLPH

MINAVILLE

BIRMINGHAM

Shoal Creek

Blud Sand Bar

Paseo Bridge

ASB Bridge

Clay Co.
Jackson Co.

Jackson Co.
Clay Co.

Manchester Trafficway

Point

Point

High Bank

Blue Creek

Rock Creek

EXPLORATIONS OF LEWIS AND CLARK   1804 - 1806
CARTOGRAPHIC RECONSTRUCTION

Missouri

CONTOUR INTERVAL 50 FEET

**BLUE WATER RIVER**

UTM ZONE 15
MAP NUMBER 40

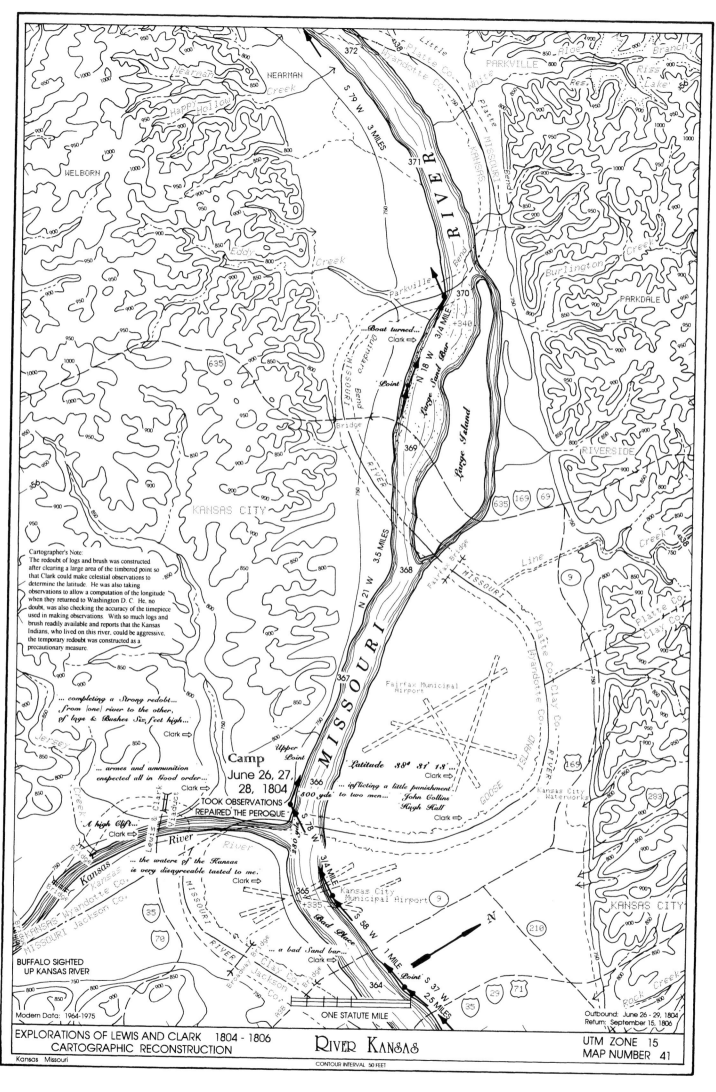

Cartographer's Note:
The redoubt of logs and brush was constructed
after clearing a large area of the timbered point so
that Clark could make celestial observations to
determine the latitude. He was also taking
observations to allow a computation of the longitude
when they returned to Washington D. C. He, no
doubt, was also checking the accuracy of the timepiece
used in making observations. With so much logs and
brush readily available and reports that the Kansas
Indians, who lived on this river, could be aggressive,
the temporary redoubt was constructed as a
precautionary measure.

*...completing a Strong redobt...*
*from [one] river to the other,*
*of logs & Bushes Six feet high...*
            Clark ⇨

*... armes and ammunition*
*enspected all in Good order...*
            Clark ⇨

*A high Clift...*
    Clark ⇨

*... the waters of the Kansas*
*is very disagreeable tasted to me.*
            Clark ⇨

BUFFALO SIGHTED
UP KANSAS RIVER

Modern Data: 1964-1975

Camp
June 26, 27,
28, 1804
TOOK OBSERVATIONS
REPAIRED THE PEROQUE

Upper
Point

*...Boat turned...*
Clark ⇨

Point

*Latitude 38° 31' 13"...*
        Clark ⇨

*... inflicting a little punishment*
*500 yds to two men...*
        *John Collins*
        *High Hall*
            Clark ⇨

*... a bad Sand bar...*
    Clark ⇨

Bad Place

ONE STATUTE MILE

Outbound: June 26 - 29, 1804
Return: September 15, 1806

EXPLORATIONS OF LEWIS AND CLARK   1804 - 1806
CARTOGRAPHIC RECONSTRUCTION
Kansas   Missouri
River Kansas
CONTOUR INTERVAL 50 FEET
UTM ZONE  15
MAP NUMBER  41

65

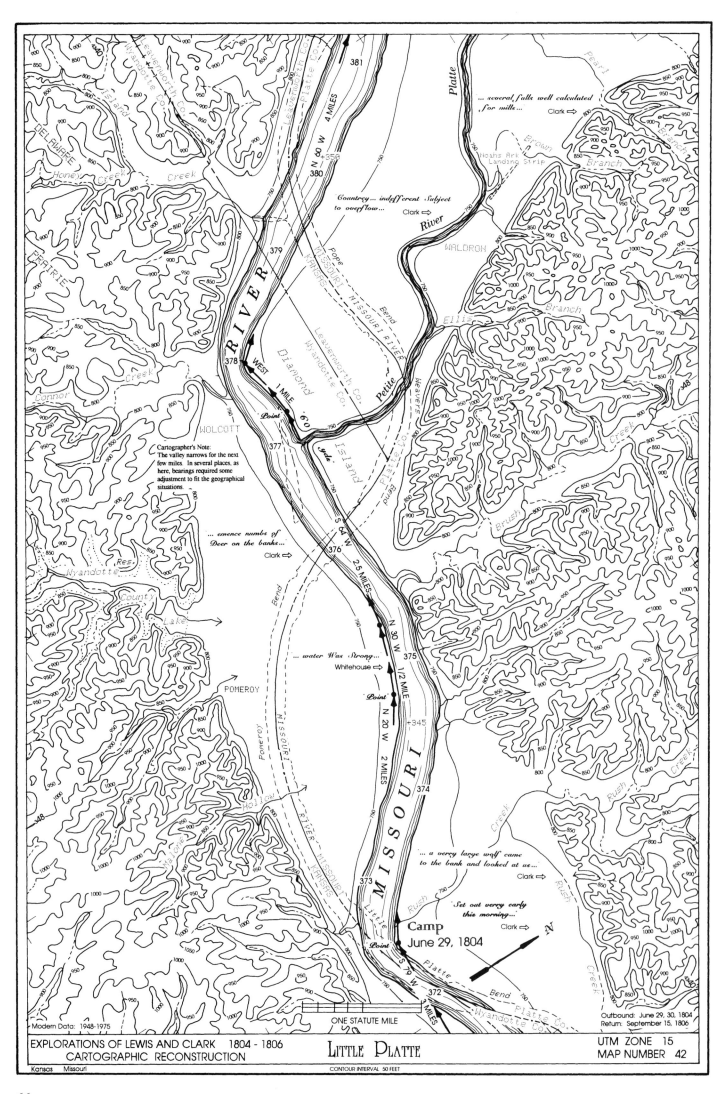

Leavenworth Co.
Wyandotte Co.

DELAWARE

Honey Creek

Island

900
850
900
850
900
850

Creek

PRAIRIE

Connor

Creek

950
900
850

WOLCOTT

Cartographer's Note:
The valley narrows for the next
few miles. In several places, as
here, bearings required some
adjustment to fit the geographical
situations.

... emence numbs of
Deer on the banks...
Clark ⇨

Res.
Wyandotte

County

Lake

POMEROY

Hollow

Leavenworth Co.
Platte Co.

N 80 W
4 MILES

381

+350

380

Pope

Kansas Missouri River

Bend

Leavenworth Co.
Wyandotte Co.

379

378

WEST
1 MILE

Point

6.0

377

RIVER

Diamond

Petite

Island

Bend

S 64 W

376

Bend

Pomeroy

MISSOURI RIVER

KANSAS

... water Was Strong...
Whitehouse ⇨

375

2.5 MILES

N 30 W

1/2 MILE

Point

N 20 W
2 MILES

+345

374

Missouri

373

River

Little

372

S 79 W
5 MILES

Country... indifferent Subject
to overflow...
Clark ⇨

... several falls well calculated
for mills...
Clark ⇨

Platte

River

WALDRON

Ellis

Weavers

Noahs Ark
Landing Strip

Brown Branch

Pearl

Branch

Branch

Brush

Creek

Creek

Rush

Rush

... a verry large wolf came
to the bank and looked at us...
Clark ⇨

Set out verry early
this morning...
Clark ⇨

N

Camp
June 29, 1804

Point

Platte

Bend

Platte Co.
Wyandotte Co.

Creek

Outbound: June 29, 30, 1804
Return: September 15, 1806

UTM ZONE 15
MAP NUMBER 42

Modern Data: 1948-1975

ONE STATUTE MILE

EXPLORATIONS OF LEWIS AND CLARK 1804 - 1806
CARTOGRAPHIC RECONSTRUCTION

Kansas    Missouri

LITTLE PLATTE

CONTOUR INTERVAL 50 FEET

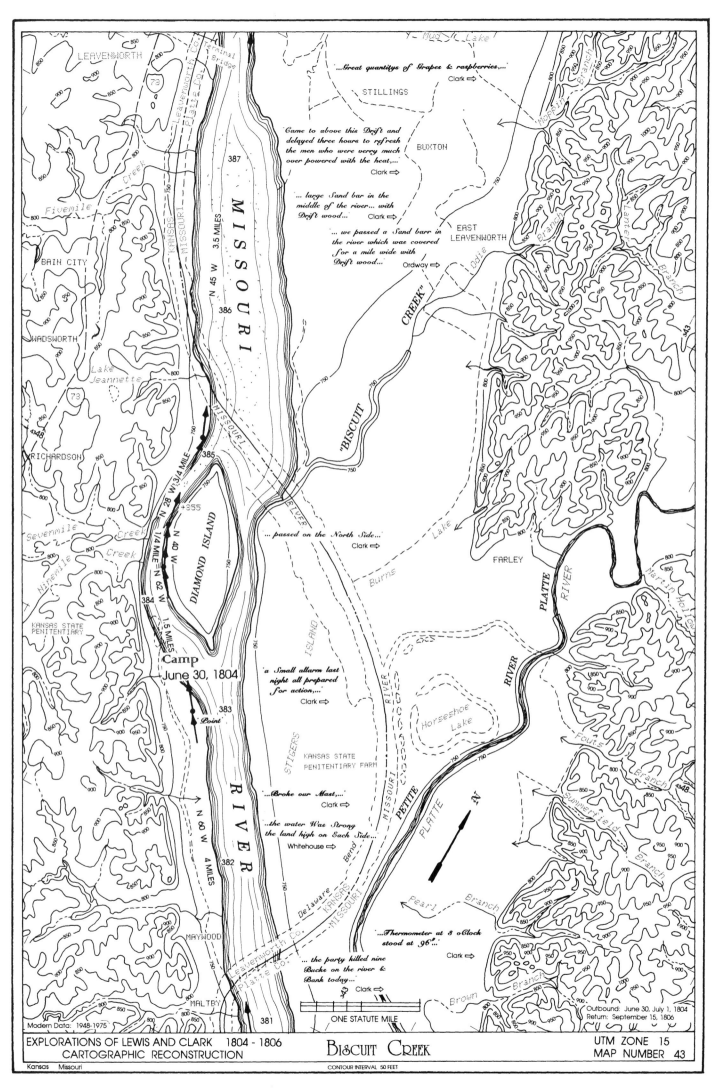

LEAVENWORTH

73

Terminal Bridge

387

MISSOURI

3.5 MILES

N 45 W

386

BAIN CITY

WADSWORTH

Lake
Jeannette

73

4348

RICHARDSON

385

N 28 W 3/4 MILE

+355

1/4 MILE

N 40 W

N 62 W

384

DIAMOND ISLAND

1.5 MILES

KANSAS STATE
PENITENTIARY

Sevenmile Creek

Ninemile Creek

Fivemile Creek

KANSAS CITY, MISSOURI

Camp
June 30, 1804

383

*Point*

N 8 W

4 MILES

382

MAYWOOD

381

MALTBY

Leavenworth Co.

Platte Co.

Leavenworth Co.

Platte Co.

...Great quantitys of Grapes & raspberries,...
Clark ⇨

STILLINGS

Came to above this Drift and
delayed three hours to refresh
the men who were verry much
over powered with the heat,...
Clark ⇨

BUXTON

... large Sand bar in the
middle of the river... with
Drift wood...
Clark ⇨

...we passed a Sand barr in
the river which was covered
for a mile wide with
Drift wood...
Ordway ⇨

EAST
LEAVENWORTH

"BISCUIT

CREEK"

Odie Lake

Morein Branch

Lantern Branch

Branch

4348

...passed on the North Side...
Clark ⇨

FARLEY

Burns Lake

STIGERS ISLAND

a Small allarm last
night all prepared
for action,...
Clark ⇨

KANSAS STATE
PENITENTIARY FARM

...Broke our Mast,...
Clark ⇨

...the water Was Strong
the land high on Each Side...
Whitehouse ⇨

Bend

Delaware

KANSAS

MISSOURI

PETITE PLATTE RIVER

MISSOURI RIVER

PLATTE RIVER

Horseshoe Lake

Martin Hollow

Fouts Branch

Summerfield Branch

Branch

N

Pearl Branch

...Thermometer at 8 o'Clock
stood at 96°...
Clark ⇨

... the party killed nine
Bucks on the river &
Bank today...
Clark ⇨

Brown Branch

ONE STATUTE MILE

Modern Data: 1948-1975

Outbound: June 30, July 1, 1804
Return: September 15, 1806

EXPLORATIONS OF LEWIS AND CLARK   1804 - 1806
CARTOGRAPHIC RECONSTRUCTION

BISCUIT CREEK

UTM ZONE  15
MAP NUMBER  43

Kansas   Missouri

CONTOUR INTERVAL 50 FEET

67

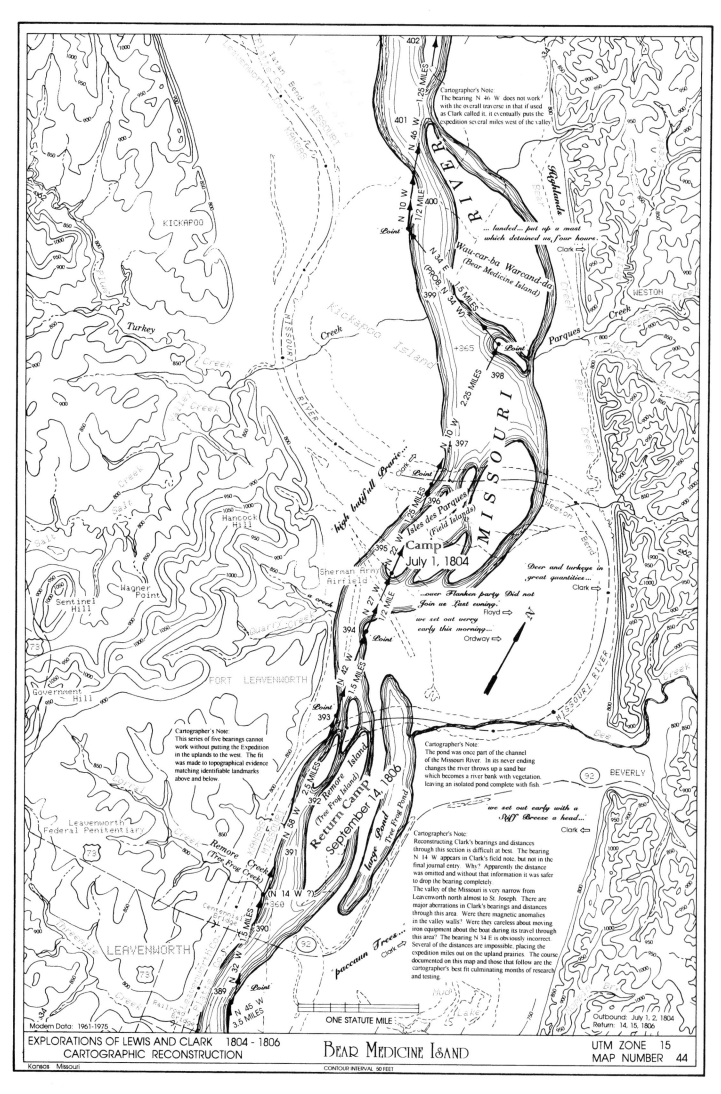

KICKAPOO

Turkey

Hancock
Hill

Wagner
Point

Sentinel
Hill

73

Government
Hill

FORT LEAVENWORTH

**Cartographer's Note:**
This series of five bearings cannot
work without putting the Expedition
in the uplands to the west. The fit
was made to topographical evidence
matching identifiable landmarks
above and below.

Leavenworth
Federal Penitentiary

73

Remore
(Tree Frog Creek)

Centennial
Bridge

390

LEAVENWORTH

73

389

RIVER

402

401

N 46 W

**Cartographer's Note:**
The bearing N 46 W does not work
with the overall traverse in that if used
as Clark called it, it eventually puts the
expedition several miles west of the valley

N 10 W
1/2 MILE

400

*Point*

Highlands

*...landed...put up a mast
which detained us four hours.*

Clark ⇨

N 34 E
(PROB. N 34 W)
1.5 MILES

399

Wau-car-ba Warcand-da
(Bear Medicine Island)

WESTON

Parques

Creek

Kickapoo
Island

KICKAPOO

RIVER

Creek

+965

*Point*

398

2.25 MILES

N 10 W

397

*Point*

MISSOURI

Weston
Bend

*Point*

Isles des Parques
(Field Islands)

1.25 MILES

N 22 W

396

395

Camp
July 1, 1804

Sherman Army
Airfield

*high bluff all Prairie...*

Clark ⇨

a creek

N 27 W
1/2 MILE

394

*Point*

Quarry Creek

*Deer and turkeys in
great quantities...*
Clark ⇨

*...over Flanken party Did not
Join us Last evening.*
Floyd ⇨

*we set out verry
early this morning...*
Ordway ⇨

N

MISSOURI RIVER

N 42 W
1.5 MILES

*Point*
393

92

BEVERLY

**Cartographer's Note:**
The pond was once part of the channel
of the Missouri River. In its never ending
changes the river throws up a sand bar
which becomes a river bank with vegetation,
leaving an isolated pond complete with fish.

N 58 W
2.5 MILES

392

Remore Island
(Tree Frog Island)

Return Camp
September 14, 1806

large Pond

Tree Frog Pond

*we set out early with a
Stiff Breeze a head...*
Clark ⇦

391

**Cartographer's Note:**
Reconstructing Clark's bearings and distances
through this section is difficult at best. The bearing
N 14 W appears in Clark's field note, but not in the
final journal entry. Why? Apparently the distance
was omitted and without that information it was safer
to drop the bearing completely.
The valley of the Missouri is very narrow from
Leavenworth north almost to St. Joseph. There are
major aberrations in Clark's bearings and distances
through this area. Were there magnetic anomalies
in the valley walls? Were they careless about moving
iron equipment about the boat during its travel through
this area? The bearing N 34 E is obviously incorrect.
Several of the distances are impossible, placing the
expedition miles out on the upland prairies. The course
documented on this map and those that follow are the
cartographer's best fit culminating months of research
and testing.

(N 14 W ?)
+960

2.5 MILES
N 58 W

1.5 MILES

Kansas River

Railroad Bridge

Threemile Creek

34

N 32 W
1.5 MILES

*Point*

N 45 W
3.5 MILES

*...paccaun Trees...*
Clark ⇨

92

Mud
Lake

Branch

950

**ONE STATUTE MILE**

EXPLORATIONS OF LEWIS AND CLARK   1804 - 1806
CARTOGRAPHIC RECONSTRUCTION

Kansas  Missouri

BEAR MEDICINE ISLAND

CONTOUR INTERVAL  50 FEET

UTM ZONE   15
MAP NUMBER   44

Modern Data: 1961-1975

Outbound: July 1, 2, 1804
Return: 14, 15, 1806

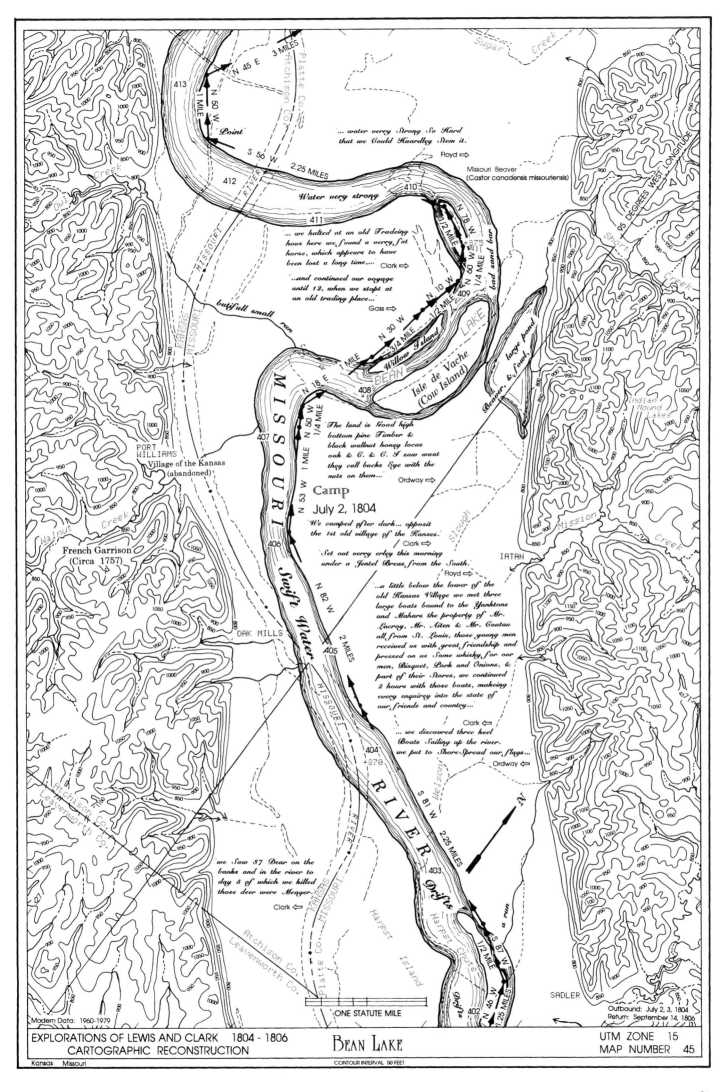

EXPLORATIONS OF LEWIS AND CLARK 1804 - 1806
CARTOGRAPHIC RECONSTRUCTION

Bean Lake

UTM ZONE 15
MAP NUMBER 45

Kansas Missouri

ONE STATUTE MILE

CONTOUR INTERVAL 50 FEET

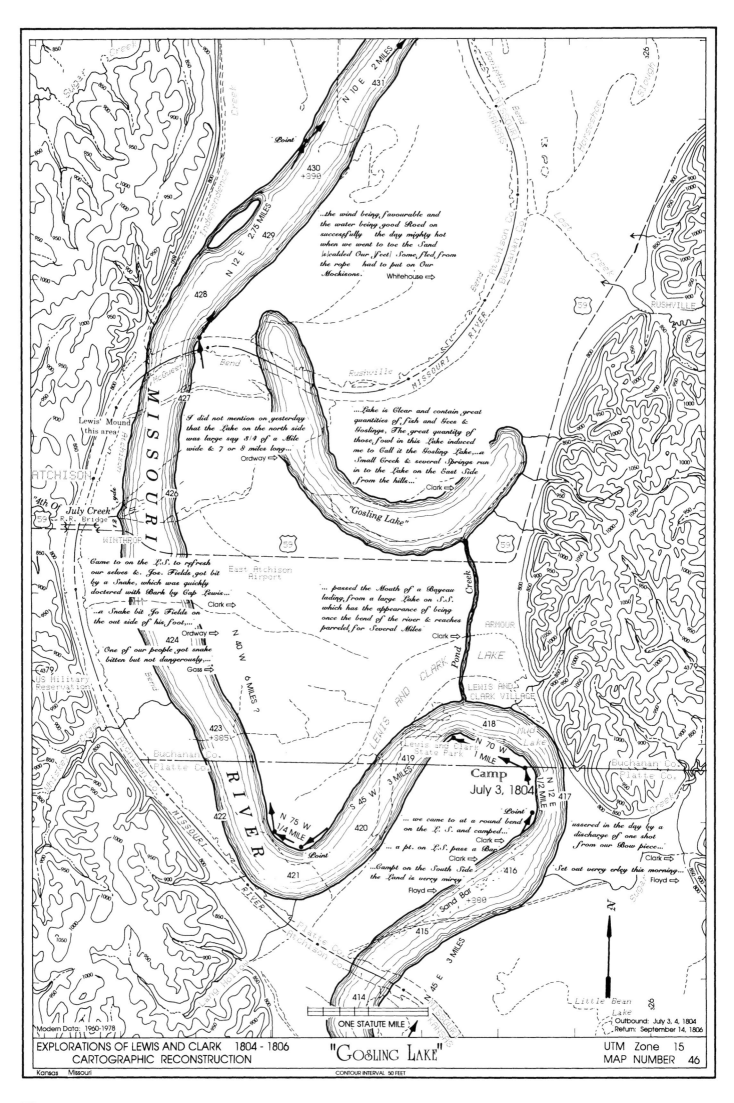

...the wind being favourable and the water being good Roed on successfully the day mighty hot when we went to toe the Sand [scalded Our feet] Some fled from the rope had to put on Our Mochisons. Whitehouse ⇒

...Lake is Clear and contain great quantities of fish and Gees & Goslings, The great quantity of those fowl in this Lake induced me to Call it the Gosling Lake,...a Small Creek & several Springs run in to the Lake on the East Side from the hills... Clark ⇒

I did not mention on yesterday that the Lake on the north side was large say 3/4 of a Mile wide & 7 or 8 miles long... Ordway ⇒

"Gosling Lake"

Came to on the L.S. to refresh our selves &. Jos. Fields got bit by a Snake, which was quickly doctered with Bark by Cap Lewis... Clark ⇒

...a Snake bit Jo Fields on the out side of his foot,...

One of our people got snake bitten but not dangerously,... Gass ⇒

... passed the Mouth of a Bayeau lading from a large Lake on S.S. which has the appearance of being once the bend of the river & reaches parrelel for Several Miles Clark ⇒

... we came to at a round bend on the L. S. and camped... Clark ⇒

... a pt. on L.S. pass a Bar Clark ⇒

...Campt on the South Side the Land is verry mirey Floyd ⇒

Camp July 3, 1804

...assered in the day by a discharge of one shot from our Bow piece... Clark ⇒

Set out verry erley this morning... Floyd ⇒

Modern Data: 1960-1978

ONE STATUTE MILE

Outbound: July 3, 4, 1804
Return: September 14, 1806

EXPLORATIONS OF LEWIS AND CLARK    1804 - 1806
CARTOGRAPHIC RECONSTRUCTION

"GOSLING LAKE"

UTM Zone  15
MAP NUMBER  46

Kansas   Missouri                    CONTOUR INTERVAL 50 FEET

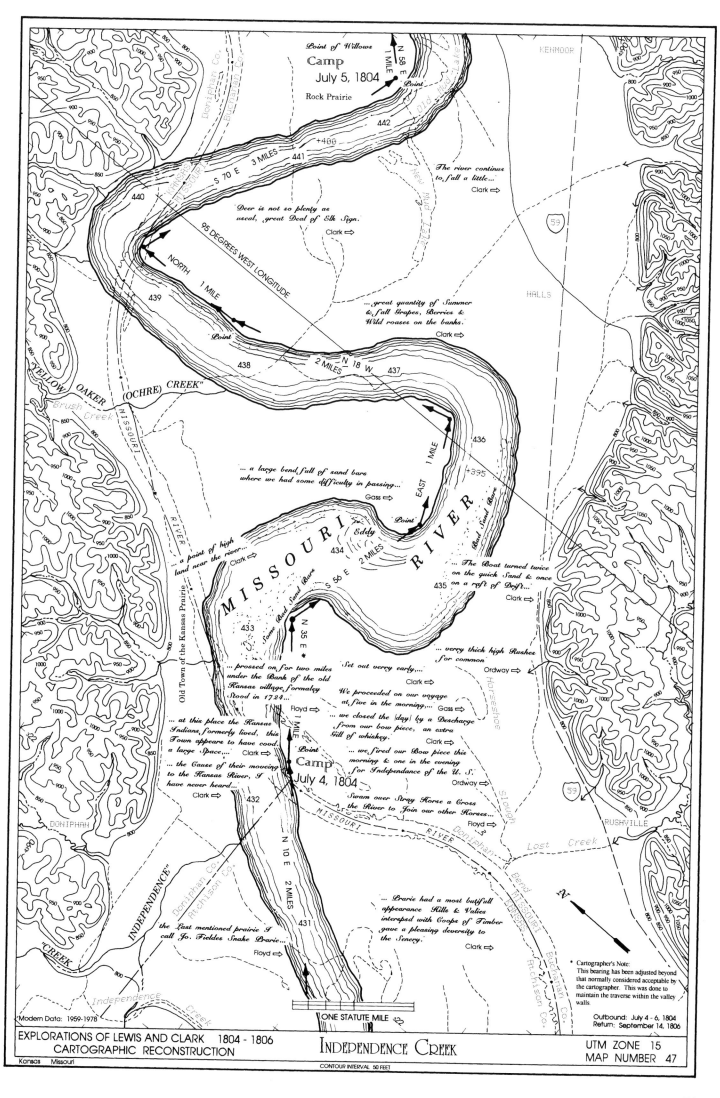

Point of Willows
**Camp**
**July 5, 1804**
Rock Prairie

N 58 E
1 MILE

Point

KENMOOR

442

The river continues
to fall a little...
Clark ⇨

59

HALLS

+400

S 70 E  3 MILES  441

440

95 DEGREES WEST LONGITUDE

*Deer is not so plenty as
useal, great Deal of Elk Sign.*
Clark ⇨

NORTH  1 MILE

439

Point

438

2 MILES  N 18 W  437

*...great quantity of Summer
& fall Grapes, Berries &
Wild roases on the banks.*
Clark ⇨

"YELLOW OAKER (OCHRE) CREEK"

Brush Creek

MISSOURI RIVER

436

EAST  1 MILE

*... a large bend, full of sand bars
where we had some difficulty in passing...*
Gass ⇨

+395

Bad Sand Bars

435

*... The Boat turned twice
on the quick Sand & once
on a raft of Drift...*
Clark ⇨

Eddy

434

S 56 E  2 MILES

M I S S O U R I    R I V E R

*...a point of high
land near the river...*
Clark ⇨

Some Bad Sand Bars

433

N 35 E *

*...verry thick high Rushes
for common*
Ordway ⇨

Horseshoe

*...prossed on, for two miles
under the Bank of the old
Kansas village, formaley
stood in 1724...*
Clark ⇨

Set out verry early,....
Clark ⇨

*We proceeded on our voyage
at five in the morning,....*
Gass ⇨

*...at this place the Kansas
Indians, formerly lived, this
Town appears to have covd.
a large Space,....*

Floyd ⇨

*...we closed the [day] by a Descharge
from our bow piece, an extra
Gill of whiskey.*
Clark ⇨

*... the Cause of their moveing
to the Kansas River, I
have never heard...*
Clark ⇨

Point

**Camp
July 4, 1804**

*...we fired our Bow piece this
morning & one in the evening
for Independance of the U. S.*
Ordway ⇨

432

N 10 E  2 MILES

*Swam over Stray Horse a Cross
the River to Join our other Horses...*
Floyd ⇨

MISSOURI   RIVER

Doniphan Co.   Atchison Co.

DONIPHAN

Old Town of the Kansas Prairie

59

RUSHVILLE

Doniphan Bend Missouri Slough

Lost  Creek

"INDEPENDENCE"

*Prarie had a most butifull
appearance Hills & Valies
interapsd with Coops of Timber
gave a pleasing deversity to
the Senery.*
Clark ⇨

431

*the Last mentioned prairie I
call Jo. Fieldes Snake Prarie...*
Floyd ⇨

"CREEK"

Independence

N

Buchanan Co.   Atchison Co.

Modern Data: 1959-1978

**ONE STATUTE MILE**

* Cartographer's Note:
This bearing has been adjusted beyond
that normally considered acceptable by
the cartographer. This was done to
maintain the traverse within the valley
walls.

Outbound: July 4 - 6, 1804
Return:  September 14, 1806

**EXPLORATIONS OF LEWIS AND CLARK   1804 - 1806**
**CARTOGRAPHIC RECONSTRUCTION**

Kansas   Missouri

**INDEPENDENCE CREEK**

CONTOUR INTERVAL 50 FEET

UTM ZONE  15
MAP NUMBER  47

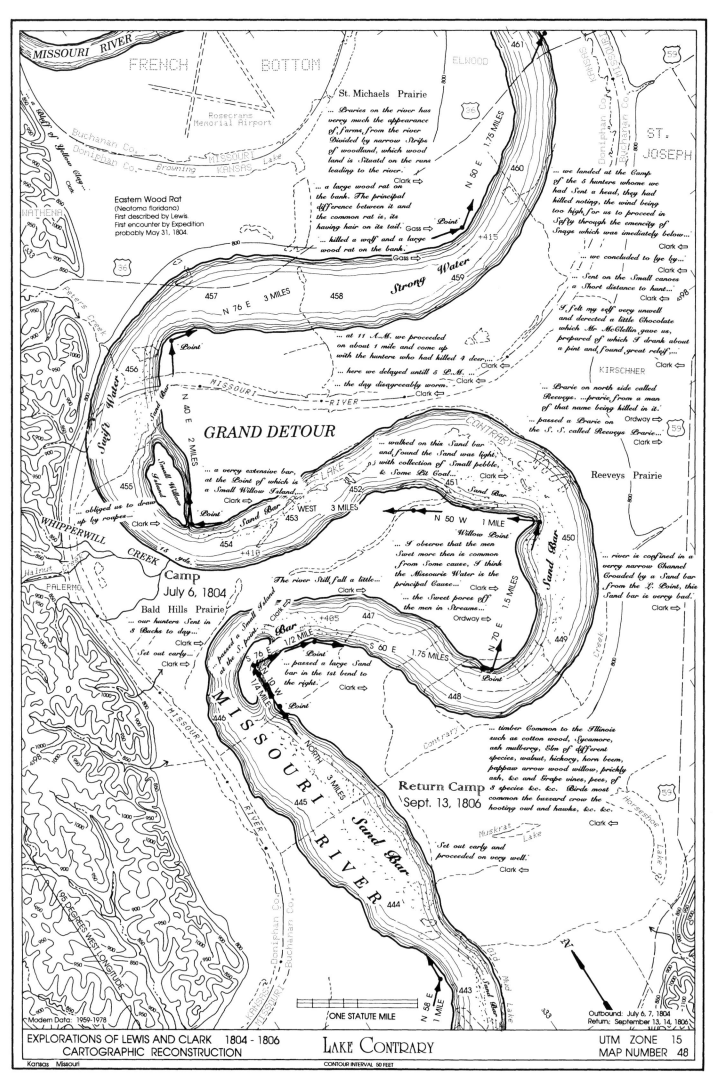

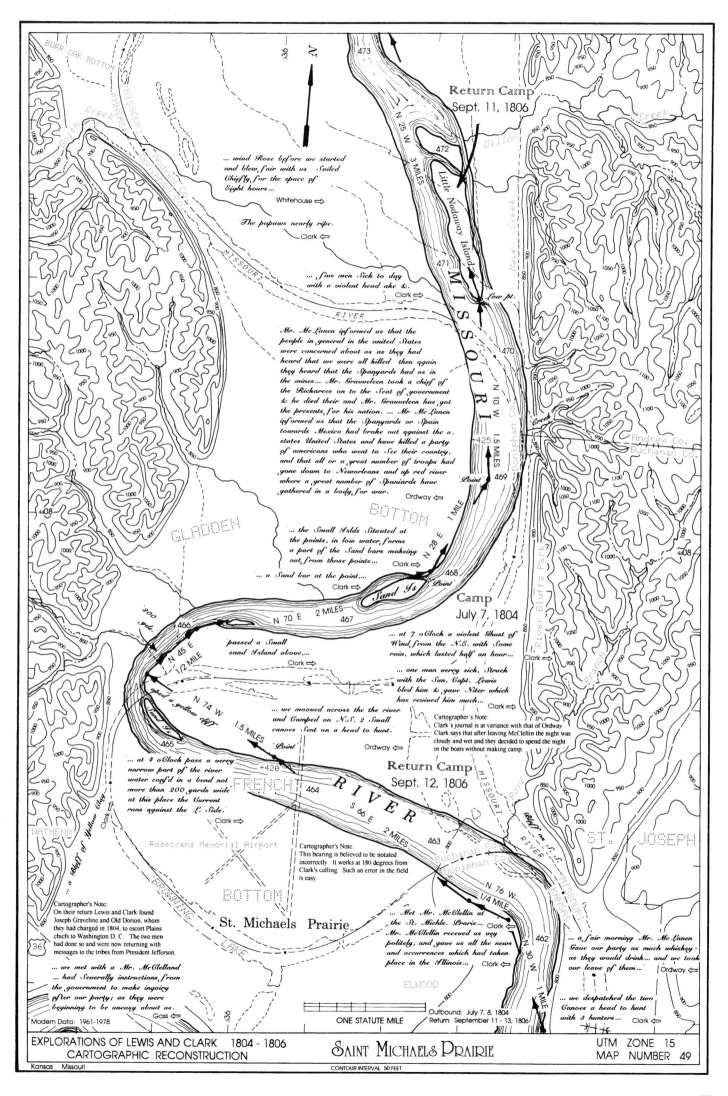

... wind Rose before we started
and blew fair with us Sailed
Chiefly for the space of
Eight hours ...

Whitehouse ⇒

The papaws nearly ripe.
⎯ Clark ⇐

... five men Sick to day
with a violent head ake &.
⎯ Clark ⇒

Mr. McLanen informed us that the
people in general in the united States
were concerned about us as they had
heard that we were all killed then again
they heard that the Spanyards had us in
the mines ... Mr. Gravveleen took a chief of
the Rickarees on to the Seat of government
& he died their and Mr. Gravveleen has got
the presents for his nation. ... Mr. McLanen
informed us that the Spanyards or Spain
towards Mexico had broke out against the u.
states United States and have killed a party
of americans who went to See their country,
and that all or a great number of troops had
gone down to Neworleans and up red river
where a great number of Spaniards have
gathered in a body for war.
⎯ Ordway ⇐

... the Small Islds Situated at
the points, in low water forms
a part of the Sand bars makeing
out from those points ...
⎯ Clark ⇒

... a Sand bar at the point, ...
⎯ Clark ⇒

Camp
July 7, 1804

... at 7 oClock a violent Ghust of
Wind from the N.E. with Some
rain, which lasted half an hour ...

... one man verry sick, Struck
with the Sun, Capt. Lewis
bled him & gave Niter which
has revived him much ...
⎯ Clark ⇒

Cartographer's Note:
Clark's journal is at variance with that of Ordway.
Clark says that after leaving McClellin the night was
cloudy and wet and they decided to spend the night
in the boats without making camp.

passed a Small
sand Island above, ...
⎯ Clark ⇒

... we mooved across the the river
and Camped on N.S. 2 Small
canoes Sent on a head to hunt.
⎯ Ordway ⇐

Return Camp
Sept. 12, 1806

... at 4 oClock pass a verry
narrow part of the river
water conf'd in a bend not
more than 200 yards wide
at this place the Current
runs against the L. Side.
⎯ Clark ⇒

Cartographer's Note:
This bearing is believed to be notated
incorrectly. It works at 180 degrees from
Clark's calling. Such an error in the field
is easy.

Cartographer's Note:
On their return Lewis and Clark found
Joseph Graveline and Old Dorion, whom
they had charged in 1804, to escort Plains
chiefs to Washington D. C. The two men
had done so and were now returning with
messages to the tribes from President Jefferson.

... we met with a Mr. McClelland
... had Severally instructions from
the government to make inquiry
after our party; as they were
beginning to be uneasy about us.
⎯ Gass ⇐

St. Michaels Prairie

... Met Mr. McClellin at
the St. Michls. Prairie ...
Mr. McClellin received us very
politely, and gave us all the news
and occurrences which had taken
place in the Illinois ...
⎯ Clark ⇒

... a fair morning Mr. McLanen
Gave our party as much whiskey
as they would drink ... and we took
our leave of them ...
⎯ Ordway ⇐

... we despatched the two
Canoes a head to hunt
with 5 hunters ...
⎯ Clark ⇒

Modern Data: 1961-1978

ONE STATUTE MILE

Outbound: July 7, 8, 1804
Return: September 11 - 13, 1806

EXPLORATIONS OF LEWIS AND CLARK   1804 - 1806
CARTOGRAPHIC RECONSTRUCTION

Saint Michaels Prairie

UTM   ZONE   15
MAP   NUMBER   49

Kansas   Missouri

CONTOUR INTERVAL 50 FEET

73

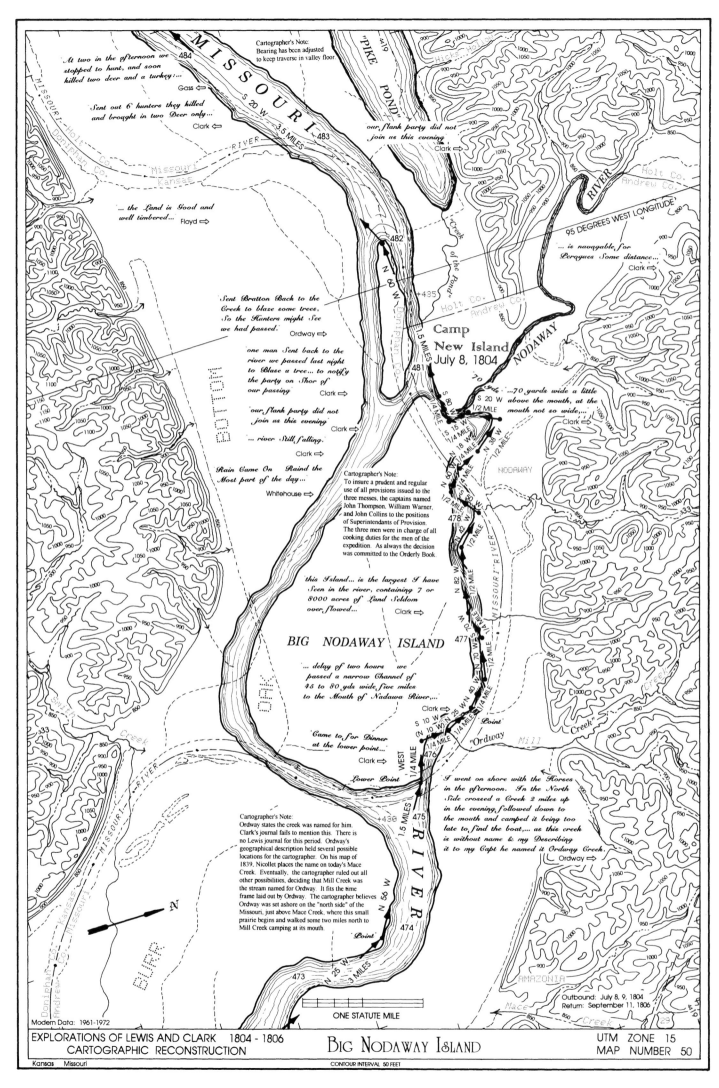

At two in the afternoon we
stopped to hunt, and soon
killed two deer and a turkey:...
Gass ⇐

Sent out 6 hunters they killed
and brought in two Deer only...
Clark ⇐

... the Land is Good and
well timbered... Floyd ⇒

Cartographer's Note:
Bearing has been adjusted
to keep traverse in valley floor.

MISSOURI

S 20 W — 35 MILES

RIVER

484

483

482

N 80 W — Doniphan Co.

481

"PIKE
POND"

4419

Hicks Hollow

our flank party did not
join us this evening
Clark ⇐

95 DEGREES WEST LONGITUDE

Holt Co.
Andrew Co.

... is navigable for
Perogues Some distance...
Clark ⇒

Sent Bratton Back to the
Creek to blaze some trees,
So the Hunters might See
we had passed.
Ordway ⇒

one man Sent back to the
river we passed last night
to Blaze a tree... to notify
the party on Shore of
our passing Clark ⇒

our flank party did not
join us this evening
Clark ⇐

... river Still falling.
Clark ⇒

Rain Came On   Raind the
Most part of the day...
Whitehouse ⇒

+435

Camp
New Island
July 8, 1804

1.5 MILES

NODAWAY

RIVER

70 Yds
S 20 W
1/2 MILE

S 80 W
1/4 MILE

...70 yards wide a little
above the mouth, at the
mouth not so wide,...
Clark ⇐

S 15 W
1/4 MILE

N 18 W
1/4 MILE

N 38 W
1/2 MILE

N 60 W
1/4 MILE

S 60 W
1/2 MILE

NODAWAY

478

Cartographer's Note:
To insure a prudent and regular
use of all provisions issued to the
three messes, the captains named
John Thompson, William Warner,
and John Collins to the positions
of Superintendants of Provision.
The three men were in charge of all
cooking duties for the men of the
expedition. As always the decision
was committed to the Orderly Book.

this Island... is the largest I have
Seen in the river, containing 7 or
8000 acres of Land Seldom
over flowed...
Clark ⇒

BIG   NODAWAY   ISLAND

... delay of two hours   we
passed a narrow Channel of
45 to 80 yds wide, five miles
to the Mouth of Nadawa River,...
Clark ⇒

N 82 W
1/2 MILE

477

MISSOURI RIVER

Came to, for Dinner
at the lower point...
Clark ⇒

N 70 WEST
1/4 MILE

N 40 W
1/4 MILE

N 25 W
1/4 MILE

S 10 W
1/4 MILE

N 10 W
1/4 MILE

476

Point

"Ordway

Mill

Creek"

Lower Point

WEST
1/4 MILE

475

1.5 MILES

I went on shore with the Horses
in the afternoon. In the North
Side crossed a Creek 2 miles up
in the evening, followed down to
the mouth and camped it being too
late to find the boat,... as this creek
is without name & my Describing
it to my Capt he named it Ordway Creek.
Ordway ⇒

Cartographer's Note:
Ordway states the creek was named for him.
Clark's journal fails to mention this. There is
no Lewis journal for this period. Ordway's
geographical description held several possible
locations for the cartographer. On his map of
1839, Nicollet places the name on today's Mace
Creek. Eventually, the cartographer ruled out all
other possibilities, deciding that Mill Creek was
the stream named for Ordway. It fits the time
frame laid out by Ordway. The cartographer believes
Ordway was set ashore on the "north side" of the
Missouri, just above Mace Creek, where this small
prairie begins and walked some two miles north to
Mill Creek camping at its mouth.

+430

N

N 56 W

RIVER

474

Point

473

N 25 W
3 MILES

Modern Data: 1961-1972

AMAZONIA

Mace
Creek

ONE STATUTE MILE

Outbound: July 8, 9, 1804
Return: September 11, 1806

EXPLORATIONS OF LEWIS AND CLARK   1804 - 1806
CARTOGRAPHIC RECONSTRUCTION

Kansas   Missouri

BIG NODAWAY ISLAND

CONTOUR INTERVAL 50 FEET

UTM   ZONE   15
MAP   NUMBER   50

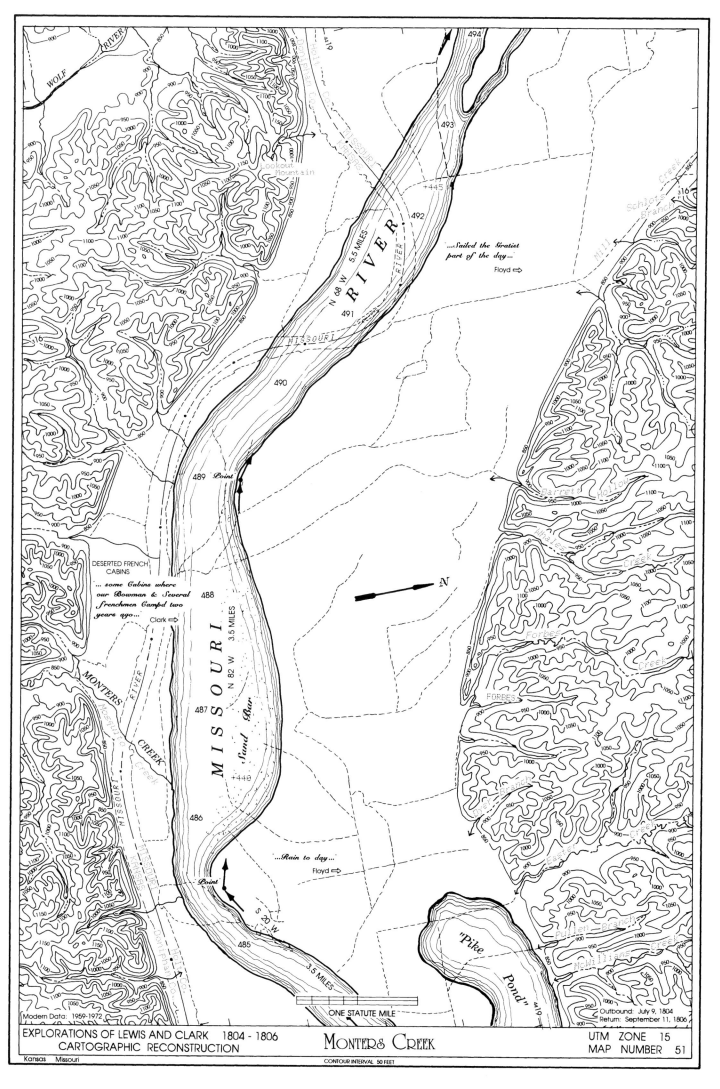

WOLF RIVER

Lookout Mountain

RIVER

N 68 W 5.5 MILES

MISSOURI

...Sailed the Gratist part of the day...
Floyd ⇨

494

493

+445

492

491

490

489 Point

DESERTED FRENCH CABINS

... some Cabins where our Bowman & Several Frenchmen Camp'd two years ago...
Clark ⇨

488

MONTERS

CREEK

MISSOURI

MISSOURI KANSAS

N 82 W 3.5 MILES

Sand Bar

487

+440

486

485

3.5 MILES

Point

S 20 W

...Rain to day...
Floyd ⇨

N

Barrett Hollow

Whales Creek

Forbes Creek

FORBES

River Branch

Easter Creek

"Pike Pond"

Pullen Branch

McWilliams Creek

316

Mill Creek

Schlots Branch

419

Outbound: July 9, 1804
Return: September 11, 1806

ONE STATUTE MILE

Modern Data: 1959-1972

EXPLORATIONS OF LEWIS AND CLARK 1804 - 1806
CARTOGRAPHIC RECONSTRUCTION

Kansas   Missouri

MONTERS CREEK

CONTOUR INTERVAL 50 FEET

UTM ZONE 15
MAP NUMBER 51

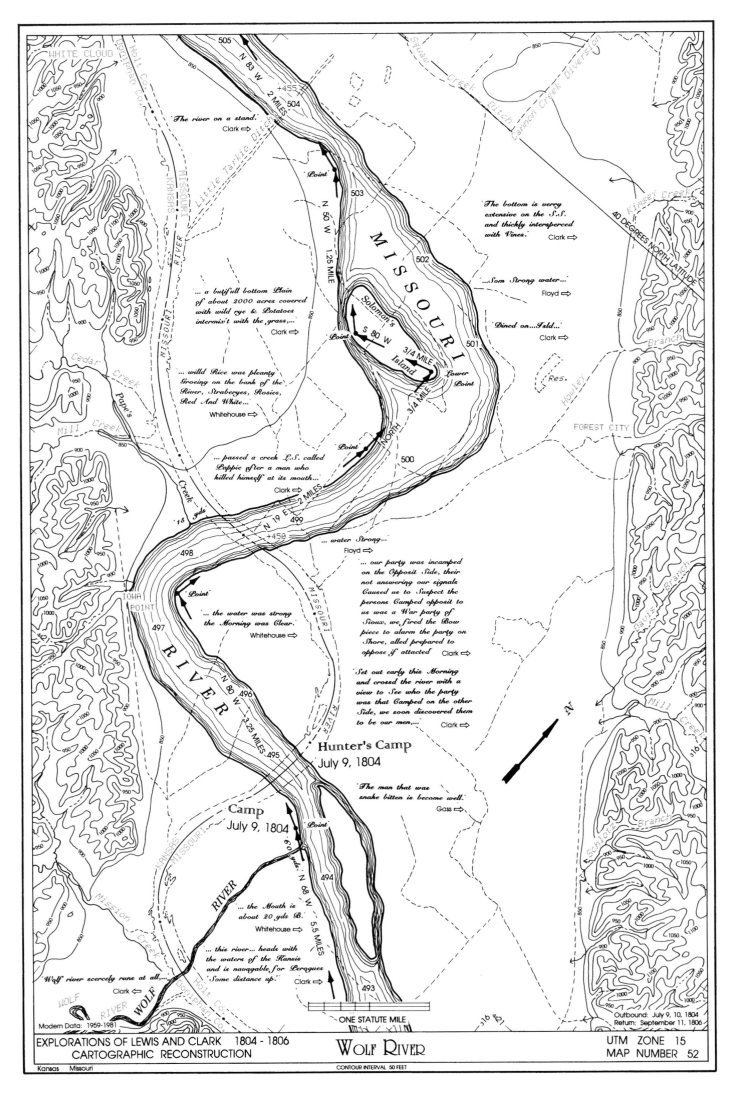

WHITE CLOUD

MISSOURI

*The river on a stand.*
Clark ⇒

505
N 83 W 2 MILES
+455
504

*Point*

503
N 50 W 1.25 MILE

*The bottom is very
extensive on the S.S.
and thickly interspersed
with Vines.*
Clark ⇒

502

*... a butifull bottom Plain
of about 2000 acres covered
with wild rye & Potatoes
intermix't with the grass,...*
Clark ⇒

Solomon's
*Point*
S 80 W
3/4 MILE
Island

*...Som Strong water...*
Floyd ⇒

*Dined on....Isld...*
Clark ⇒

501
Lower
Point
3/4 MILE

Res.

FOREST CITY

*willd Rice was pleanty
Groeing on the bank of the
River, Straberyes, Rosies,
Red And White...*
Whitehouse ⇒

NORTH
500

*Point*

40 DEGREES NORTH LATITUDE

*...passed a creek L.S. called
Pappie after a man who
killed himself at its mouth...*
Clark ⇒

15 yds

Creek

N 19 E 2 MILES
499
+450
498

*... water Strong...*
Floyd ⇒

IOWA
POINT

*Point*

MISSOURI RIVER

497

*... the water was strong
the Morning was Clear.*
Whitehouse ⇒

*... our party was incamped
on the Opposit Side, their
not answering our signals
Caused us to Suspect the
persons Camped opposit to
us was a War party of
Sioux, we, fired the Bow
piece to alarm the party on
Shore, alled prepared to
oppose if attacted*   Clark ⇒

*Set out early this Morning
and crossd the river with a
view to See who the party
was that Camped on the other
Side, we soon discovered them
to be our men,...*
Clark ⇒

R I V E R

N 80 W
496
3.25 MILES
495

**Hunter's Camp**
**July 9, 1804**

*The man that was
snake bitten is become well.*
Gass ⇒

**Camp**
**July 9, 1804**

*Point*

N

60 yds
N 68 W
5.5 MILES
494

*... the Mouth is
about 20 yds B.*
Whitehouse ⇒

*... this river... heads with
the waters of the Kansis
and is navagable for Peroques
Some distance up.*
Clark ⇒

WOLF RIVER

*Wolf river scercely runs at all,...*
Clark ⇐

493

ONE STATUTE MILE

Modern Data: 1959-1981

Outbound: July 9, 10, 1804
Return: September 11, 1806

EXPLORATIONS OF LEWIS AND CLARK  1804-1806
CARTOGRAPHIC RECONSTRUCTION

WOLF RIVER

UTM ZONE 15
MAP NUMBER 52

Kansas   Missouri

CONTOUR INTERVAL 50 FEET

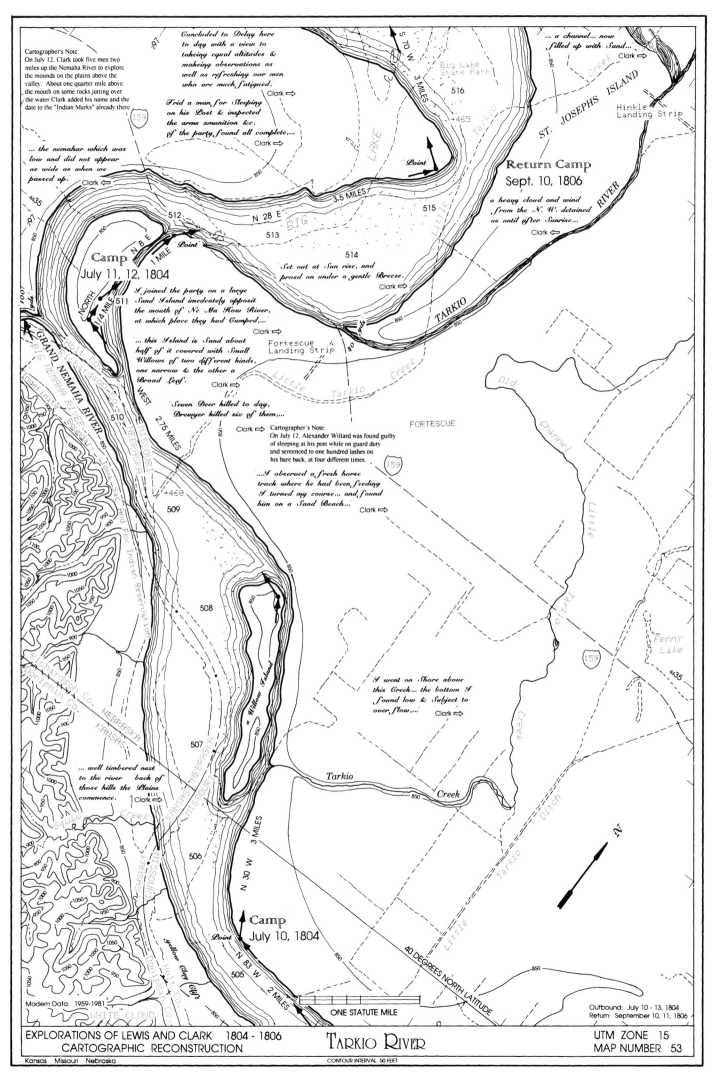

Cartographer's Note:
On July 12, Clark took five men two miles up the Nemaha River to explore the mounds on the plains above the valley. About one quarter mile above the mouth on some rocks jutting over the water Clark added his name and the date to the "Indian Marks" already there.

*Concluded to Delay here to day with a view to takeing equal altitudes & making observations as well as refreshing our men who are much fatigued.* Clark ⇨

*Trid a man for Sleeping on his Post & inspected the arms amunition &c. of the party found all complete,...* Clark ⇨

*... a channel... now filled up with Sand...* Clark ⇨

Hinkle Landing Strip

Big Lake State Park

516

+465

Point

N 28 E

3.5 MILES

515

514

513

512

*... the nemahar which was low and did not appear as wide as when we passed up.* Clark ⇦

N 8 E Point

Camp
July 11, 12, 1804

1 MILE

NORTH

1/4 MILE

511

*I joined the party on a large Sand Island imedeately opposit the mouth of Ne Ma How River, at which place they had Camped,...* Clark ⇨

*... this Island is Sand about half of it covered with Small Willows of two different kinds, one narrow & the other a Broad Leaf.* Clark ⇨

*Seven Deer killed to day, Drewyer killed six of them,...* Clark ⇨

Return Camp
Sept. 10, 1806

*a heavy cloud and wind from the N. W. detained us until after Sunrise...* Clark ⇦

*Set out at Sun rise, and prosd on under a gentle Breeze.* Clark ⇨

TARKIO RIVER

ST. JOSEPHS ISLAND

Little Tarkio

Fortescue Landing Strip

FORTESCUE

Old Channel

159

GRAND NEMAHA RIVER

WEST 2.75 MILES

510

+468

509

508

507

506

505

Cartographer's Note:
On July 12, Alexander Willard was found guilty of sleeping at his post while on guard duty and sentenced to one hundred lashes on his bare back, at four different times.

*...I observed a fresh horse track where he had been feeding I turned my course... and found him on a Sand Beach...* Clark ⇨

*I went on Shore above this Creek... the bottom I found low & Subject to over flow,...* Clark ⇨

a Willow Island

*... well timbered next to the river back of those hills the Plains commence.* Clark ⇨

Tarkio

Creek

159

Fenny Lake

4435

Little Tarkio Ditch

40 DEGREES NORTH LATITUDE

Little Tarkio Creek

Camp
July 10, 1804
Point

N 30 W
3 MILES

N 83 W
2 MILES

Modern Data: 1959-1981

WHITE CLOUD

Yellow Clay Bluff

ONE STATUTE MILE

Outbound: July 10 - 13, 1804
Return: September 10, 11, 1806

EXPLORATIONS OF LEWIS AND CLARK   1804 - 1806
CARTOGRAPHIC RECONSTRUCTION

TARKIO RIVER

UTM ZONE  15
MAP NUMBER  53

Kansas  Missouri  Nebraska

CONTOUR INTERVAL 50 FEET

77

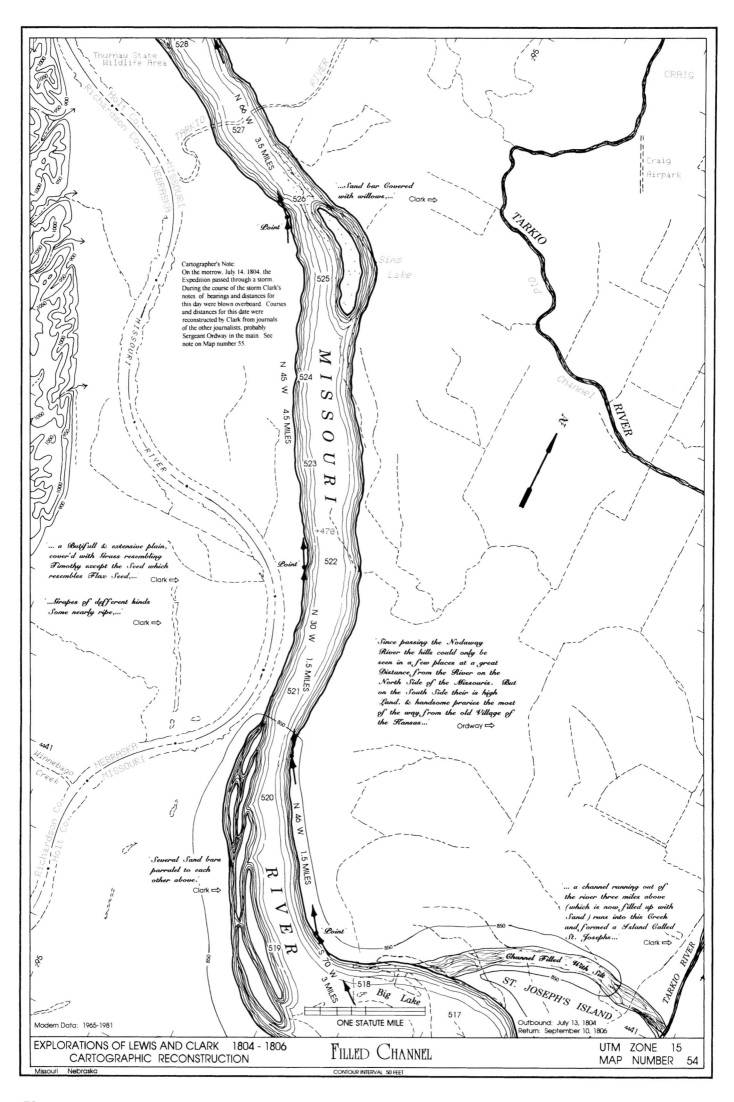

Thurnau State
Wildlife Area

CRAIG

Craig
Airpark

528

527

N 8 W
3.5 MILES

526

...Sand bar Covered
with willows,...
Clark ⇨

*Point*

525

*Sins
Lake*

TARKIO

Old

Channel

RIVER

Cartographer's Note:
On the morrow, July 14, 1804, the
Expedition passed through a storm.
During the course of the storm Clark's
notes of bearings and distances for
this day were blown overboard. Courses
and distances for this date were
reconstructed by Clark from journals
of the other journalists, probably
Sergeant Ordway in the main. See
note on Map number 55.

N 45 W
4.5 MILES

524

N

523

522

+470

N 30 W
1.5 MILES

*... a Butifull & extensive plain,
cover'd with Grass resembling
Timothy except the Seed which
resembles Flax Seed,...*
Clark ⇨

*Point*

*...Grapes of defferent kinds
Some nearly ripe,...*
Clark ⇨

521

*Since passing the Nodaway
River the hills could only be
seen in a few places at a great
Distance from the River on the
North Side of the Missouris. But
on the South Side their is high
Land. & handsome praries the most
of the way from the old Village of
the Kansas...* Ordway ⇨

850

520

N 46 W
1.5 MILES

*Several Sand bars
parralel to each
other above.*
Clark ⇨

519

*Point*

*... a channel running out of
the river three miles above
(which is now filled up with
Sand ) runs into this Creek
and formed a Island Called
St. Josephs...*
Clark ⇨

850

850

Channel Filled With Silt

ST. JOSEPH'S ISLAND

TARKIO RIVER

S 70 W
3 MILES

518

*Big Lake*

517

Winnebago
Creek

NEBRASKA
MISSOURI

Richardson Co.
Holt Co.

Modern Data: 1965-1981

ONE STATUTE MILE

Outbound: July 13, 1804
Return: September 10, 1806

EXPLORATIONS OF LEWIS AND CLARK   1804 - 1806
CARTOGRAPHIC RECONSTRUCTION

FILLED CHANNEL

UTM  ZONE   15
MAP  NUMBER   54

Missouri   Nebraska

CONTOUR INTERVAL  50 FEET

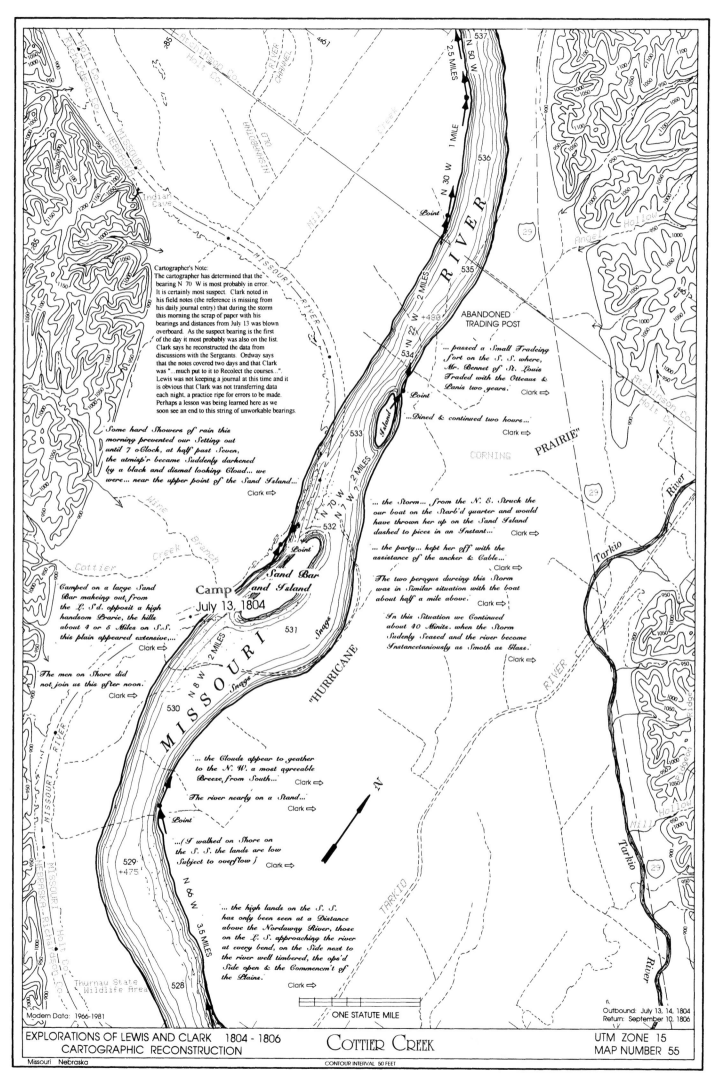

**Cartographer's Note:**
The cartographer has determined that the bearing N 70 W is most probably in error. It is certainly most suspect. Clark noted in his field notes (the reference is missing from his daily journal entry) that during the storm this morning the scrap of paper with his bearings and distances from July 13 was blown overboard. As the suspect bearing is the first of the day it most probably was also on the list. Clark says he reconstructed the data from discussions with the Sergeants. Ordway says that the notes covered two days and that Clark was "...much put to it to Recolect the courses...". Lewis was not keeping a journal at this time and it is obvious that Clark was not transferring data each night, a practice ripe for errors to be made. Perhaps a lesson was being learned here as we soon see an end to this string of unworkable bearings.

*Some hard Showers of rain this morning prevented our Setting out until 7 oClock, at half past Seven, the atmisp'r became Suddenly darkened by a black and dismal looking Cloud... we were... near the upper point of the Sand Island...* Clark ⇨

*Camped on a large Sand Bar makeing out from the L. S'd. opposit a high handsom Prarie, the hills about 4 or 5 Miles on S.S. this plain appeared extensive,...* Clark ⇨

*The men on Shore did not join us this after noon.* Clark ⇨

Camp
July 13, 1804

Sand Bar and Island

**"HURRICANE"**

*... the Clouds appear to geather to the N. W. a most agreeable Breeze from South...* Clark ⇨

*The river nearly on a Stand...* Clark ⇨

*...( I walked on Shore on the S. S. the lands are low Subject to overflow )* Clark ⇨

*... the high lands on the S. S. has only been seen at a Distance above the Nordawqy River, those on the L. S. approaching the river at every bend, on the Side next to the river well timbered, the ops'd Side open & the Commencm't of the Plains.* Clark ⇨

**ABANDONED TRADING POST**

*... passed a Small Tradeing Sort on the S. S. where, Mr. Bennet of St. Louis Traded with the Otteaus & Panis two years.* Clark ⇨

*...Dined & continued two hours...* Clark ⇨

CORNING PRAIRIE"

*... the Storm... from the N. E. Struck the our boat on the Starb'd quarter and would have thrown her up on the Sand Island dashed to pices in an Instant...* Clark ⇨

*... the party... kept her off with the assistance of the ancher & Cable...* Clark ⇨

*The two peroqus dureing this Storm was in Similar situation with the boat about half a mile above.* Clark ⇨

*In this Situation we Continued about 40 Minits. when the Storm Sudenly Seased and the river become Instancetaniously as Smoth as Glass.* Clark ⇨

ONE STATUTE MILE

Modern Data: 1966-1981

Outbound: July 13, 14, 1804
Return: September 10, 1806

**EXPLORATIONS OF LEWIS AND CLARK   1804 - 1806**
**CARTOGRAPHIC RECONSTRUCTION**

**COTTIER CREEK**

UTM ZONE 15
MAP NUMBER 55

Missouri   Nebraska

CONTOUR INTERVAL 50 FEET

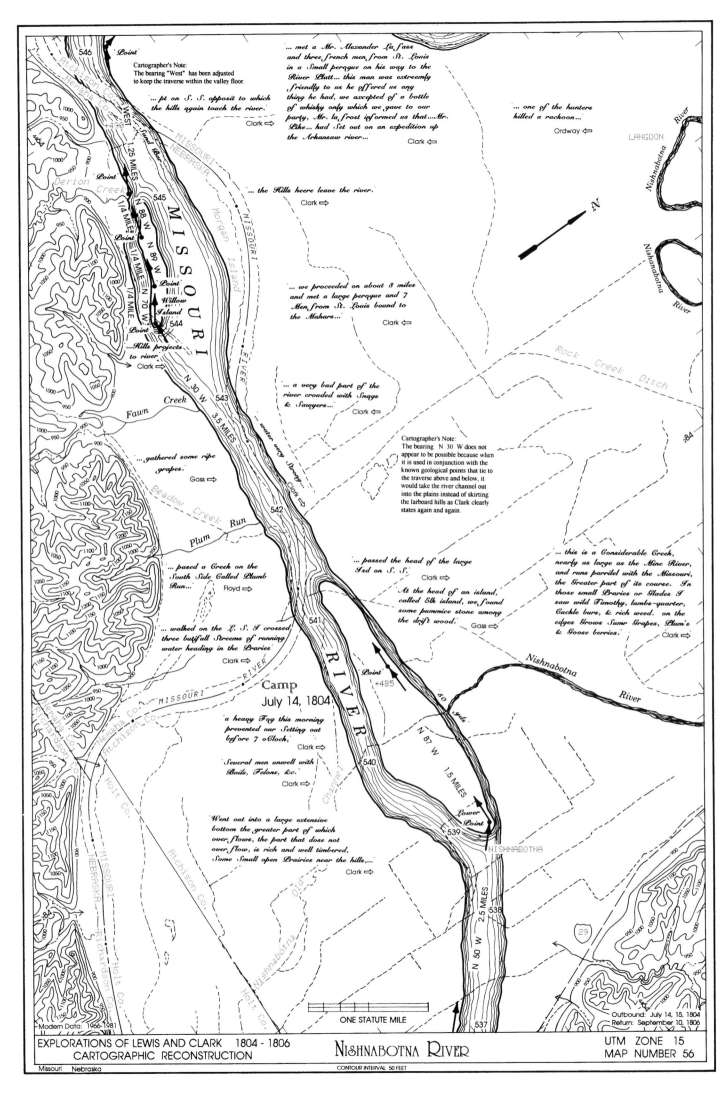

546 Point

Cartographer's Note:
The bearing "West" has been adjusted
to keep the traverse within the valley floor.

... pt on S. S. opposit to which
the hills again touch the river.

Clark ⇨

... met a Mr. Alexander La fass
and three french men from St. Louis
in a Small perogue on his way to the
River Platt ... this man was extreemly
friendly to us he offered us any
thing he had, we accepted of a bottle
of whisky only which we gave to our
party, Mr. la frost informed us that ....Mr.
Pike ... had set out on an expedition up
the Arkansaw river ...
                              Clark ⇦

... one of the hunters
killed a rackoon ...

Ordway ⇦                LANGDON

WEST         +450

N 88 W
1/4 MILE
N 89 W        545
1/4 MILE
N 70 W
1/4 MILE
Point
Willow
Island
544
Point

.. the Hills heere leave the river.
              Clark ⇨

... we proceeded on about 3 miles
and met a large perogue and 7
Men from St. Louis bound to
the Mahars ...
              Clark ⇦

...Hills projects
to river
Clark ⇨

N 30 W
3.5 MILES   543

Fawn   Creek

... water very Shoal ...

Clark

... gathered some ripe
grapes.
       Gass ⇨

... a very bad part of the
river crouded with Snags
& Sawyers ...
              Clark ⇦

Cartographer's Note:
The bearing N 30 W does not
appear to be possible because when
it is used in conjunction with the
known geological points that tie to
the traverse above and below, it
would take the river channel out
into the plains instead of skirting
the larboard hills as Clark clearly
states again and again.

.284

542

Plum   Run

... pased a Creek on the
South Side Called Plumb
Run ...
            Floyd ⇨

... passed the head of the large
Srd on S. S.
            Clark ⇨

At the head of an island,
called Elk island, we found
some pummice stone among
the drift wood.
            Gass ⇨

... this is a Considerable Creek,
nearly as large as the Mine River,
and runs parrilel with the Missouri,
the Greater part of its course. In
those small Praries or Glades I
saw wild Timothy, lambs-quarter,
Cuckle burs, & rich weed. on the
edges Grows Sumr Grapes, Plum's
& Goose berries.
                    Clark ⇨

541

... walked on the L. S. I crossed
three butifull Streems of running
water heading in the Praries ...
                 Clark ⇨

Point
+485

Nishnabotna

River

Camp
July 14, 1804

MISSOURI

a heavy Fog this morning
prevented our Setting out
before 7 oClock.
            Clark ⇨

Several men unwell with
Boils, Felons, &c.
            Clark ⇨

540

N 87 W
1.5 MILES

Lower
Point

539

NISHNABOTNA

Went out into a large extensive
bottom the greater part of which
over flows, the part that dose not
over flow, is rich and well timbered,
Some Small open Praries near the hills, ...
                    Clark ⇨

538
N 50 W
2.5 MILES

29

Modern Data: 1966-1981

ONE STATUTE MILE

537

Outbound: July 14, 15, 1804
Return: September 10, 1806

EXPLORATIONS OF LEWIS AND CLARK   1804 - 1806
CARTOGRAPHIC RECONSTRUCTION

Nishnabotna River

UTM ZONE 15
MAP NUMBER 56

Missouri   Nebraska

CONTOUR INTERVAL 50 FEET

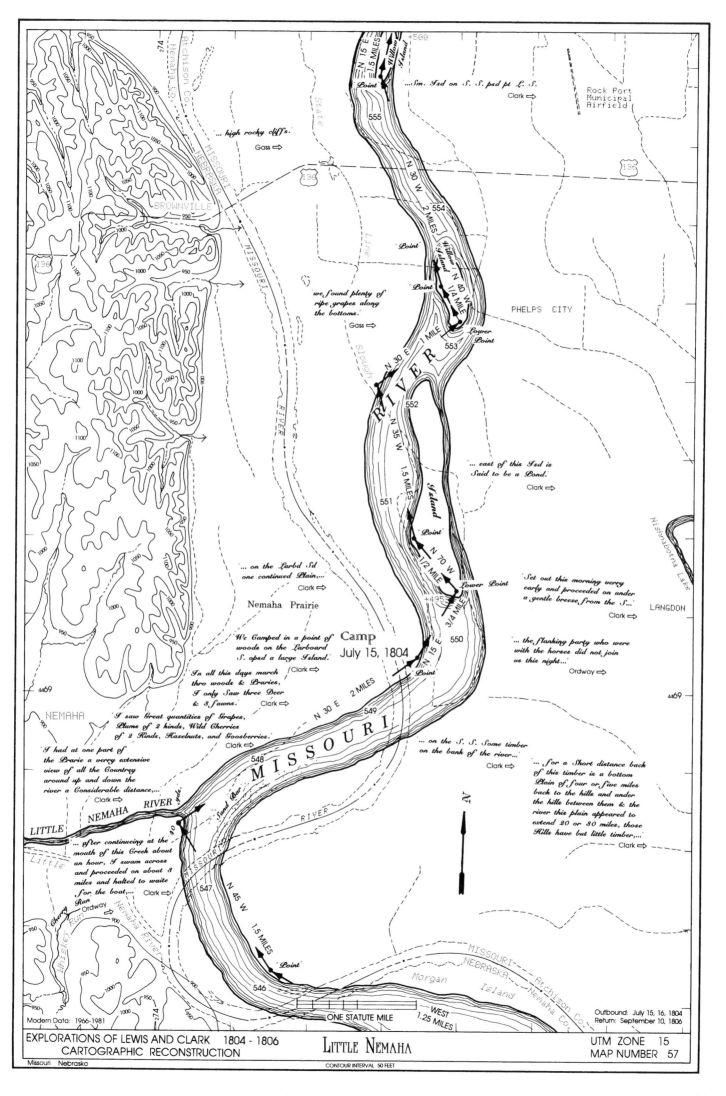

... high rocky cliffs.

Gass ⟹

...Sm. Isd on S. S. psd pt L. S.

Clark ⟹

Rock Port
Municipal
Airfield

BROWNVILLE

we found plenty of
ripe grapes along
the bottoms.

Gass ⟹

PHELPS CITY

Lower
Point

... east of this Isd is
Said to be a Pond.

Clark ⟹

LANGDON

Hismaboina Lake

... on the Larbd Sd
one continued Plain,...

Clark ⟹

Nemaha Prairie

We Camped in a point of
woods on the Larboard
S. opsd a large Island.

Clark ⟹

Camp
July 15, 1804

Set out this morning verry
early and proceeded on under
a gentle breeze from the S...

Clark ⟹

... the flanking party who were
with the horses did not join
us this night...

Ordway ⟹

In all this days march
thro woods & Praries,
I only Saw three Deer
& 3 fawns.

Clark ⟹

I saw Great quantities of Grapes,
Plums of 2 kinds, Wild Cherries
of 2 Kinds, Hazelnuts, and Goosberries.

Clark ⟹

NEMAHA

I had at one part of
the Prarie a very extensive
view of all the Country
around up and down the
river a Considerable distance,...

Clark ⟹

... on the S. S. Some timber
on the bank of the river...

Clark ⟹

... for a Short distance back
of this timber is a bottom
Plain of four or five miles
back to the hills and under
the hills between them & the
river this plain appeared to
extend 20 or 30 miles, those
Hills have but little timber,...

Clark ⟹

LITTLE NEMAHA RIVER

... after continueing at the
mouth of this Creek about
an hour, I swam across
and proceeded on about 3
miles and halted to waite
for the boat,...

Ordway ⟹

Cherry Run

Whiskey Run

MISSOURI
NEBRASKA ⟍ ATCHISON CO.
⟍ NEMAHA CO.

Morgan

Island

N

ONE STATUTE MILE

WEST
1.25 MILES

Outbound: July 15, 16, 1804
Return: September 10, 1806

Modern Data: 1966-1981

EXPLORATIONS OF LEWIS AND CLARK     1804 - 1806
CARTOGRAPHIC RECONSTRUCTION

Missouri   Nebraska

LITTLE NEMAHA

CONTOUR INTERVAL 50 FEET

UTM ZONE   15
MAP NUMBER   57

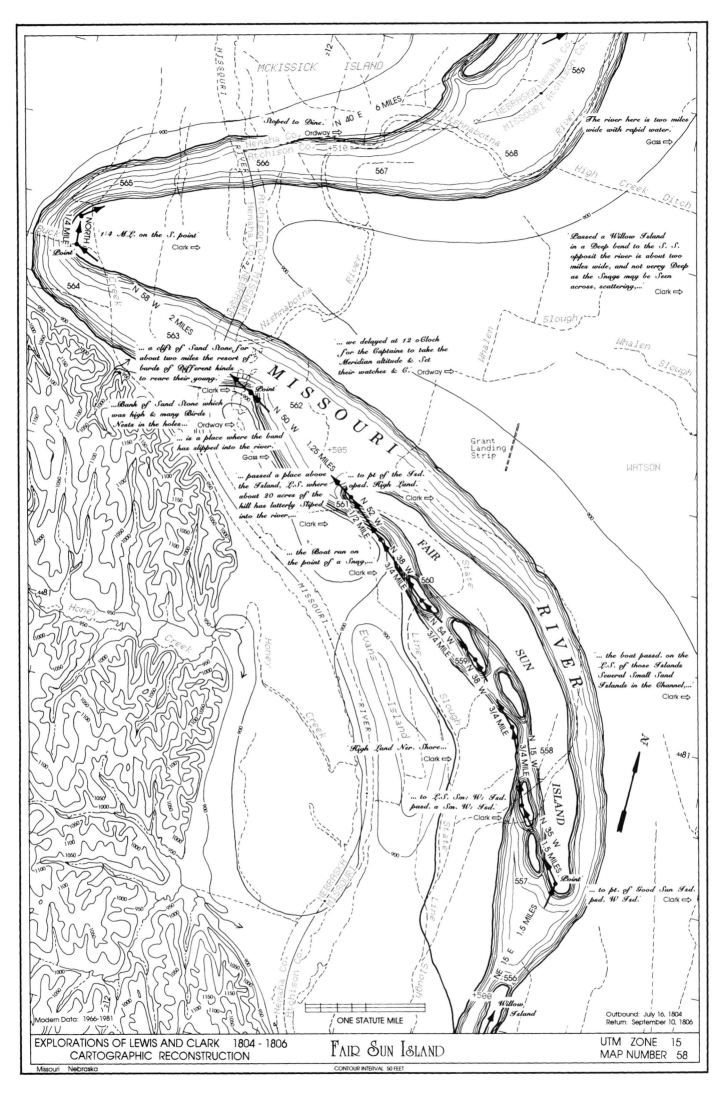

MCKISSICK ISLAND

*Stoped to Dine.*
N 40 E    6 MILES
Ordway ⇒

*The river here is two miles wide with rapid water.*
Gass ⇒

569

568

567

566

565

564

563

562

*1/4 M.L. on the S. point*
Clark ⇒

NORTH
1/4 MILE
*Buck Point*

MISSOURI

N 58 W    2 MILES

*... a clift of Sand Stone for about two miles the resort of burds of Different kinds to reare their young.*
Clark ⇒
*Point*
N 50 W

*...Bank of Sand Stone which was high & many Birds Nests in the holes...*
Ordway ⇒

*... is a place where the band has slipped into the river.*
Gass ⇒

*... passed a place above the Island, L.S. where about 20 acres of the hill has latterly Sliped into the river,...*
Clark ⇒

1.25 MILES
+565

N 52 W
1/2 MILE
561

*... the Boat run on the point of a Snag,...*
Clark ⇒

N 38 W
3/4 MILE

*... we delayed at 12 oClock for the Captains to take the Meridian altitude & Set their watches & C.*
Ordway ⇒

*... to pt of the Isd. opsd. High Land.*
Clark ⇒

*Passed a Willow Island in a Deep bend to the S. S. opposit the river is about two miles wide, and not verry Deep as the Snags may be Seen across, scattering,...*
Clark ⇒

Whalen Slough

Whalen Slough

WATSON

Grant Landing Strip

560

FAIR

N 54 W
3/4 MILE

N 38 W
3/4 MILE
559

SUN

*High Land Ner. Shore....*
Clark ⇒

Evans Island

State Line Slough

*... the boat passd. on the L.S. of those Islands Several Small Sand Islands in the Channel,...*
Clark ⇒

N 15 W
3/4 MILE
558

*... to L.S. Sm: W: Isd. passd. a Sm: W: Isd.*
Clark ⇒

N 35 W
1.5 MILES
*Point*

ISLAND

557

RIVER

*... to pt. of Good Sun Isd. psd. W Isd.*
Clark ⇒

Honey Creek

Honey Creek

MISSOURI

NEBRASKA
MISSOURI

State Line Slough

NE 15 E
1.5 MILES
556

+566
*Willow Island*

Modern Data: 1966-1981

ONE STATUTE MILE

Outbound: July 16, 1804
Return: September 10, 1806

EXPLORATIONS OF LEWIS AND CLARK    1804 - 1806
CARTOGRAPHIC RECONSTRUCTION

FAIR SUN ISLAND

UTM ZONE    15
MAP NUMBER    58

Missouri    Nebraska

CONTOUR INTERVAL 50 FEET

82

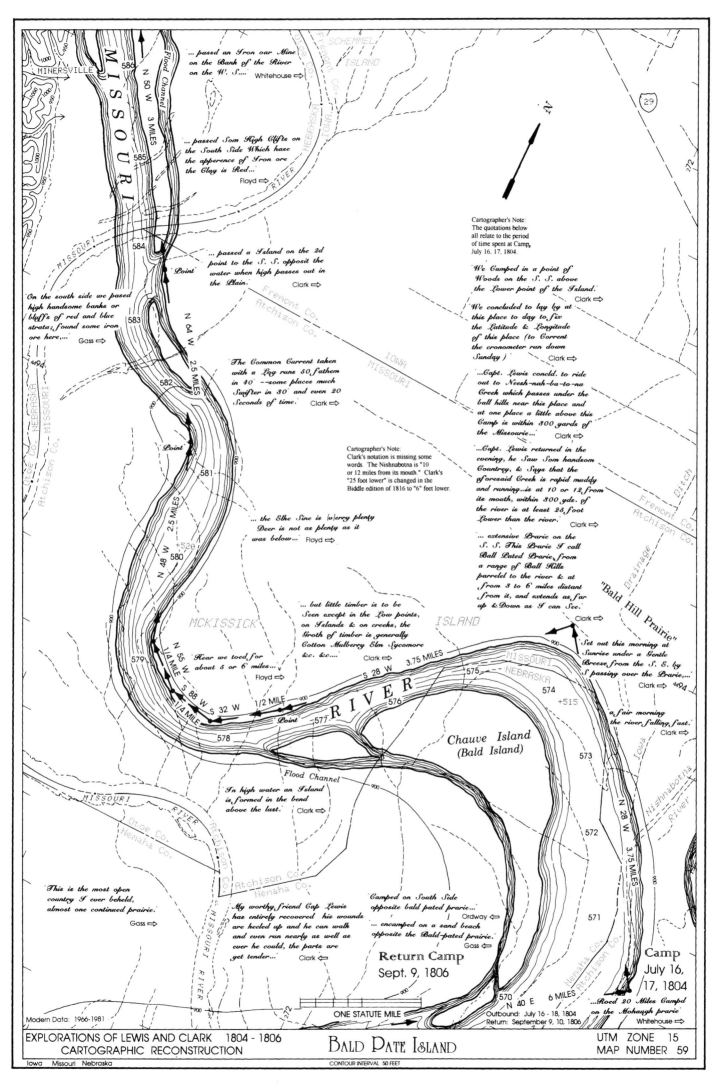

MINERSVILLE

586

N 50 W
3 MILES
Flood Channel

...passed an Iron oar Mine
on the Bank of the River
on the W. S.....    Whitehouse ⇒

585

...passed Som High Clifts on
the South Side Which hase
the apperence of Iron ore
the Clay is Red....
Floyd ⇒

SCHEMMEL
ISLAND

FREMONT CO.
ATCHISON CO.

29

N

Cartographer's Note:
The quotations below
all relate to the period
of time spent at Camp,
July 16, 17, 1804.

584

Point

...passed a Island on the 2d
point to the S. S. opposit the
water when high passes out in
the Plain.    Clark ⇒

We Camped in a point of
Woods on the S. S. above
the Lower point of the Island.
Clark ⇒

On the south side we passed
high handsome banks or
bluffs of red and blue
strata; found some iron
ore here,...    Gass ⇒

583

N 64 W
2.5 MILES

FREMONT CO.
ATCHISON CO.

IOWA
MISSOURI

We concluded to lay by at
this place to day to fix
the Latitude & Longitude
of this place (to Corrent
the cronometer run down
Sunday )    Clark ⇒

582

The Common Current taken
with a Log runs 50 fathem
in 40' --some places much
Swifter in 30' and even 20
Seconds of time.    Clark ⇒

...Capt. Lewis concld. to ride
out to Neesh-nah-ba-to-na
Creek which passes under the
ball hills near this place and
at one place a little above this
Camp is within 800 yards of
the Missourie...    Clark ⇒

Point

581

2.5 MILES
N 48 W
580
+520

Cartographer's Note:
Clark's notation is missing some
words. The Nishnabotna is "10
or 12 miles from its mouth." Clark's
"25 foot lower" is changed in the
Biddle edition of 1816 to "6" feet lower.

...the Elke Sine is |v|erry plenty
Deer is not as plenty as it
was below...    Floyd ⇒

...Capt. Lewis returned in the
evening, he Saw Som handsom
Countrey, & Says that the
aforesaid Creek is rapid muddy
and running...is at 10 or 12 from
its mouth, within 800 yds. of
the river is at least 25 foot
Lower than the river...    Clark ⇒

494

MCKISSICK

N 55 W
1/4 MILE
Near we toed, for
about 5 or 6 miles...
Floyd ⇒

579

S 88 W
1/4 MILE
S 32 W
578
Point
577    S 28 W    3.75 MILES
1/2 MILE
576

...but little timber is to be
Seen except in the Low points,
on Islands & on creeks, the
Groth of timber is generally
Cotton Mulberry Elm Sycomore
&c. &c....    Clark ⇒

ISLAND

RIVER

... extensive Prarie on the
S. S. This Prarie I call
Ball Pated Prarie, from
a range of Ball Hills
parrelel to the river & at
from 3 to 6 miles distant
from it, and extends as far
up & Down as I can See.
Clark ⇒

"Bald Hill Prairie"

900

MISSOURI
NEBRASKA

575

574
+515

Set out this morning at
Sunrise under a Gentle
Breeze from the S. E. by
S passing over the Prarie,...
Clark ⇒    494

a fair morning
the river falling fast.
Clark ⇒

573

Chauve Island
(Bald Island)

Flood Channel

In high water an Island
is formed in the bend
above the last.    Clark ⇒

900

572

N 28 W
3.75 MILES

Nishnabotna River

Iowa

MISSOURI
RIVER

Otoe Co.
Nemaha Co.

Atchison Co.

This is the most open
country I ever beheld,
almost one continued prairie.
Gass ⇒

MISSOURI
RIVER

272

Atchison Co.
Nemaha Co.

My worthy friend Cap Lewis
has entirely recovered his wounds
are heeled up and he can walk
and even run nearly as well as
ever he could, the parts are
yet tender...    Clark ⇒

Camped on South Side
opposite bald pated prarie...
Ordway ⇐

... encamped on a sand beach
opposite the Bald-pated prairie.
Gass ⇒

Return Camp
Sept. 9, 1806

900

ONE STATUTE MILE

570
N 40 E    6 MILES

Outbound: July 16 - 18, 1804
Return: September 9, 10, 1806

571

Nemaha Co.
Atchison Co.

Camp
July 16,
17, 1804

...Roed 20 Miles Campd
on the Mohaugh prarie
Whitehouse ⇒

Modern Data: 1966-1981

272

EXPLORATIONS OF LEWIS AND CLARK    1804 - 1806
CARTOGRAPHIC RECONSTRUCTION

Iowa    Missouri    Nebraska

BALD PATE ISLAND

CONTOUR INTERVAL 50 FEET

UTM ZONE    15
MAP NUMBER    59

83

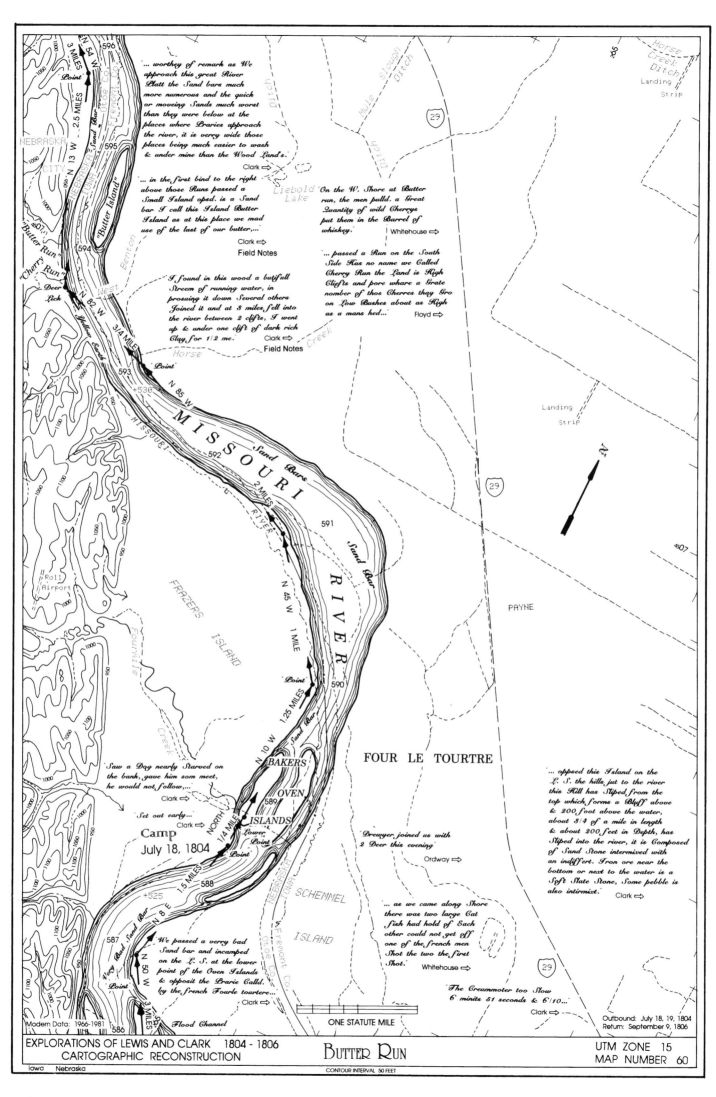

... worthey of remark as We
approach this great River
Platt the Sand bars much
more numerous and the quick
or moveing Sands much worst
than they were below at the
places where Praries approach
the river, it is verry wide those
places being much easier to wash
& under mine than the Wood Land's.
Clark ⇨

... in the first bind to the right
above those Runs passed a
Small Island opsd. is a Sand
bar I call this Island Butter
Island as at this place we mad
use of the last of our butter,...
Clark ⇨
Field Notes

On the W. Shore at Butter
run, the men pulld. a Great
Quantity of wild Cherrys
put them in the Barrel of
whiskey.
Whitehouse ⇨

I found in this wood a butifull
Streem of running water, in
prosuing it down Several others
Joined it and at 3 miles, fell into
the river between 2 clifts, I went
up & under one clift of dark rich
Clay for 1/2 me.
Clark ⇨
Field Notes

... passed a Run on the South
Side Has no name we Called
Cherry Run the Land is High
Cliefts and pore whare a Grate
nomber of thos Cherres thay Gro
on Low Bushes about as High
as a mans hed...
Floyd ⇨

FOUR LE TOURTRE

Saw a Dog nearly Starved on
the bank, gave him som meet,
he would not follow,...
Clark ⇨

Set out early...
Clark ⇨

Camp
July 18, 1804

Drewyer, joined us with
2 Deer this evening
Ordway ⇨

... opposed this Island on the
L. S. the hills jut to the river
this Hill has Sliped from the
top which forms a Bluff above
& 200 foot above the water,
about 3/4 of a mile in length
& about 200 feet in Depth, has
Sliped into the river, it is Composed
of Sand Stone intermixed with
an indiffert. Iron ore near the
bottom or next to the water is a
Soft Slate Stone, Some pebble is
also intirmixt.
Clark ⇨

... as we came along Shore
there was two large Cat
fish had hold of Each
other could not get off
one of the french men
Shot the two the first
Shot.
Whitehouse ⇨

We passed a verry bad
Sand bar and incamped
on the L. S. at the lower
point of the Oven Islands
& opposit the Prarie Calld.
by the french Fourle tourtere...
Clark ⇨

The Creummoter too Slow
6' minits 51 seconds & 6/10...
Clark ⇨

Outbound: July 18, 19, 1804
Return: September 9, 1806

ONE STATUTE MILE

Modern Data: 1966-1981

EXPLORATIONS OF LEWIS AND CLARK    1804 - 1806
CARTOGRAPHIC RECONSTRUCTION
Butter Run
UTM ZONE  15
MAP NUMBER  60
Iowa    Nebraska
CONTOUR INTERVAL 50 FEET

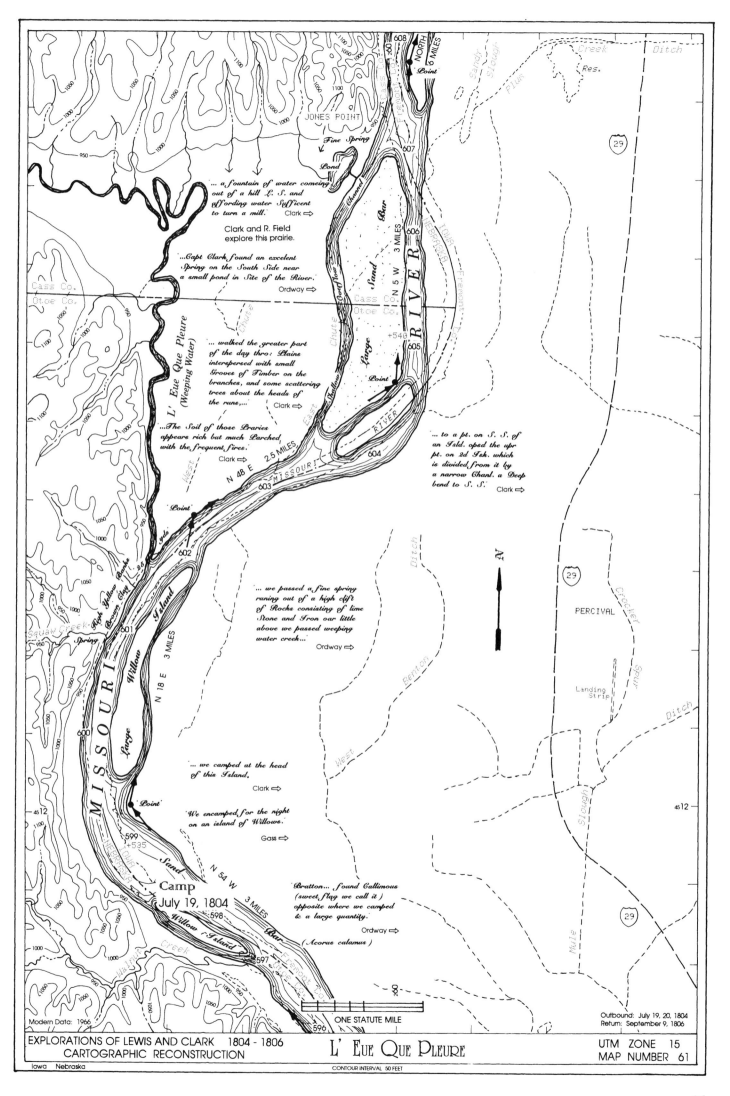

... a fountain of water comeing out of a hill L. S. and affording water Sufficent to turn a mill.  Clark ⇒

Clark and R. Field explore this prairie.

...Capt Clark found an excelent Spring on the South Side near a small pond in Site of the River.  Ordway ⇒

... walked the greater part of the day thro: Plains interspersed with small Groves of Timber on the branches, and some scattering trees about the heads of the runs,...  Clark ⇒

...The Soil of those Praries appears rich but much Parched with the frequent fires.  Clark ⇒

... to a pt. on S. S. of an Isld. opsd the upr pt. on 2d Ish. which is divided from it by a narrow Chanl. a Deep bend to S. S.  Clark ⇒

... we passed a fine spring runing out of a high clift of Rocks consisting of lime Stone and Iron oar little above we passed weeping water creek...  Ordway ⇒

... we camped at the head of this Island.  Clark ⇒

We encamped for the night on an island of Willows.  Gass ⇒

Bratton... found Callimous (sweet flag we call it ) opposite where we camped & a large quantity.  Ordway ⇒
(Acorus calamus )

Camp
July 19, 1804

PERCIVAL

Landing Strip

N

JONES POINT
Fine Spring
Pond
NORTH POINT
6 MILES

MISSOURI RIVER

L' Eue Que Pleure
(Weeping Water)

Large Willow Island

ONE STATUTE MILE

Outbound: July 19, 20, 1804
Return: September 9, 1806

EXPLORATIONS OF LEWIS AND CLARK   1804 - 1806
CARTOGRAPHIC RECONSTRUCTION

Modern Data: 1966

Iowa   Nebraska

CONTOUR INTERVAL 50 FEET

L' Eue Que Pleure

UTM ZONE 15
MAP NUMBER 61

85

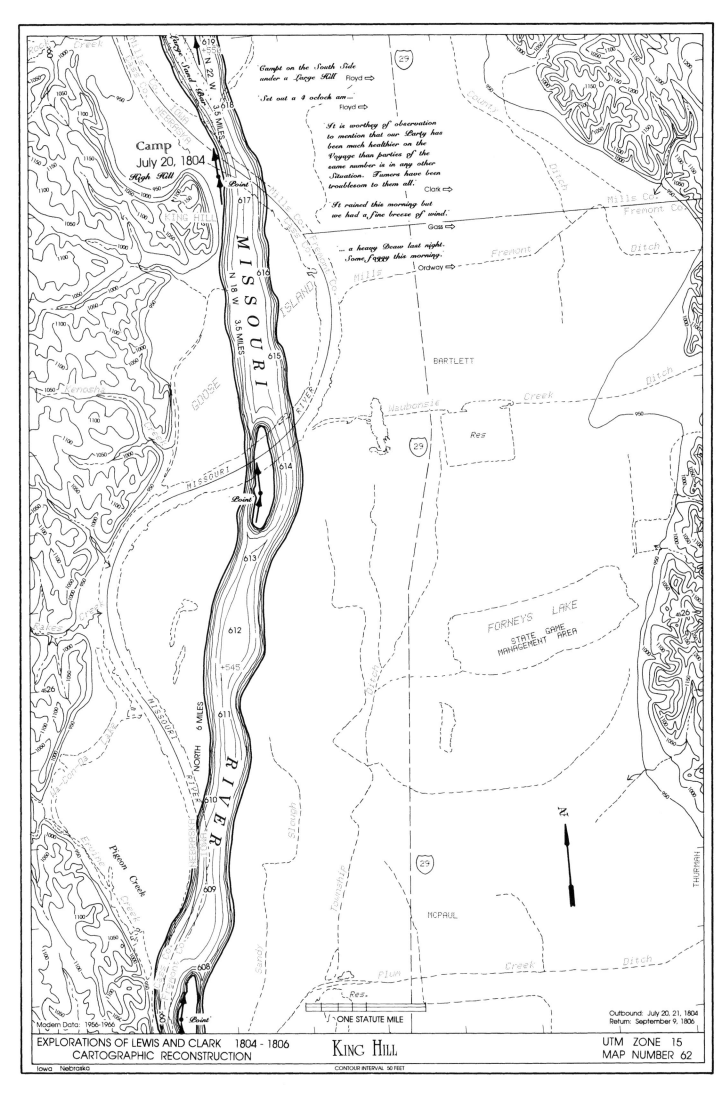

Camp
July 20, 1804

*Campt on the South Side
under a Large Hill* Floyd ⟹

*Set out a 4 oclock am...*
Floyd ⟹

*It is worthey of observation
to mention that our Party has
been much healthier on the
Voyage than parties of the
same number is in any other
Situation. Tumers have been
troublesom to them all.* Clark ⟹

*It rained this morning but
we had a fine breeze of wind.* Gass ⟹

*... a heavy Deaw last night.
Some foggy this morning.* Ordway ⟹

BARTLETT

Waubonsie

Res

FORNEYS LAKE
STATE GAME
MANAGEMENT AREA

MCPAUL

ONE STATUTE MILE

Outbound: July 20, 21, 1804
Return: September 9, 1806

UTM ZONE 15
MAP NUMBER 62

EXPLORATIONS OF LEWIS AND CLARK   1804 - 1806
CARTOGRAPHIC RECONSTRUCTION

KING HILL

Iowa   Nebraska

Modern Data: 1956-1966

CONTOUR INTERVAL 50 FEET

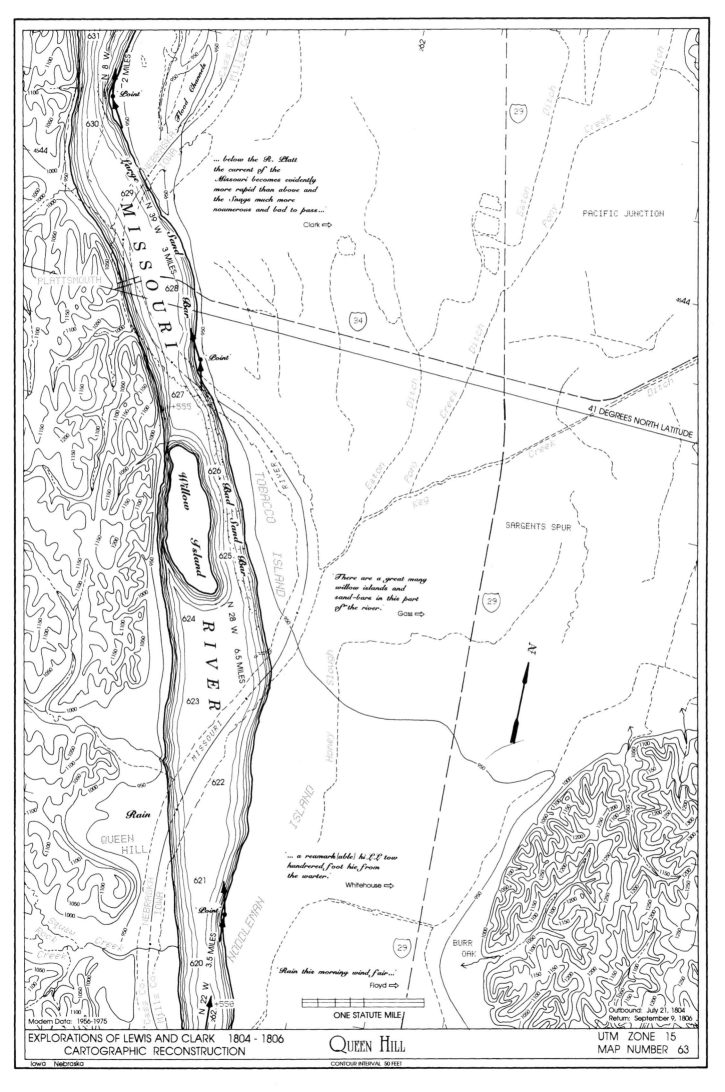

... below the R. Platt
the current of the
Missouri becomes evidently
more rapid than above and
the Snags much more
noumerous and bad to pass...

Clark ⇒

PACIFIC JUNCTION

There are a great many
willow islands and
sand-bars in this part
of the river.

Gass ⇒

SARGENTS SPUR

41 DEGREES NORTH LATITUDE

... a reamark[able] hi.LL tow
hundrered foot hie from
the warter.

Whitehouse ⇒

QUEEN HILL

BURR OAK

Rain this morning wind fair...

Floyd ⇒

ONE STATUTE MILE

Modern Data: 1956-1975

Outbound: July 21, 1804
Return: September 9, 1806

EXPLORATIONS OF LEWIS AND CLARK   1804 - 1806
CARTOGRAPHIC RECONSTRUCTION

QUEEN HILL

UTM ZONE 15
MAP NUMBER 63

Iowa   Nebraska

CONTOUR INTERVAL 50 FEET

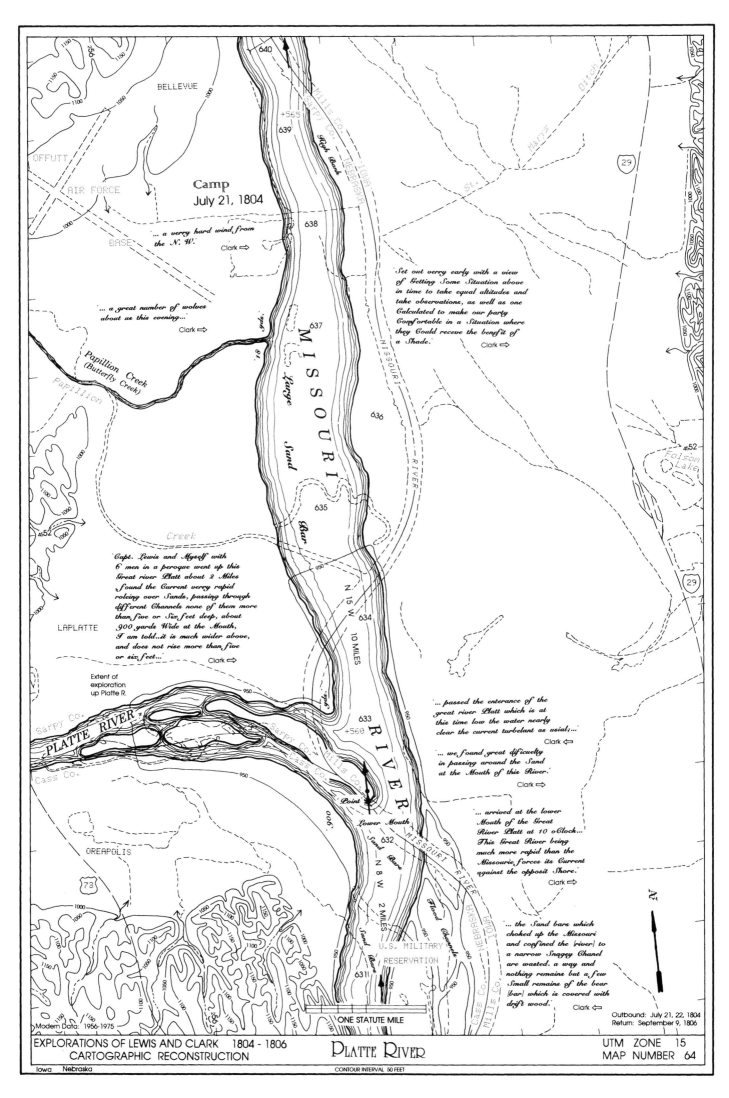

BELLEVUE

640

+565

639

Camp
July 21, 1804

638

*... a verry hard wind from the N. W.*

Clark ⇨

*... a great number of wolves about us this evening...*

Clark ⇨

OFFUTT

AIR FORCE

BASE

Papillion Creek
(Butterfly Creek)

Papillion

LAPLATTE

*Capt. Lewis and Myself with 6 men in a perogue went up this Great river Platt about 2 Miles found the Current verry rapid roleing over Sands, passing through different Channels none of them more than five or Six feet deep, about 900 yards Wide at the Mouth, I am told...it is much wider above, and does not rise more than five or six feet...*

Clark ⇨

Extent of exploration up Platte R.

Creek

950

950

637

M
I
S
S
O
U
R
I

Large
Sand
Bar

636

635

N
15
W

10
MILES

634

*Set out verry early with a view of Getting Some Situation above in time to take equal altitudes and take observations, as well as one Calculated to make our party Comfortable in a Situation where they Could receve the benefit of a Shade.*

Clark ⇨

M
I
S
S
O
U
R
I

R
I
V
E
R

4552

Folsom
Lake

29

29

950

PLATTE RIVER

Sarpy Co.

PLATTE RIVER

Cass Co.

950

950

Sarpy Co.    Mills Co.

Cass Co.

.006.

633

+560

R
I
V
E
R

950

*... passed the enterance of the great river Platt which is at this time low the water nearly clear the current turbelant as usial;...*

Clark ⇦

*... we found great dificuelty in passing around the Sand at the Mouth of this River.*

Clark ⇨

Point

Lower Mouth

632

N
8
W

2
MILES

Sand
Bar

Sand
Bar

Flood Channels

M
I
S
S
O
U
R
I
R
I
V
E
R

NEBRASKA    IOWA

Mills Co.    Cass Co.

950

*... arrived at the lower Mouth of the Great River Platt at 10 oClock... This Great River being much more rapid than the Missourie, forces its Current against the opposit Shore.*

Clark ⇨

OREAPOLIS

73

U.S. MILITARY
RESERVATION

6311

*... the Sand bare which choked up the Missouri and coffined the [river] to a narrow Snaggy Chanel are wasted. a way and nothing remains but a few Small remains of the bear [bar] which is covered with drift wood.*

Clark ⇦

N↑

1000

1050

1100

1150

Modern Data: 1956-1975

ONE STATUTE MILE

Outbound: July 21, 22, 1804
Return: September 9, 1806

EXPLORATIONS OF LEWIS AND CLARK    1804 - 1806
CARTOGRAPHIC RECONSTRUCTION

PLATTE RIVER

UTM ZONE    15
MAP NUMBER    64

Iowa    Nebraska

CONTOUR INTERVAL 50 FEET

88

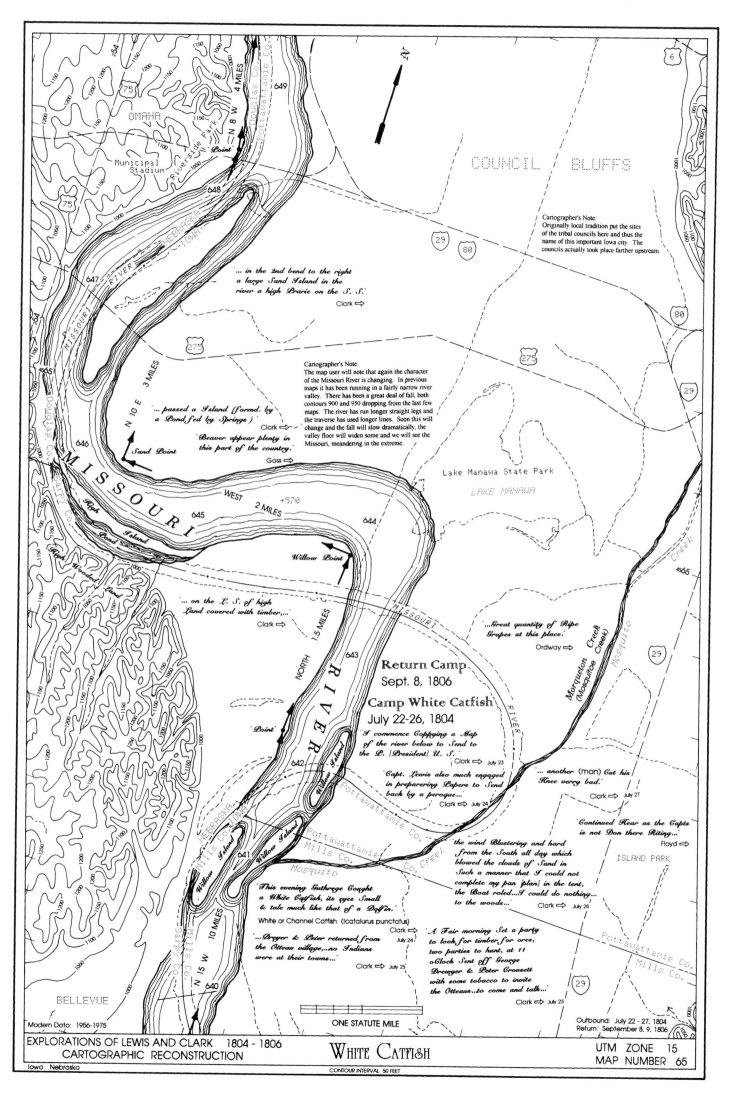

OMAHA

Municipal
Stadium

Riverside Park

Point

649

648

647

... in the 2nd bend to the right
a large Sand Island in the
river a high Prarie on the S. S.
Clark ⇒

646

... passed a Island (formd. by
a Pond fed by Springs)
Clark ⇒

Sand Point

Beaver appear plenty in
this part of the country.
Gass ⇒

645

644

Willow Point

... on the L. S. of high
Land covered with timber,...
Clark ⇒

Point

643

642

Willow Island

641

Willow Island

Willow Island

640

BELLEVUE

COUNCIL BLUFFS

Cartographer's Note:
Originally local tradition put the sites
of the tribal councils here and thus the
name of this important Iowa city. The
councils actually took place farther upstream.

Cartographer's Note:
The map user will note that again the character
of the Missouri River is changing. In previous
maps it has been running in a fairly narrow river
valley. There has been a great deal of fall, both
contours 900 and 950 dropping from the last few
maps. The river has run longer straight legs and
the traverse has used longer lines. Soon this will
change and the fall will slow dramatically, the
valley floor will widen some and we will see the
Missouri, meandering in the extreme.

Lake Manawa State Park
LAKE MANAWA

...Great quantity of Ripe
Grapes at this place.
Ordway ⇒

Return Camp
Sept. 8, 1806

Camp White Catfish
July 22-26, 1804

I commence Coppying a Map
of the river below to Send to
the P. [President] U. S.
Clark ⇒   July 23

Capt. Lewis also much engaged
in preparering Papers to Send
back by a peroque...
Clark ⇒   July 24

... another (man) Cut his
Knee verry bad.
Clark ⇒   July 27

Continued Hear as the Capts
is not Don there Riting...
Floyd ⇒

ISLAND PARK

the wind Blustering and hard
from the South all day which
blowed the clouds of Sand in
Such a manner that I could not
complete my pan [plan] in the tent,
the Boat roled...I could do nothing...
to the woods...
Clark ⇒   July 26

This evening Guthrege Cought
a White Catfish, its eyes Small
& tale much like that of a Dolffin.
White or Channel Catfish (Icatalurus punctatus)
Clark ⇒   July 24

...Dreyer & Peter returned from
the Otteau village,...no Indians
were at their towns...
Clark ⇒   July 25

A Fair morning Set a party
to look for timber for ores,
two parties to hunt, at 11
oClock Sent off George
Dreuyer & Peter Crousett
with some tobacco to invite
the Otteaus...to come and talk...
Clark ⇒   July 23

Modern Data: 1956-1975

ONE STATUTE MILE

Outbound: July 22 - 27, 1804
Return: September 8, 9, 1806

EXPLORATIONS OF LEWIS AND CLARK   1804 - 1806
CARTOGRAPHIC RECONSTRUCTION

Iowa   Nebraska

WHITE CATFISH

CONTOUR INTERVAL 50 FEET

UTM ZONE   15
MAP NUMBER 65

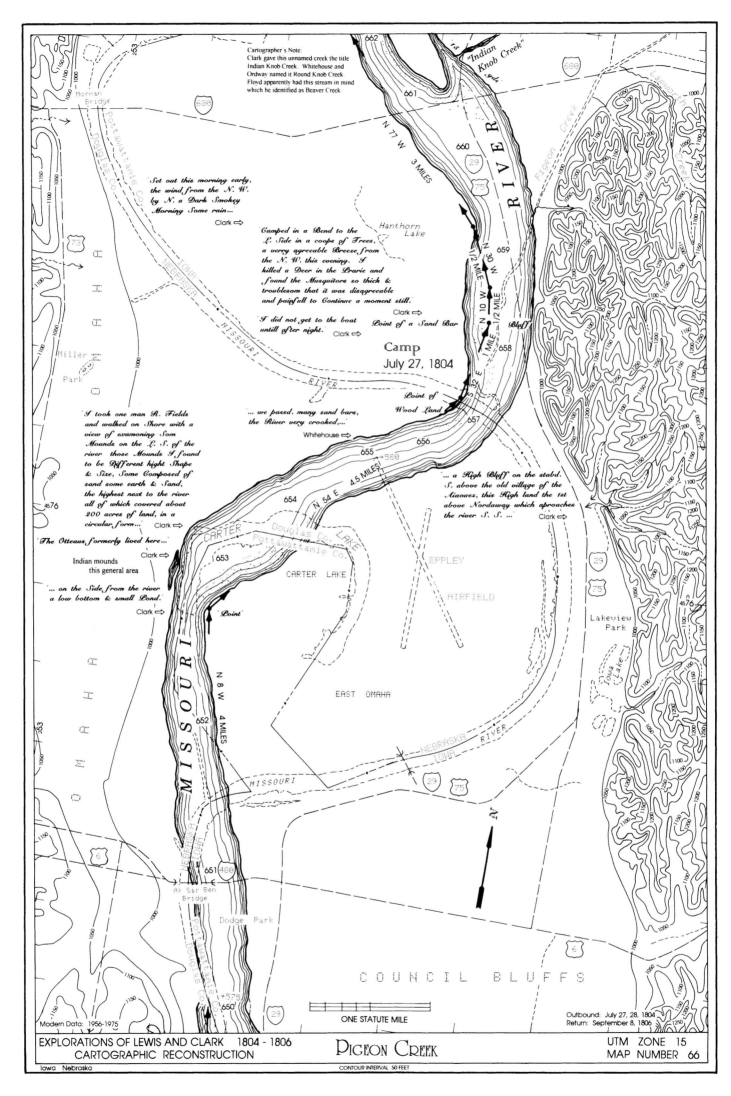

Cartographer's Note:
Clark gave this unnamed creek the title Indian Knob Creek. Whitehouse and Ordway named it Round Knob Creek. Floyd apparently had this stream in mind which he identified as Beaver Creek.

"Indian Knob Creek"

*Set out this morning early, the wind from the N. W. by N. a Dark Smokey Morning Some rain...*
Clark ⇨

*Camped in a Bend to the L. Side in a coops of Trees, a verry agreeable Breeze from the N. W. this evening. I killed a Deer in the Prarie and found the Musquitors so thick & troublesom that it was disagreeable and painfull to Continue a moment still.*

*I did not get to the boat untill after night.*
Clark ⇨

*Point of a Sand Bar*
Clark ⇨

Camp
July 27, 1804

*Point of Wood Land*

*I took one man R. Fields and walked on Shore with a view of examoning Som Mounds on the L. S. of the river those Mounds I found to be Different hight Shape & Size, Some Composed of sand some earth & Sand, the highest next to the river all of which covered about 200 acres of land, in a circular form...*
Clark ⇨

*The Otteaus, formerly lived here...*
Clark ⇨

Indian mounds this general area

*... on the Side from the river a low bottom & small Pond.*
Clark ⇨

*... we passd. many sand bars, the River very crooked,...*
Whitehouse ⇨

*... a High Bluff on the stabd. S. above the old village of the Aiaouez, this High land the 1st above Nordaway which aproaches the river S. S. ...*
Clark ⇨

CARTER LAKE

EPPLEY AIRFIELD

EAST OMAHA

Lakeview Park

Point

Dodge Park

COUNCIL BLUFFS

ONE STATUTE MILE

Modern Data: 1956-1975

Outbound: July 27, 28, 1804
Return: September 8, 1806

EXPLORATIONS OF LEWIS AND CLARK   1804 - 1806
CARTOGRAPHIC RECONSTRUCTION

PIGEON CREEK

UTM ZONE 15
MAP NUMBER 66

Iowa   Nebraska

CONTOUR INTERVAL 50 FEET

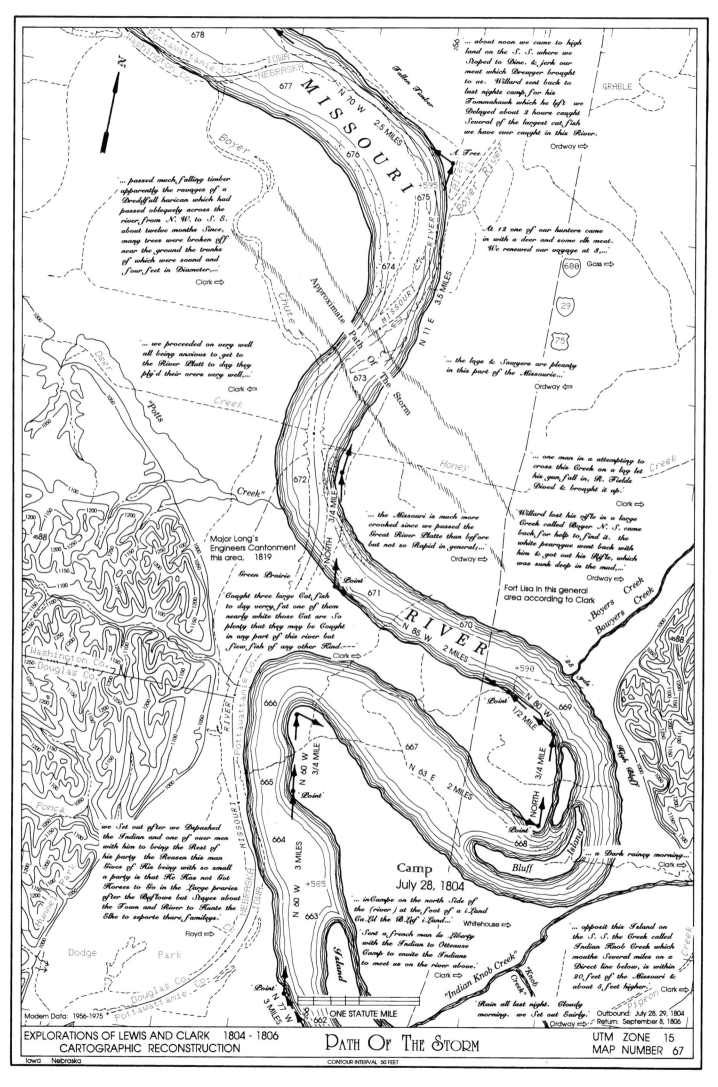

MISSOURI

678

677

676

675

674

673

672

671

670

IOWA
NEBRASKA

N 70 W 2.5 MILES

+595

Fallen Timber

Boyer

Chute

MISSOURI CITY

N 11 E 3.5 MILES

Boyer Creek

Boyer River

GRABLE

... about noon we came to high
land on the S. S. where we
Stoped to Dine. & jerk our
meat which Drewyer brought
to us. Willard sent back to
last nights camp for his
Tommahawk which he left we
Delayed about 2 hours caught
Several of the largest cat fish
we have ever caught in this River.

A Tree

Ordway ⇒

At 12 one of our hunters came
in with a deer and some elk meat.
We renewed our voyage at 3,...

680   Gass ⇒

29

75

... the logs & Sawyers are plenty
in this part of the Missourie...

Ordway ⇐

... one man in a attempting to
cross this Creek on a log let
his gun fall in, R. Fields
Dived & brought it up.

Clark ⇒

Willard lost his rifle in a large
Creek called Boyer N. S. came
back for help to find it. the
white pearogue went back with
him & got out his Rifle, which
was sunk deep in the mud,...

Ordway ⇒

Honey Creek

Boyers Creek

Bouyers Creek

Fort Lisa In this general
area according to Clark

... passed much falling timber
apparently the ravages of a
Dreddfull harican which had
passed obliquely across the
river from N. W. to S. E.
about twelve months Since,
many trees were broken off
near the ground the trunks
of which were sound and
four feet in Diameter,...

Clark ⇒

N
2.5 MILES

Approximate Path Of The Storm

... we proceeded on very well
all being anxious to get to
the River Platt to day they
ply'd their orers very well,...

Clark ⇐

Deer Creek

"Potts

1000

1050

1100

1200
1150
1200
4588
1200

1250  1100
1150

Washington Co.
Douglas Co.

1200

1100

1050

1200
1150
1150

1100

1050

Ponca

1150
1200

1100

1050

Hummel Park

Dodge      Park

Douglas Co.
Pottawattamie Co.

Washington Co.
Pottawattamie Co.

NEBRASKA
IOWA

MISSOURI

Major Long's
Engineers Cantonment
this area, 1819

Green Prairie

Cought three large Cat fish
to day verry fat one of them
nearly white those Cat are So
plenty that they may be Cought
in any part of this river but
fiew fish of any other Kind.---

Clark ⇒

... the Missouri is much more
crooked since we passed the
Great River Platte than before
but not so Rapid in general;...

Ordway ⇒

NORTH 3/4 MILE

Point

N 85 W
2 MILES

+590

Point  1/2 MILE

N 80 W  669

NORTH 3/4 MILE

Fish Bluff

4588

666

667

665

N 60 W
3/4 MILE

Point

664

N 60 W
3 MILES

663

N 63 E
2 MILES

Point

668

Island

Bluff

... a Dark rainey morning...

Clark ⇒

we Set out after we Dispashed
the Indian and one of ouer men
with him to bring the Rest of
his party the Reasen this man
Gives of His being with so small
a party is that He Has not got
Horses to Go in the Large praries
after the Byflows but Stayes about
the Town and River to Hunte the
Elke to seporte thare famileys.

Floyd ⇒

Camp
July 28, 1804

... inCampe on the north Side of
the (river) at the foot of a iLand
CaLd the B Luf i Land...

Sent a french man la Liberty
with the Indian to Otteauze
Camp to envite the Indians
to meet us on the river above.

Clark ⇒

Whitehouse ⇒

"Indian Knob Creek"

"Knob Creek"

... opposit this Island on
the S. S. the Creek called
Indian Knob Creek which
mouths Several miles on a
Direct line below, is within
20 feet of the Missouri &
about 5 feet higher,...

Clark ⇒

Pigeon Creek

Point

N 77 W
3 MILES

662

ONE STATUTE MILE

Rain all last night. Cloudy
morning. we Set out Eairly.

Ordway ⇒

Outbound: July 28, 29, 1804
Return: September 8, 1806

EXPLORATIONS OF LEWIS AND CLARK   1804 - 1806
CARTOGRAPHIC RECONSTRUCTION

PATH OF THE STORM

UTM ZONE 15
MAP NUMBER 67

Iowa  Nebraska

CONTOUR INTERVAL 50 FEET

Modern Data: 1956-1975

91

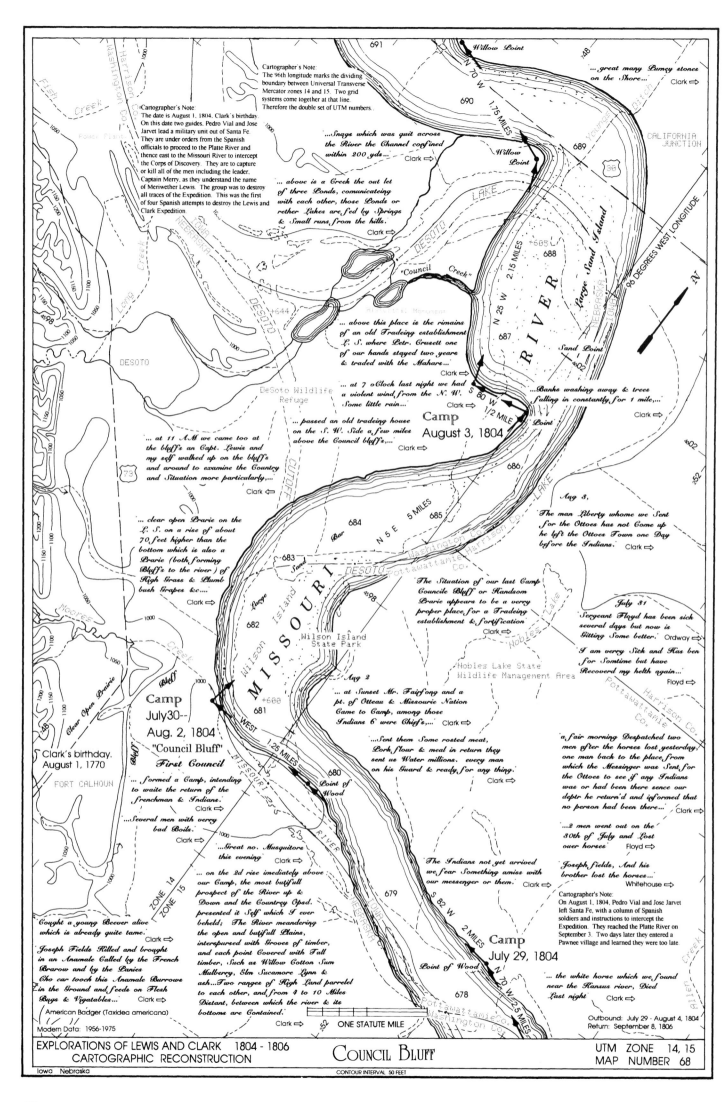

Cartographer's Note:
The 96th longitude marks the dividing boundary between Universal Transverse Mercator zones 14 and 15. Two grid systems come together at that line. Therefore the double set of UTM numbers.

Cartographer's Note:
The date is August 1, 1804. Clark's birthday. On this date two guides, Pedro Vial and Jose Jarvet lead a military unit out of Santa Fe. They are under orders from the Spanish officials to proceed to the Platte River and thence east to the Missouri River to intercept the Corps of Discovery. They are to capture or kill all of the men including the leader, Captain Merry, as they understand the name of Meriwether Lewis. The group was to destroy all traces of the Expedition. This was the first of four Spanish attempts to destroy the Lewis and Clark Expedition.

...Snqgs which was quit across the River the Channel confined within 200 yds... Clark ⇨

... above is a Creek the out let of three Ponds, comunicateing with each other, those Ponds or rether Lakes are fed by Springs & Small runs from the hills. Clark ⇨

...great many Pumey stones on the Shore... Clark ⇨

... above this place is the rimains of an old Tradeing establishment L. S. where Petr. Crusett one of our hands stayed two years & traded with the Mahars... Clark ⇨

... at 7 oClock last night we had a violent wind from the N. W. Some little rain...

...Banks washing away & trees falling in constantly for 1 mile,... Clark ⇨

Camp August 3, 1804

... passed an old tradeing house on the S. W. Side a few miles above the Council bluffs,... Clark ⇨

... at 11 AM we came too at the bluffs an Capt. Lewis and my self walked up on the bluffs and around to examine the Country and Situation more particularly,... Clark ⇦

Aug 3,
The man Liberty whome we Sent for the Ottoes has not Come up he left the Ottoes Town one Day before the Indians. Clark ⇨

... clear open Prarie on the L. S. on a rise of about 70 feet higher than the bottom which is also a Prarie (both forming Bluffs to the river) of High Grass & Plumb bush Grapes &c.... Clark ⇦

The Situation of our last Camp Councile Bluff or Handsom Prarie appears to be a verry proper place for a Tradeing establishment & fortification Clark ⇨

July 31
Sergeant Floyd has been sick several days but now is Gitting Some better. Ordway ⇨
I am verry Sick and Has ben for Somtime but have Recoverd my helth again... Floyd ⇨

Camp July 30-- Aug. 2, 1804 "Council Bluff" First Council

Clark's birthday. August 1, 1770

... at Sunset Mr. Fairfong and a pt. of Otteau & Missourie Nation Came to Camp, among those Indians 6 were Chiefs,... Clark ⇨

...Sent them Some rosted meat, Pork, flour & meal in return they sent us Water millions. every man on his Guard & ready for any thing. Clark ⇨

a fair morning Despatched two men after the horses lost yesterday, one man back to the place from which the Messinger was Sent for the Ottoes to see if any Indians was or had been there sence our deptr he return'd and informed that no person had been there... Clark ⇨

... formed a Camp, intending to waite the return of the frenchman & Indians. Clark ⇨

...Several men with verry bad Boils. Clark ⇨

...2 men went out on the 30th of July and Lost ouer horses Floyd ⇨

...Great no. Musquitors this evening Clark ⇨

Joseph fields, And his brother lost the horses... Whitehouse ⇨

... on the 2d rise imediately above our Camp, the most butifull prospect of the River up & Down and the Countrey Opsd. presented it Self which I ever beheld; The River meandering the open and butifull Plains, interspused with Groves of timber, and each point Covered with Tall timber, Such as Willow Cotton Sum Mulberry, Elm Sucamore Lynn & ash...Two ranges of High Land parrelel to each other, and from 4 to 10 Miles Distant, between which the river & its bottoms are Contained. Clark ⇨

The Indians not yet arrived we fear Something amiss with our messenger or them. Clark ⇨

Cartographer's Note:
On August 1, 1804, Pedro Vial and Jose Jarvet left Santa Fe, with a column of Spanish soldiers and instructions to intercept the Expedition. They reached the Platte River on September 3. Two days later they entered a Pawnee village and learned they were too late.

Cought a young Beever alive which is already quite tame. Clark ⇨

Joseph Fields Killed and brought in an Anamale Called by the French Brarow and by the Panies Cho car tooch this Anamale Burrows in the Ground and feeds on Flesh Bugs & Vigatables... Clark ⇨

American Badger (Taxidea americana)
Modern Data: 1956-1975

Camp July 29, 1804

Point of Wood

... the white horse which we found near the Kanzus river, Died Last night Clark ⇨

Outbound: July 29 - August 4, 1804
Return: September 8, 1806

ONE STATUTE MILE

EXPLORATIONS OF LEWIS AND CLARK 1804 - 1806
CARTOGRAPHIC RECONSTRUCTION
COUNCIL BLUFF
UTM ZONE 14, 15
MAP NUMBER 68
Iowa Nebraska
CONTOUR INTERVAL 50 FEET

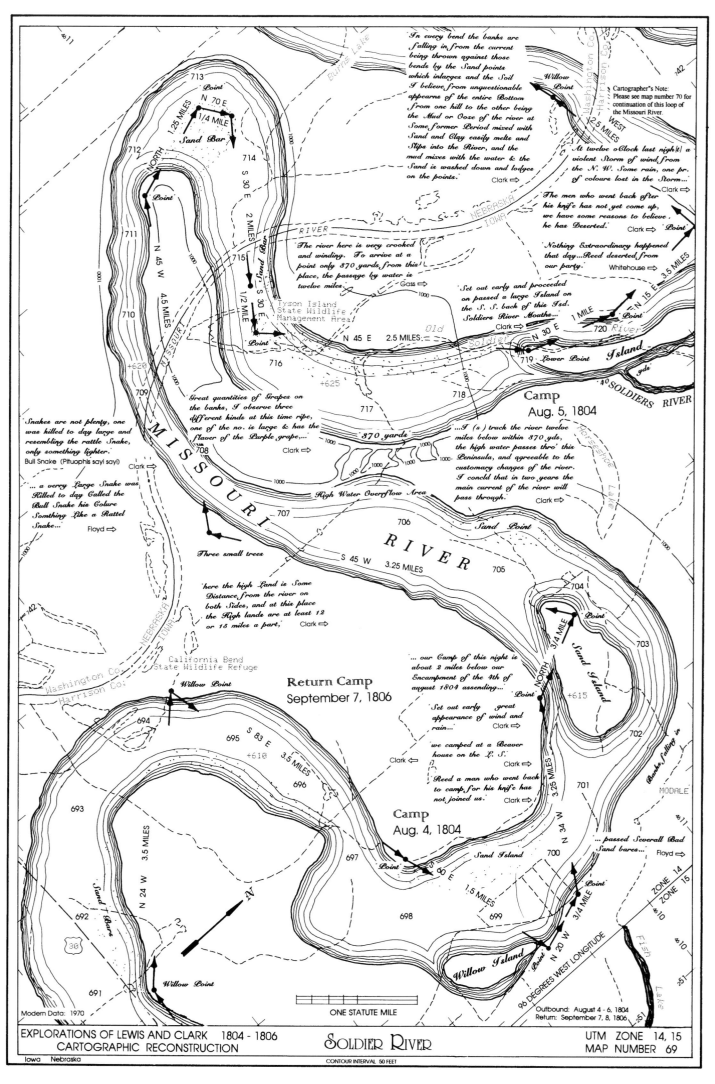

In every bend the banks are falling in from the current being thrown against those bends by the Sand points which inlarges and the Soil I believe from unquestionable appearns of the entire Bottom from one hill to the other being the Mud or Ooze of the river at Some former Period mixed with Sand and Clay easily melts and Slips into the River, and the mud mixes with the water & the Sand is washed down and lodges on the points. Clark ⇒

Cartographer's Note: Please see map number 70 for continuation of this loop of the Missouri River.

At twelve o'Clock last nigh[t] a violent Storm of wind from the N. W. Some rain, one pr. of coloures lost in the Storm... Clark ⇒

The men who went back after his knife has not yet come up, we have some reasons to believe he has Deserted. Clark ⇒

Nothing Extraordinary happened that day...Reed deserted from our party. Whitehouse ⇒

The river here is very crooked and winding. To arrive at a point only 370 yards from this place, the passage by water is twelve miles. Gass ⇒

Tyson Island State Wildlife Management Area

Set out early and proceeded on passed a large Island on the S. S. back of this Isd. Soldiers River Mouths... Clark ⇒

Camp Aug. 5, 1804

...I (s) truck the river twelve miles below within 370 yds, the high water passes thro' this Peninsula, and agreeable to the customary changes of the river, I concld that in two years the main current of the river will pass through. Clark ⇒

Great quantities of Grapes on the banks, I observe three different kinds at this time ripe, one of the no. is large & has the flavor of the Purple grape,... Clark ⇒

Snakes are not plenty, one was killed to day large and resembling the rattle Snake, only something lighter. Bull Snake (Pituophis sayi sayi)

... a verry Large Snake was Killed to day Called the Bull Snake his Colure Somthing Like a Rattel Snake... Floyd ⇒

High Water Overflow Area

Three small trees

here the high Land is Some Distance from the river on both Sides, and at this place the High lands are at least 12 or 15 miles a part, Clark ⇒

California Bend State Wildlife Refuge

Return Camp September 7, 1806

... our Camp of this night is about 2 miles below our Encampment of the 4th of august 1804 ascending... Clark ⇒

Set out early great appearance of wind and rain... Clark ⇒

we camped at a Beaver house on the L. S. Clark ⇒

Reed a man who went back to camp for his knife has not joined us. Clark ⇒

Camp Aug. 4, 1804

... passed Severall Bad Sand bares... Floyd ⇒

MODALE

Modern Data: 1970

ONE STATUTE MILE

Outbound: August 4 - 6, 1804
Return: September 7, 8, 1806

EXPLORATIONS OF LEWIS AND CLARK 1804 - 1806
CARTOGRAPHIC RECONSTRUCTION

SOLDIER RIVER

UTM ZONE 14, 15
MAP NUMBER 69

Iowa    Nebraska

CONTOUR INTERVAL 50 FEET

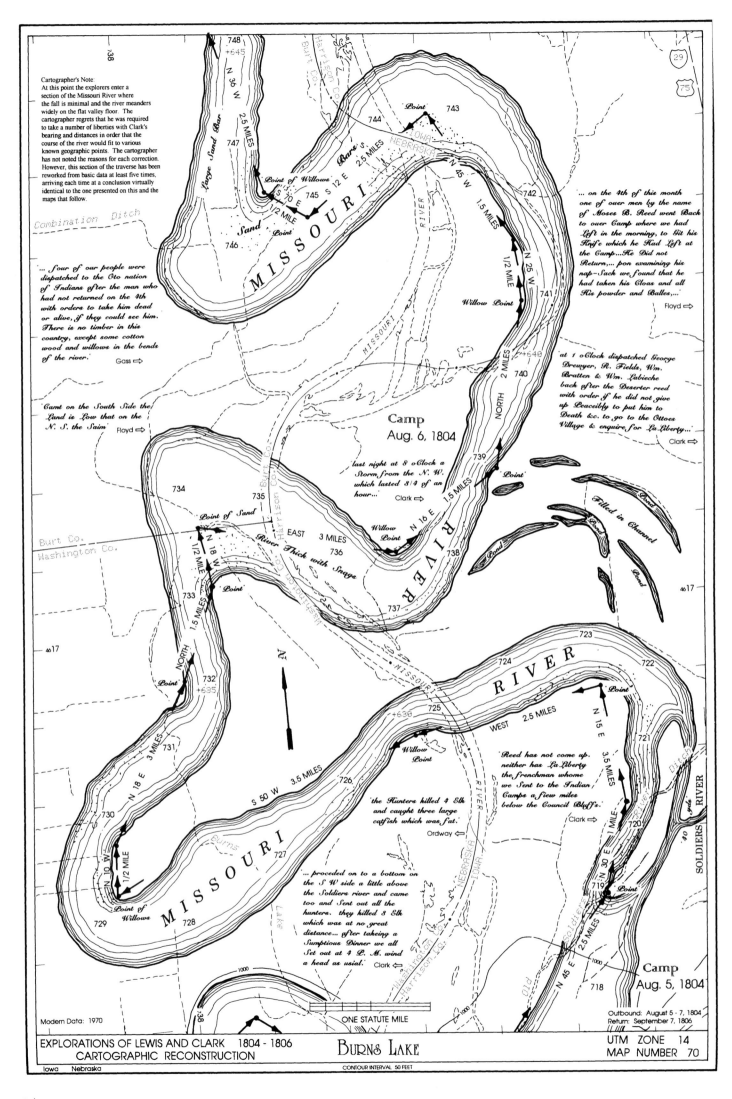

EXPLORATIONS OF LEWIS AND CLARK 1804 - 1806
CARTOGRAPHIC RECONSTRUCTION

BURNS LAKE

UTM ZONE 14
MAP NUMBER 70

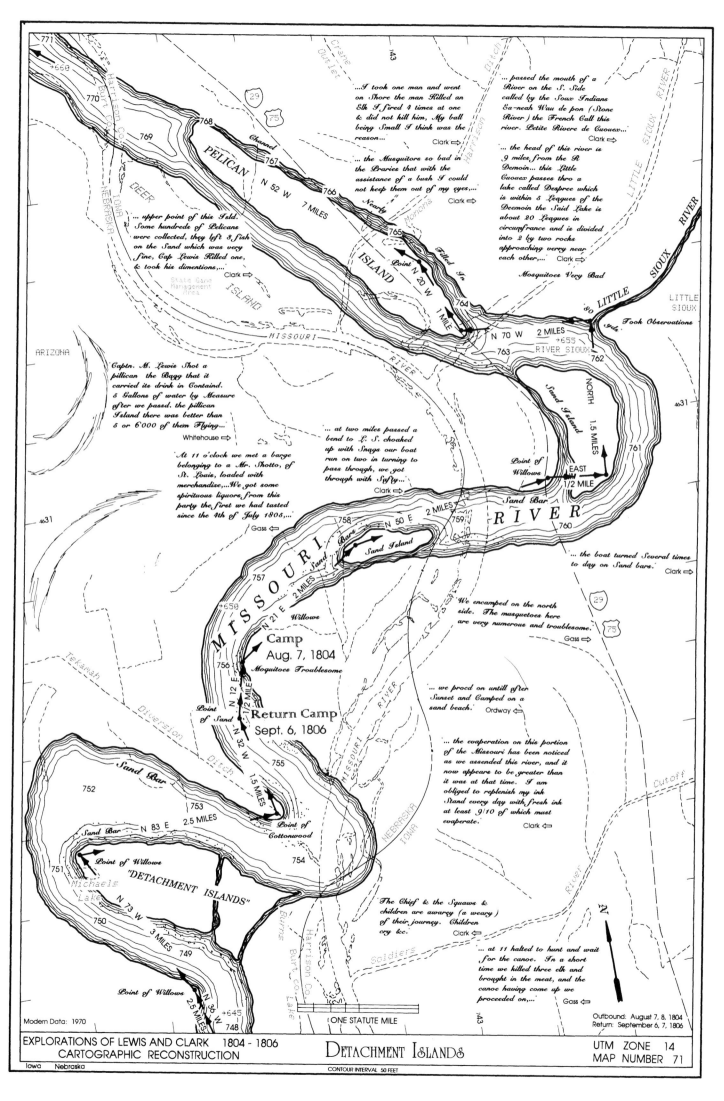

771
+650
770
769
768
767
766
765
764
763
762
761
760
759
758
757
756
755
754
753
752
751
750
749
748
743

PELICAN

DEER

IOWA
NEBRASKA

ISLAND

Channel

N 52 W
7 MILES

ISLAND

State Game
Management
Area

ARIZONA

MISSOURI

RIVER

Nearly
Filled In

Point
N 20 W
1 Mile

N 70 W    2 MILES
RIVER SIOUX

LITTLE SIOUX

LITTLE
SIOUX
Side

Took Observations

Sand Island

NORTH    1.5 MILES

Point of
Willows
EAST
1/2 MILE

Sand Bar

Sand Bar

RIVER

+655

+650

Crane Outlet

743

Harrison

Monona

Little Sioux

29
75

LITTLE SIOUX RIVER

80

431

...I took one man and went
on Shore the man killed an
Elk I fired 4 times at one
& did not kill him, My ball
being Small I think was the
reason...                     Clark ⇨

... the Musquitors so bad in
the Praries that with the
assistance of a bush I could
not keep them out of my eyes,...
                              Clark ⇨

... upper point of this Isld.
Some hundreds of Pelicans
were collected, they left 3 fish
on the Sand which was very
fine, Cap Lewis killed one,
& took his dimentions,...
                    Clark ⇨

Captn. M. Lewis Shot a
pillican the Bagg that it
carried its drink in Containd.
5 Gallons of water by Measure
after we passd. the pillican
Island there was better than
5 or 6'000 of them Flying...
              Whitehouse ⇨

At 11 o'clock we met a barge
belonging to a Mr. Shotto, of
St. Louis, loaded with
merchandize,...We got some
spirituous liquors from this
party the first we had tasted
since the 4th of July 1806,...
              Gass ⇨

...passed the mouth of a
River on the S. Side
called by the Soux Indians
Ea-neah Wau de pon (Stone
River) the French Call this
river. Petite Rivere de Cuouex...
                        Clark ⇨

... the head of this river is
9 miles from the R.
Demoin... this Little
Cuouex passes thro a
lake called Despree which
is within 5 Leagues of the
Decmoin the Said Lake is
about 20 Leagues in
circumfrance and is divided
into 2 by two rocks
approaching verry near
each other,...    Clark ⇨

Mosquitoes Very Bad

... at two miles passed a
bend to L. S. choaked
up with Snags our boat
run on two in turning to
pass through, we got
through with Safty...
              Clark ⇨

N 50 E
2 MILES

2 MILES

758
759
760

Sand Bars

Sand
Bars

N 21 E
2 MILES

Sand Island

... the boat turned Several times
to day on Sand bars.
                        Clark ⇨

We encamped on the north
side. The musquetoes here
are very numerous and troublesome.
                        Gass ⇨

Willows

Camp
Aug. 7, 1804

Moquitoes Troublesome

N 21 E
1/2 MILE

756

Point
of Sand

Return Camp
Sept. 6, 1806

N 32 W
1.5 MILES

755

MISSOURI RIVER

... we procd on untill after
Sunset and Camped on a
sand beach.    Ordway ⇨

... the evaperation on this portion
of the Missouri has been noticed
as we assended this river, and it
now appears to be greater than
it was at that time. I am
obliged to replenish my ink
Stand every day with fresh ink
at least 9/10 of which must
evaperate.        Clark ⇦

Tekamah Diversion Ditch

Sand Bar

752

Sand Bar

751

Michaels
Lake

N 83 E
2.5 MILES

753

N 73 W
3 MILES

750

N 36 W
2.5 MILES

Point of Willows

749

+645

748

"DETACHMENT ISLANDS"

Point of
Cottonwood

754

Point of Willows

The Chief & the Squaws &
children are awarey (a weary)
of their journey. Children
cry &c.            Clark ⇦

... at 11 halted to hunt and wait
for the canoe. In a short
time we killed three elk and
brought in the meat, and the
canoe having come up we
proceeded on,...    Gass ⇦

Harrison Co.
Burt Co.
Soldiers
Burt Co. Lake

NEBRASKA
IOWA

Missouri River

Cutoff

River

29
75

743

N

Modern Data: 1970

ONE STATUTE MILE

Outbound: August 7, 8, 1804
Return: September 6, 7, 1806

EXPLORATIONS OF LEWIS AND CLARK    1804 - 1806
CARTOGRAPHIC RECONSTRUCTION

Iowa    Nebraska

DETACHMENT ISLANDS

CONTOUR INTERVAL 50 FEET

UTM  ZONE  14
MAP NUMBER  71

95

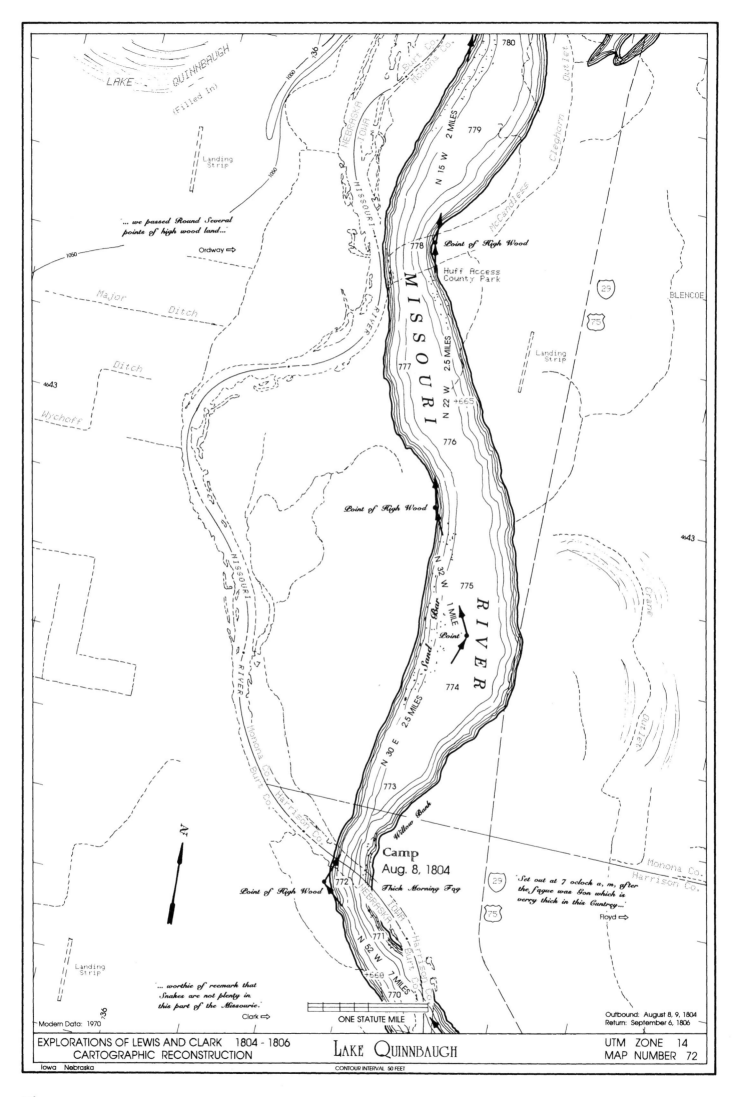

LAKE QUINNBAUGH
(Filled In)

Landing
Strip

*... we passed Round Several
points of high wood land...*

Ordway ⇒

Major    Ditch

Ditch

Wychoff

Buff Co.
Monona Co.

MISSOURI

MISSOURI

RIVER

N 15 W
2 MILES

780

779

778    *Point of High Wood*

Huff Access
County Park

N 22 W
2.5 MILES    +665

777

776

*Point of High Wood*

N 32 W
1 MILE

Sand Bar

*Point*

N 30 E
2.5 MILES

775

774

773

*Willow Bank*

**Camp**
**Aug. 8, 1804**

*Thick Morning Fog*

Cleghorn    Outlet

29

75    BLENCOE

Landing
Strip

4643

Crane    Outlet

4643

Monona Co.
Harrison Co.

29    *Set out at 7 oclock a, m, after
the fague was Gon which is
verry thick in this Cuntrey...*

75    Floyd ⇒

N

*Point of High Wood*

772

N 52 W
7 MILES    +668

771

770

Landing
Strip

736

*... worthie of reemark that
Snakes are not plenty in
this part of the Missourie.*

Clark ⇒

ONE STATUTE MILE

Outbound: August 8, 9, 1804
Return: September 6, 1806

Modern Data: 1970

EXPLORATIONS OF LEWIS AND CLARK    1804 - 1806
CARTOGRAPHIC RECONSTRUCTION

Iowa    Nebraska

LAKE QUINNBAUGH

CONTOUR INTERVAL 50 FEET

UTM ZONE    14
MAP NUMBER  72

96

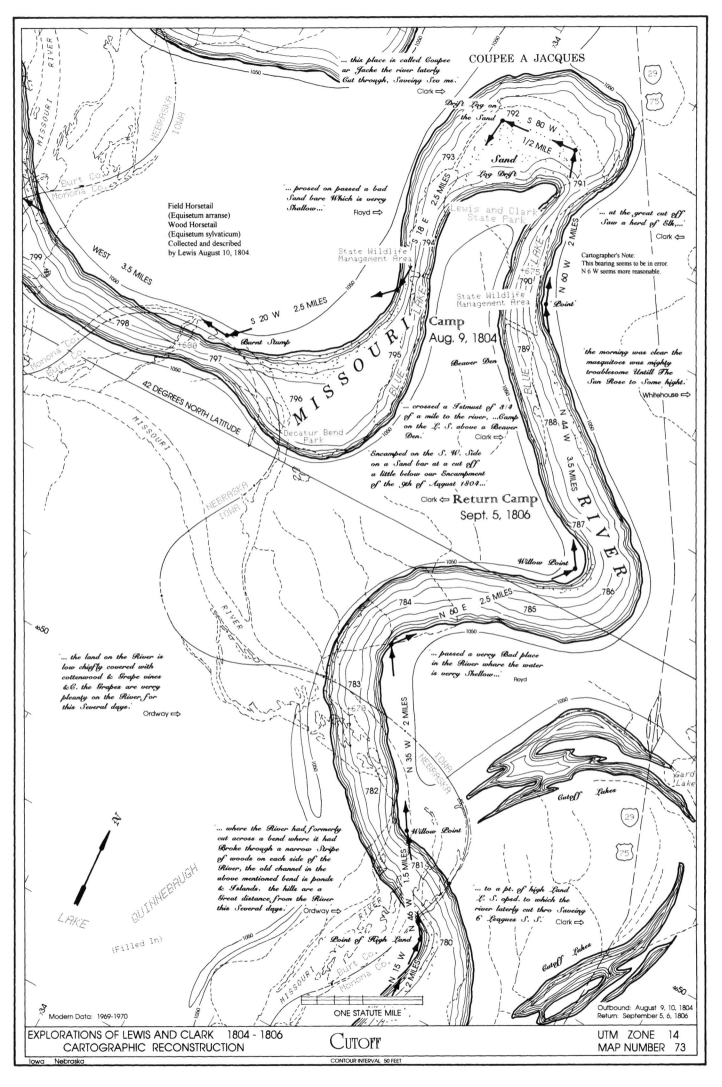

... this place is called Coupee
ar Jacke the river lately
Cut through, Saveing Sev ms.
Clark ⇒

COUPEE A JACQUES

Drift Log on
the Sand
792
S 80 W
1/2 MILE

793
Sand
Log Drift
791

2.5 MILES

S 18 E

Lewis and Clark
State Park

794

State Wildlife
Management Area

... proed on passed a bad
Sand bare Which is verry
Shallow...
Floyd ⇒

Field Horsetail
(Equisetum arranse)
Wood Horsetail
(Equisetum sylvaticum)
Collected and described
by Lewis August 10, 1804.

799

WEST
3.5 MILES

1050

MISSOURI RIVER

HEBRASKA
IOWA

Burt Co.
Moncia Co.

Missouri
River

S 20 W    2.5 MILES

798

+680

S 20 W
2.5 MILES

797

Burnt Stump

Moncia Co.
Burt Co.

796

1050

42 DEGREES NORTH LATITUDE

Decatur Bend
Park

MISSOURI

RIVER

795

Beaver Den

BLUE

... crossed a Istmust of 3/4
of a mile to the river, ...Camp
on the L. S. above a Beaver
Den.
Clark ⇒

+675

790

State Wildlife
Management Area

Point

N 60 W

... at the great cut off
Saw a herd of Elk,...
Clark ⇐

Cartographer's Note:
This bearing seems to be in error.
N 6 W seems more reasonable.

789

BLUE    LAKE

788

N 44 W

3.5 MILES

the morning was clear the
musquitoes was mighty
troublesome Untill The
Sun Rose to Some hight.
Whitehouse ⇒

Camp
Aug. 9, 1804

Encamped on the S. W. Side
on a Sand bar at a cut off
a little below our Encampment
of the 9th of August 1804...

Clark ⇐ Return Camp
Sept. 5, 1806

787

Willow Point

786

RIVER

784

N 60 E    2.5 MILES

785

1050

... passed a verry Bad place
in the River whare the water
is verry Shallow...
Floyd

... the land on the River is
low chiefly covered with
cottenwood & Grape vines
&c. the Grapes are verry
pleanty on the River, for
this Several days.
Ordway ⇒

783

+670

N 35 W    2 MILES

IOWA
HEBRASKA

1050

Cutoff    Lakes

Gard
Lake

29

782

... where the River had formerly
cut across a bend where it had
Broke through a narrow Stripe
of woods on each side of the
River, the old channel in the
above mentioned bend is ponds
& Islands. the hills are a
Great distance from the River
this Several days.
Ordway ⇒

N
LAKE

QUINNEBAUGH

(Filled In)

Willow Point

781

1.5 MILES

N 46 W

... to a pt. of high Land
L. S. opsd. to which the
river laterly cut thro Saveing
6 Leagues S. S.
Clark ⇒

75

780

Point of High Land

N 15 W
2 MILES

MISSOURI RIVER

Burt Co.
Moncia Co.

Cutoff Lakes

1050

ONE STATUTE MILE

Modern Data: 1969-1970

Outbound: August 9, 10, 1804
Return: September 5, 6, 1806

EXPLORATIONS OF LEWIS AND CLARK   1804 - 1806
CARTOGRAPHIC RECONSTRUCTION

CUTOFF

CONTOUR INTERVAL 50 FEET

UTM ZONE   14
MAP NUMBER   73

Iowa    Nebraska

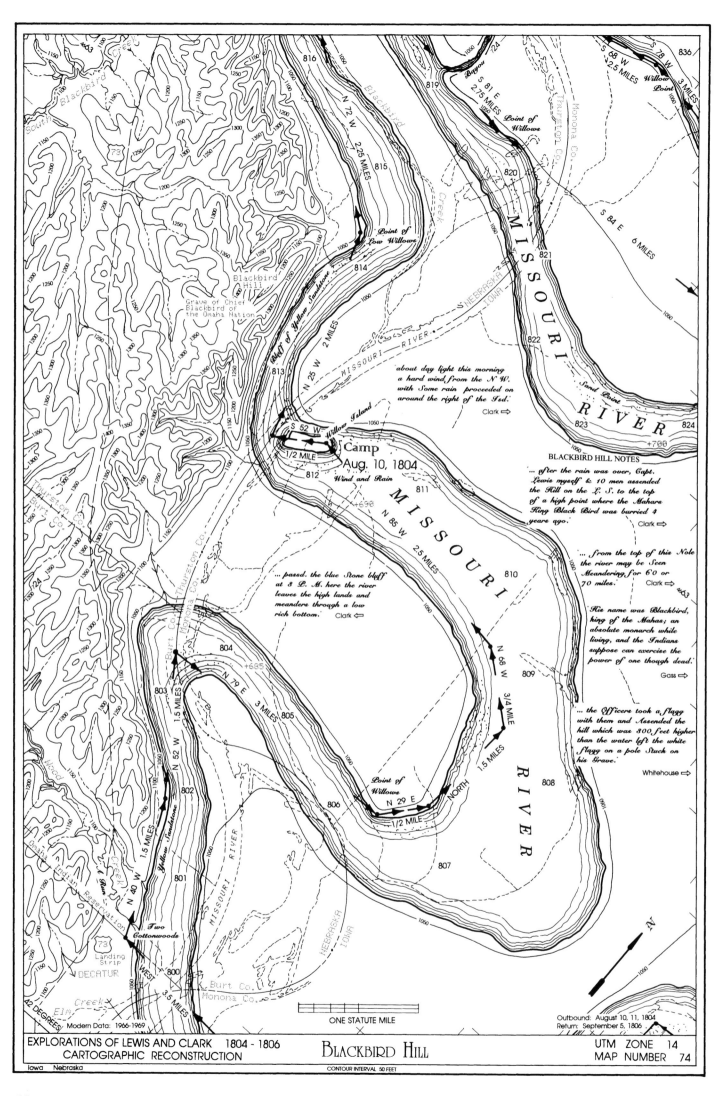

**BLACKBIRD HILL NOTES**

... after the rain was over, Capt.
Lewis myself & 10 men assended
the Hill on the L. S. to the top
of a high point where the Mahars
King Black Bird was burried 4
years ago.
Clark ⇨

... from the top of this Nole
the river may be Seen
Meandering for 60 or
70 miles.
Clark ⇨

His name was Blackbird,
king of the Mahas; an
absolute monarch while
living, and the Indians
suppose can exercise the
power of one though dead.
Gass ⇨

... the Officers took a flagg
with them and Assended the
hill which was 300 feet higher
than the water left the white
flagg on a pole Stuck on
his Grave.
Whitehouse ⇨

about day light this morning
a hard wind from the N W.
with Some rain proceeded on
around the right of the Isd.
Clark ⇨

... passd. the blue Stone bluff
at 3 P. M. here the river
leaves the high lands and
meanders through a low
rich bottom.
Clark ⇦

Camp
Aug. 10, 1804
Wind and Rain

Blackbird
Hill
Grave of Chief
Blackbird of
the Omaha Nation

Point of
Low Willows

Point of
Willows

Point of
Willows

Point of
Willows

Two
Cottonwoods

DECATUR
Landing
Strip

Modern Data: 1966-1969

Outbound: August 10, 11, 1804
Return: September 5, 1806

ONE STATUTE MILE

EXPLORATIONS OF LEWIS AND CLARK  1804 - 1806
CARTOGRAPHIC RECONSTRUCTION

BLACKBIRD HILL

UTM ZONE  14
MAP NUMBER  74

Iowa  Nebraska

CONTOUR INTERVAL 50 FEET

98

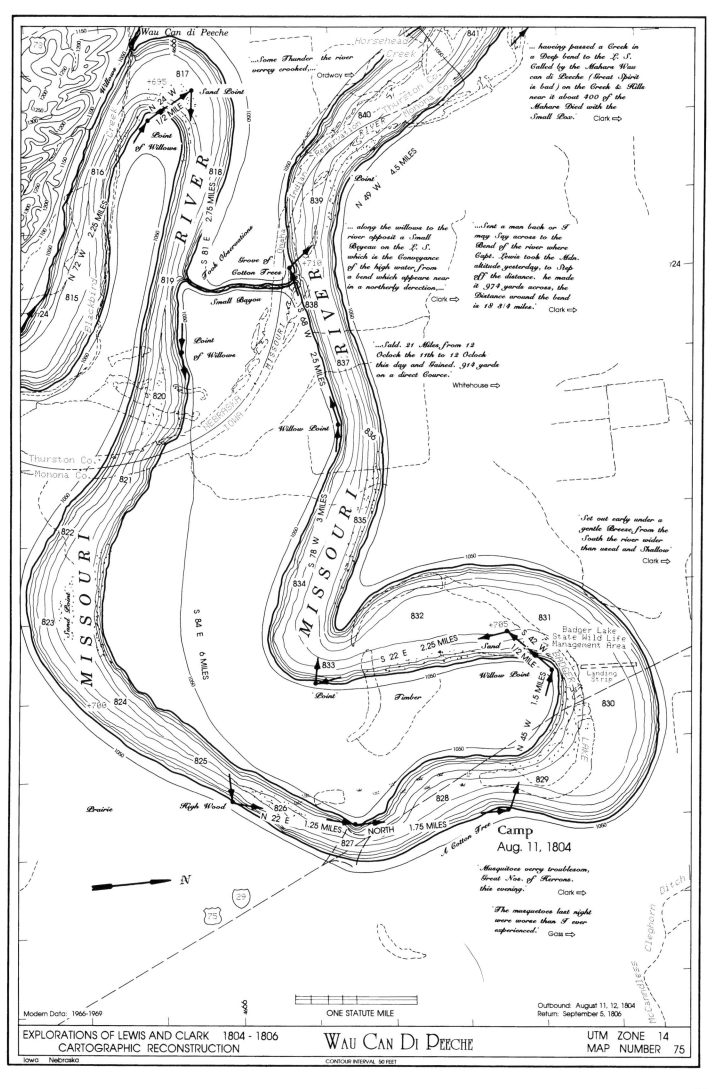

Wau Can di Peeche

1150
1200
73
1100
1050
1000

Willow Creek
695

817
Sand Point

N 24 W
1/2 MILE

Point of Willows

816

818

815

Blackbird Creek
N 72 W
2.25 MILES
S 81 E
2.75 MILES

819

724

Took Observations

Grove of Cotton Trees

Small Bayou

Point of Willows

820

Thurston Co.
Monona Co.

821

822

Sand Point

823

824
+700

825

High Wood
826
N 22 E
1.25 MILES
827

Prairie

...Some Thunder the river verrey crooked,...
Ordway ⇒

Horsehead Creek

841

840

Indian Reservation Thurston Co. Monona Co.

839

838

S 68 W
2.5 MILES

Missouri

Nebraska
Iowa

...having passed a Creek in a Deep bend to the L. S. Called by the Mahars Wau can di Peeche (Great Spirit is bad) on the Creek & Hills near it about 400 of the Mahars Died with the Small Pox.   Clark ⇒

Point
N 49 W
4.5 MILES

... along the willows to the river opposit a Small Beyeau on the L. S. which is the Conveyance of the high water, from a bend which appears near in a northerly derection,...

...Sent a man back or I may Say across to the Bend of the river where Capt. Lewis took the Mdn. altitude yesterday, to Step off the distance. he made it .974 yards across, the Distance around the bend is 18 3/4 miles.'   Clark ⇒

724

...Said .21 Miles, from 12 Oclock the 11th to 12 Oclock this day and Gained .914 yards on a direct Cource.'
Whitehouse ⇒

837

836

Willow Point

3 MILES
S 78 W

835

834

RIVER

MISSOURI

'Set out early under a gentle Breeze, from the South the river wider than useal and Shallow'   Clark ⇒

1050

832

831
+705
S 42 W
1/2 MILE

Sand

Badger Lake State Wild Life Management Area

Landing Strip

833
S 22 E   2.25 MILES

Point

Timber

Willow Point
1.5 MILES

BADGER LAKE

830

N 45 W

828
1.75 MILES

829

MISSOURI

1050

826
N 22 E
1.25 MILES   NORTH
827

A Cotton Tree

Camp
Aug. 11, 1804

Musquitoes verry troublesom, Great Nos. of Herrons. this evening.   Clark ⇒

'The musquetoes last night were worse than I ever experienced.'   Gass ⇒

McCandless Cleghorn Ditch

N

29

75

ONE STATUTE MILE

Modern Data: 1966-1969

Outbound: August 11, 12, 1804
Return: September 5, 1806

EXPLORATIONS OF LEWIS AND CLARK   1804 - 1806
CARTOGRAPHIC RECONSTRUCTION

Iowa   Nebraska

Wau Can Di Peeche

CONTOUR INTERVAL 50 FEET

UTM ZONE   14
MAP NUMBER   75

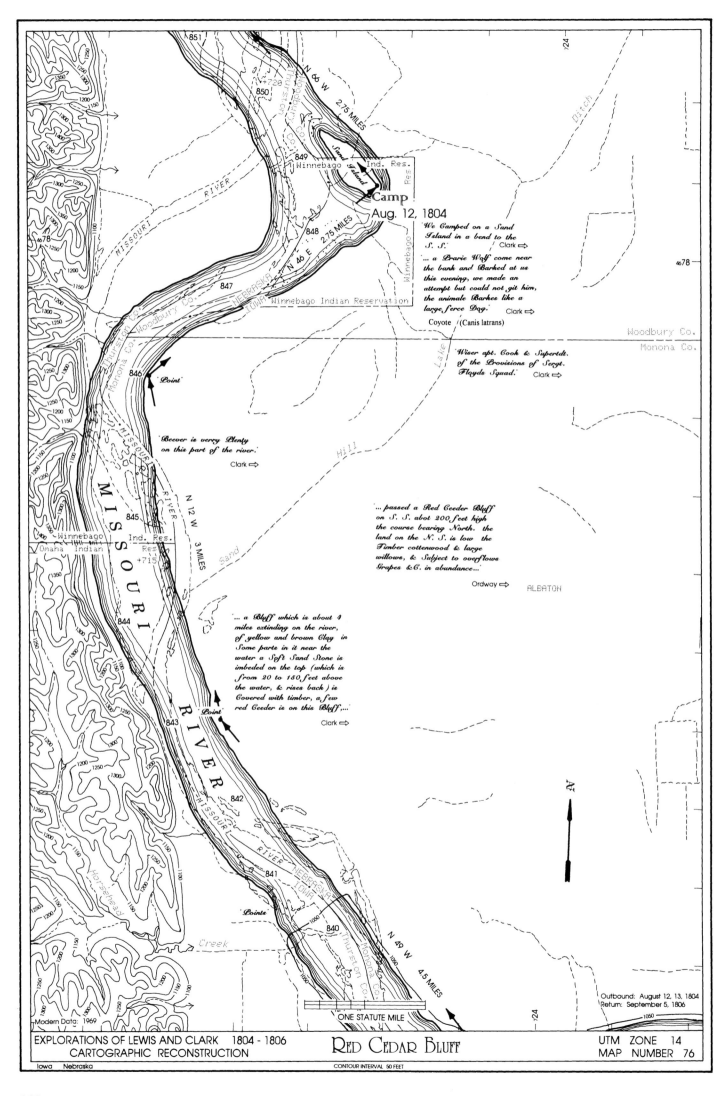

851
850
849
Winnebago
848
N 8 W
2.75 MILES
Ind. Res.
Sand Island
Camp
Aug. 12, 1804

847
N 46 E
2.75 MILES
Winnebago Indian Reservation

We Camped on a Sand
Island in a bend to the
S. S.          Clark ⟹

... a Prarie Wolf come near
the bank and Barked at us
this evening, we made an
attempt but could not git him,
the animale Barkes like a
large ferce Dog.
                    Clark ⟹

Coyote  (Canis latrans)

Woodbury Co.
Monona Co.

846
Point

Wiser apt. Cook & Superidt.
of the Provisions of Sergt.
Floyds Squad.     Clark ⟹

Beever is very Plenty
on this part of the river.

          Clark ⟹

845
Winnebago
Omaha Indian
Ind. Res.
Res
+715

N 12 W
3 MILES

... passed a Red Ceeder Bluff
on S. S. abot 200 feet high
the course bearing North. the
land on the N. S. is low the
Timber cottenwood & large
willows, & Subject to overflows
Grapes &C. in abundance...

          Ordway ⟹     ALBATON

844

... a Bluff which is about 4
miles extinding on the river,
of yellow and brown Clay  in
Some parts in it near the
water a Soft Sand Stone is
imbeded on the top (which is
from 20 to 150 feet above
the water, & rises back ) is
Covered with timber, a few
red Ceeder is on this Bluff,...
                    Clark ⟹

843
Point

842

N

841

Points

N 49 W
4.5 MILES

840

ONE STATUTE MILE

Outbound: August 12, 13, 1804
Return: September 5, 1806

Modern Data: 1969

EXPLORATIONS OF LEWIS AND CLARK   1804 - 1806
CARTOGRAPHIC RECONSTRUCTION

RED CEDAR BLUFF

UTM ZONE  14
MAP  NUMBER  76

Iowa    Nebraska

CONTOUR INTERVAL 50 FEET

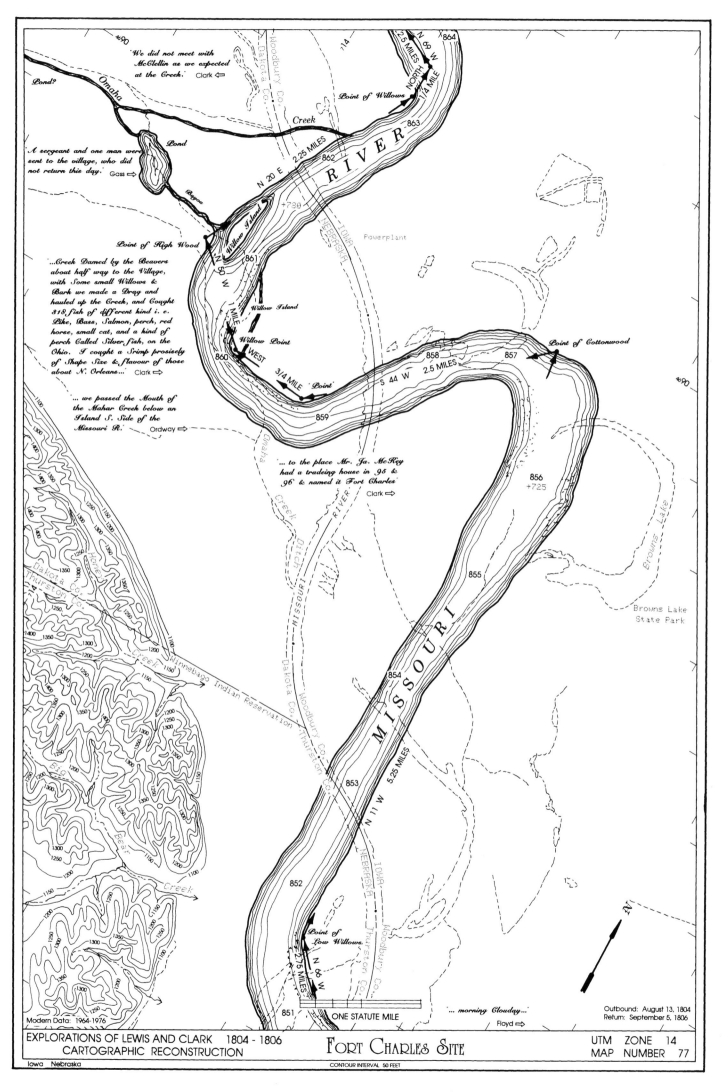

'We did not meet with McClellin as we expected at the Creek.' Clark ⇐

Pond?

Omaha

Creek

Point of Willows

RIVER

864

863

862

N 69 W

2.25 MILES

NORTH

1/4 MILE

N 20 E

2.25 MILES

Pond

'A sergeant and one man were sent to the village, who did not return this day.' Gass ⇒

Bayou

Willow Island

+790

861

Point of High Wood

Powerplant

'...Creek Damed by the Beavers about half way to the Village, with Some small Willows & Bark we made a Drag and hauled up the Creek, and Cought 318 fish of different kind i. e. Pike, Bass, Salmon, perch, red horse, small cat, and a kind of perch Called Silver fish, on the Ohio. I cought a Srimp prosisely of Shape Size & flavour of those about N. Orleans...' Clark ⇒

N 50 W

1 MILE

Willow Island

Willow Point

860

WEST

3/4 MILE

Point

858

859

S 44 W

2.5 MILES

857

Point of Cottonwood

'... we passed the Mouth of the Mahar Creek below an Island S. Side of the Missouri R.' Ordway ⇒

Omaha

Creek

+490

856

+725

Browns Lake

'... to the place Mr. Ja. McKey had a tradeing house in ,95 & ,96 & named it Fort Charles.' Clark ⇒

Ditch

River

855

Browns Lake State Park

1300

1400

1350

1250

1300

1200

1350

1300

Dakota Co.

Thurston Co.

Horse

Creek

Winnebago Indian Reservation

Woodbury Co.

Dakota Co.

Thurston Co.

854

MISSOURI

1250

1300

1350

1200

1250

1300

1350

Big

Bear

853

N 11 W

5.25 MILES

852

MISSOURI

1150

1200

1350

1250

1300

1250

1350

Creek

Point of Low Willows

2.275 MILES

N 66 W

851

ONE STATUTE MILE

'... morning Clouday...' Floyd ⇒

N

Outbound: August 13, 1804
Return: September 5, 1806

Modern Data: 1964-1976

| EXPLORATIONS OF LEWIS AND CLARK 1804 - 1806 CARTOGRAPHIC RECONSTRUCTION | FORT CHARLES SITE | UTM ZONE 14 MAP NUMBER 77 |
|---|---|---|
| Iowa Nebraska | CONTOUR INTERVAL 50 FEET | |

101

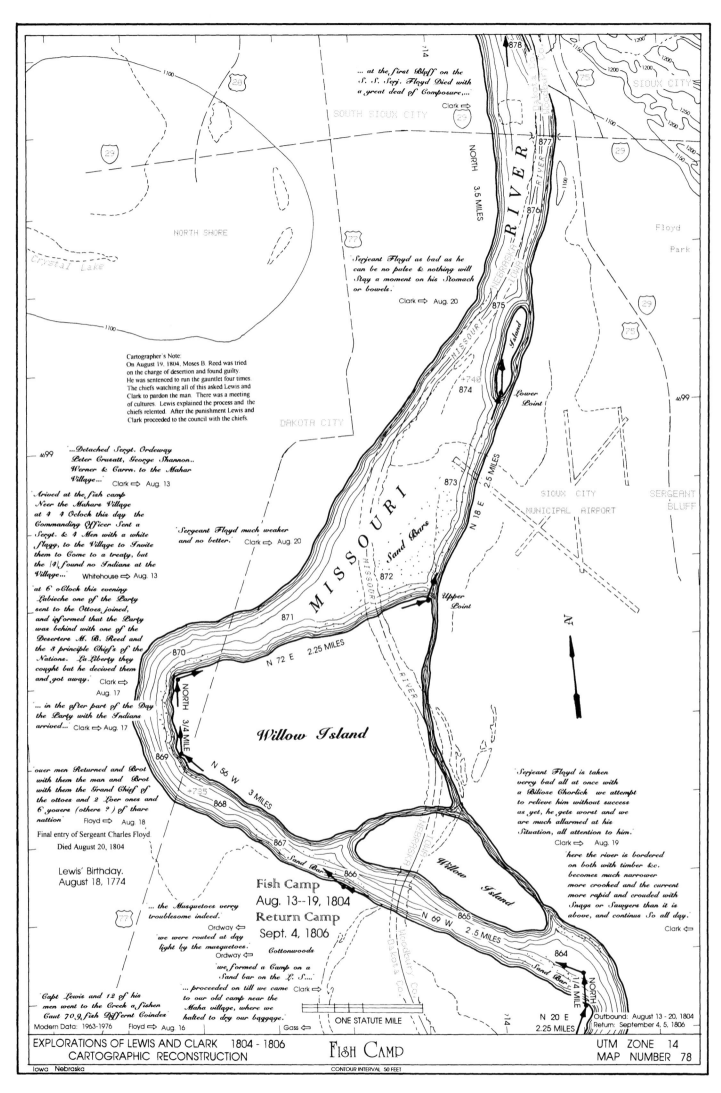

... at the first Bluff on the
S. S. Serj. Floyd Died with
a great deal of Composure,...
Clark ⇨ Aug. 20

Serjeant Floyd as bad as he
can be no pulse & nothing will
Stay a moment on his Stomach
or bowels.
Clark ⇨ Aug. 20

Cartographer's Note:
On August 19, 1804, Moses B. Reed was tried
on the charge of desertion and found guilty.
He was sentenced to run the gauntlet four times.
The chiefs watching all of this asked Lewis and
Clark to pardon the man. There was a meeting
of cultures. Lewis explained the process and the
chiefs relented. After the punishment Lewis and
Clark proceeded to the council with the chiefs.

...Detached Sergt. Ordeway
Peter Crusatt, George Shannon..
Werner & Carrn. to the Mahar
Village...
Clark ⇨ Aug. 13

Arived at the fish camp
Neer the Mahars Village
at 4 4 Oclock this day the
Commanding Officer Sent a
Sergt. & 4 Men with a white
flagg, to the Village to Invite
them to Come to a treaty, but
the [4] found no Indians at the
Village...
Whitehouse ⇨ Aug. 13

Sergeant Floyd much weaker
and no better.
Clark ⇨ Aug. 20

at 6 o'Clock this evening
Labieche one of the Party
sent to the Ottoes joined,
and informed that the Party
was behind with one of the
Deserters M. B. Reed and
the 3 principle Chiefs of the
Nations. La Liberty they
cought but he decived them
and got away.
Clark ⇨
Aug. 17

... in the after part of the Day
the Party with the Indians
arrived...
Clark ⇨ Aug. 17

ower men Returned and Brot
with them the man and Brot
with them the Grand Chief of
the ottoes and 2 Loer ones and
6 youers (others ?) of thare
nattion
Floyd ⇨ Aug. 18

Final entry of Sergeant Charles Floyd.
Died August 20, 1804

Lewis' Birthday.
August 18, 1774

... the Musquetoes verry
troublesome indeed.
Ordway ⇦

we were routed at day
light by the musquetoes.
Ordway ⇦

Cottonwoods

we formed a Camp on a
Sand bar on the L. S...
Clark ⇨

... proceeded on till we came
to our old camp near the
Maha village, where we
halted to dry our baggage.
Gass ⇦ Aug. 16

Capt Lewis and 12 of his
men went to the Creek a fishen
Gaut 70.9 Fish Differnt Coindes
Modern Data: 1963-1976    Floyd ⇨ Aug. 16

Serjeant Floyd is taken
verry bad all at once with
a Biliose Chorlick we attempt
to relieve him without success
as yet, he gets worst and we
are much allarmed at his
Situation, all attention to him.
Clark ⇨    Aug. 19

here the river is bordered
on both with timber &c.
becomes much narrower
more crooked and the current
more rapid and crouded with
Snags or Sawyers than it is
above, and continus So all day.
Clark ⇦

Willow Island

Willow Island

Fish Camp
Aug. 13--19, 1804
Return Camp
Sept. 4, 1806

ONE STATUTE MILE

Outbound: August 13 - 20, 1804
Return: September 4, 5, 1806

UTM ZONE 14
MAP NUMBER 78

EXPLORATIONS OF LEWIS AND CLARK  1804 - 1806
CARTOGRAPHIC RECONSTRUCTION

FISH CAMP

Iowa  Nebraska

CONTOUR INTERVAL 50 FEET

102

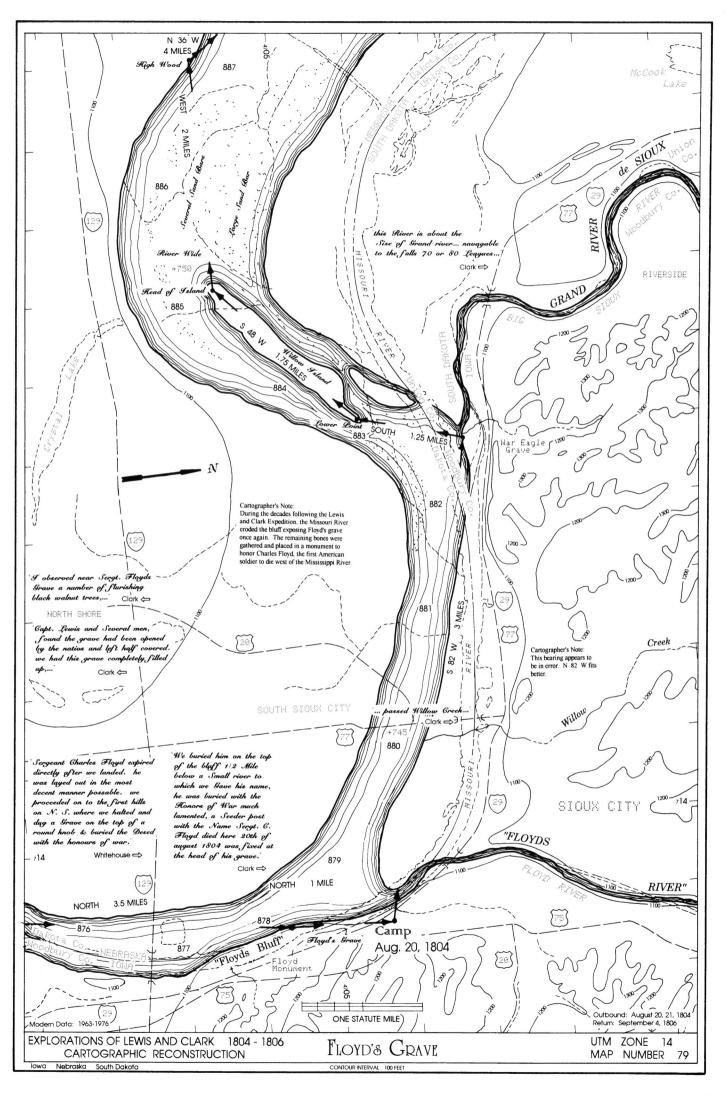

N 36 W
4 MILES

High Wood

887

WEST 2 MILES

886

Several Sand Bars

Large Sand Bar

River Wide

+750

Head of Island

885

S 48 W 1.75 MILES

Willow Island

884

Lower Point

883

SOUTH

1.25 MILES

this River is about the Size of Grand river... navagable to the falls 70 or 80 Leagues...'
Clark ⇒

RIVERSIDE

War Eagle Grave

882

N

Cartographer's Note:
During the decades following the Lewis and Clark Expedition, the Missouri River eroded the bluff exposing Floyd's grave once again. The remaining bones were gathered and placed in a monument to honor Charles Floyd, the first American soldier to die west of the Mississippi River.

881

S 82 W 3 MILES

'I observed near Sergt. Floyds Grave a number of flurishing black walnut trees,...'  Clark ⇐

NORTH SHORE

'Capt. Lewis and Several men, found the grave had been opened by the natives and left half covered. we had this grave completely filled up,...'
Clark ⇐

SOUTH SIOUX CITY

Creek

Cartographer's Note:
This bearing appears to be in error.  N 82 W fits better.

Willow

... passed Willow Creek...
Clark ⇒

+745

880

'Sergeant Charles Floyd expired directly after we landed. he was layed out in the most decent manner possable. we proceeded on to the first hills on N. S. where we halted and dug a Grave on the top of a round knob & buried the Desed with the honours of war.'
714    Whitehouse ⇒

'We buried him on the top of the bluff 1/2 Mile below a Small river to which we Gave his name, he was buried with the Honors of War much lamented, a Seeder post with the Name Sergt. C. Floyd died here 20th of august 1804 was fixed at the head of his grave.'
Clark ⇒

SIOUX CITY

714

"FLOYDS

879

NORTH 1 MILE

NORTH  3.5 MILES

876

878

877

"Floyds Bluff"

Floyd's Grave

Camp
Aug. 20, 1804

FLOYD RIVER

RIVER"

Floyd Monument

Modern Data: 1963-1976

ONE STATUTE MILE

Outbound: August 20, 21, 1804
Return: September 4, 1806

EXPLORATIONS OF LEWIS AND CLARK   1804 - 1806
CARTOGRAPHIC RECONSTRUCTION

Iowa   Nebraska   South Dakota

FLOYD'S GRAVE

CONTOUR INTERVAL  100 FEET

UTM  ZONE   14
MAP  NUMBER  79

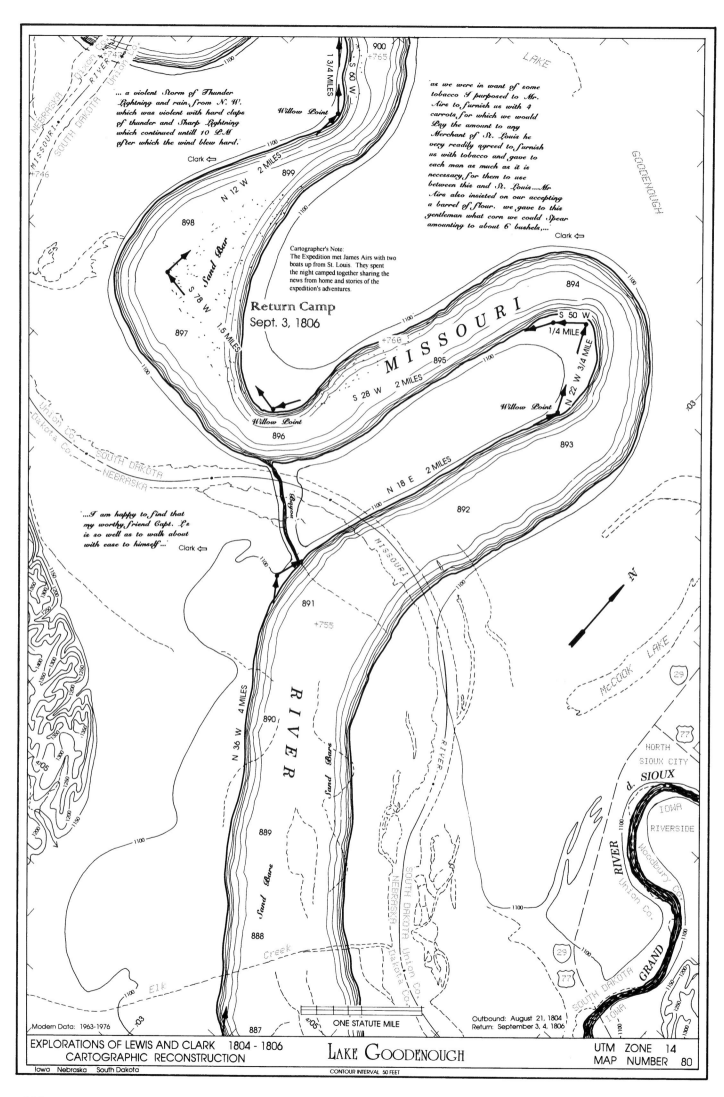

... a violent Storm of Thunder
Lightning and rain from N. W.
which was violent with hard claps
of thunder and Sharp Lightning
which continued untill 10 P.M.
after which the wind blew hard.

Clark ⇐

as we were in want of some
tobacco I purposed to Mr.
Airs to furnish us with 4
carrots, for which we would
Pay the amount to any
Merchant of St. Louis he
very readily agreed to furnish
us with tobacco and gave to
each man as much as it is
necessary for them to use
between this and St. Louis...Mr
Airs also insisted on our accepting
a barrel of flour. we gave to this
gentleman what corn we could Spear
amounting to about 6 bushels,...

Clark ⇐

Cartographer's Note:
The Expedition met James Airs with two
boats up from St. Louis. They spent
the night camped together sharing the
news from home and stories of the
expedition's adventures.

Return Camp
Sept. 3, 1806

...I am happy to find that
my worthy friend Capt. L.
is so well as to walk about
with ease to himself...

Clark ⇐

Outbound: August 21, 1804
Return: September 3, 4, 1806

Modern Data: 1963-1976

ONE STATUTE MILE

EXPLORATIONS OF LEWIS AND CLARK   1804 - 1806
CARTOGRAPHIC RECONSTRUCTION

Iowa   Nebraska   South Dakota

LAKE GOODENOUGH

CONTOUR INTERVAL 50 FEET

UTM   ZONE   14
MAP   NUMBER   80

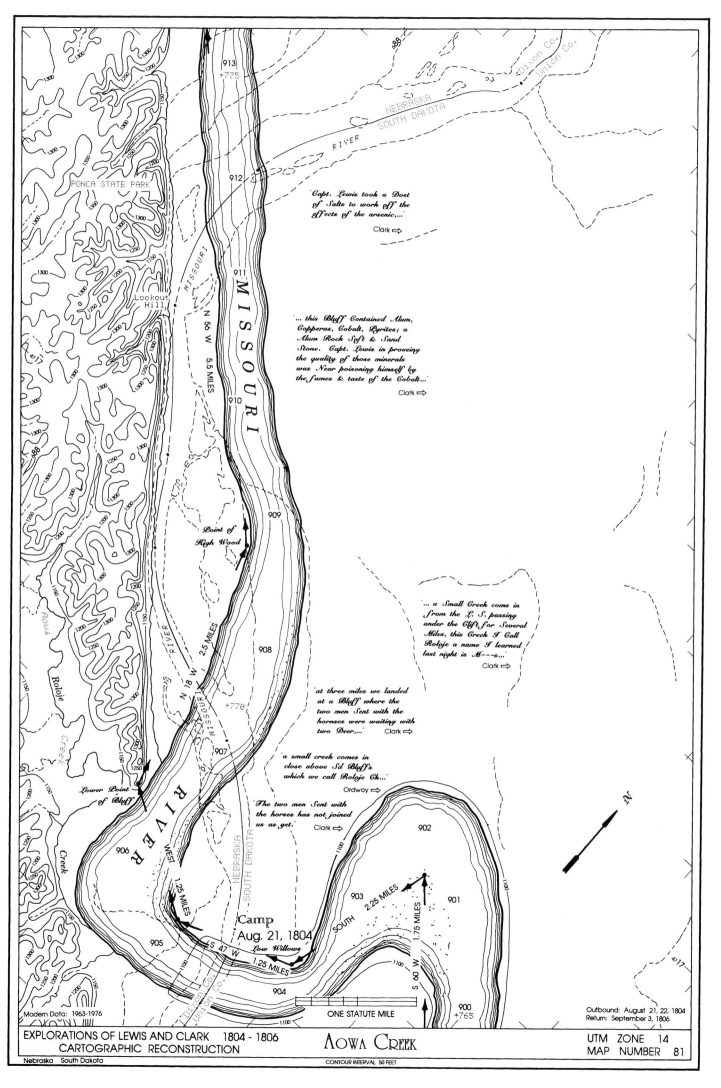

PONCA STATE PARK

Lookout Hill

MISSOURI

N 56 W 5.5 MILES

910

909

*Point of High Wood*

908

907

Roloje Creek

*Lower Point of Bluff*

906

N 18 W 2.5 MILES

913
+775

912

911

NEBRASKA
SOUTH DAKOTA

RIVER

Dixon Co.
Union Co.

888

"*Capt. Lewis took a Dost of Salts to work off the effects of the arsenic,...*"
Clark ⇒

"*... this Bluff Contained Alum, Copperas, Cobalt, Pyrites; a Alum Rock Soft & Sand Stone. Capt. Lewis in proving the quality of those minerals was Near poisoning himself by the fumes & taste of the Cobalt...*"
Clark ⇒

"*... a Small Creek comes in from the L. S. passing under the Clift for Several Miles, this Creek I Call Roloje a name I learned last night is M---s...*"
Clark ⇒

"*at three miles we landed at a Bluff where the two men Sent with the hornses were waiting with two Deer,...*" Clark ⇒

"*a small creek comes in close above Sd Bluff's which we call Roloje Ck...*"
Ordway ⇒

"*The two men Sent with the horses has not joined us as yet.*"
Clark ⇒

902

903

901

2.25 MILES

S 60 W 1.75 MILES

WEST 1.25 MILES

Camp
Aug. 21, 1804

*Low Willows*

S 47 W 1.25 MILES

SOUTH

905

904

900
+765

+770

MISSOURI RIVER

NEBRASKA SOUTH DAKOTA

Dixon Co. Union Co.

N

Modern Data: 1963-1976

ONE STATUTE MILE

Outbound: August 21, 22, 1804
Return: September 3, 1806

EXPLORATIONS OF LEWIS AND CLARK   1804 - 1806
CARTOGRAPHIC RECONSTRUCTION
Nebraska   South Dakota

AOWA CREEK

CONTOUR INTERVAL 50 FEET

UTM ZONE 14
MAP NUMBER 81

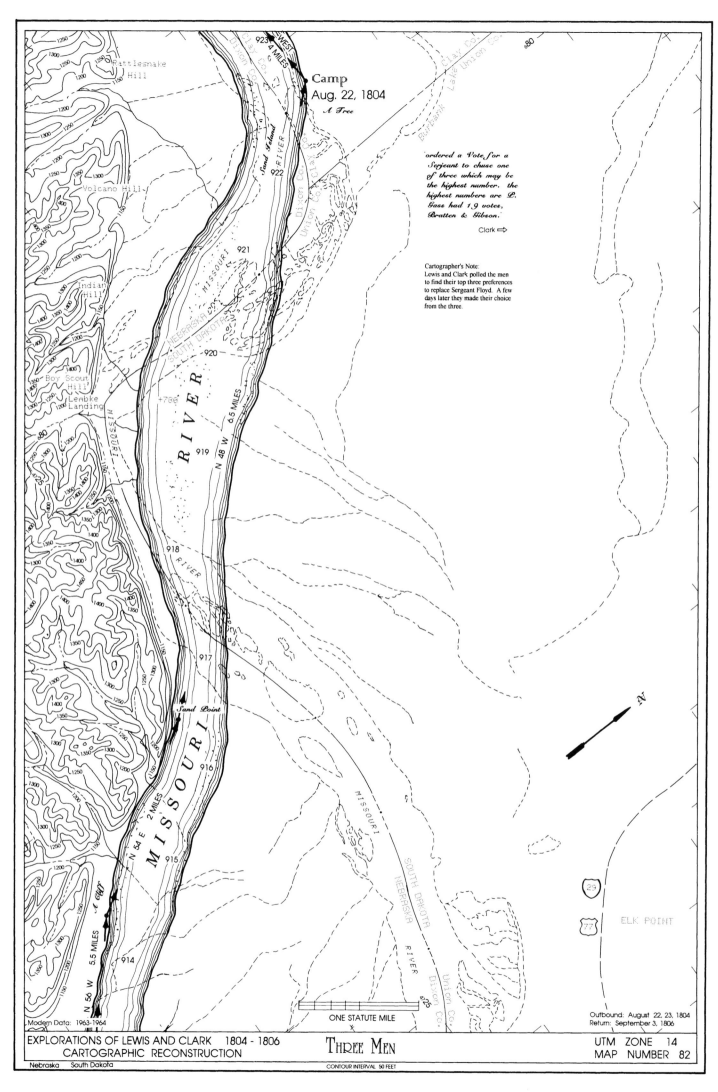

Camp
Aug. 22, 1804
A Tree

*ordered a Vote for a Serjeant to chuse one of three which may be the highest number. the highest numbers are P. Gass had 19 votes, Bratten & Gibson.*

Clark ⟹

Cartographer's Note:
Lewis and Clark polled the men to find their top three preferences to replace Sergeant Floyd. A few days later they made their choice from the three.

Rattlesnake Hill

Volcano Hill

Indian Hill

Boy Scout Hill
Lembke Landing

Sand Island

MISSOURI RIVER

N 48 W  6.5 MILES

N 54 E  2 MILES

Sand Point

MISSOURI

A 600'

N 56 W  5.5 MILES

Modern Data: 1963-1964

ONE STATUTE MILE

ELK POINT

Outbound: August 22, 23, 1804
Return: September 3, 1806

EXPLORATIONS OF LEWIS AND CLARK   1804 - 1806
CARTOGRAPHIC RECONSTRUCTION

THREE MEN

UTM ZONE  14
MAP NUMBER 82

Nebraska    South Dakota

CONTOUR INTERVAL  50 FEET

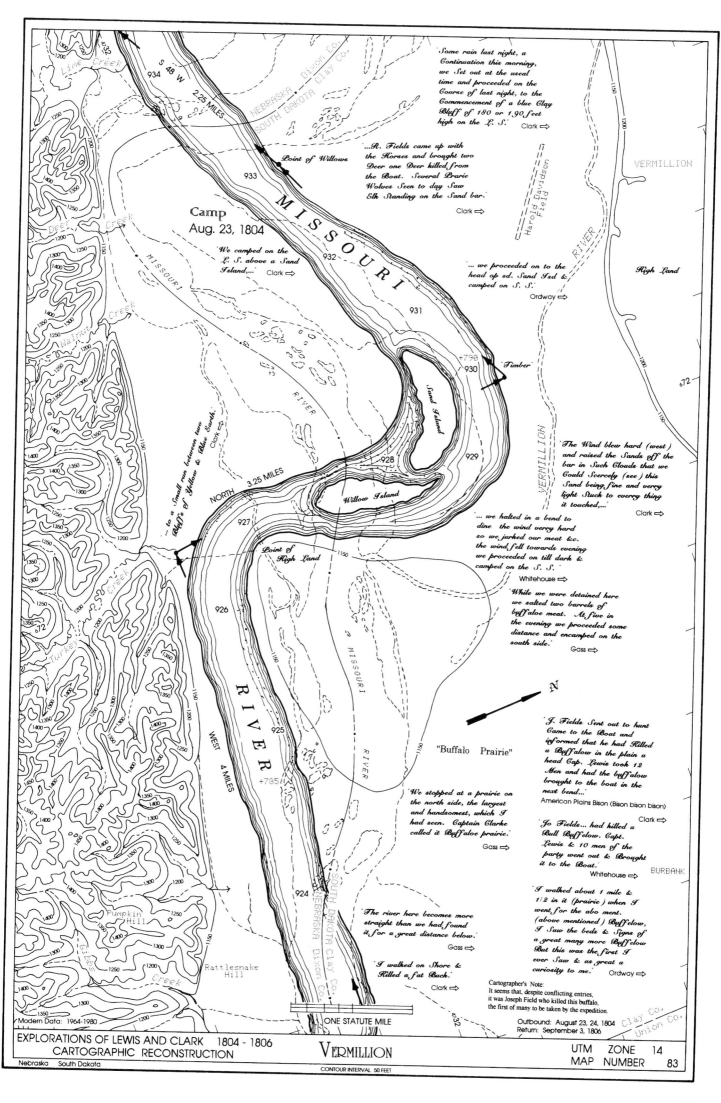

Some rain last night, a Continuation this morning, we Set out at the useal time and proceeded on the Course of last night, to the Commencement of a blue Clay Bluff of 180 or 190 feet high on the L. S.
Clark ⇒

....R. Fields came up with the Horses and brought two Deer one Deer killed from the Boat. Several Prarie Wolves Seen to day Saw Elk Standing on the Sand bar.
Clark ⇒

VERMILLION

Camp
Aug. 23, 1804

We camped on the L. S. above a Sand Island,...
Clark ⇒

... we proceeded on to the head of sd. Sand Isd & camped on S. S.
Ordway ⇒

High Land

Timber

The Wind blew hard (west) and raised the Sands off the bar in Such Cloudes that we Could Scarcely (see) this Sand being fine and verry light Stuck to everry thing it touched,...
Clark ⇒

Sand Island

Willow Island

... we halted in a bend to dine the wind verry hard so we jurked our meat &c. the wind fell towards evening we proceeded on till dark & camped on the S. S.
Whitehouse ⇒

Point of High Land

...to a Small run between two Bluffs of Yellow & Blue Earth.
Clark ⇒

NORTH 3.25 MILES

While we were detained here we salted two barrels of buffaloe meat. At five in the evening we proceeded some distance and encamped on the south side.
Gass ⇒

N

"Buffalo Prairie"

J. Fields Sent out to hunt Came to the Boat and informed that he had killed a Buffalow in the plain a head Cap. Lewis took 12 Men and had the buffalow brought to the boat in the next bend...
American Plains Bison (Bison bison bison)
Clark ⇒

We stopped at a prairie on the north side, the largest and handsomest, which I had seen. Captain Clarke called it Buffaloe prairie.
Gass ⇒

Jo Fields... had killed a Bull Buffalow. Capt. Lewis & 10 men of the party went out & Brought it to the Boat.
Whitehouse ⇒

BURBANK

WEST 4 MILES

I walked about 1 mile & 1/2 in it (prairie) when I went for the abo ment. (above mentioned) Buffalow, I Saw the beds & Signs of a great many more Buffalow But this was the first I ever Saw & as great a curiosity to me.
Ordway ⇒

Pumpkin Hill

The river here becomes more straight than we had found it for a great distance below.
Gass ⇒

Rattlesnake Hill

I walked on Shore & Killed a fat Buck.
Clark ⇒

Cartographer's Note:
It seems that, despite conflicting entries, it was Joseph Field who killed this buffalo, the first of many to be taken by the expedition.

Outbound: August 23, 24, 1804
Return: September 3, 1806

Modern Data: 1964-1980

ONE STATUTE MILE

EXPLORATIONS OF LEWIS AND CLARK 1804 - 1806
CARTOGRAPHIC RECONSTRUCTION
Nebraska    South Dakota

VERMILLION

CONTOUR INTERVAL 50 FEET

UTM ZONE 14
MAP NUMBER 83

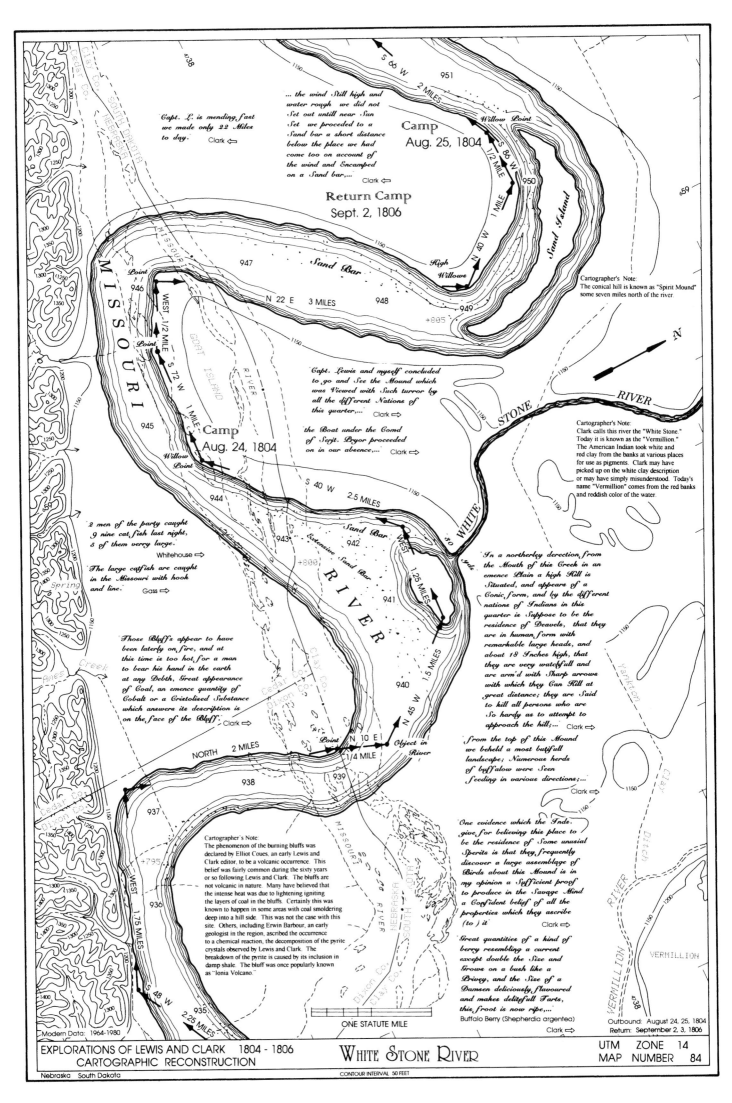

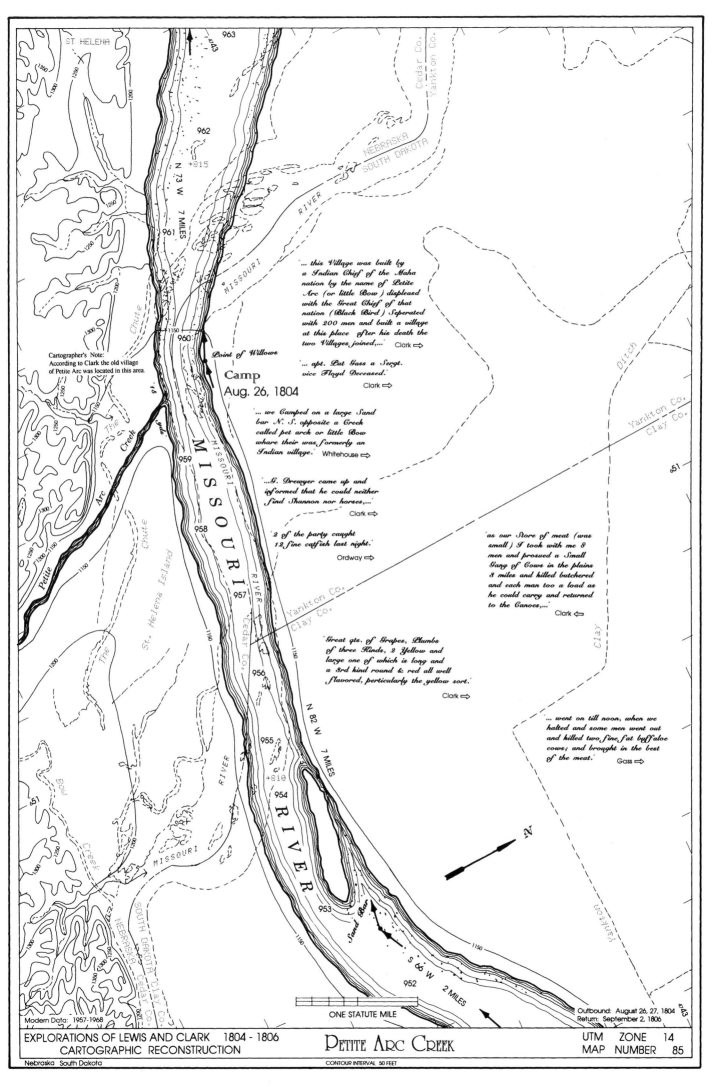

ST HELENA

963

962

N 73 W    7 MILES

+915

961

MISSOURI    RIVER

Cartographer's Note:
According to Clark the old village
of Petite Arc was located in this area.

1150

960

*Point of Willows*

**Camp**
**Aug. 26, 1804**

959

958

957

956

955

+810

954

953

*Sand Bar*

952

*... this Village was built by
a Indian Chief of the Maha
nation by the name of Petite
Arc (or little Bow) displeasd
with the Great Chief of that
nation (Black Bird) Seperated
with 200 men and built a village
at this place after his death the
two Villages joined,...*     Clark ⇨

*... apt. Pat Gass a Sergt.
vice Floyd Deceased.*     Clark ⇨

*... we Camped on a large Sand
bar N. S. opposite a Creek
called pet arch or little Bow
whare their was formerly an
Indian village.*     Whitehouse ⇨

*...G. Drewyer came up and
informed that he could neither
find Shannon nor horses,...*
Clark ⇨

*2 of the party caught
12 fine catfish last night.*
Ordway ⇨

*Great qts. of Grapes, Plumbs
of three Kinds, 2 Yellow and
large one of which is long and
a 3rd kind round & red all well
flavored, perticularly the yellow sort.*
Clark ⇨

*as our Store of meat (was
small) I took with me 8
men and prosued a Small
Gang of Cows in the plains
8 miles and killed butchered
and each man too a load as
he could carry and returned
to the Canoes,...*     Clark ⇦

*... went on till noon, when we
halted and some men went out
and killed two fine fat buffaloe
cows; and brought in the best
of the meat.*     Gass ⇨

N

ONE STATUTE MILE

Outbound: August 26, 27, 1804
Return: September 2, 1806

Modern Data: 1957-1968

EXPLORATIONS OF LEWIS AND CLARK    1804 - 1806
CARTOGRAPHIC RECONSTRUCTION

Nebraska  South Dakota

PETITE ARC CREEK

CONTOUR INTERVAL 50 FEET

UTM    ZONE    14
MAP    NUMBER    85

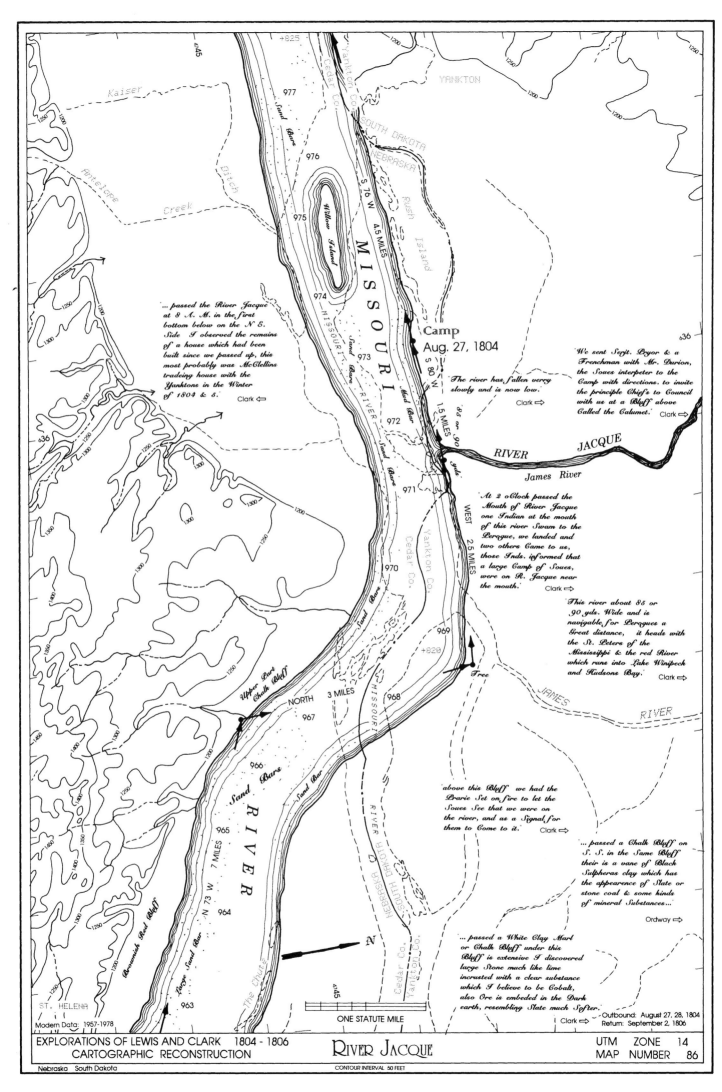

... passed the River Jacque at 8 A. M. in the first bottom below on the N. E. Side. I observed the remains of a house which had been built since we passed up, this most probably was McClellins tradeing house with the Yanktons in the Winter of 1804 & 5.
Clark ⇐

Camp
Aug. 27, 1804

The river has fallen verry slowly and is now low.
Clark ⇒

We sent Serjt. Pryor & a Frenchman with Mr. Durion, the Soues interpeter to the Camp with directions. to invite the principle Chiefs to Council with us at a Bluff above Called the Calumet.
Clark ⇒

RIVER JACQUE

James River

At 2 oClock passed the Mouth of River Jacque one Indian at the mouth of this river Swam to the Perogue, we landed and two others Came to us, those Inds. informed that a large Camp of Soues, were on R. Jacque near the mouth.
Clark ⇒

This river about 85 or 90 yds. Wide and is navigable for Perogues a Great distance, it heads with the St. Peters of the Mississippi & the red River which runs into Lake Winipeck and Hudsons Bay.
Clark ⇒

Tree

JAMES RIVER

NORTH 3 MILES

above this Bluff we had the Prarie Set on fire to let the Soues See that we were on the river, and as a Signal for them to Come to it.
Clark ⇒

... passed a Chalk Bluff on S. S. in the Same Bluff their is a vane of Black Sulpheras clay which has the appearence of Slate or stone coal & some kinds of mineral Substances...
Ordway ⇒

... passed a White Clay Marl or Chalk Bluff under this Bluff is extensive I discovered large Stone much like lime incrusted with a clear substance which I believe to be Cobalt, also Ore is embeded in the Dark earth, resembling Slate much Softer.
Clark ⇒

Modern Data: 1957-1978

ONE STATUTE MILE

Outbound: August 27, 28, 1804
Return: September 2, 1806

EXPLORATIONS OF LEWIS AND CLARK   1804 - 1806
CARTOGRAPHIC RECONSTRUCTION
RIVER JACQUE
UTM   ZONE   14
MAP   NUMBER   86

Nebraska   South Dakota

CONTOUR INTERVAL 50 FEET

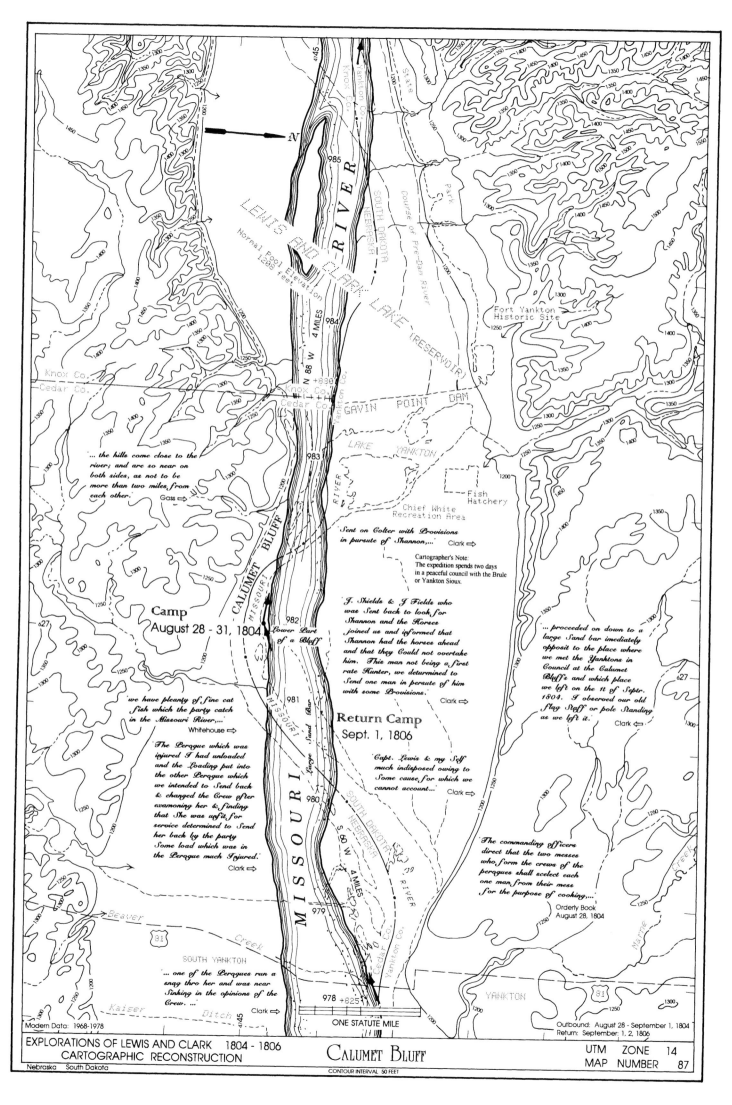

N

985

984

N 88 W  4 MILES

N +898

Knox Co.
Cedar Co.

Knox Co.     Yankton Co.
Cedar Co.

983

*... the hills come close to the river; and are so near on both sides, as not to be more than two miles, from each other.*
Gass ⟹

*Camp*
**August 28 - 31, 1804**

982

*Lower Part of a Bluff*

981

*we have pleasty of fine cat fish which the party catch in the Missouri River,...*
Whitehouse ⟹

*The Perague which was injured I had unloaded and the Loading put into the other Perague which we intended to Send back & changed the Crew after examoning her & finding that She was unfit for service determined to Send her back by the party Some load which was in the Perague much Injured.*
Clark ⟹

980

979

978 +825

*... one of the Perogues run a snag thro her and was near Sinking in the opinions of the Crew. ...*
Clark ⟹

**ONE STATUTE MILE**

SOUTH YANKTON

*Sent on Colter with Provisions in pursute of Shannon,...*
Clark ⟹

Cartographer's Note:
The expedition spends two days in a peaceful council with the Brule or Yankton Sioux.

*J. Shields & J Fields who was Sent back to look for Shannon and the Horses joined us and informed that Shannon had the horses ahead and that they Could not overtake him. This man not being a first rate Hunter, we deturmined to Send one man in persute of him with some Provisions.*
Clark ⟹

**Return Camp**
**Sept. 1, 1806**

*Capt. Lewis & my Self much indisposed owing to Some cause for which we cannot account...*
Clark ⟹

*... proceeded on down to a large Sand bar imediately opposit to the place where we met the Yanktons in Council at the Calumet Bluff's and which place we left on the 1t of Septr. 1804. I observed our old Flag Staff or pole Standing as we left it.*
Clark ⟹

*The commanding officers direct that the two messes who, form the crews of the perogues shall scelect each one man from their mess for the purpose of cooking,...*
Orderly Book
August 28, 1804

Fort Yankton
Historic Site

GAVIN POINT DAM

LAKE YANKTON

Fish Hatchery

Chief White Recreation Area

627

627

LEWIS AND CLARK LAKE (RESERVOIR)

*Normal Pool Elevation 1208 feet*

RIVER

SOUTH DAKOTA
NEBRASKA

Course of Pre-Dam River

CALUMET BLUFF

MISSOURI

MISSOURI

Large Sand Bar

Missouri Sand Bar

S 88 W  4 MILES

SOUTH DAKOTA
NEBRASKA

JAMES RIVER

YANKTON

Beaver Creek

Kaiser Ditch

Marne Creek

Modern Data: 1968-1978

Outbound: August 28 - September 1, 1804
Return: September: 1, 2, 1806

**EXPLORATIONS OF LEWIS AND CLARK   1804 - 1806**
**CARTOGRAPHIC RECONSTRUCTION**
Nebraska   South Dakota

**CALUMET BLUFF**

CONTOUR INTERVAL 50 FEET

UTM   ZONE   14
MAP NUMBER   87

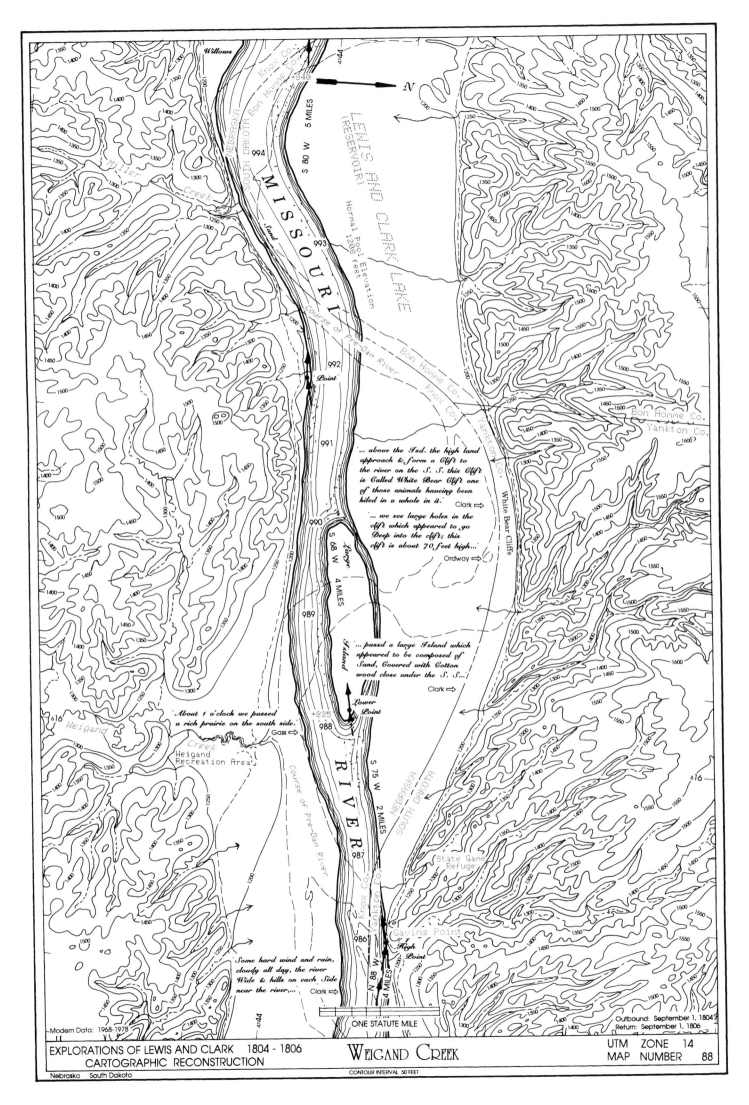

Willows

Knox Co.
Bon Homme Co. +640

1350
1400
1400
1350
1300
1350
1400
1450
1350

S 80 W
5 MILES

NORTH DAKOTA
SOUTH DAKOTA
NEBRASKA

994

MISSOURI

Miller
Creek

Sand

993

Course of Pre-Dam River

LEWIS AND CLARK LAKE (RESERVOIR)
Normal Pool Elevation 1208 feet

N

Bon Homme Co.
Knox Co.

992

Point

991

Bon Homme Co.
Yankton Co.

White Bear Cliffs

Yankton Co.

... above the Isd. the high land
approach & form a Clift to
the river on the S. S. this Clift
is Called White Bear Clift one
of those animals haveing been
kiled in a whole in it.

Clark ⇒

990

S 68 W
4 MILES

Large

... we see large holes in the
clift which appeared to go
Deep into the clift; this
clift is about 70 feet high...

Ordway ⇒

989

... passd a large Island which
appeared to be composed of
Sand, Covered with Cotton
wood close under the S. S...

Clark ⇒

Island

Lower
Point

About 1 o'clock we passed
a rich prairie on the south side.

+835

988

616
Weigand

Gass ⇒

Creek
Weigand
Recreation Area

Course of Pre-Dam River

RIVER

S 75 W
2 MILES

NEBRASKA
SOUTH DAKOTA

987

State Game
Refuge

616

Knox Co.
Yankton Co.

986

Gavins Point
High
Point

N 88 W
4 MILES

Some hard wind and rain,
cloudy all day, the river
Wide & hills on each Side
near the river,...

Clark ⇒

ONE STATUTE MILE

Modern Data: 1968-1978

Outbound: September 1, 1804
Return: September 1, 1806

EXPLORATIONS OF LEWIS AND CLARK    1804 - 1806
CARTOGRAPHIC RECONSTRUCTION

Weigand Creek

UTM   ZONE   14
MAP   NUMBER   88

Nebraska    South Dakota

CONTOUR INTERVAL 50 FEET

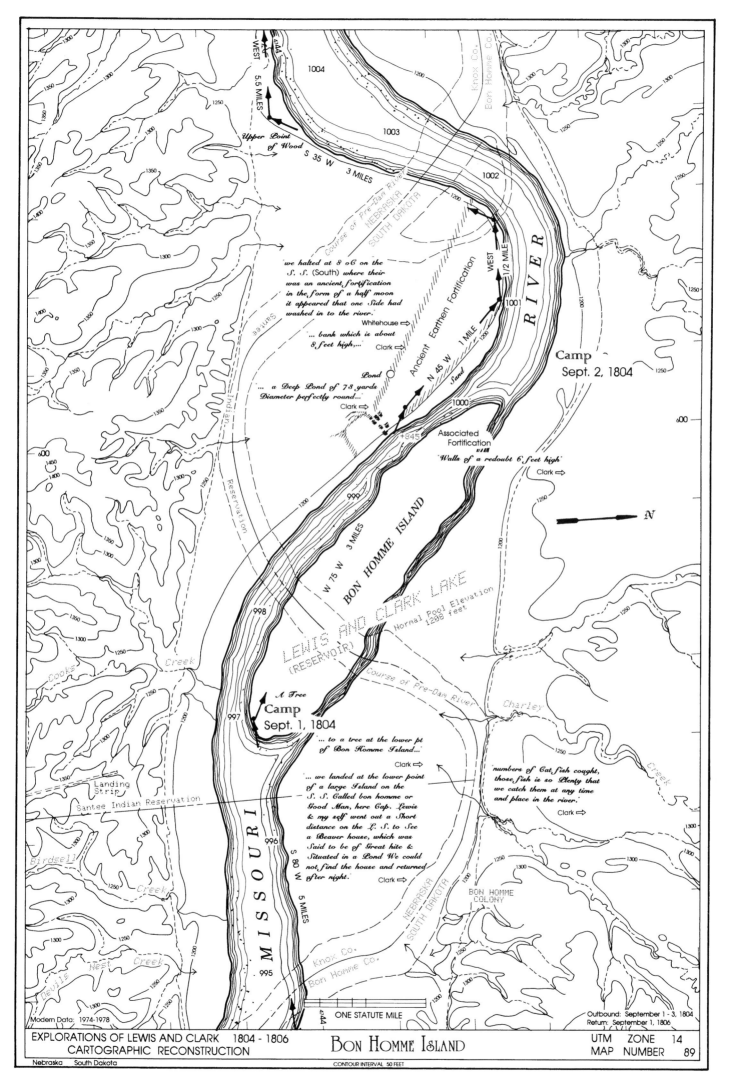

WEST
5.5 MILES

1004

1003

Upper Point
of Wood S 35 W
3 MILES

Knox Co.

Bon Homme Co.

1002

WEST 1/2 MILE

we halted at 8 oC on the
S. S. (South) where their
was an ancient fortification
in the form of a half moon
it appeared that one Side had
washed in to the river.

Whitehouse ⇒

Clark ⇒

... bank which is about
8 feet high,...

Pond

... a Deep Pond of 73 yards
Diameter perfectly round...

Clark ⇒

+845

Ancient Earthen Fortification

N 45 W 1 MILE

Sand

1001

1000

Associated
Fortification

'Walls of a redoubt 6 feet high'

Clark ⇒

Camp
Sept. 2, 1804

600

R I V E R

999

BON HOMME ISLAND

W 75 W 3 MILES

998

LEWIS AND CLARK LAKE
(RESERVOIR)

Normal Pool Elevation
1208 feet

Course of Pre-Dam River

N

Charley

Creek

A Tree

997

Camp
Sept. 1, 1804

... to a tree at the lower pt
of Bon Homme Island...

Clark ⇒

... we landed at the lower point
of a large Island on the
S. S. Called bon homme or
Good Man, here Cap. Lewis
& my self went out a Short
distance on the L. S. to See
a Beaver house, which was
Said to be of Great hite &
Situated in a Pond We could
not find the house and returned
after night.

Clark ⇒

numbers of Cat fish cought,
those fish is so Plenty that
we catch them at any time
and place in the river.

Clark ⇒

Cooks

Creek

1450
1400

600

Indian

Reservation

Landing
Strip

Santee Indian Reservation

Birdsell

Creek

996

S 80 W
5 MILES

M I S S O U R I

995

Devils Nest Creek

Knox Co.
Bon Homme Co.

NEBRASKA
SOUTH DAKOTA

BON HOMME
COLONY

Modern Data: 1974-1978

ONE STATUTE MILE

Outbound: September 1 - 3, 1804
Return: September 1, 1806

EXPLORATIONS OF LEWIS AND CLARK   1804 - 1806
CARTOGRAPHIC RECONSTRUCTION

BON HOMME ISLAND

UTM   ZONE   14
MAP   NUMBER   89

Nebraska   South Dakota

CONTOUR INTERVAL 50 FEET

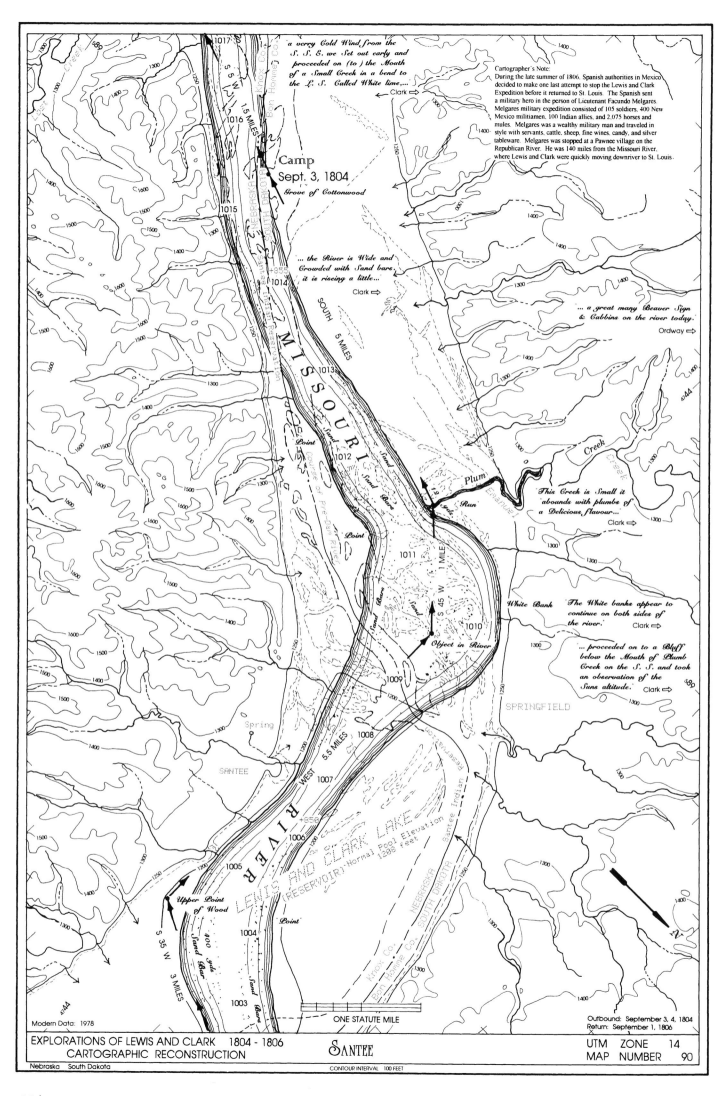

a verry Cold Wind from the
S. S. E. we Set out early and
proceeded on (to ) the Mouth
of a Small Creek in a bend to
the L. S. Called White lime,...

Clark ⇨

Cartographer's Note:
During the late summer of 1806, Spanish authorities in Mexico
decided to make one last attempt to stop the Lewis and Clark
Expedition before it returned to St. Louis. The Spanish sent
a military hero in the person of Lieutenant Facundo Melgares.
Melgares military expedition consisted of 105 soldiers, 400 New
Mexico militiamen, 100 Indian allies, and 2,075 horses and
mules. Melgares was a wealthy military man and traveled in
style with servants, cattle, sheep, fine wines, candy, and silver
tableware. Melgares was stopped at a Pawnee village on the
Republican River. He was 140 miles from the Missouri River,
where Lewis and Clark were quickly moving downriver to St. Louis.

1017

1016

1015

Camp
Sept. 3, 1804
Grove of Cottonwood

1014

... the River is Wide and
Crowded with Sand bars.
it is riseing a little...
Clark ⇨

... a great many Beaver Sign
& Cabbins on the river today.
Ordway ⇨

MISSOURI

SOUTH 5 MILES

1013

1012
Point

Sand Bars

Plum
Run

Creek

This Creek is Small it
abounds with plumbs of
a Delicious flavour...
Clark ⇨

1011
Sand Bars

White Bank

The White banks appear to
continue on both sides of
the river.
Clark ⇨

1010
Object in River

... proceeded on to a Bluff
below the Mouth of Plumb
Creek on the S. S. and took
an observation of the
Suns altitude.
Clark ⇨

1009

SPRINGFIELD

1008

Spring

SANTEE

1007

1006

LEWIS AND CLARK LAKE
(RESERVOIR) Normal Pool Elevation
1208 feet

1005

Upper Point
of Wood

S 35 W
3 MILES

Point

1004

Sand Bars

1003

N

ONE STATUTE MILE

Modern Data: 1978

EXPLORATIONS OF LEWIS AND CLARK    1804 - 1806
CARTOGRAPHIC RECONSTRUCTION

Santee

Nebraska    South Dakota
CONTOUR INTERVAL  100 FEET

Outbound: September 3, 4, 1804
Return: September 1, 1806

UTM  ZONE  14
MAP  NUMBER  90

114

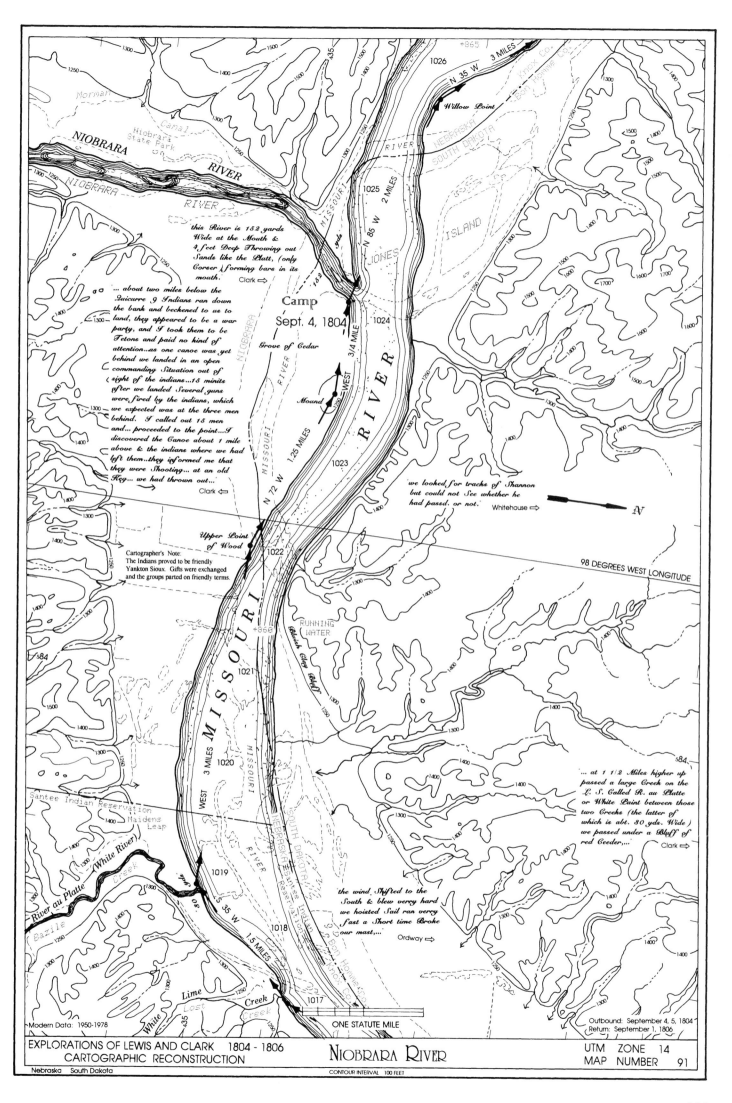

NIOBRARA RIVER

this River is 152 yards Wide at the Mouth & 4 feet Deep Throwing out Sands like the Platt, (only Corser) forming bars in its mouth.

Clark ⇒

... about two miles below the Quicurre 9 Indians ran down the bank and beckened to us to land, they appeared to be a war party, and I took them to be Tetons and paid no kind of attention...as one canoe was yet behind we landed in an open commanding Situation out of sight of the indians...15 minits after we landed Several guns were fired by the indians, which we expected was at the three men behind. I called out 15 men and... proceeded to the point....I discovered the Canoe about 1 mile above & the indians where we had left them...they informed me that they were Shooting... at an old Keg... we had thrown out...

Clark ⇐

Cartographer's Note:
The Indians proved to be friendly Yankton Sioux. Gifts were exchanged and the groups parted on friendly terms.

Camp Sept. 4, 1804

Grove of Cedar

Mound

WEST 3/4 MILE

Willow Point

N 35 W 3 MILES

N 85 W 2 MILES

JONES ISLAND

we looked for tracks of Shannon but could not See whether he had passd. or not.

Whitehouse ⇒

N

98 DEGREES WEST LONGITUDE

RUNNING WATER

Bluish Clay Bluff

N 72 W 1.25 MILES

Upper Point of Wood

Santee Indian Reservation

Maidens Leap

WEST 3 MILES

White River

River au Platte

Bazile Creek

N 35 W 1.5 MILES

Lime Creek

White

Lost Creek

... at 1 1/2 Miles higher up passed a large Creek on the L. S. called R. au Platte or White Paint between those two Creeks (the latter of which is abt. 30 yds. Wide) we passed under a Bluff of red Ceeder,...

Clark ⇒

the wind Shifted to the South & blew verry hard we hoisted Sail ran verry fast a Short time Broke our mast,...

Ordway ⇒

ONE STATUTE MILE

Outbound: September 4, 5, 1804
Return: September 1, 1806

EXPLORATIONS OF LEWIS AND CLARK   1804 - 1806
CARTOGRAPHIC RECONSTRUCTION

Nebraska   South Dakota

NIOBRARA RIVER

CONTOUR INTERVAL  100 FEET

Modern Data: 1950-1978

UTM   ZONE   14
MAP  NUMBER   91

115

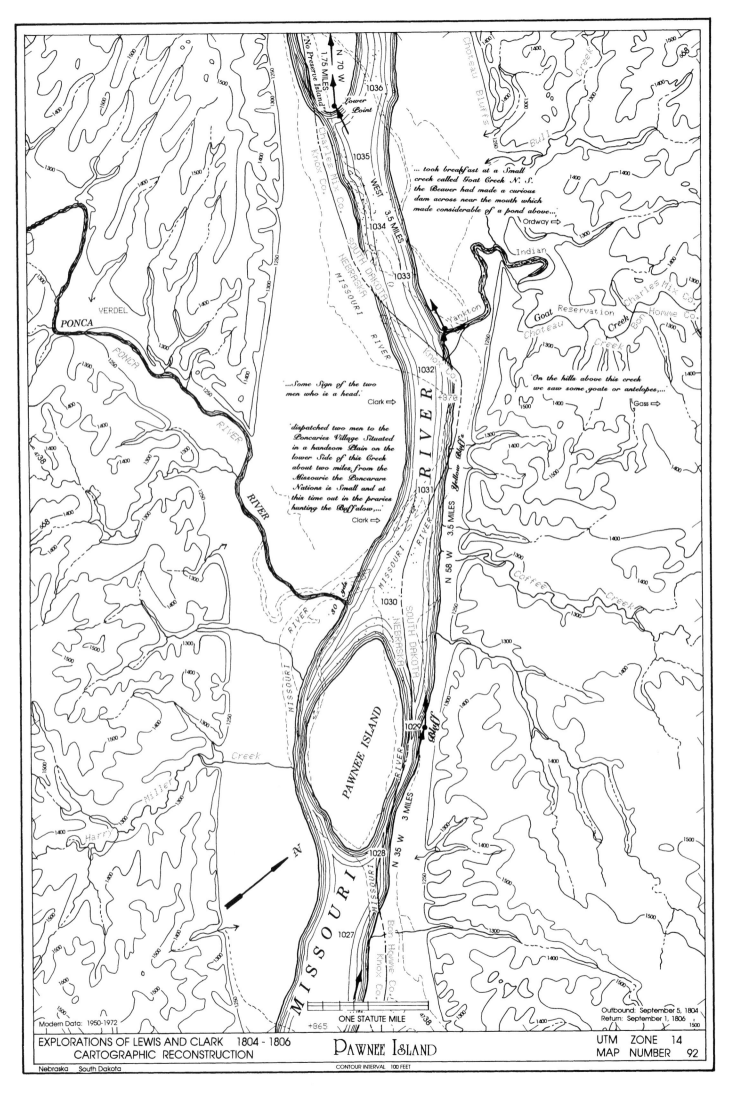

"No Preserve Island"
1.75 MILES
N 70 W
1036
Lower Point

... took breakfast at a Small creek called Goat Creek N. S. the Beaver had made a curious dam across near the mouth which made considerable of a pond above...

1035

WEST 3.5 MILES

1034

Ordway ⇨

1033

Indian

Yankton

Goat Reservation

Choteau Creek    Bon Homme Co.

...Some Sign of the two men who is a head."
Clark ⇨

+376

On the hills above this creek we saw some goats or antelopes,...
Gass ⇨

dispatched two men to the Poncaries Village Situated in a handsom Plain on the lower Side of this Creek about two miles from the Missourie the Poncararn Nations is Small and at this time out in the praries hunting the Buffalow,...
Clark ⇨

1031

1032

N 58 W 3.5 MILES

1030

Coffee Creek

VERDEL

PONCA

PONCA RIVER

RIVER

MISSOURI RIVER

MISSOURI RIVER

PAWNEE ISLAND

N 3 MILES

1029    Bluff

N 35 W

1028

N

1027

MISSOURI

Miller    Creek

Harry

+865

ONE STATUTE MILE

Modern Data: 1950-1972

Outbound: September 5, 1804
Return: September 1, 1806

EXPLORATIONS OF LEWIS AND CLARK    1804 - 1806
CARTOGRAPHIC RECONSTRUCTION

PAWNEE ISLAND

UTM ZONE 14
MAP NUMBER 92

Nebraska    South Dakota

CONTOUR INTERVAL 100 FEET

116

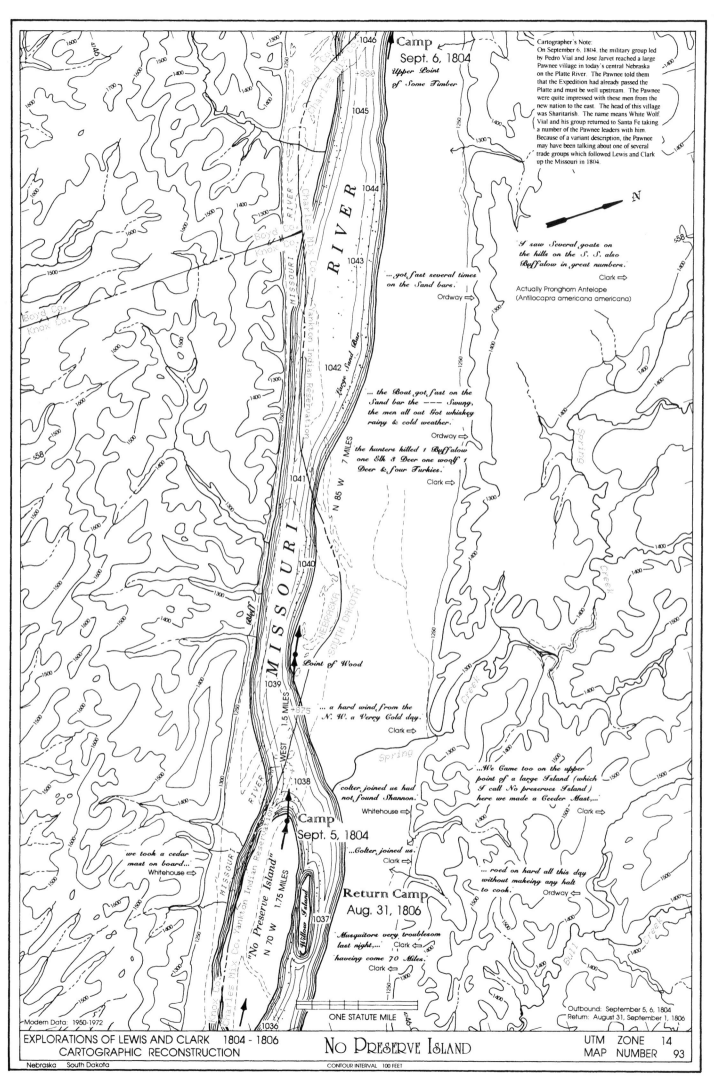

Camp
Sept. 6, 1804
*Upper Point
of Some Timber*

1046
1045
1044
1043
1042
1041
1040
1039
1038
1037
1036

RIVER

MISSOURI

MISSOURI RIVER

Boyd Co.
Knox Co.

Charles Mix Co.
Yankton Indian Reservation

Boyd Co.
Knox Co.

Charles Mix Co.

NEBRASKA
SOUTH DAKOTA

7 MILES

N 85 W

1.5 MILES

WEST

N 70 W    1.75 MILES

Knox Co. Nix Co.
Charles Mix Co.
Yankton Indian Reservation

"No Preserve Island"

Willow Island

*...got fast several times
on the Sand bars.*
Ordway ⇨

*... the Boat got fast on the
Sand bar the ——— Swung,
the men all out Got whiskey
rainy & cold weather.*
Ordway ⇨

*the hunters killed 1 Buffalow
one Elk 3 Deer one woolf 1
Deer & four Turkies.*
Clark ⇨

*Point of Wood*

*... a hard wind from the
N. W. a Very Cold day.*
Clark ⇨

*colter joined us had
not found Shannon.*
Whitehouse ⇨

*...Colter joined us.*
Clark ⇨

Camp
Sept. 5, 1804

*we took a cedar
mast on board...*
Whitehouse ⇨

Return Camp
Aug. 31, 1806

*Musquitors very troublesom
last night,...* Clark ⇨
*haveing come 70 Miles.*
Clark ⇨

Spring

*I saw Several goats on
the hills on the S. S. also
Buffalow in great numbers.*
Clark ⇨
Actually Pronghorn Antelope
(Antilocapra americana americana)

*...We Came too on the upper
point of a large Island (which
I call No preserves Island)
here we made a Ceeder Mast,...*
Clark ⇨

*... roed on hard all this day
without makeing any halt
to cook.*
Ordway ⇨

N

Cartographer's Note:
On September 6, 1804, the military group led
by Pedro Vial and Jose Jarvet reached a large
Pawnee village in today's central Nebraska
on the Platte River. The Pawnee told them
that the Expedition had already passed the
Platte and must be well upstream. The Pawnee
were quite impressed with these men from the
new nation to the east. The head of this village
was Sharitarish. The name means White Wolf.
Vial and his group returned to Santa Fe taking
a number of the Pawnee leaders with him.
Because of a variant description, the Pawnee
may have been talking about one of several
trade groups which followed Lewis and Clark
up the Missouri in 1804.

ONE STATUTE MILE

Outbound: September 5, 6, 1804
Return: August 31, September 1, 1806

EXPLORATIONS OF LEWIS AND CLARK    1804 - 1806
CARTOGRAPHIC RECONSTRUCTION

Nebraska    South Dakota

No Preserve Island

CONTOUR INTERVAL   100 FEET

UTM   ZONE   14
MAP NUMBER   93

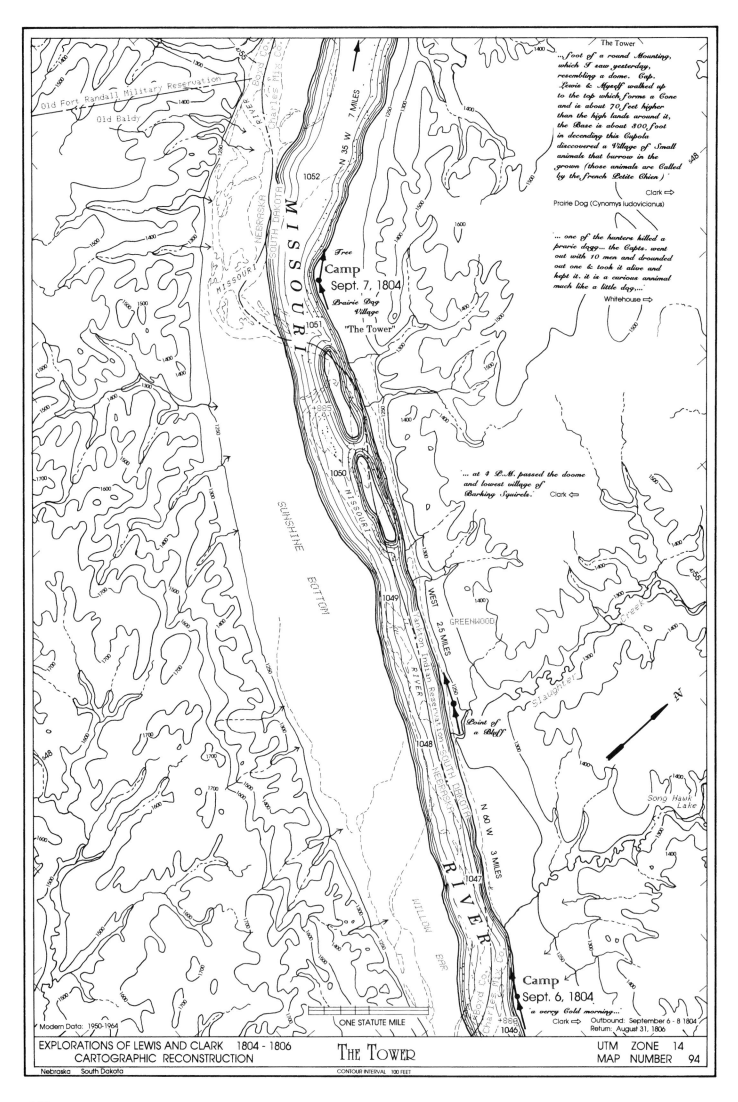

The Tower

...foot of a round Mounting, which I saw yesterday, resembling a dome. Cap. Lewis & Myself walked up to the top which, forms a Cone and is about 70 feet higher than the high lands around it, the Base is about 300 foot in decending this Cupola disccovered a Village of Small animals that burrow in the grown (those animals are Called by the french Petite Chien)

Clark ⇨

Prairie Dog (Cynomys ludovicianus)

... one of the hunters killed a prarie dogg... the Capts. went out with 10 men and drounded out one & took it alive and kept it. it is a curious annimal much like a little dog,...

Whitehouse ⇨

... at 4 P.M. passed the doome and lowest village of Barking Squirels.    Clark ⇦

Old Fort Randall Military Reservation

Old Baldy

RIVER BOYD CO.
Charles Mix Co.

NEBRASKA
SOUTH DAKOTA

MISSOURI

N 35 W   7 MILES

1052

1051

Tree
Camp
Sept. 7, 1804

Prairie Dog Village
"The Tower"

+885

1050

SUNSHINE BOTTOM

1049

MISSOURI

WEST   2.5 MILES   GREENWOOD

Yankton Indian Reservation–SOUTH DAKOTA
NEBRASKA

Point of
a Bluff

1048

Slaughter   Creek

Song Hawk Lake

N

N 60 W
3 MILES

1047

WILLOW BAR

Charles Mix Co.
Boyd Co.

Camp
Sept. 6, 1804

'a verry Cold morning...'

Clark ⇨   Outbound: September 6 - 8 1804
Return: August 31, 1806

+889
1046

Modern Data: 1950-1964

ONE STATUTE MILE

EXPLORATIONS OF LEWIS AND CLARK   1804 - 1806
CARTOGRAPHIC RECONSTRUCTION

THE TOWER

UTM   ZONE   14
MAP   NUMBER   94

Nebraska   South Dakota

CONTOUR INTERVAL   100 FEET

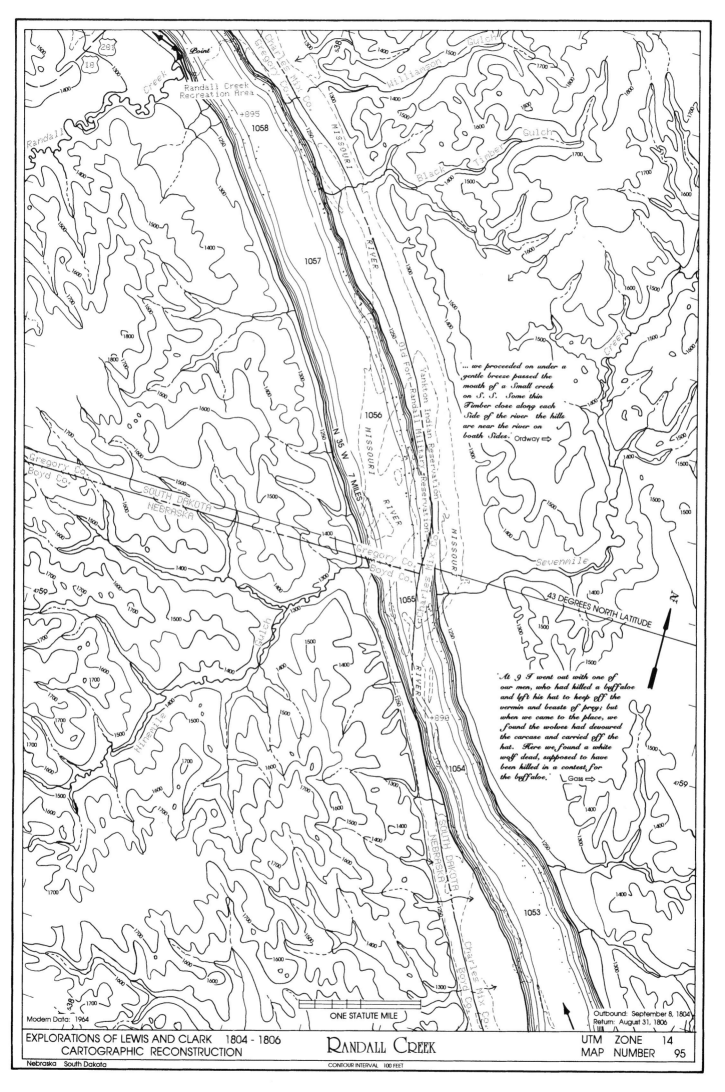

... we proceeded on under a
gentle breeze passed the
mouth of a Small creek
on S. S. Some thin
Timber close along each
Side of the river the hills
are near the river on
boath Sides. Ordway ⇒

At 9 I went out with one of
our men, who had killed a buffaloe
and left his hat to keep off the
vermin and beasts of prey; but
when we came to the place, we
found the wolves had devoured
the carcase and carried off the
hat. Here we found a white
wolf dead, supposed to have
been killed in a contest for
the buffaloe.
⎩ Gass ⇒

43 DEGREES NORTH LATITUDE

N

ONE STATUTE MILE

Modern Data: 1964

Outbound: September 8, 1804
Return: August 31, 1806

EXPLORATIONS OF LEWIS AND CLARK   1804 - 1806
CARTOGRAPHIC RECONSTRUCTION

RANDALL CREEK

UTM   ZONE   14
MAP   NUMBER   95

Nebraska   South Dakota

CONTOUR INTERVAL   100 FEET

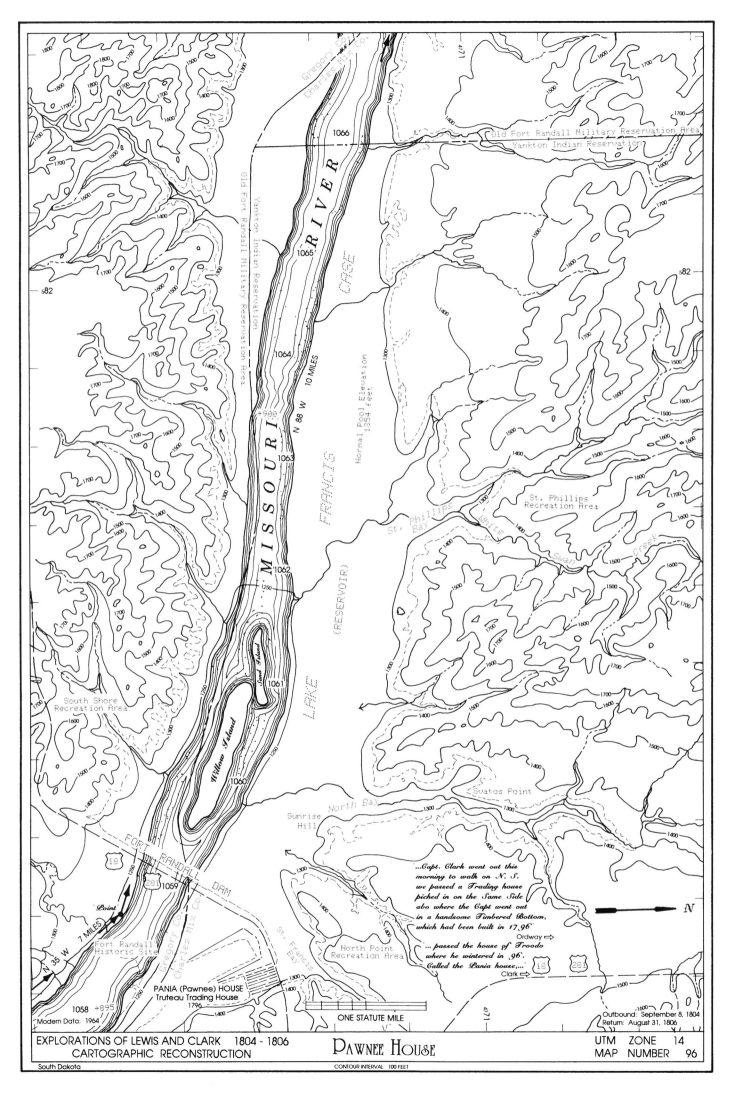

...Capt. Clark went out this
morning to walk on N. S.
we passed a Trading house
piched in on the Same Side
abo where the Capt went out
in a handsome Timbered Bottom,
which had been built in 17.96̈

... passed the house of Troodo
where he wintered in .96̈.
Called the Pania house,...

Ordway ⇨

Clark ⇨

Outbound: September 8, 1804
Return: August 31, 1806

EXPLORATIONS OF LEWIS AND CLARK   1804 - 1806
CARTOGRAPHIC RECONSTRUCTION

PAWNEE HOUSE

UTM   ZONE   14
MAP   NUMBER   96

South Dakota

CONTOUR INTERVAL   100 FEET

PANIA (Pawnee) HOUSE
Truteau Trading House
1796

ONE STATUTE MILE

Modern Data: 1964

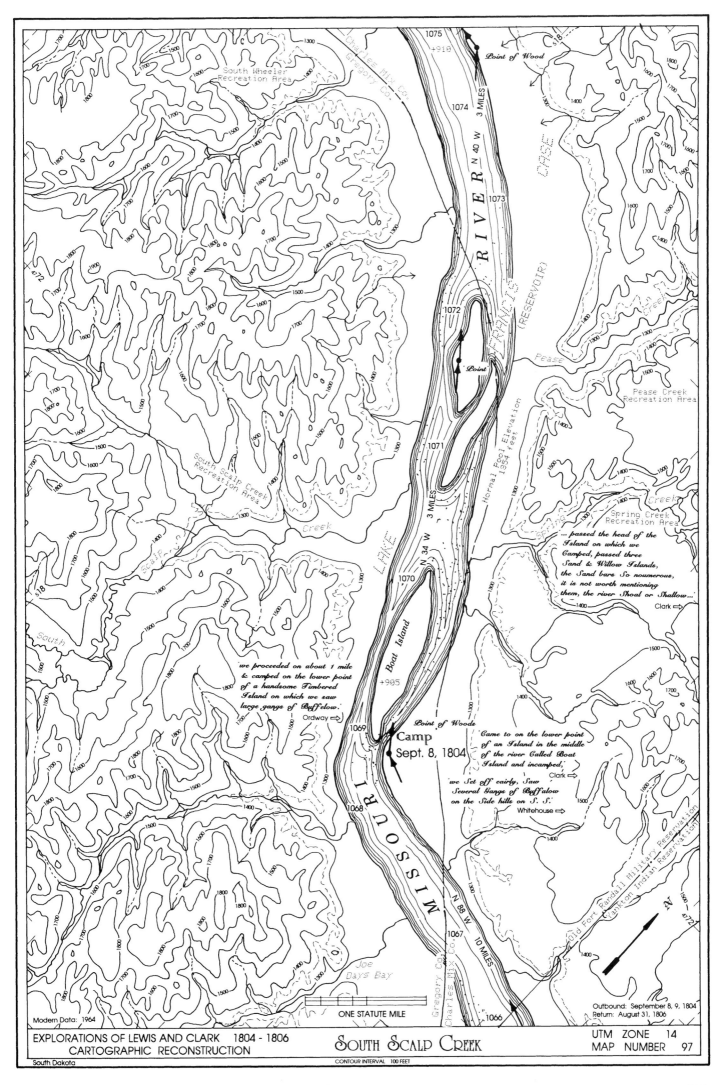

1075
+910
Point of Wood

1074

1073

Point

1072

1071

1070

...passed the head of the
Island on which we
Camped, passed three
Sand & Willow Islands,
the Sand bars so noumerous,
it is not worth mentioning
them, the river Shoal or Shallow...
Clark ⇨

Boat Island
+995

Point of Woods

Camp
Sept. 8, 1804

Came to on the lower point
of an Island in the middle
of the river Called Boat
Island and incamped;
Clark ⇨

we proceeded on about 1 mile
& camped on the lower point
of a handsome Timbered
Island on which we saw
large gangs of Buffelow.
Ordway ⇨

1069

1068

we Set off early, Saw
Several Gangs of Buffalow
on the Side hills on S. S.
Whitehouse ⇨

1067

Joe
Days Bay

1066

South Wheeler
Recreation Area

Charles Mix Co.
Gregory Co.

RIVER N 40 W 3 MILES

PEASE

(RESERVOIR)

Normal Pool Elevation
1354 feet

Pease Creek
Recreation Area

Pease Creek

Spring Creek
Recreation Area

Spring Creek

South Scalp Creek
Recreation Area

Creek

Scalp

South

LAKE FRANCIS CASE

MISSOURI

N 34 W 3 MILES

N 88 W 10 MILES

Gregory Co.
Charles Mix Co.

Old Fort Randall Military Reservation
Yankton Indian Reservation

N

+172

ONE STATUTE MILE

Outbound: September 8, 9, 1804
Return: August 31, 1806

Modern Data: 1964

EXPLORATIONS OF LEWIS AND CLARK   1804 - 1806
CARTOGRAPHIC RECONSTRUCTION

South Dakota

South Scalp Creek

CONTOUR INTERVAL   100 FEET

UTM ZONE   14
MAP NUMBER   97

121

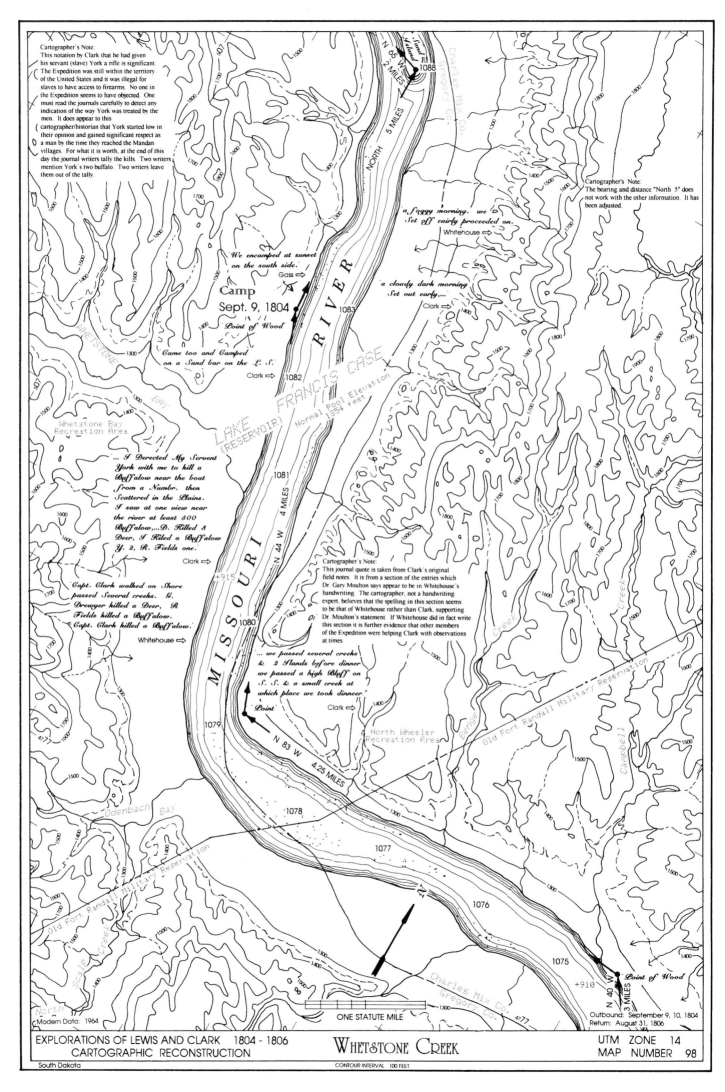

Cartographer's Note:
This notation by Clark that he had given his servant (slave) York a rifle is significant. The Expedition was still within the territory of the United States and it was illegal for slaves to have access to firearms. No one in the Expedition seems to have objected. One must read the journals carefully to detect any indication of the way York was treated by the men. It does appear to this cartographer/historian that York started low in their opinion and gained significant respect as a man by the time they reached the Mandan villages. For what it is worth, at the end of this day the journal writers tally the kills. Two writers mention York's two buffalo. Two writers leave them out of the tally.

N 65 W
2 MILES
1088

NORTH 5 MILES

Cartographer's Note:
The bearing and distance "North 5" does not work with the other information. It has been adjusted.

*a foggy morning. we Set off early proceeded on.*
Whitehouse ⇨

*We encamped at sunset on the south side.*
Gass ⇨

Camp
Sept. 9, 1804

*Point of Wood*

*a cloudy dark morning Set out early,...*
Clark ⇨

1083

RIVER

*Came too and Camped on a Sand bar on the L. S.*
Clark ⇨ 1082

LAKE FRANCIS CASE

(RESERVOIR) Normal Pool Elevation 1354 feet

Whetstone Bay
Recreation Area

*... I Derected My Servent York with me to kill a Buffalow near the boat from a Numbr. then Scattered in the Plains. I saw at one view near the river at least 500 Buffalow,...D. Killed 3 Deer, I Killed a Buffalow Y. 2, R. Fields one.*
Clark ⇨

1081

N 44 W 4 MILES

+915

MISSOURI

*Capt. Clark walked on Shore passed Several creeks. G. Dreuyer killed a Deer, R. Fields killed a Buffalow. Capt. Clark killed a Buffalow.*
Whitehouse ⇨

1080

Cartographer's Note:
This journal quote is taken from Clark's original field notes. It is from a section of the entries which Dr. Gary Moulton says appear to be in Whitehouse's handwriting. The cartographer, not a handwriting expert, believes that the spelling in this section seems to be that of Whitehouse rather than Clark, supporting Dr. Moulton's statement. If Whitehouse did in fact write this section it is further evidence that other members of the Expedition were helping Clark with observations at times.

*... we passed several creeks & 2 Islands before dinner we passed a high Bluff on S. S. & a small creek at which place we took dinneer"*
*Point*
Clark ⇨

1079

N 83 W 4.25 MILES

North Wheeler
Recreation Area

Old Fort Randall Military Reservation

Charles Mix Co.
Gregory Co.

4777

Odenbach Bay

1078

1077

1076

1075

+910

*Point of Wood*

N 40 W 3 MILES

Old Fort Randall Military Reservation

ONE STATUTE MILE

Outbound: September 9, 10, 1804
Return: August 31, 1806

North

Modern Data: 1964

EXPLORATIONS OF LEWIS AND CLARK    1804 - 1806
CARTOGRAPHIC RECONSTRUCTION

WHETSTONE CREEK

UTM  ZONE  14
MAP  NUMBER  98

South Dakota

CONTOUR INTERVAL  100 FEET

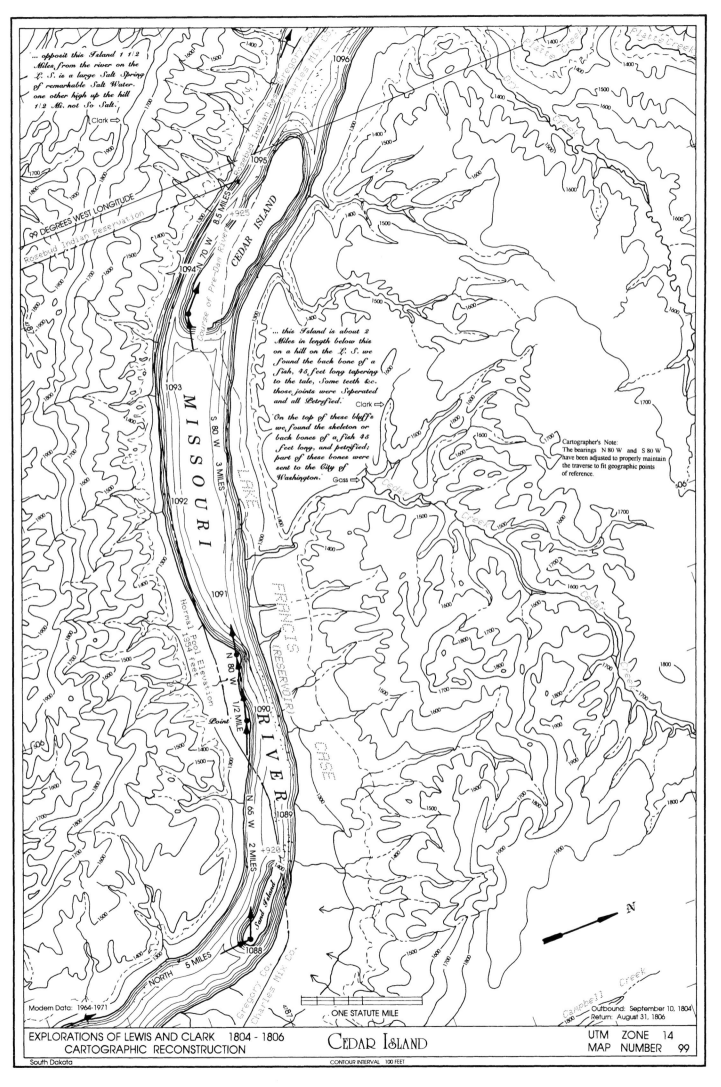

... opposit this Island 1 1/2
Miles, from the river on the
L. S. is a large Salt Spring
of remarkable Salt Water.
one other high up the hill
1/2 Mi. not So Salt.

Clark ⇒

99 DEGREES WEST LONGITUDE

Rosebud Indian Reservation

Course of Pre-Dam River

CEDAR ISLAND

N 70 W 8.5 MILES

+925

1096

1095

1094

1093

MISSOURI

S 80 W 3 MILES

1092

LAKE

... this Island is about 2
Miles in length below this
on a hill on the L. S. we
found the back bone of a
fish, 45 feet long tapering
to the tale, Some teeth &c.
those joints were Seperated
and all Petrefied.

Clark ⇒

On the top of these bluffs
we found the skeleton or
back bones of a fish 45
feet long, and petrified;
part of these bones were
sent to the City of
Washington.

Gass ⇒

Cartographer's Note:
The bearings N 80 W and S 80 W
have been adjusted to properly maintain
the traverse to fit geographic points
of reference.

Cedar Creek

1091

Normal Pool Elevation 1354 feet

FRANCIS (RESERVOIR)

N 80 W 1/2 MILE

Point

1090

CASE

RIVER

N 65 W 2 MILES

+920

1089

Sand Island

NORTH 5 MILES

Gregory Co. Charles Mix Co.

1088

Modern Data: 1964-1971

ONE STATUTE MILE

Campbell Creek

Outbound: September 10, 1804
Return: August 31, 1806

N

EXPLORATIONS OF LEWIS AND CLARK   1804 - 1806
CARTOGRAPHIC RECONSTRUCTION

CEDAR ISLAND

UTM   ZONE   14
MAP   NUMBER   99

South Dakota

CONTOUR INTERVAL 100 FEET

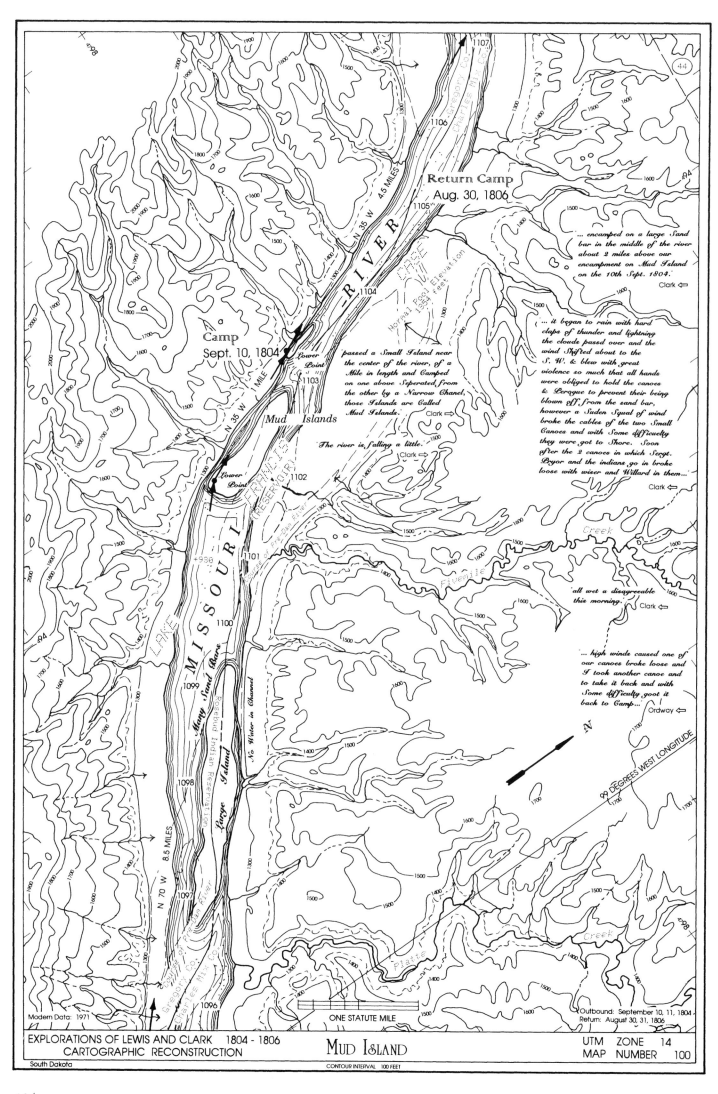

Return Camp
Aug. 30, 1806

Camp
Sept. 10, 1804

Lower Point

Mud Islands

Lower Point

Course of Firedan River

+930

Missouri

Many Sand Bars

Rosebud Indian Reservation

No Water in Channel

Large Island

N 35 W    4.5 MILES

N 35 W    1 MILE

N 70 W    8.5 MILES

Lake Francis Case Reservoir

Normal Pool Elevation 1354 feet

Gregory Co.
Charles Mix Co.

Fivemile

Creek

Creek

Platte

... encamped on a large Sand
bar in the middle of the river
about 2 miles above our
encampment on Mud Island
on the 10th Sept. 1804.
Clark ⇐

... it began to rain with hard
claps of thunder and lightning
the clouds passed over and the
wind Shifted about to the
S. W. & blew with great
violence so much that all hands
were obliged to hold the canoes
& Perogue to prevent their being
blown off from the sand bar,
however a Suden Squal of wind
broke the cables of the two Small
Canoes and with Some difficulty
they were got to Shore. Soon
after the 2 canoes in which Sergt.
Pryor and the indians go in broke
loose with wiser and Willard in them...
Clark ⇐

passed a Small Island near
the center of the river, of a
Mile in length and Camped
on one above Seperated from
the other by a Narrow Chanel,
those Islands are Called
Mud Islands.
Clark ⇒

The river is falling a little.
Clark ⇒

all wet a disagreeable
this morning.
Clark ⇐

... high winds caused one of
our canoes broke loose and
I took another canoe and
to take it back and with
Some difficulty goot it
back to Camp...
Ordway ⇐

N

99 DEGREES WEST LONGITUDE

Modern Data: 1971

ONE STATUTE MILE

Outbound: September 10, 11, 1804
Return: August 30, 31, 1806

EXPLORATIONS OF LEWIS AND CLARK    1804 - 1806
CARTOGRAPHIC RECONSTRUCTION

MUD ISLAND

South Dakota

CONTOUR INTERVAL 100 FEET

UTM    ZONE    14
MAP    NUMBER    100

124

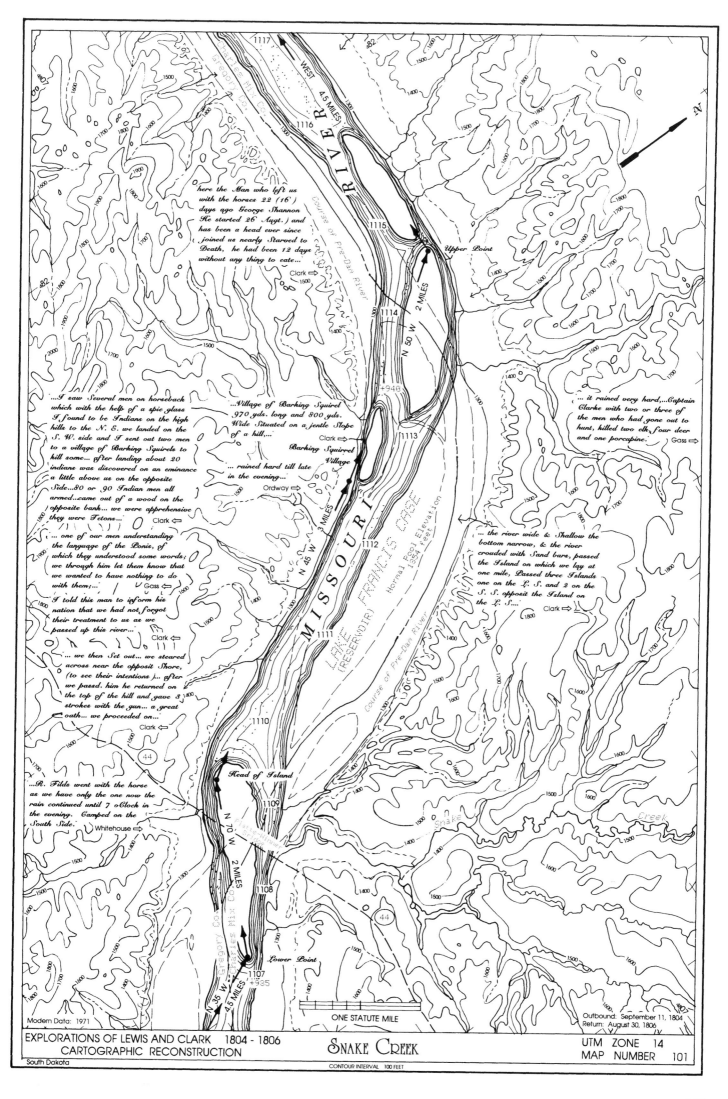

here the Man who left us
with the horses 22 (16')
days ago George Shannon
He started 26' Augt.) and
has been a head ever since
joined us nearly Starved to
Death, he had been 12 days
without any thing to eate...

Clark ⇒

...I saw Several men on horseback
which with the help of a spie glass
I found to be Indians on the high
hills to the N. E. we landed on the
S. W. side and I sent out two men
to a village of Barking Squirels to
kill some... after landing about 20
indians was discovered on an eminance
a little above us on the opposite
Side...80 or 90 Indian men all
armed...came out of a wood on the
opposite bank... we were apprehensive
they were Tetons...

Clark ⇐

... one of our men understanding
the language of the Ponis, of
which they understood some words;
we through him let them know that
we wanted to have nothing to do
with them;...

⤵ Gass ⇐

I told this man to inform his
nation that we had not forgot
their treatment to us as we
passed up this river...

Clark ⇐

... we then Set out... we steared
across near the opposit Shore,
(to see their intentions )... after
we passd. him he returned on
the top of the hill and gave 3
strokes with the gun... a great
oath... we proceeded on...

Clark ⇐

...R. Fields went with the horse
as we have only the one now the
rain continued until 7 o'clock in
the evening. Camped on the
South Side.

Whitehouse ⇒

...Village of Barking Squirel
970 yds. long and 800 yds.
Wide Situated on a jentle Slope
of a hill,...

Clark ⇐

Barking Squirrel
Village

... rained hard till late
in the evening...

Ordway ⇒

... it rained very hard,...Captain
Clarke with two or three of
the men who had gone out to
hunt, killed two elk, four deer
and one porcupine.

Gass ⇒

... the river wide & Shallow the
bottom narrow, & the river
crouded with Sand bars, passed
the Island on which we lay at
one mile, Passed three Islands
one on the L. S. and 2 on the
S. S. opposit the Island on
the L. S....

Clark ⇒

Upper Point

Head of Island

Lower Point

ONE STATUTE MILE

Modern Data: 1971

Outbound: September 11, 1804
Return: August 30, 1806

EXPLORATIONS OF LEWIS AND CLARK  1804 - 1806
CARTOGRAPHIC RECONSTRUCTION

South Dakota

SNAKE CREEK

CONTOUR INTERVAL  100 FEET

UTM  ZONE  14
MAP  NUMBER  101

125

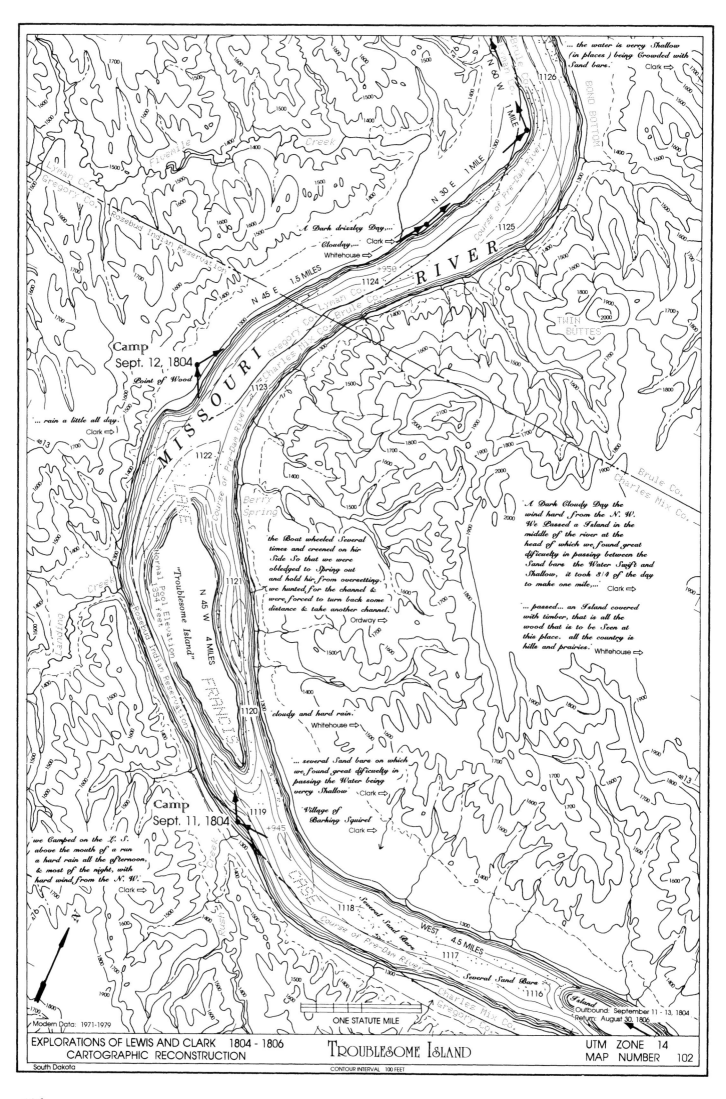

... the water is very Shallow (in places) being Crowded with Sand bars.
Clark ⇒

1126

BOND BOTTOM

N 8 W 1 MILE

N 30 E 1 MILE

A Dark drizzley Day,...
Cloudy,....
Clark ⇒
Whitehouse ⇒

N 45 E 1.5 MILES

1124

1125

Course of Pre-Dam River

RIVER

+950

TWIN BUTTES

2000
1900
1800

Camp
Sept. 12, 1804
Point of Wood

MISSOURI

1123

Gregory Co. Lyman Co. Brule Co.
Charles Mix Co. Brule Co.

... rain a little all day.
Clark ⇒

4813

1122

Course of Pre-Dam River

2100
2000

1900
1800

A Dark Cloudy Day the wind hard from the N. W. We Passed a Island in the middle of the river at the head of which we found great dificuelty in passing between the Sand bars the Water Swift and Shallow, it took 3/4 of the day to make one mile,...
Clark ⇒

Berry Spring

the Boat wheeled Several times and creened on hir Side So that we were obledged to Spring out and hold hir from oversetting, we hunted for the channel & were forced to turn back some distance & take another channel.
Ordway ⇒

"Troublesome Island"

Normal Pool Elevation 1354 feet

Rosebud Indian Reservation

N 45 W 4 MILES

1121

... passed... an Island covered with timber, that is all the wood that is to be Seen at this place. all the country is hills and prairies.
Whitehouse ⇒

1120

cloudy and hard rain.
Whitehouse ⇒

... several Sand bars on which we found great dificuelty in passing the Water being verry Shallow
Clark ⇒

Camp
Sept. 11, 1804

1119

+945

Village of Barking Squirel
Clark ⇒

we Camped on the L. S. above the mouth of a run a hard rain all the afternoon, & most of the night, with hard wind from the N. W.
Clark ⇒

N

1118

WEST 4.5 MILES

1117

Course of Pre-Dam River

Several Sand Bars

1116

Several Sand Bars

Island
Outbound: September 11 - 13, 1804
Return: August 30, 1806

Gregory Co.
Charles Mix Co.

Modern Data: 1971-1979

ONE STATUTE MILE

EXPLORATIONS OF LEWIS AND CLARK   1804 - 1806
CARTOGRAPHIC RECONSTRUCTION

South Dakota

TROUBLESOME ISLAND

CONTOUR INTERVAL 100 FEET

UTM ZONE   14
MAP NUMBER   102

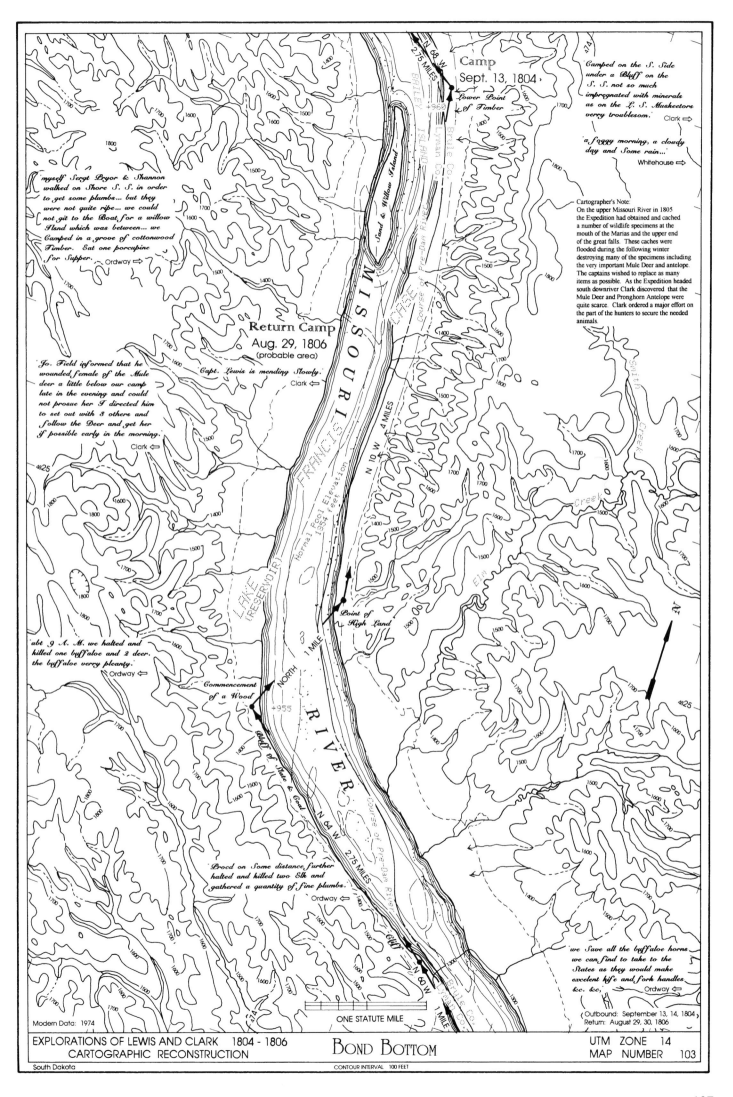

Camp
Sept. 13, 1804

*Lower Point of Timber*

*Camped on the S. Side under a Bluff on the S. S. not so much impregnated with minerals as on the L. S. Muskeetors verry troublesom.*
Clark ⇒

*a foggy morning, a cloudy day and Some rain...*
Whitehouse ⇒

Cartographer's Note:
On the upper Missouri River in 1805 the Expedition had obtained and cached a number of wildlife specimens at the mouth of the Marias and the upper end of the great falls. These caches were flooded during the following winter destroying many of the specimens including the very important Mule Deer and antelope. The captains wished to replace as many items as possible. As the Expedition headed south downriver Clark discovered that the Mule Deer and Pronghorn Antelope were quite scarce. Clark ordered a major effort on the part of the hunters to secure the needed animals.

*myself Sergt Pryor & Shannon walked on Shore S. S. in order to get some plumbs... but they were not quite ripe... we could not git to the Boat for a willow Sland which was between... we Camped in a grove of cottonwood Timber. Eat one porcupine for Supper.*
Ordway ⇒

Return Camp
Aug. 29, 1806
(probable area)

*Capt. Lewis is mending Slowly.*
Clark ⇐

*Jo. Field informed that he wounded female of the Mule deer a little below our camp late in the evening and could not prosue her I directed him to set out with 3 others and follow the Deer and get her if possible early in the morning.*
Clark ⇐

*abt 9 A. M. we halted and killed one buffaloe and 2 deer. the buffaloe verry pleanty.*
Ordway ⇐

*Point of High Land*

*Commencement of a Wood*

*Proed on Some distance further halted and killed two Elk and gathered a quantity of fine plumbs.*
Ordway ⇐

*we Save all the buffaloe horns we can find to take to the States as they would make excelent kife and fork handles &c. &c,*
Ordway ⇐

Outbound: September 13, 14, 1804
Return: August 29, 30, 1806

ONE STATUTE MILE

Modern Data: 1974

EXPLORATIONS OF LEWIS AND CLARK   1804 - 1806
CARTOGRAPHIC RECONSTRUCTION

BOND BOTTOM

CONTOUR INTERVAL   100 FEET

South Dakota

UTM ZONE   14
MAP NUMBER   103

127

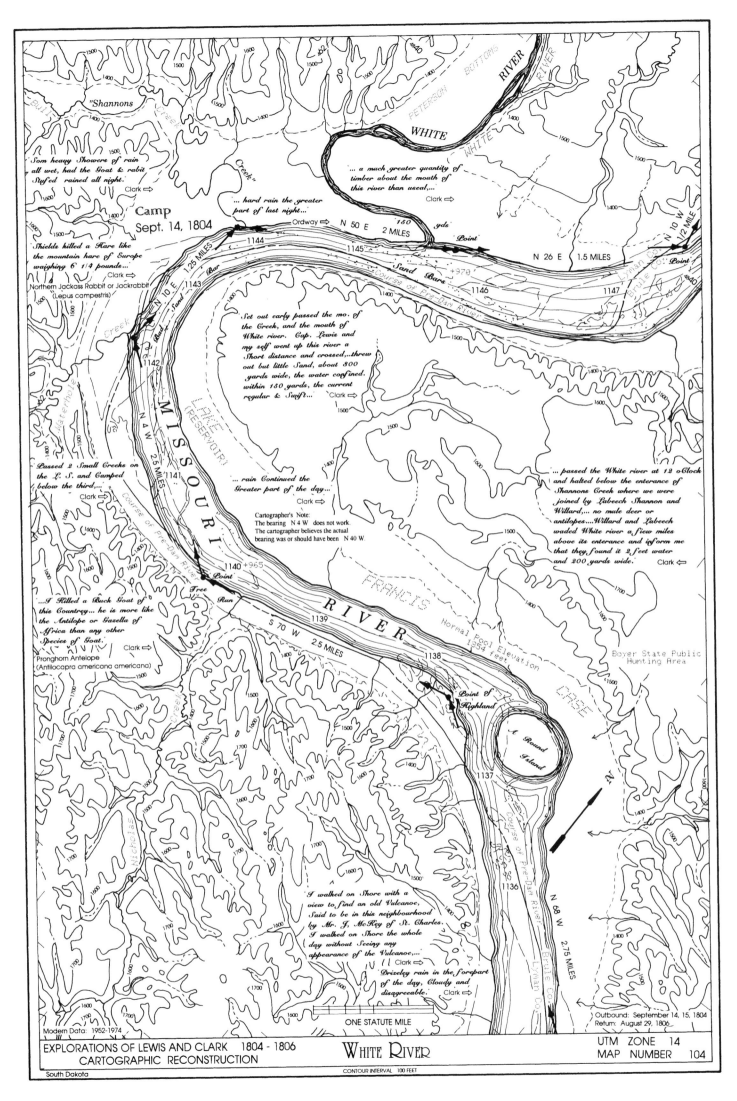

"Shannons

Som heavy Showers of rain
all wet, had the Goat & rabit
Stafed rained all night.
Clark ⇒

... hard rain the greater
part of last night...
Ordway ⇒  N 50 E
2 MILES

... a much greater quantity of
timber about the mouth of
this river than useal,...
Clark ⇒

WHITE                    RIVER

PETERSON BOTTOMS

Camp
Sept. 14, 1804

150
yds
Point

N 26 E    1.5 MILES

N 10 W    1/2 MILE
Point

Shields killed a Hare like
the mountain hare of Europe
waighing 6' 1/4 pounds...
Clark ⇒
Northern Jackass Rabbit or Jackrabbit
(Lepus campestris)

1144
1145
Sand    Bars
1146    +979
1147

1143
Bar    Sand

N 10 E    1.25 MILES

Creek"

Brule Co.
Lyman Co.

1142
Bad    Sand

Set out early passed the mo. of
the Creek, and the mouth of
White river. Cap. Lewis and
my self went up this river a
Short distance and crossed,...threw
out but little Sand, about 800
yards wide, the water coffined,
within 150 yards, the current
regular & Swift...
Clark ⇒

Waterhole

Creek

MISSOURI

N 4 W    2.5 MILES

LAKE
(RESERVOIR)

1141

... rain Continued the
Greater part of the day...
Clark ⇒

Cartographer's Note:
The bearing N 4 W does not work.
The cartographer believes the actual
bearing was or should have been N 40 W.

... passed the White river at 12 oClock
and halted below the entrance of
Shannons Creek where we were
joined by Labeech Shannon and
Willard,... no mule deer or
antilopes....Willard and Labeech
waded White river a few miles
above its entrance and inform me
that they found it 2 feet water
and 200 yards wide.
Clark ⇐

Passed 2 Small Creeks on
the L. S. and Camped
below the third,...
Clark ⇒

Course of Pre-Dam River

... I Killed a Buck Goat of
this Country... he is more like
the Antilope or Gazella of
Africa than any other
Species of Goat.
Clark ⇒
Pronghorn Antelope
(Antilocapra americana americana)

1140    +965
Point

Tree
Run

S 70 W    2.5 MILES

1139

R  I  V  E  R

FRANCIS

Normal Pool Elevation
1354 feet

Boyer State Public
Hunting Area

1138

Point of
Highland

CASE

1137

Round
Island

N

Jackass    Creek

Nicholas    Creek

1136

I walked on Shore with a
view to find an old Vulcanoe,
said to be in this neighbourhood
by Mr. J. McKey of St. Charles.
I walked on Shore the whole
day without Seeing any
appearance of the Vulcanoe,...
Clark ⇒

Drizeley rain in the forepart
of the day, Cloudy and
disagreeable.
Clark ⇒

Course of Pre-Dam River

Brule Co.
Lyman Co.

N 68 W    2.75 MILES

ONE STATUTE MILE

Outbound: September 14, 15, 1804
Return: August 29, 1806

Modern Data: 1952-1974

EXPLORATIONS OF LEWIS AND CLARK    1804 - 1806
CARTOGRAPHIC RECONSTRUCTION

South Dakota

WHITE RIVER

CONTOUR INTERVAL  100 FEET

UTM ZONE  14
MAP NUMBER  104

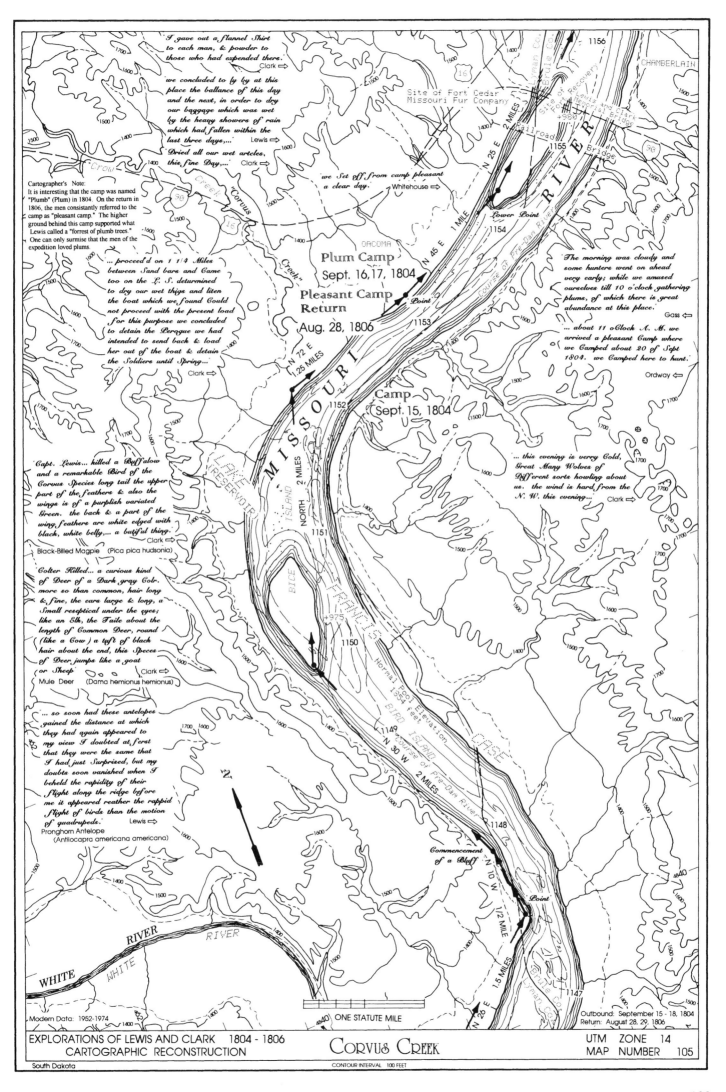

I gave out a flannel Shirt to each man, & powder to those who had expended there. — Clark ⇒

we concluded to ly by at this place the ballance of this day and the next, in order to dry our baggage which was wet by the heavy showers of rain which had fallen within the last three days,... — Lewis ⇒

Dried all our wet artcles, this fine Day,... — Clark ⇒

Cartographer's Note:
It is interesting that the camp was named "Plumb" (Plum) in 1804. On the return in 1806, the men consistantly referred to the camp as "pleasant camp." The higher ground behind this camp supported what Lewis called a "forrest of plumb trees." One can only surmise that the men of the expedition loved plums.

...proceed'd on 1 1/4 Miles between Sand bars and Came too on the L. S. deturmined to dry our wet thigs and liten the boat which we found Could not proceed with the present load for this purpose we concluded to detain the Perogue we had intended to send back & load her out of the boat & detain the Soldiers until Spring... — Clark ⇒

Capt. Lewis... killed a Buffalow and a remarkable Bird of the Corvus Species long tail the upper part of the feathers & also the wings is of a purplish variated Green. the back & a part of the wing feathers are white edged with black, white belly,... a butiful thing. — Clark ⇒
Black-Billed Magpie (Pica pica hudsonia)

Colter Killed... a curious kind of Deer of a Dark gray Colr. more so than common, hair long & fine, the ears large & long, a Small reseptical under the eyes; like an Elk, the Taile about the length of Common Deer, round (like a Cow) a tuft of black hair about the end, this Speces of Deer jumps like a goat or Sheep — Clark ⇒
Mule Deer (Dama hemionus hemionus)

... so soon had these antelopes gained the distance at which they had again appeared to my view I doubted at ferst that they were the same that I had just Surprised, but my doubts soon vanished when I beheld the rapidity of their flight along the ridge before me it appeared reather the rappid flight of birds than the motion of quadrupeds. — Lewis ⇒
Pronghorn Antelope (Antilocapra americana americana)

Modern Data: 1952-1974

we Set off from camp pleasant a clear day. — Whitehouse ⇒

Plum Camp
Sept. 16, 17, 1804

Pleasant Camp
Return
Aug. 28, 1806

Site of Fort Cedar
Missouri Fur Company

CHAMBERLAIN

The morning was cloudy and some hunters went on ahead very early; while we amused ourselves till 10 o'clock gathering plums, of which there is great abundance at this place. — Gass ⇐

... about 11 oClock A. M. we arrived a pleasant Camp where we Camped about 20 of Sept 1804. we Camped here to hunt. — Ordway ⇐

... this evening is verry Cold, Great Many Wolves of Different sorts howling about us. the wind is hard from the N. W. this evening... — Clark ⇒

Camp
Sept. 15, 1804

Commencement
of a Bluff

ONE STATUTE MILE

Outbound: September 15-18, 1804
Return: August 28, 29, 1806

EXPLORATIONS OF LEWIS AND CLARK   1804 - 1806
CARTOGRAPHIC RECONSTRUCTION

CORVUS CREEK

UTM   ZONE   14
MAP NUMBER   105

South Dakota

CONTOUR INTERVAL 100 FEET

129

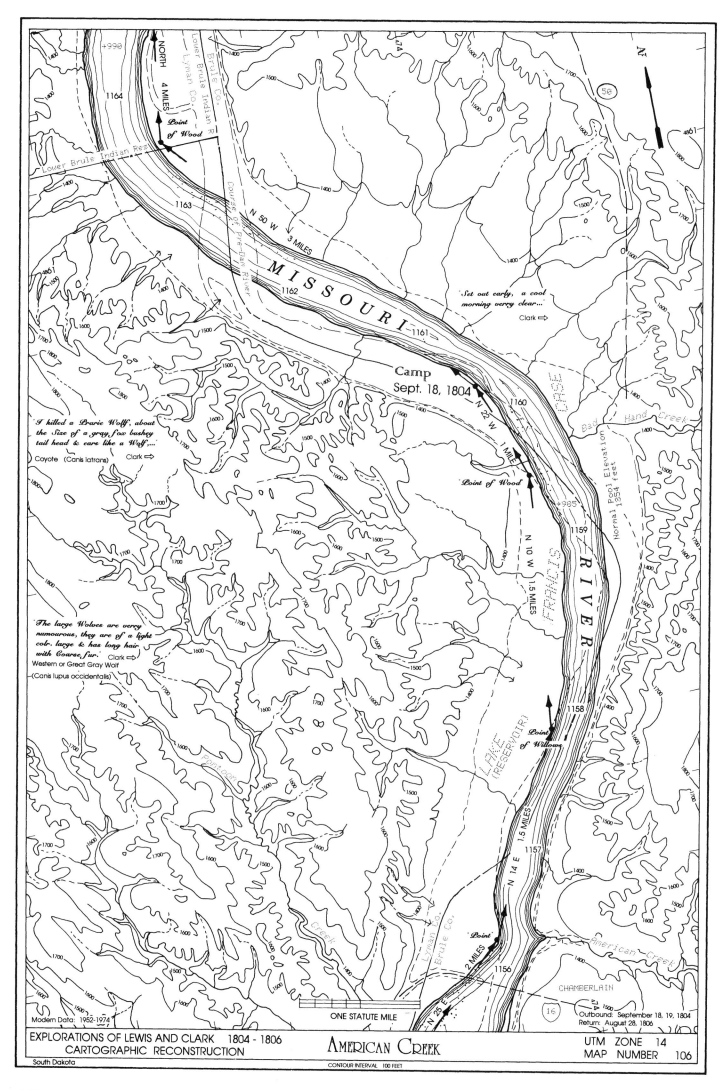

NORTH

4 MILES

*Point of Wood*

1164

+990

Lower Brule Indian Res.

Lower Brule Indian Res.

Lyman Co.

Brule Co.

Course of Pre-Dam River

1163

1162

M I S S O U R I

1161

N 50 W 3 MILES

4861

4861

56

N

474

1700

Set out early, a cool
morning verry clear...

Clark ⇒

1400

1500

1800

Camp
Sept. 18, 1804

N 22 W 1 MILE

1160

"I killed a Prarie Wolff, about
the Size of a gray fox bushey
tail head & ears like a Wolf,..."

Coyote (Canis latrans)  Clark ⇒

*Point of Wood*

+985

N 10 W 1.5 MILES

1159

Bad Hand Creek

Normal Pool Elevation 1354 feet

CROW

FRANCIS

ST.

R I V E R

"The large Wolves are verry
numourous, they are of a light
colr. large & has long hair
with Coarse fur."   Clark ⇒
Western or Great Gray Wolf
(Canis lupus occidentalis)

1700

1800

1600

1500

Portage Creek

LAKE (RESERVOIR)

*Point of Willow*

1158

N 14 E 1.5 MILES

1157

1400

1600

1800

Lyman Co.

Brule Co.

Creek

*Point*

N 25 E 2 MILES

1156

American Creek

CHAMBERLAIN

474

16

Modern Data: 1952-1974

ONE STATUTE MILE

Outbound: September 18, 19, 1804
Return: August 28, 1806

EXPLORATIONS OF LEWIS AND CLARK   1804 - 1806
CARTOGRAPHIC RECONSTRUCTION

South Dakota

AMERICAN CREEK

CONTOUR INTERVAL  100 FEET

UTM  ZONE  14
MAP  NUMBER  106

130

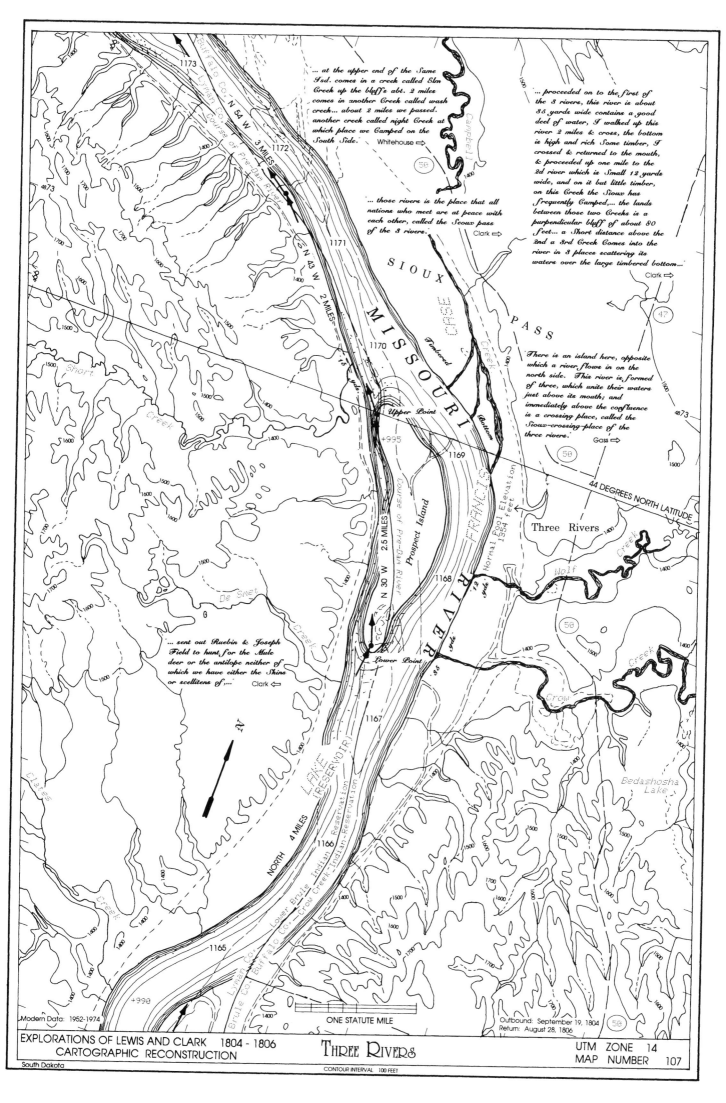

... at the upper end of the Same Isd. comes in a creek called Elm Creek up the bluff's abt. 2 miles comes in another Creek called wash creek.... about 2 miles we passed another creek called night Creek at which place we Camped on the South Side. Whitehouse ⟹

... those rivers is the place that all nations who meet are at peace with each other, called the Seoux pass of the 3 rivers. Clark ⟹

... proceeded on to the first of the 3 rivers, this river is about 85 yards wide contains a good deed of water, I walked up this river 2 miles & cross, the bottom is high and rich Some timber, I crossed & returned to the mouth, & proceeded up one mile to the 2d river which is Small 12 yards wide, and on it but little timber, on this Creek the Sioux has frequently Camped,... the lands between those two Creeks is a purpendicular bluff of about 80 feet... a Short distance above the 2nd a 3rd Creek Comes into the river in 3 places scattering its waters over the large timbered bottom... Clark ⟹

There is an island here, opposite which a river flows in on the north side. This river is formed of three, which unite their waters just above its mouth; and immediately above the confluence is a crossing place, called the Sioux-crossing-place of the three rivers. Gass ⟸

Three Rivers

44 DEGREES NORTH LATITUDE

... sent out Ruebin & Joseph Field to hunt for the Mule deer or the antelope neither of which we have either the Skins or scellitens of,... Clark ⟸

N

Normal Pool Elevation 1354 feet

ONE STATUTE MILE

Modern Data: 1952-1974

Outbound: September 19, 1804
Return: August 28, 1806

EXPLORATIONS OF LEWIS AND CLARK 1804 - 1806
CARTOGRAPHIC RECONSTRUCTION

THREE RIVERS

UTM ZONE 14
MAP NUMBER 107

South Dakota

CONTOUR INTERVAL 100 FEET

131

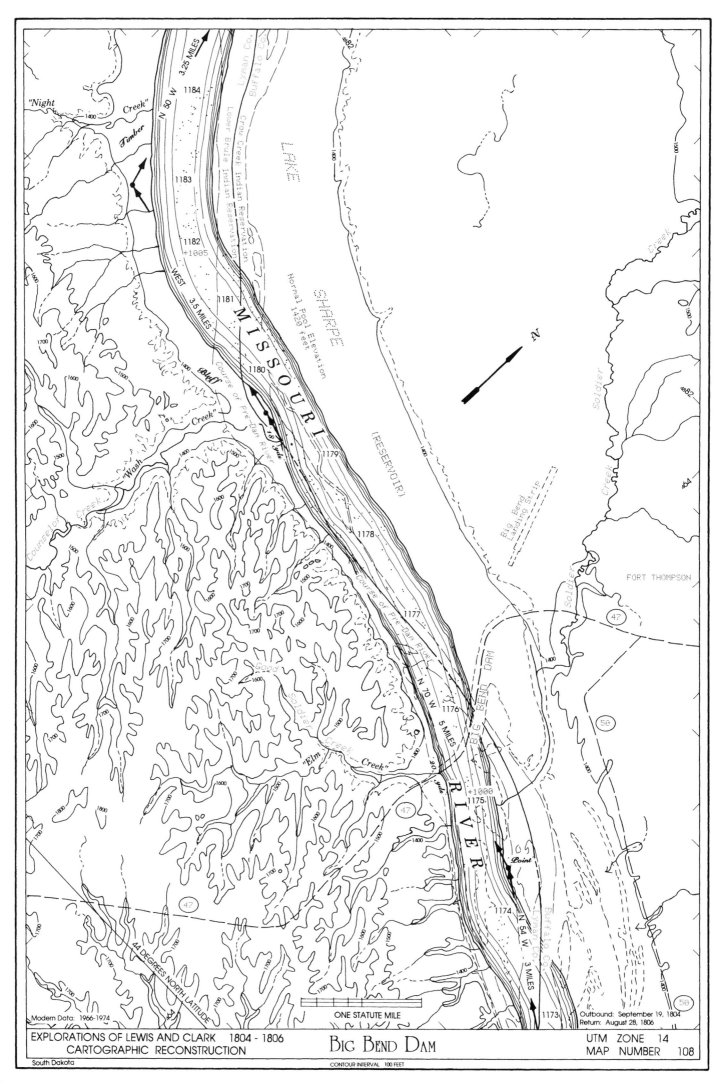

"Night

Creek"

Timber

1184

1183

1182
+1005

1181

1180

Bluff

Creek"

"8 yds

1179

"Wash

Creek"

1178

Counselor Creek

1177

Good

1176

"Elm — Creek — Creek"

N 70 W 5 MILES

Soldier Creek

+1000

1175

Point

1174 N 54 W 3 MILES

1173

Outbound: September 19, 1804
Return: August 28, 1806

WEST 3.5 MILES

N 50 W 3.25 MILES

M I S S O U R I

Course of Pre-Dam River

Crow Creek Indian Reservation

Buffalo Co.

Lyman Co.

Lower Brule Indian Reservation

L A K E

S H A R P E

Normal Pool Elevation 1420 feet

(RESERVOIR)

N

Course of Pre-Dam River

Big Bend Landing Strip

Soldier Creek

Soldier

Creek

FORT THOMPSON

47

50

BIG BEND DAM

R I V E R

Buffalo Co.
Lyman Co.

47

44 DEGREES NORTH LATITUDE

ONE STATUTE MILE

Modern Data: 1966-1974

South Dakota

EXPLORATIONS OF LEWIS AND CLARK   1804 - 1806
CARTOGRAPHIC RECONSTRUCTION

BIG BEND DAM

CONTOUR INTERVAL   100 FEET

UTM  ZONE   14
MAP  NUMBER   108

132

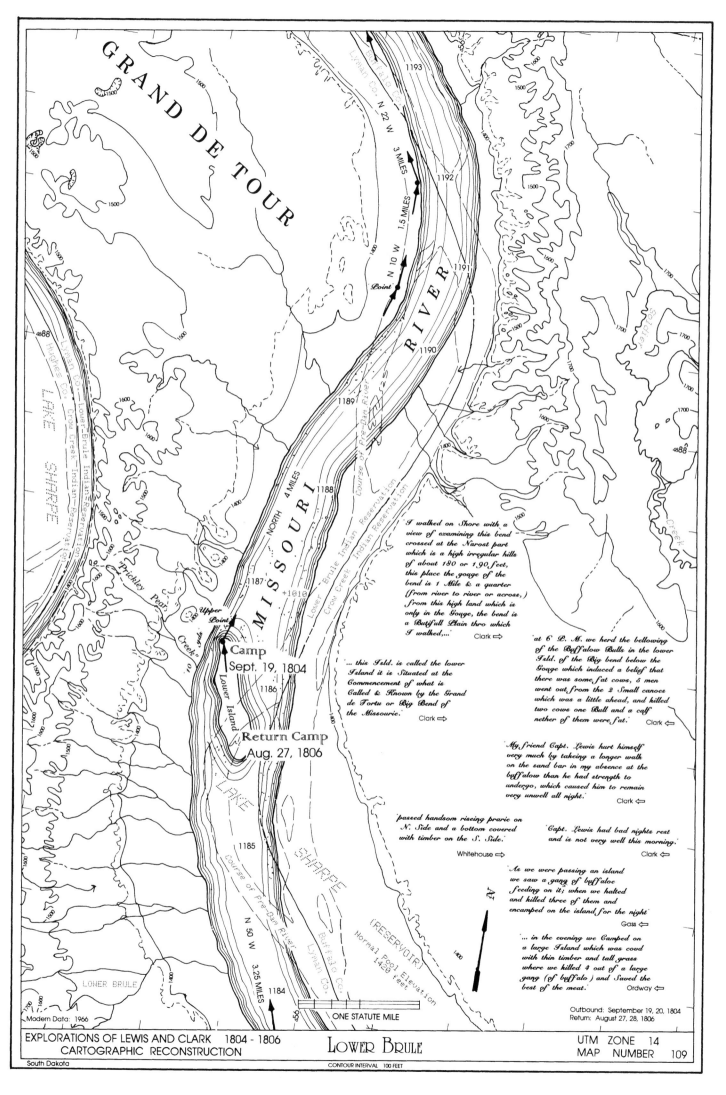

GRAND DE TOUR

LAKE SHARPE

MISSOURI RIVER

Point

N 22 W
3 MILES

N 10 W
1.5 MILES

1193

1192

1191

1190

1189

1188

NORTH
4 MILES

1187

+1010

Upper
Point

Camp
Sept. 19, 1804

Lower Island

1186

Return Camp
Aug. 27, 1806

LAKE SHARPE

1185

N 50 W
3.25 MILES

1184

I walked on Shore with a
view of examining this bend
crossed at the Narost part
which is a high irregular hills
of about 180 or 190 feet,
this place the gouge of the
bend is 1 Mile & a quarter
(from river to river or across,)
from this high land which is
only in the Gouge, the bend is
a Butifull Plain thro which
I walked,...                    Clark ⇨

... this Isld. is called the lower
Island it is Situated at the
Commencement of what is
Called & Known by the Grand
de Tortu or Big Bend of
the Missourie.                 Clark ⇨

at 6 P. M. we herd the bellowing
of the Buffalow Bulls in the lower
Isld. of the Big bend below the
Gouge which induced a belief that
there was some fat cows, 5 men
went out from the 2 Small canoes
which was a little ahead, and killed
two cows one Bull and a calf
nether of them were fat.       Clark ⇦

My friend Capt. Lewis hurt himself
very much by takeing a longer walk
on the sand bar in my absence at the
buffalow than he had strength to
undergo, which caused him to remain
very unwell all night.          Clark ⇦

passed handsom riseing prarie on
N. Side and a bottom covered
with timber on the S. Side.

Whitehouse ⇨

Capt. Lewis had bad nights rest
and is not very well this morning.

Clark ⇦

As we were passing an island
we saw a gang of buffaloe
feeding on it; when we halted
and killed three of them and
encamped on the island for the night

Gass ⇦

... in the evening we Camped on
a large Island which was covd
with thin timber and tall grass
where we killed 4 out of a large
gang (of buffalo) and Saved the
best of the meat.               Ordway ⇦

Modern Data: 1966

LOWER BRULE

Normal Pool Elevation 1420 feet

(RESERVOIR)

ONE STATUTE MILE

Outbound: September 19, 20, 1804
Return: August 27, 28, 1806

EXPLORATIONS OF LEWIS AND CLARK   1804 - 1806
CARTOGRAPHIC RECONSTRUCTION

LOWER BRULE

South Dakota

CONTOUR INTERVAL 100 FEET

UTM ZONE   14
MAP NUMBER   109

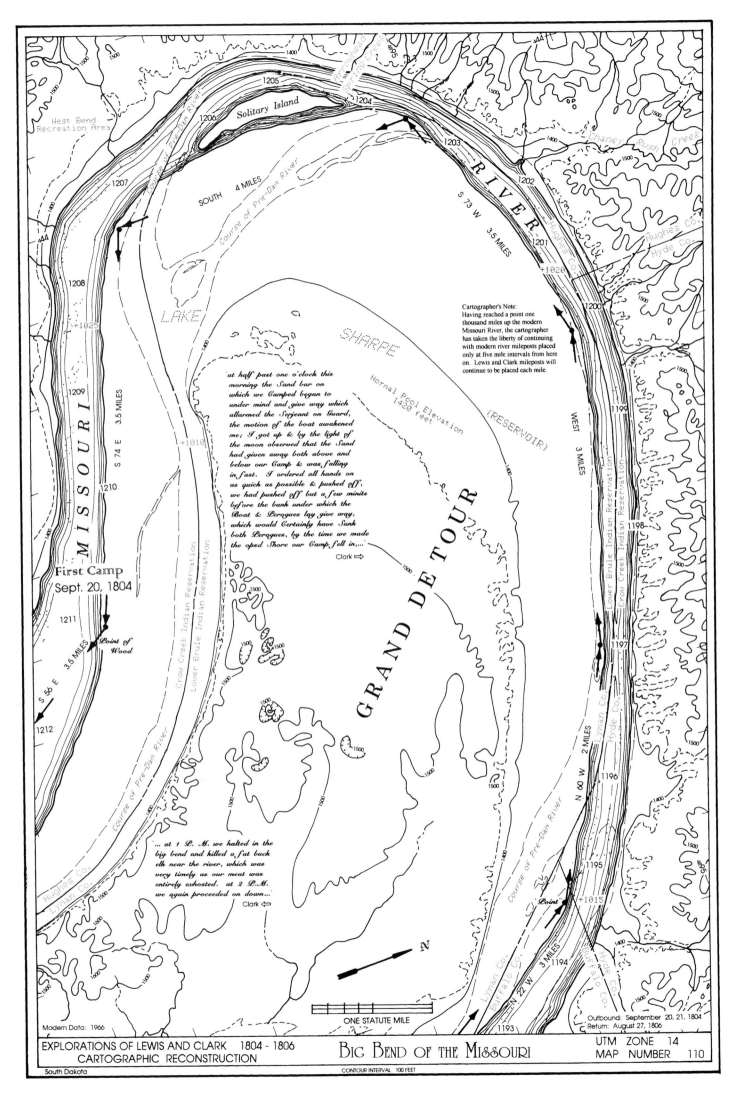

1500 1500 1400 1205 1206 1204 1207

West Bend Recreation Area

Solitary Island

Course of Pre-Dam River

1203

RIVER

S 73 W    3.5 MILES

Hughes Co.

Chaney Rush Creek

Hughes Co.

Hyde Co.

SOUTH    4 MILES

1202

1201

+1020

Cartographer's Note:
Having reached a point one thousand miles up the modern Missouri River, the cartographer has taken the liberty of continuing with modern river mileposts placed only at five mile intervals from here on. Lewis and Clark mileposts will continue to be placed each mile.

LAKE

+1025

SHARPE

Normal Pool Elevation 1420 feet

(RESERVOIR)

WEST    3 MILES

1208

1209

MISSOURI

S 74 E    3.5 MILES

+1018

1210

at half past one o'clock this morning the Sand bar on which we Camped began to under mind and give way which allarmed the Serjeant on Guard, the motion of the boat awakened me; I got up & by the light of the moon observed that the Sand had given away both above and below our Camp & was falling in fast. I ordered all hands on as quick as possible & pushed off, we had pushed off but a few minits before the bank under which the Boat & Peroques lay give way, which would Certainly have Sunk both Peroques, by the time we made the opsd Shore our Camp fell in,....
Clark ⇨

GRAND DETOUR

1199

1198

First Camp
Sept. 20, 1804

Crow Creek Indian Reservation

Lower Brule Indian Reservation

1211

Point of Wood

S 56 E    3.5 MILES

1500

1500

1500

1500

1500

1197

Lower Brule Indian Reservation

Crow Creek Indian Reservation

1212

1500

1500

N 00 W    2 MILES

Lyman Co.

Hyde Co.

1196

... at 1 P. M. we halted in the big bend and killed a fat buck elk near the river, which was very timely as our meat was entirely exhosted. at 2 P.M. we again proceeded on down...
Clark ⇦

1195

Course of Pre-Dam River

+1015

Point

Hughes Co.

Lyman Co.

N

N 22 W    3 MILES

1194

Lyman Co.

Buffalo Co.

Hyde Co.

Buffalo Co.

1193

ONE STATUTE MILE

Outbound: September 20, 21, 1804
Return: August 27, 1806

Modern Data: 1966

EXPLORATIONS OF LEWIS AND CLARK    1804 - 1806
CARTOGRAPHIC RECONSTRUCTION

South Dakota

CONTOUR INTERVAL 100 FEET

BIG BEND OF THE MISSOURI

UTM  ZONE    14
MAP  NUMBER    110

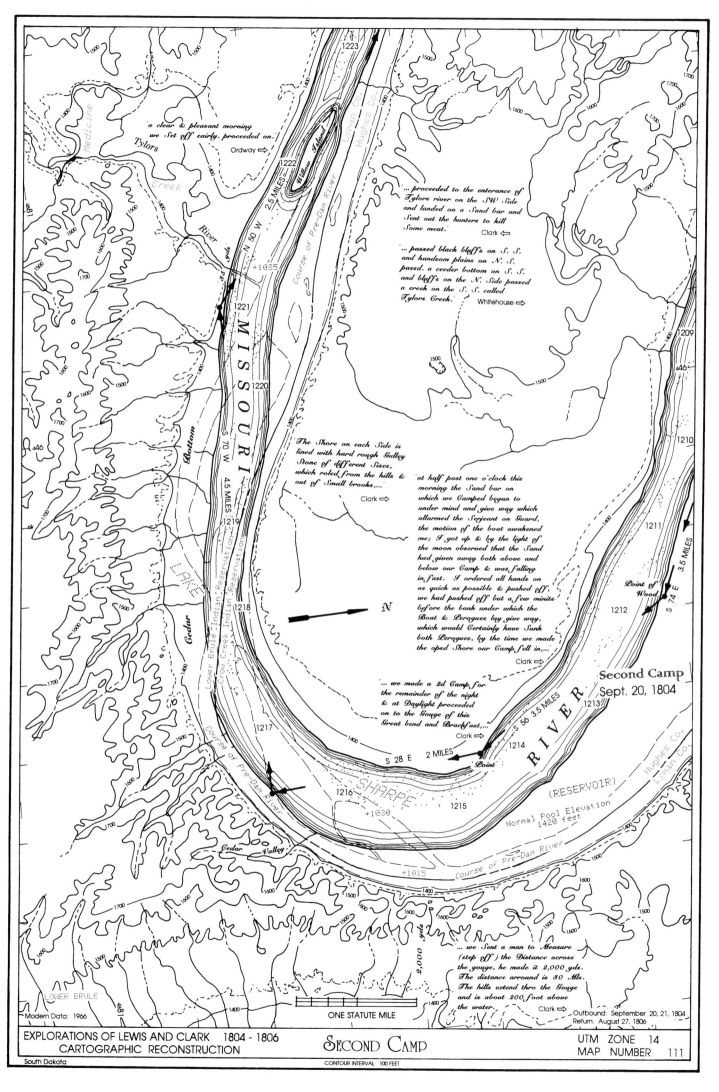

a clear & pleasant morning we Set off eairly, proceeded on." Ordway ⇒

Tylors

Medicine Creek

River

Willow Island

N 50 W 2.5 MILES

+1335

.6 yds

Course of Pre-Dam River

Lyman Co.
Hughes Co.

1223

1222

1221

1220

S 70 W 4.5 MILES

MISSOURI

1219

1218

... proceeded to the enterance of Tylors river on the SW Side and landed on a Sand bar and Sent out the hunters to kill Some meat." Clark ⇐

... passed black bluffs on S. S. and handsom plains on N. S. passd. a ceeder bottom on S. S. and bluffs on the N. Side passed a creek on the S. S. called Tylors Creek." Whitehouse ⇒

1209

1210

1211

Point of Wood

1212

S 74 E 3.5 MILES

The Shore on each Side is lined with hard rough Gulley Stone of different Sises, which roled from the hills & out of Small brooks,... Clark ⇒

at half past one o'clock this morning the Sand bar on which we Camped began to under mind and give way which allarmed the Serjeant on Guard, the motion of the boat awakened me; I got up & by the light of the moon observed that the Sand had given away both above and below our Camp & was falling in fast. I ordered all hands on as quick as possible & pushed off, we had pushed off but a few minits before the bank under which the Boat & Peroques lay give way, which would Certainly have Sunk both Peroques, by the time we made the opsd Shore our Camp fell in,... Clark ⇒

N

Lower Brule Indian Reservation
Crow Creek Indian Reservation

Cedar Bottom

446

1700

... we made a 2d Camp for the remainder of the night & at Daylight proceeded on to the Gouge of this Great bend and Brackfast,... Clark ⇒

S 56 3.5 MILES

1213

RIVER

Second Camp
Sept. 20, 1804

1214

S 28 E 2 MILES

Point

1217

1216

SHARPE

+1090

1215

(RESERVOIR)

Normal Pool Elevation 1420 feet

LAKE

Cedar Valley

Course of Pre-Dam River

+1015

Course of Pre-Dam River

2,000 yds

... we Sent a man to Measure (step off) the Distance across the gouge, he made it 2,000 yds. The distance arround is 30 Mls. The hills extend thro the Gouge and is about 200 foot above the water." Clark ⇒

Outbound: September 20, 21, 1804
Return: August 27, 1806

LOWER BRULE

Modern Data: 1966

ONE STATUTE MILE

EXPLORATIONS OF LEWIS AND CLARK 1804 - 1806
CARTOGRAPHIC RECONSTRUCTION

SECOND CAMP

UTM ZONE 14
MAP NUMBER 111

South Dakota

CONTOUR INTERVAL 100 FEET

135

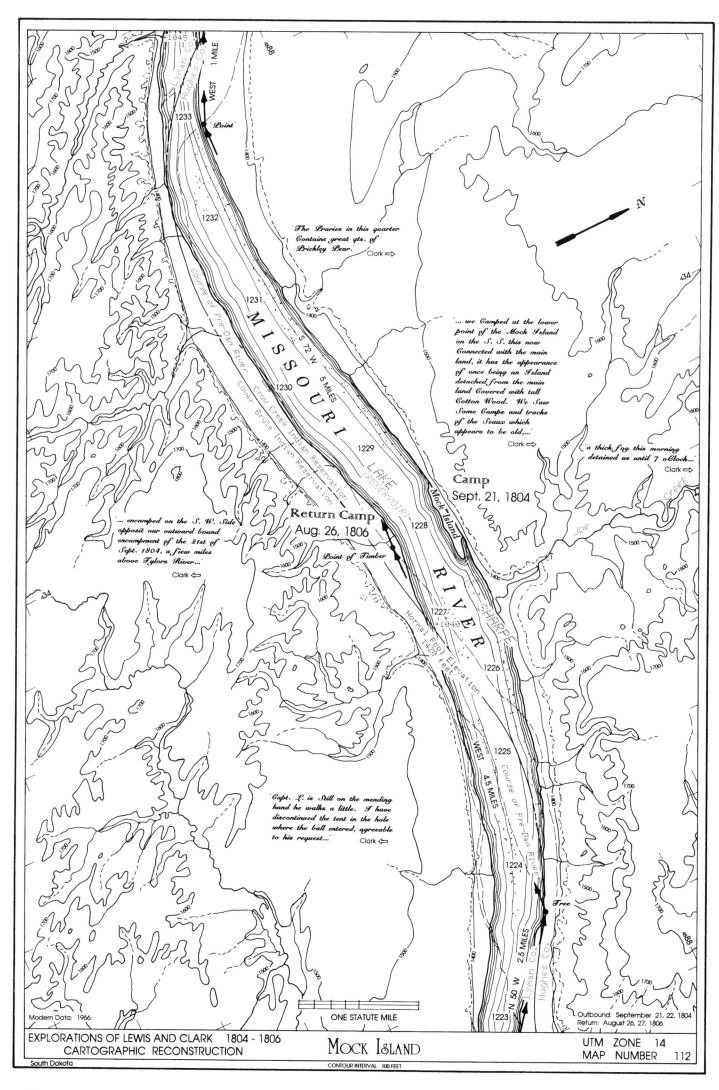

The Praries in this quarter
Contains great qts. of
Prickley Pear.
Clark ⟹

... we Camped at the lower
point of the Mock Island
on the S. S. this now
Connected with the main
land, it has the appearance
of once being an Island
detached from the main
land Covered with tall
Cotton Wood. We Saw
Some Camps and tracks
of the Seaux which
appears to be old,...
Clark ⟹

a thick fog this morning
detained us until 7 oClock...
Clark ⟹

Camp
Sept. 21, 1804

Return Camp
Aug. 26, 1806

... encamped on the S. W. Side
opposit our outward bound
encampment of the 21st of
Sept. 1804, a fiew miles
above Tylors River...
Clark ⟸

Point of Timber

Capt. L. is Still on the mending
hand he walks a little. I have
discontinued the tent in the hole
where the ball entered, agreeable
to his request...
Clark ⟸

WEST 1 MILE
Point

MISSOURI

S 72 W 5 MILES

RIVER

Normal Pool Elevation 1420 feet

WEST 4.5 MILES

N 50 W 2.5 MILES

Tree

ONE STATUTE MILE

Modern Data: 1966

Outbound: September 21, 22, 1804
Return: August 26, 27, 1806

EXPLORATIONS OF LEWIS AND CLARK   1804 - 1806
CARTOGRAPHIC RECONSTRUCTION

MOCK ISLAND

UTM  ZONE  14
MAP  NUMBER  112

South Dakota

CONTOUR INTERVAL  100 FEET

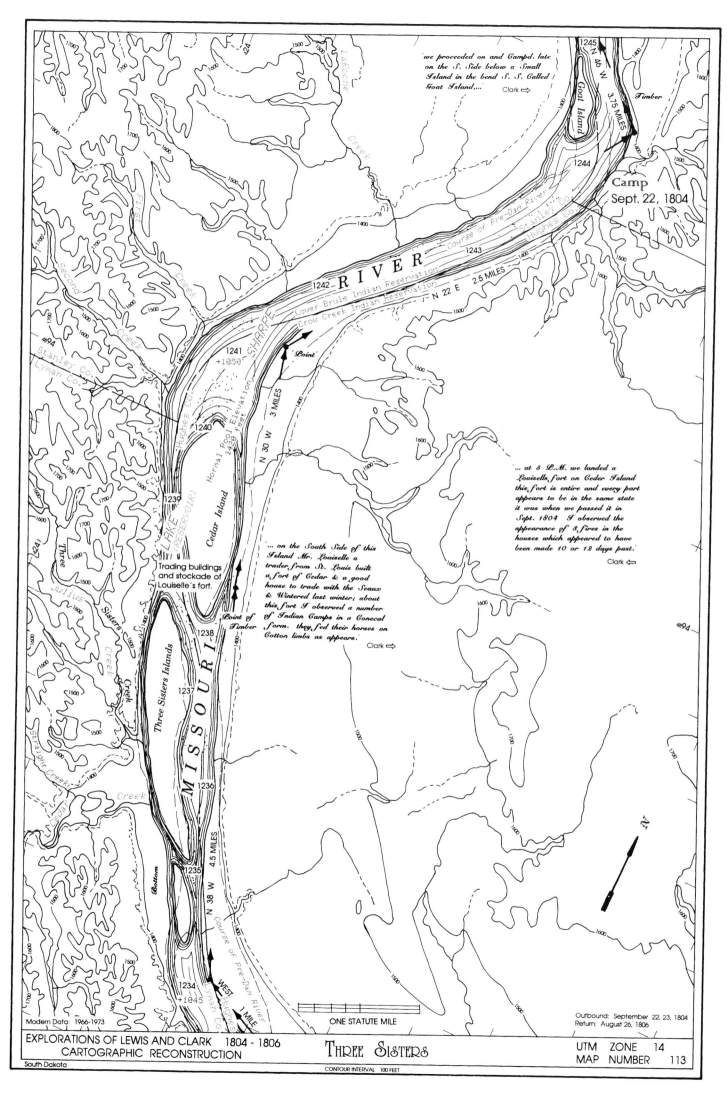

we proceeded on and Campd. late
on the S. Side below a Small
Island in the bend S. S. Called
Goat Island,...      Clark ⇨

1245
N 46 W
3.75 MILES

Goat Island

Timber

1244

Camp
Sept. 22, 1804

LaRoche Creek

Course of Pre-Dam River

1243

Stanley Co.

1242   R I V E R

Lower Brule Indian Reservation

Crow Creek Indian Reservation

N 22 E   2.5 MILES

First Creek

Second Creek

Yeckson Creek

4894

Stanley Co.
Lyman Co.
Hughes Co.

1241
+1850

Point

N 30 W   3 MILES

1240

Normal Pool Elevation
1420 feet

1239

LAKE
(RESERVOIR)

Cedar Island

... at 5 P.M. we landed a
Louisells fort on Ceder Island
this fort is entire and every part
appears to be in the same state
it was when we passed it in
Sept. 1804  I observed the
appearance of 3 fires in the
houses which appeared to have
been made 10 or 12 days past.
                    Clark ⇦

Trading buildings
and stockade of
Louiselle's fort.

Three Julius Sisters Creek

Cutright Creek

Straight Creek

Three Sisters Islands

... on the South Side of this
Island Mr. Louiselle a
trader from St. Louis built
a fort of Cedar & a good
house to trade with the Seaux
& Wintered last winter; about
this fort I observed a number
of Indian Camps in a Conecal
form. they fed their horses on
Cotton limbs as appears.
                Clark ⇨

Point of
Timber

1238

1237

M I S S O U R I

1236

Bottom

Creek

4894

4.5 MILES

1235

N 38 W

Course of Pre-Dam River

West Hughes Co.
Lyman Co.

1234
+1945

1 MILE

N

Modern Data: 1966-1973

ONE STATUTE MILE

Outbound: September 22, 23, 1804
Return: August 26, 1806

EXPLORATIONS OF LEWIS AND CLARK  1804 - 1806
CARTOGRAPHIC RECONSTRUCTION
South Dakota

THREE SISTERS

CONTOUR INTERVAL  100 FEET

UTM  ZONE  14
MAP NUMBER  113

137

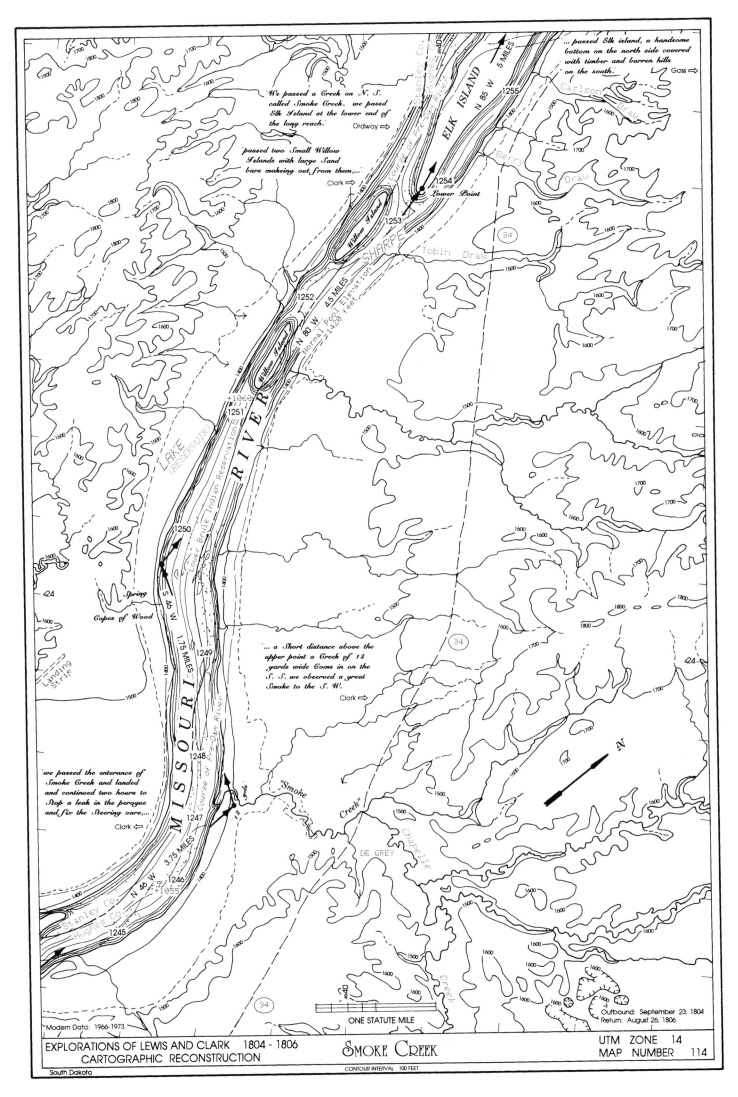

We passed a Creek on N. S.
called Smoke Creek. we passed
Elk Island at the lower end of
the long reach.
Ordway ⇒

passed two Small Willow
Islands with large Sand
bars makeing out from them,...
Clark ⇒

... passed Elk island, a handsome
bottom on the north side covered
with timber and barren hills
on the south.
Gass ⇒

ELK ISLAND

N 85 W    5 MILES

1255

Carlson Draw

Course of Pre-Dam River

Stanley Co.
Hughes Co.

1254
Lower Point

1253

SHARPE

Barry

34

Tobin Draw

1252

N 80 W    4.5 MILES

Normal Pool Elevation
1423 feet

Willow Island

1251

N 80 W

+1060

LAKE
(RESERVOIR)

Lower Brule Indian Reservation

MISSOURI    RIVER

1250

S 46 W    1.75 MILES

Spring

Copes of Wood

424

Landing
Strip

1600

1249

... a Short distance above the
upper point a Creek of 12
yards wide Coms in on the
S. S. we observed a great
Smoke to the S. W.
Clark ⇒

34

424

1248

N

1247

we passed the enterance of
Smoke Creek and landed
and continued two hours to
Stop a leak in the perogue
and fix the Steering oare,...
Clark ⇐

Course of Pre-Dam River

"Smoke
Creek"

Chapelle Creek

1246    N 46 W    3.75 MILES

+1055

DE GREY

Stanley Co.
Hughes Co.

1245

34

ONE STATUTE MILE

Outbound: September 23, 1804
Return: August 26, 1806

Modern Data: 1966-1973

EXPLORATIONS OF LEWIS AND CLARK    1804 - 1806
CARTOGRAPHIC RECONSTRUCTION

SMOKE CREEK

UTM    ZONE    14

MAP    NUMBER    114

South Dakota

CONTOUR INTERVAL    100 FEET

138

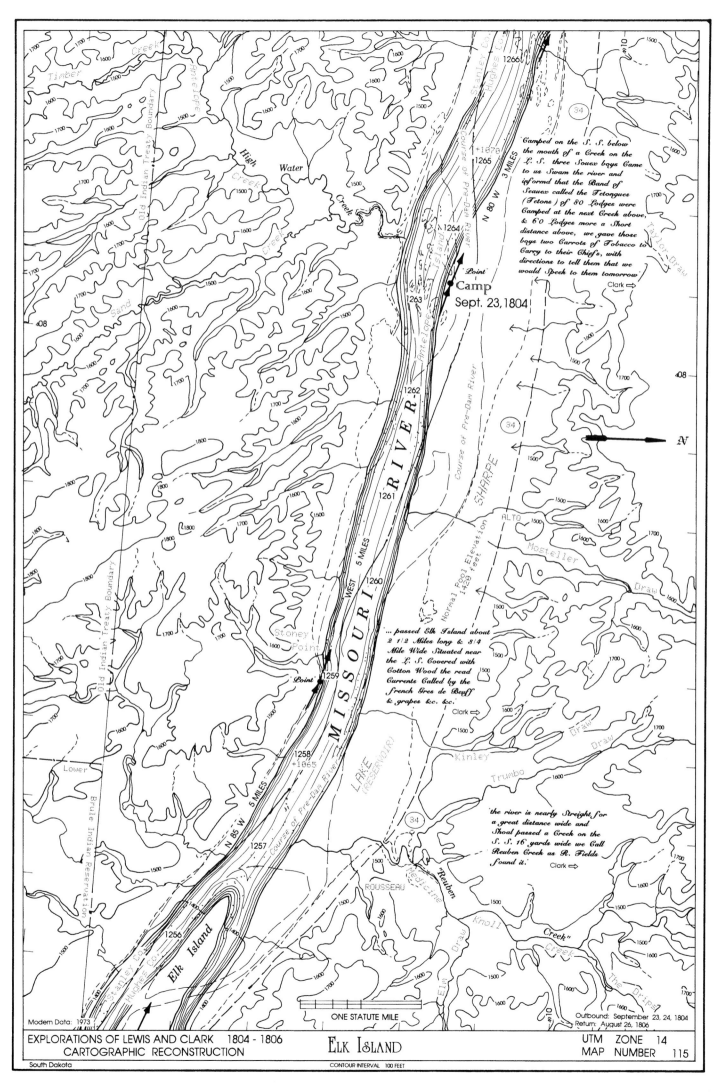

Camped on the S. S. below the mouth of a Creek on the L. S. three Souex boys Came to us Swam the river and informd that the Band of Seauex called the Tetongues (Tetons) of 80 Lodges were Camped at the next Creek above, & 60 Lodges more a Short distance above, we gave those boys two Carrots of Tobacco to Carry to their Chiefs, with directions to tell them that we would Speek to them tomorrow

Clark →

... passed Elk Island about 2 1/2 Miles long & 3/4 Mile Wide Situated near the L. S. Covered with Cotton Wood the read Currents Called by the French Gres de Beuff & grapes &c. &c.

Clark ⇒

the river is nearly Streight for a great distance wide and Shoal passed a Creek on the S. S. 16 yards wide we Call Reuben Creek as R. Fields found it.

Clark ⇒

Camp Sept. 23, 1804

Point

Point

Outbound: September 23, 24, 1804
Return: August 26, 1806

ONE STATUTE MILE

EXPLORATIONS OF LEWIS AND CLARK 1804 - 1806
CARTOGRAPHIC RECONSTRUCTION

ELK ISLAND

UTM ZONE 14
MAP NUMBER 115

South Dakota

CONTOUR INTERVAL 100 FEET

Modern Data: 1973

139

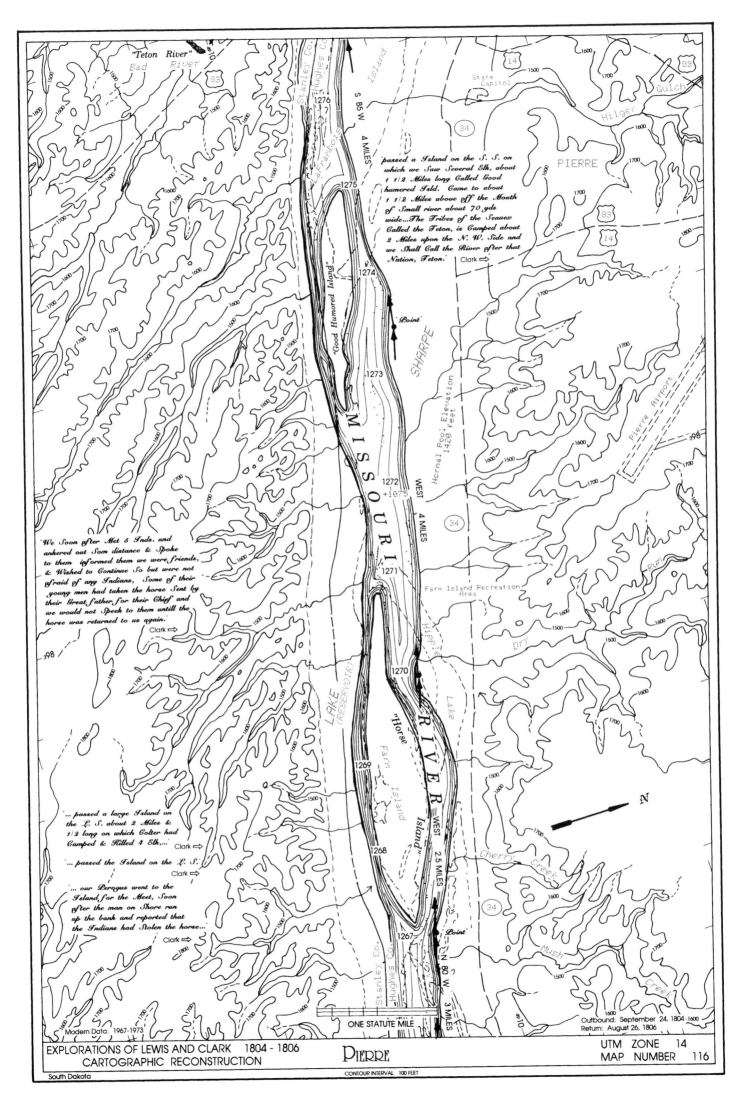

"Teton River"
Bad River

passed a Island on the S. S. on which we Saw Several Elk, about 1 1/2 Miles long Called Good humered Isld. Came to about 1 1/2 Miles above off the Mouth of Small river about 70 yds wide...The Tribes of the Seaux Called the Teton, is Camped about 2 Miles upon the N. W. Side and we Shall Call the River after that Nation, Teton. Clark ⇨

PIERRE

State Capitol

Pierre Airport

MISSOURI

"Good Humored Island"

Point

1276
1275
1274
1273
1272
+1075
1271
1270
1269
1268
1267

S 85 W 4 MILES
WEST 4 MILES

Normal Pool Elevation 1421 feet

Farm Island Recreation Area

RIVER

LAKE (RESERVOIR)

"Horse Island"

Farm Island

We Soon after Met 5 Inds. and ankered out Som distance & Spoke to them informed them we were friends, & Wished to Continue So but were not afraid of any Indians, Some of their young men had taken the horse Sent by their Great father for their Chief and we would not Speek to them untill the horse was returned to us again. Clark ⇨

...passed a large Island on the L. S. about 2 Miles & 1/2 long on which Colter had Camped & Killed 4 Elk,... Clark ⇨

...passed the Island on the L. S. Clark ⇨

...our Perogue went to the Island for the Meet, Soon after the man on Shore run up the bank and reported that the Indians had Stolen the horse... Clark ⇨

WEST 2.5 MILES

Point

N 80 W 3 MILES

N

Cherry Creek

Mush Creek

Modern Data: 1967-1973

ONE STATUTE MILE

Outbound: September 24, 1804-1806
Return: August 26, 1806

EXPLORATIONS OF LEWIS AND CLARK 1804 - 1806
CARTOGRAPHIC RECONSTRUCTION

PIERRE

UTM ZONE 14
MAP NUMBER 116

South Dakota

CONTOUR INTERVAL 100 FEET

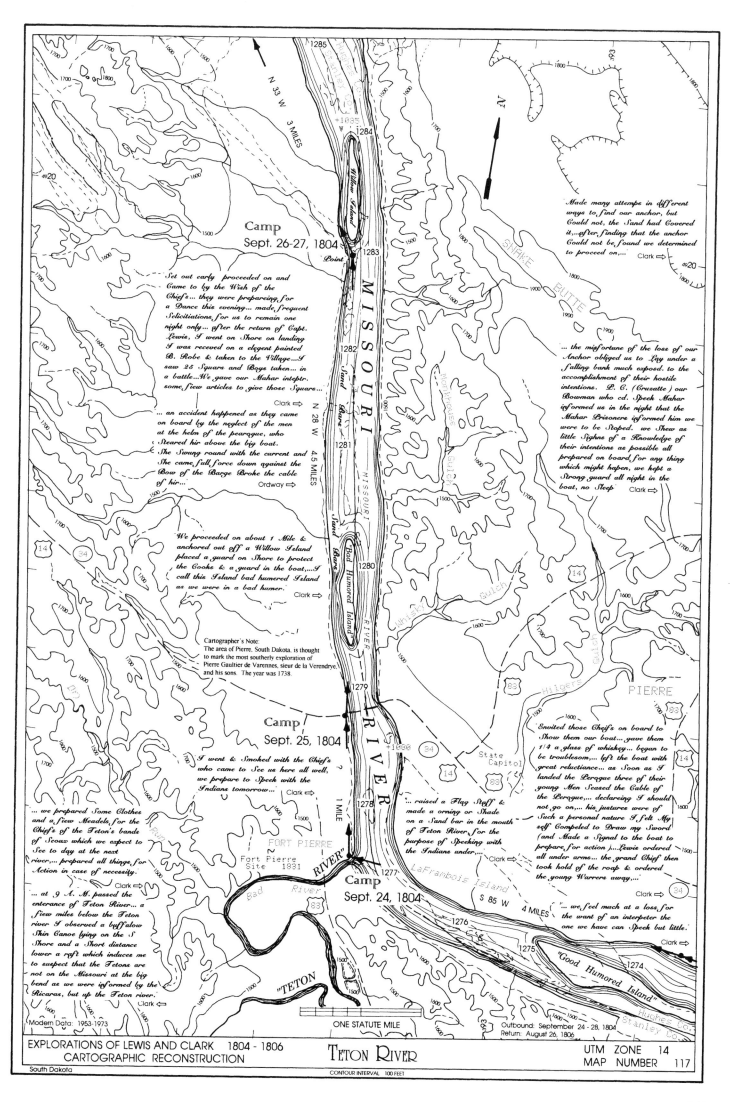

Camp
Sept. 26-27, 1804

Set out early proceeded on and
Came to by the Wish of the
Chief's... they were prepareing, for
a Dance this evening... made frequent
Solicitiations, for us to remain one
night only... after the return of Capt.
Lewis, I went on Shore on landing
I was received on a elegent painted
B. Robe & taken to the Village...I
saw 25 Squars and Boys taken... in
a battle...We gave our Mahar inteptr.
some fiew articles to give those Squars...

Clark ⇒

... an accident happened as they came
on board by the neglect of the men
at the helm of the pearogue, who
Steared hir above the big boat.
She Swung round with the current and
She came full force down against the
Bow of the Barge Broke the cable
of hir...

Ordway ⇒

We proceeded on about 1 Mile &
anchored out off a Willow Island
placed a guard on Shore to protect
the Cooks & a guard in the boat,...I
call this Island bad humered Island
as we were in a bad humer.

Clark ⇒

Cartographer's Note:
The area of Pierre, South Dakota, is thought
to mark the most southerly exploration of
Pierre Gaultier de Varennes, sieur de la Verendrye,
and his sons. The year was 1738.

Camp
Sept. 25, 1804

I went & Smoked with the Chief's
who came to See us here all well,
we prepare to Speek with the
Indians tomorrow...

Clark ⇒

... we prepared Some Clothes
and a fiew Meadels, for the
Chief's of the Teton's bands
of Seoux which we expect to
See to day at the next
river,... prepared all things for
Action in case of necessity.

Clark ⇒

... at 9 A. M. passed the
enterance of Teton River... a
fiew miles below the Teton
river I observed a buffalow
Skin Canoe lying on the S
Shore and a Short distance
lower a raft which induces me
to suspect that the Tetons are
not on the Missouri at the big
bend as we were informed by the
Ricaras, but up the Teton river.

Clark ⇐

Modern Data: 1953-1973

FORT PIERRE

Fort Pierre
Site 1831

"TETON"

ONE STATUTE MILE

EXPLORATIONS OF LEWIS AND CLARK    1804 - 1806
CARTOGRAPHIC RECONSTRUCTION

South Dakota

TETON RIVER

CONTOUR INTERVAL  100 FEET

Made many attemps in different
ways to find our anchor, but
Could not, the Sand had Covered
it,...after finding that the anchor
Could not be found we determined
to proceed on,...

Clark ⇒

SNAKE BUTTE

... the misfortune of the loss of our
Anchor obliged us to Lay under a
falling bank much exposd. to the
accomplishment of their hostile
intentions. L. C. ( Cruzatte ) our
Bowman who cd. Speek Mahar
informed us in the night that the
Mahar Prisoners informed him we
were to be Stoped. we Shew as
little Sighns of a Knowledge of
their intentions as possible all
prepared on board, for any thing
which might hapen, we kept a
Strong guard all night in the
boat, no Sleep

Clark ⇒

PIERRE

State
Capitol

Envited those Chief's on board to
Show them our boat... gave them
1/4 a glass of whiskey... began to
be troublesom,... left the boat with
great reluctiance... as Soon as I
landed the Perogue three of their
young Men Seased the Cable of
the Perogue,... declaring I should
not go on,... his justures were of
Such a personal nature I felt My
self Compeled to Draw my Sword
(and Made a Signal to the boat to
prepare for action )...Lewis ordered
all under arms... the grand Chief then
took hold of the roap & ordered
the young Warrers awey,...

Clark ⇒

...raised a Flag Staff &
made a orning or Shade
on a Sand bar in the mouth
of Teton River for the
purpose of Speeking with
the Indians under,...

Clark ⇒

Camp
Sept. 24, 1804

LaFrambois Island

S 85 W

4 MILES

... we feel much at a loss for
the want of an interpeter the
one we have can Speek but little.

Clark ⇒

"Good Humored Island"

Outbound: September 24 - 28, 1804
Return: August 26, 1806

UTM ZONE    14
MAP NUMBER   117

141

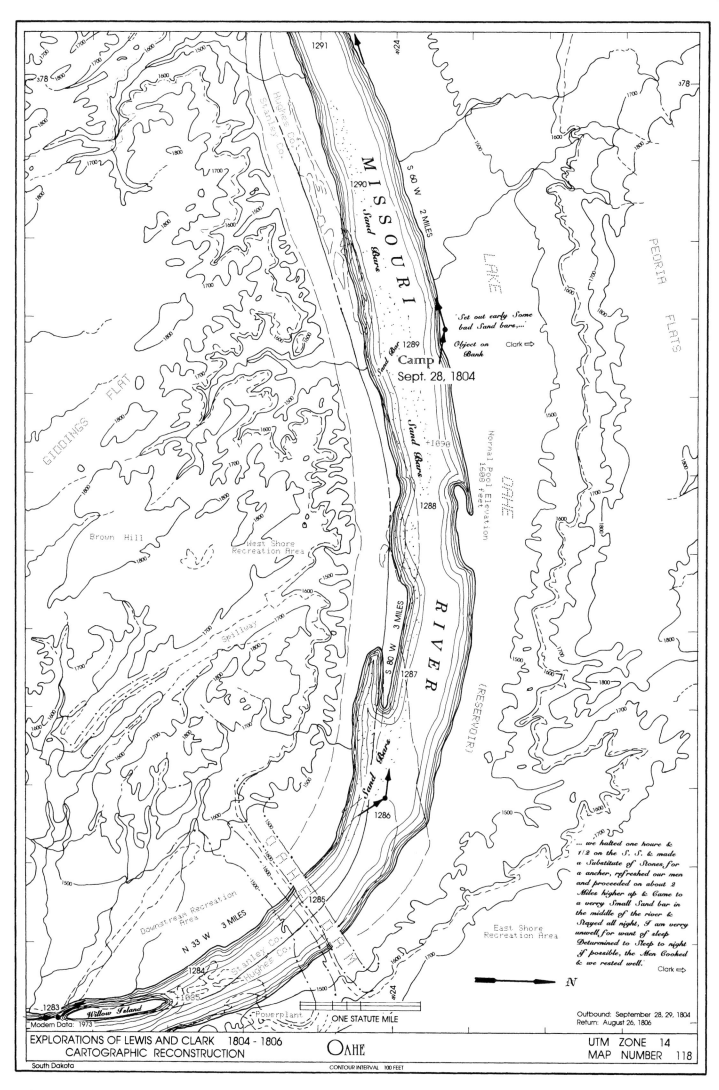

1291

ᴎ24

1290

S 60 W
2 MILES

MISSOURI

*Sand
Bars*

*Set out early Some
bad Sand bars,...*

*Sand Bar* 1289

*Object on
Bank*            Clark ⇨

Camp
Sept. 28, 1804

*Sand Bars*

+1696

LAKE

*Normal Pool Elevation
1608 feet*

1288

GIDDINGS FLAT

PEORIA FLATS

Brown Hill

West Shore
Recreation Area

OAHE

RIVER

Spillway

S 80 W
3 MILES

1287

(RESERVOIR)

*Sand Bars*

1286

*... we halted one houre &
1/2 on the S. S. & made
a Substitute of Stones, for
a ancher, refreshed our men
and proceeded on about 2
Miles higher up & Came to
a verry Small Sand bar in
the middle of the river &
Stayed all night, I am verry
unwell for want of sleep
Determined to Sleep to night
if possible, the Men Cooked
& we rested well.*

Downstream Recreation
Area

N 33 W
3 MILES

1285

East Shore
Recreation Area

Clark ⇨

Stanley Co.
Hughes Co.

N

1284

ᴎ24

+1695

1283

Willow Island

Modern Data: 1973

Powerplant

ONE STATUTE MILE

Outbound: September 28, 29, 1804
Return: August 26, 1806

EXPLORATIONS OF LEWIS AND CLARK    1804 - 1806
CARTOGRAPHIC RECONSTRUCTION

OAHE

UTM  ZONE    14
MAP  NUMBER  118

South Dakota

CONTOUR INTERVAL  100 FEET

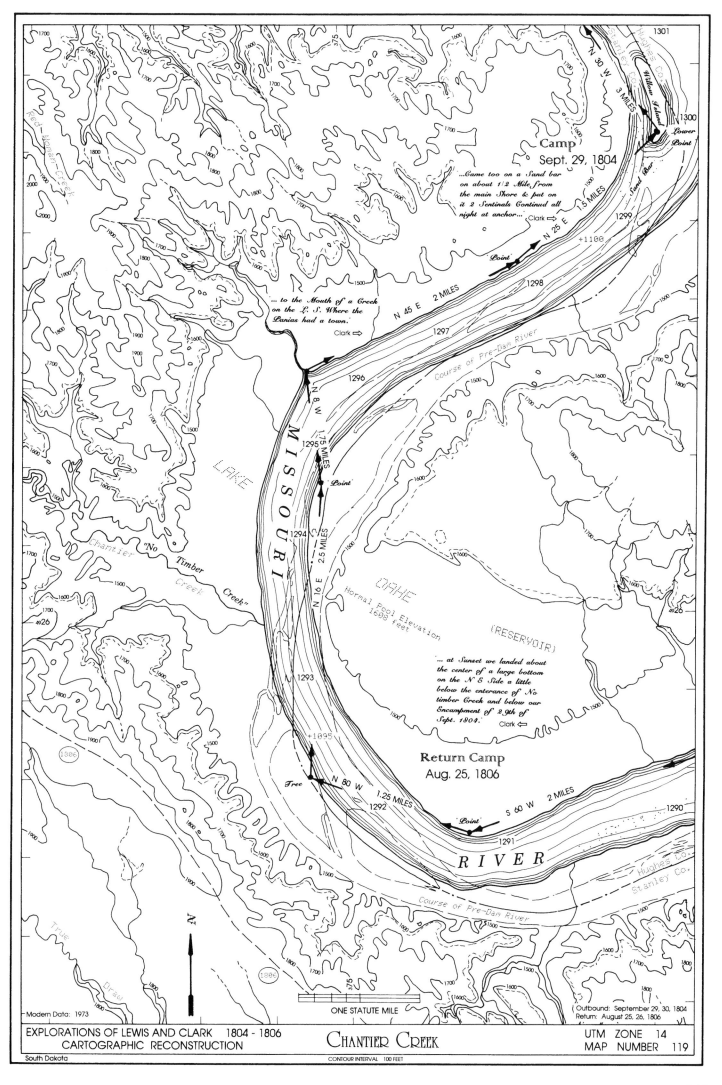

Camp
Sept. 29, 1804

*...Came too on a Sand bar
on about 1/2 Mile from
the main Shore & put on
it 2 Sentinals Continud all
night at anchor....*
Clark ⇒   N 25 E

*Point*

*... to the Mouth of a Creek
on the L. S. Where the
Panias had a town.*
Clark ⇒

N 45 E   2 MILES

1.5 MILES

+1100

1298

1297

1296

N 8 W

1.75 MILES

1295

*Point*

N 16 E   2.5 MILES

1294

1293

+1095

*Tree*   N 80 W

1.25 MILES

1292

LAKE

MISSOURI

Chantier   "No   Timber   Creek"

Course of Pre-Dam River

OAHE

Normal Pool Elevation
1608 feet

(RESERVOIR)

*... at Sunset we landed about
the center of a large bottom
on the N E Side a little
below the enterance of No
timber Creek and below our
Encampment of 29th of
Sept. 1804.*
Clark ⇐

Return Camp
Aug. 25, 1806

*Point*   S 60 W   2 MILES

1291   1290

R I V E R

Course of Pre-Dam River

N

1805

ONE STATUTE MILE

Modern Data: 1973

(Outbound: September 29, 30, 1804
Return: August 25, 26, 1806)

EXPLORATIONS OF LEWIS AND CLARK   1804 - 1806
CARTOGRAPHIC RECONSTRUCTION

CHANTIER CREEK

UTM   ZONE   14
MAP   NUMBER   119

South Dakota

CONTOUR INTERVAL   100 FEET

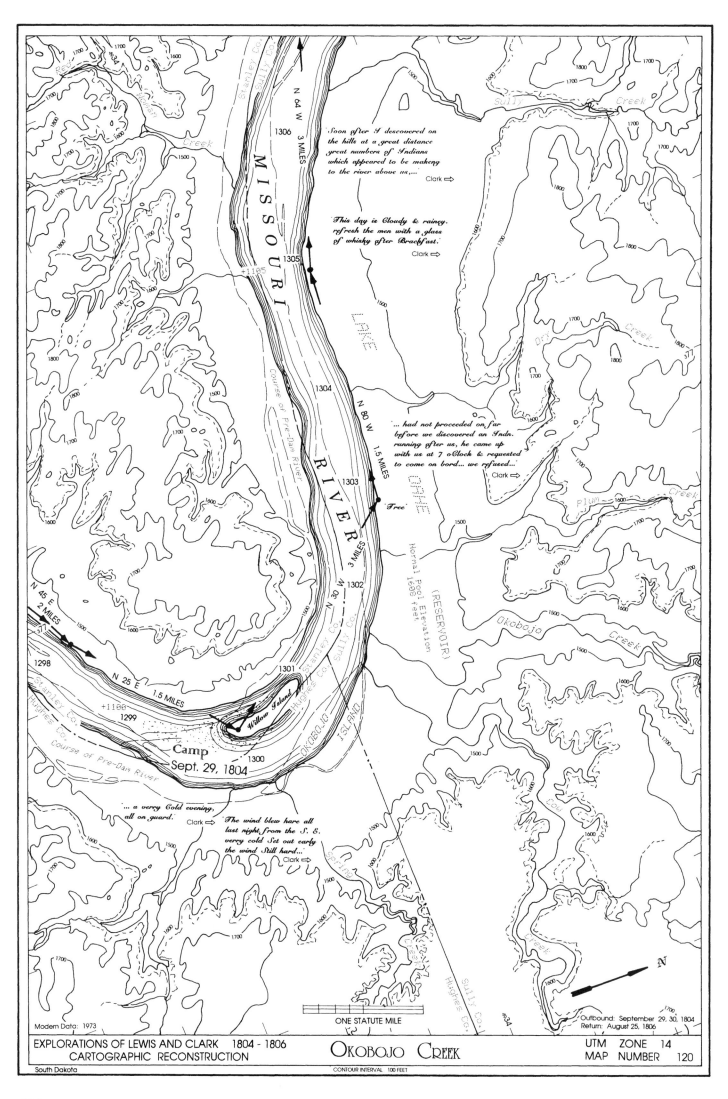

N 64 W
3 MILES

1306

*Soon after I descovered on
the hills at a great distance
great numbers of Indians
which appeared to be makeing
to the river above us,...*

Clark ⇨

*This day is Cloudy & rainey.
refresh the men with a glass
of whisky after Brackfast.*

Clark ⇨

MISSOURI

Course of Pre-Dam River

1305

+1105

LAKE

1304

N 80 W
1.5 MILES

RIVER

*... had not proceeded on far
before we discovered an Indn.
running after us, he came up
with us at 7 oClock & requested
to come on bord... we refused...*

Clark ⇨

1303

Tree

3 MILES

OAHE

Normal Pool Elevation
1600 feet

1302

1301

N 30 W

Stanley Co.

Hughes Co.

N 45 E
2 MILES

1298

N 25 E
1.5 MILES

+1100

1299

1300

Willow Island

OKOBOJO ISLAND

(RESERVOIR)

Camp
Sept. 29, 1804

Stanley Co.

Hughes Co.

Course of Pre-Dam River

*... a verry Cold evening,
all on guard.*

Clark ⇨

*The wind blew hare all
last night from the S. E.
verry cold Set out early
the wind Still hard...*

Clark ⇨

Okobojo Creek

Spring Creek

Hughes Co.

Sully Co.

N

ONE STATUTE MILE

Modern Data: 1973

Outbound: September 29, 30, 1804
Return: August 25, 1806

EXPLORATIONS OF LEWIS AND CLARK    1804 – 1806
CARTOGRAPHIC RECONSTRUCTION

OKOBOJO CREEK

UTM   ZONE   14
MAP   NUMBER   120

South Dakota

CONTOUR INTERVAL 100 FEET

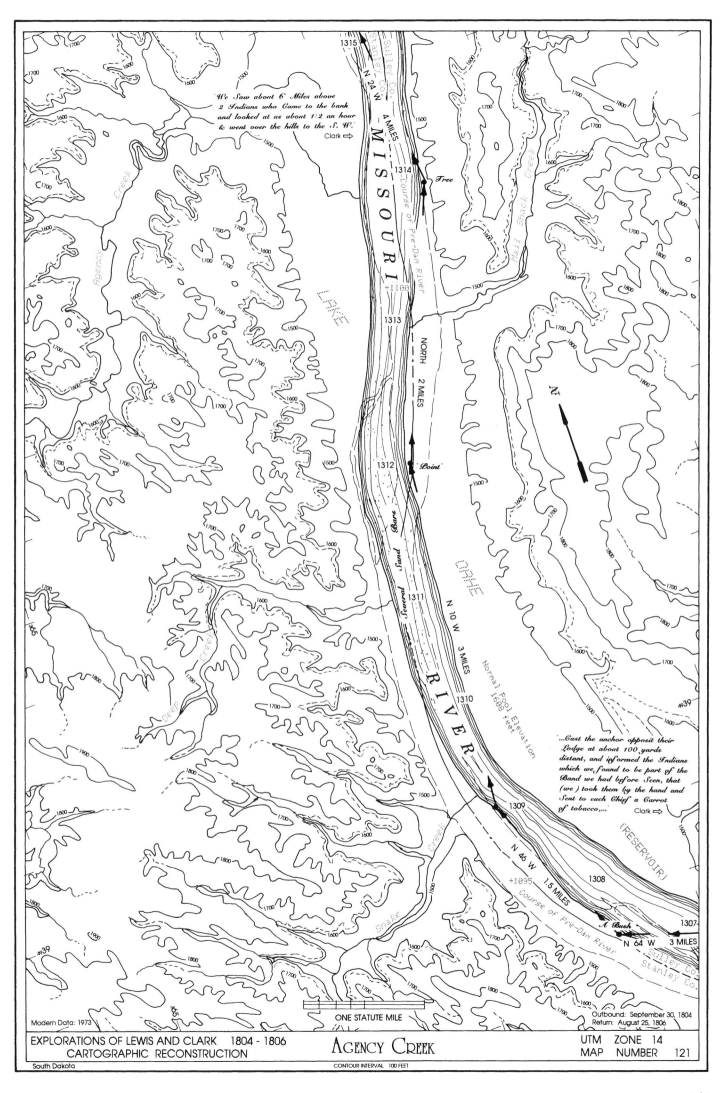

We Saw about 6 Miles above
2 Indians who Came to the bank
and looked at us about 1/2 an hour
& went over the hills to the S.W.
Clark ⇒

MISSOURI

Course of Pre-Dam River

Stanley Co.
Sulley Co.

Mail Shack Creek

1315

1314    Tree

N 24 W
4 MILES

1313

LAKE

NORTH
2 MILES

N↑

1312    Point

Several Sand Bars

OAHE

1311

N 10 W
3 MILES

Normal Pool Elevation 1692 feet

1310

RIVER

...Cast the anchor opposit their
Lodge at about 100 yards
distant, and informed the Indians
which we found to be part of the
Band we had before Seen, that
(we ) took them by the hand and
Sent to each Chief a Carrot
of tobacco,...
Clark ⇒

Agency Creek

Creek

Snake Creek

1309

(RESERVOIR)

N 46 W
+1895    1.5 MILES

Course of Pre-Dam River

1308

A Bush

N 64 W    3 MILES

1307

Sulley Co.
Stanley Co.

Modern Data: 1973

ONE STATUTE MILE

Outbound: September 30, 1804
Return: August 25, 1806

EXPLORATIONS OF LEWIS AND CLARK    1804 - 1806
CARTOGRAPHIC RECONSTRUCTION

AGENCY CREEK

UTM    ZONE    14
MAP    NUMBER    121

South Dakota

CONTOUR INTERVAL    100 FEET

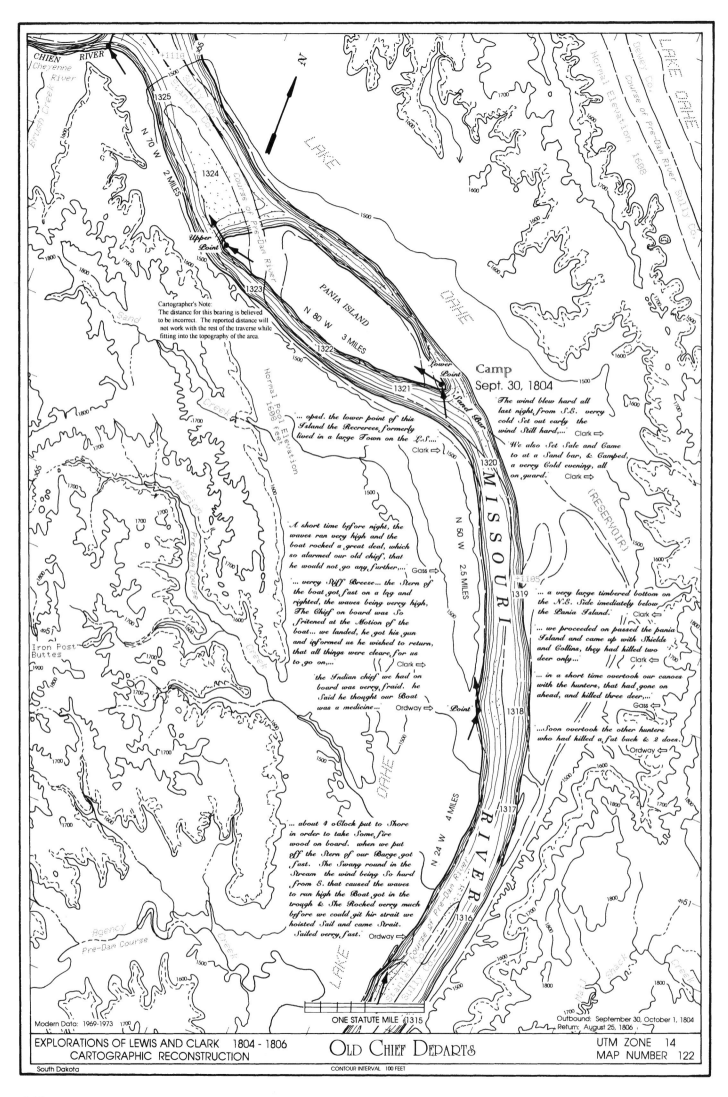

CHIEN RIVER
Cheyenne River

Brush Creek Course

+1118

1500

1325

1324

N 70 W 2 MILES

Upper Point

1500

1323

Cartographer's Note:
The distance for this bearing is believed
to be incorrect. The reported distance will
not work with the rest of the traverse while
fitting into the topography of the area.

N 80 W 3 MILES

1322

PANIA ISLAND

Lower Point

Camp
Sept. 30, 1804

The wind blew hard all
last night from S.E. verry
cold Set out early the
wind Still hard,... Clark ⇨

We also Set Sale and Came
to at a Sand bar, & Camped,
a verry Cold evening, all
on guard. Clark ⇨

... opsd. the lower point of this
Island the Recrerees, formerly
lived in a large Town on the L.S.....
Clark ⇨

Sand Bar

1320

MISSOURI

A short time before night, the
waves ran very high and the
boat rocked a great deal, which
so alarmed our old chief, that
he would not go any further,...
Gass ⇨

... verry Stiff Breeze... the Stern of
the boat got fast on a log and
righted, the waves being verry high,
The Chief on board was So
fritened at the Motion of the
boat... we landed, he got his gun
and informed us he wished to return,
that all things were cleare for us
to go on,... Clark ⇨

the Indian chief we had on
board was verry fraid. he
Said he thought our Boat
was a medicine... Ordway ⇨

N 50 W 2.5 MILES

+1105

1319

... a very large timbered bottom on
the N.E. Side imediately below
the Pania Island. Clark ⇨

... we proceeded on passed the pania
Island and came up with Shields
and Collins, they had killed two
deer only... Clark ⇨

... in a short time overtook our canoes
with the hunters, that had gone on
ahead, and killed three deer,...
Gass ⇨

.... Soon overtook the other hunters
who had killed a fat buck & 2 does.
Ordway ⇨

Point

1318

N 24 W 4 MILES

1317

... about 4 oClock put to Shore
in order to take Some fire
wood on board. when we put
off the Stern of our Barge got
fast. She Swang round in the
Stream the wind being So hard
from E. that caused the waves
to run high the Boat got in the
trough & She Rocked verry much
before we could git hir strait we
hoisted Sail and came Strait.
Sailed verry fast. Ordway ⇨

1316

Iron Post Buttes

4951

RIVER

LAKE OAHE

Course of Pre-Dam River

Normal Elevation 1608

Dewey Co.

Sully Co.

(RESERVOIR)

Stanley Co. - Bully Co.

ONE STATUTE MILE 1315

Modern Data: 1969-1973

Outbound: September 30, October 1, 1804
Return: August 25, 1806

EXPLORATIONS OF LEWIS AND CLARK 1804 - 1806
CARTOGRAPHIC RECONSTRUCTION

OLD CHIEF DEPARTS

UTM ZONE 14
MAP NUMBER 122

South Dakota

CONTOUR INTERVAL 100 FEET

146

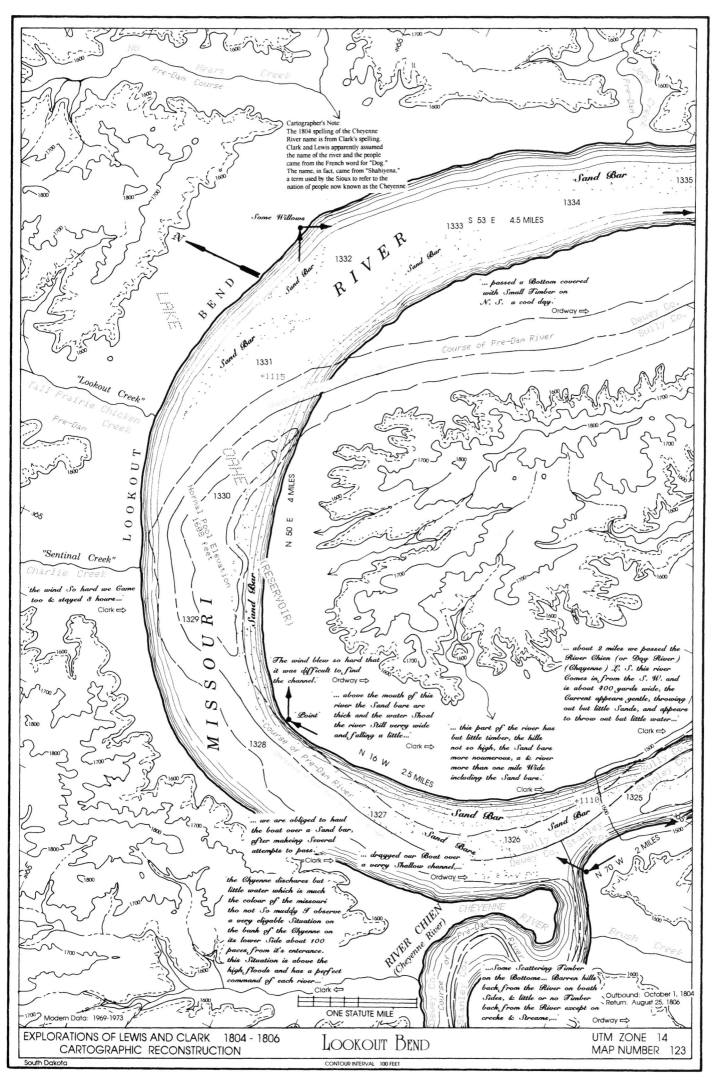

Cartographer's Note:
The 1804 spelling of the Cheyenne
River name is from Clark's spelling.
Clark and Lewis apparently assumed
the name of the river and the people
came from the French word for "Dog."
The name, in fact, came from "Shahiyena,"
a term used by the Sioux to refer to the
nation of people now known as the Cheyenne.

*Some Willows*

N

*Sand Bar* 1335

1334

1333  S 53 E   4.5 MILES

1332

*Sand Bar*

BEND

RIVER

*Sand Bar*

... passed a Bottom covered
with Small Timber on
N. S. a cool day.
Ordway ⟹

Course of Pre-Dam River

Dewey Co.
Sully Co.

*Sand Bar*

1331

+1115

"Lookout Creek"

Tall Prairie Chicken Creek

Pre-Dam

1330

N 50 E   4 MILES

LOOKOUT

"Sentinal Creek"

Charlie Creek

Normal Pool Elevation 1695 feet.

OAHE (RESERVOIR)

1329

*Sand Bar*

... about 2 miles we passed the
River Chien (or Dog River)
(Chayenne) L. S. this river
Comes in from the S. W. and
is about 400 yards wide, the
Current appears gentle, throwing
out but little Sands, and appears
to throw out but little water...
Clark ⟹

MISSOURI

the wind So hard we Came
too & stayed 3 hours...
Clark ⟹

The wind blew so hard that
it was difficult to find
the channel.
Ordway ⟹

*Point*

... above the mouth of this
river the Sand bars are
thick and the water Shoal
the river Still verry wide
and falling a little...
Clark ⟹

... this part of the river has
but little timber, the hills
not so high, the Sand bars
more noumerous, a & river
more than one mile Wide
including the Sand bars.
Clark ⟹

1328

Course of Pre-Dam River

N 16 W   2.5 MILES

+1110

*Sand Bar*

Sully Co.
Stanley Co.

1325

Stanley Co.

1327

*Sand Bar*

*Sand Bars*

1326

Sully Co.
Dewey Co.

N 70 W   2 MILES

... we are obliged to haul
the boat over a Sand bar,
after makeing Several
attempts to pass.
Clark ⟹

... dragged our Boat over
a verry Shallow channel,...
Ordway ⟹

the Chyenne dischares but
little water which is much
the colour of the missouri
tho not So muddy I observe
a very eligable Situation on
the bank of the Chyenne on
its lower Side about 100
paces from it's enterance.
this Situation is above the
high floods and has a perfect
command of each river...
Clark ⟸

RIVER CHIEN
(Cheyenne River)

Dewey Co.
Stanley Co.

CHEYENNE    RIVER

Pre-Dam River

Brush Creek

Course of

...Some Scattering Timber
on the Bottoms.... Barren hills
back from the River on boath
Sides, & little or no Timber
back from the River except on
creeks & Streams,...
Ordway ⟹

Outbound: October 1, 1804
Return: August 25, 1806

Modern Data: 1969-1973

ONE STATUTE MILE

EXPLORATIONS OF LEWIS AND CLARK   1804 - 1806
CARTOGRAPHIC RECONSTRUCTION

LOOKOUT BEND

UTM ZONE 14
MAP NUMBER 123

South Dakota

CONTOUR INTERVAL 100 FEET

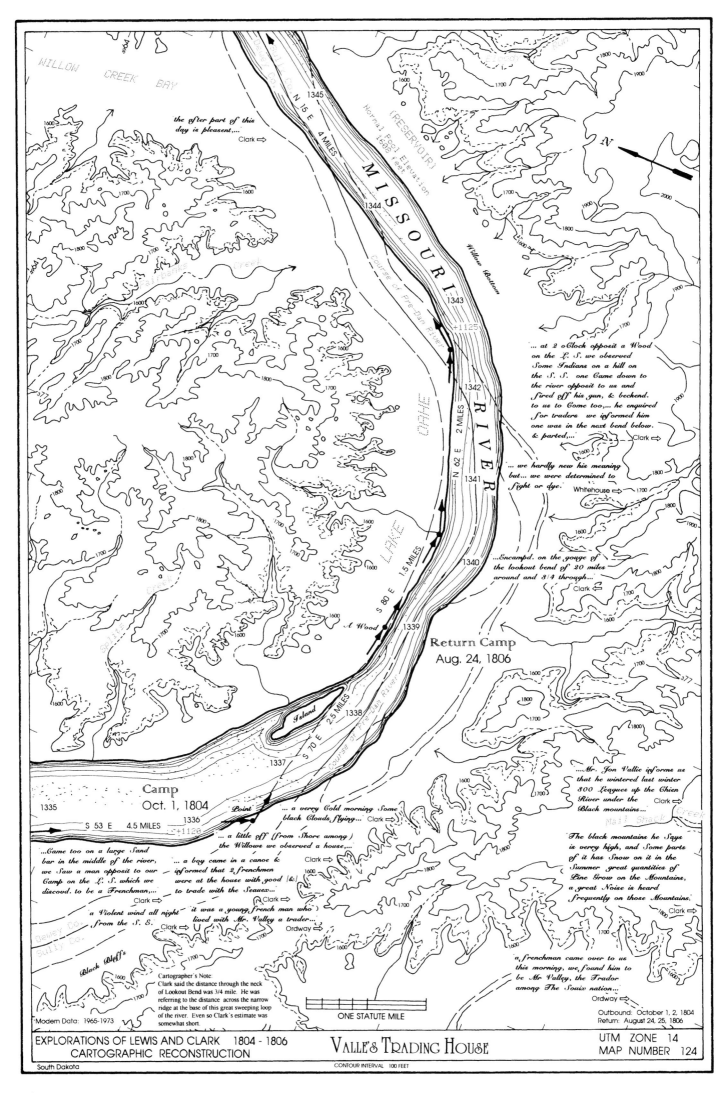

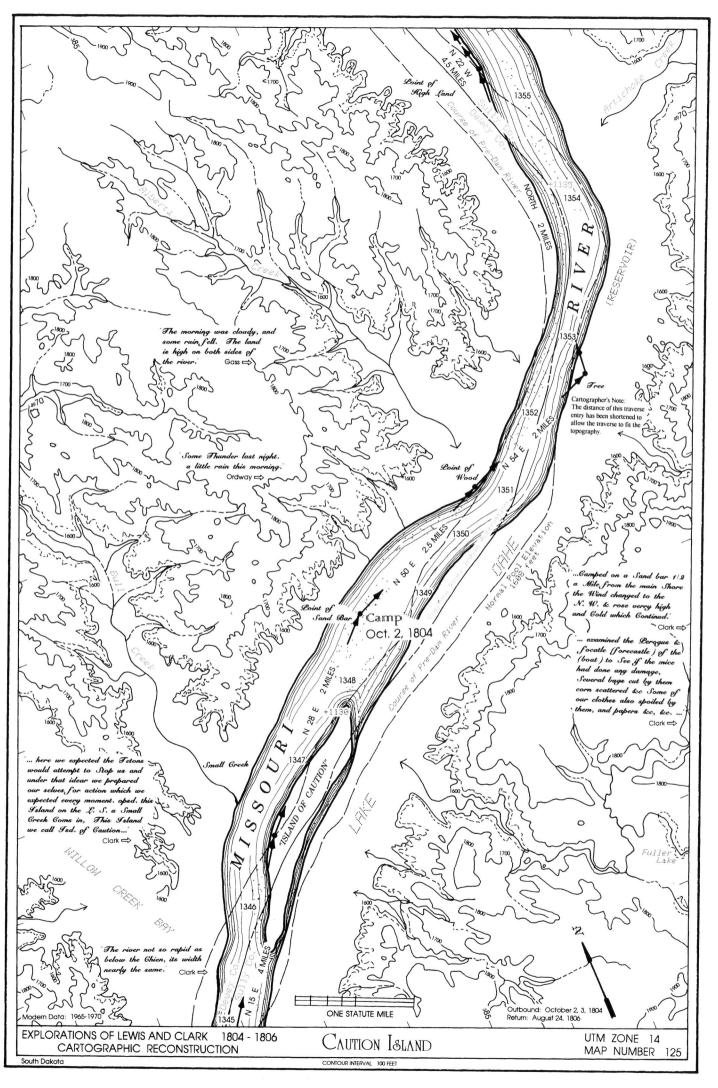

The morning was cloudy, and
some rain, fell. The land
is high on both sides of
the river.         Gass ⇨

Some Thunder last night.
a little rain this morning.
Ordway ⇨

Point of
Sand Bar      Camp
            Oct. 2, 1804

... here we expected the Tetons
would attempt to Stop us and
under that idear we prepared
our selves, for action which we
expected every moment. opsd. this
Island on the L. S. a Small
Creek Coms in, This Island
we call Isd. of Caution...
            Clark ⇨

The river not so rapid as
below the Chien, its width
nearly the same.    Clark ⇨

Modern Data: 1965-1970

Point of
High Land

Tree

Cartographer's Note:
The distance of this traverse
entry has been shortened to
allow the traverse to fit the
topography.

Point of
Wood

...Camped on a Sand bar 1/2
a Mile, from the main Shore
the Wind changed to the
N. W. & rose very high
and Cold which Continud.
            Clark ⇨

... examined the Perogus &
focatle (forecastle ) of the
(boat ) to See if the mice
had done any damage,
Several bags cut by them
corn scattered &c Some of
our clothes also spoiled by
them, and papers &c, &c. ...
            Clark ⇨

Small Creek

"ISLAND OF CAUTION"

ONE STATUTE MILE

Outbound: October 2, 3, 1804
Return: August 24, 1806

EXPLORATIONS OF LEWIS AND CLARK    1804 - 1806
CARTOGRAPHIC RECONSTRUCTION

CAUTION ISLAND

South Dakota                    CONTOUR INTERVAL  100 FEET

UTM ZONE  14
MAP NUMBER  125

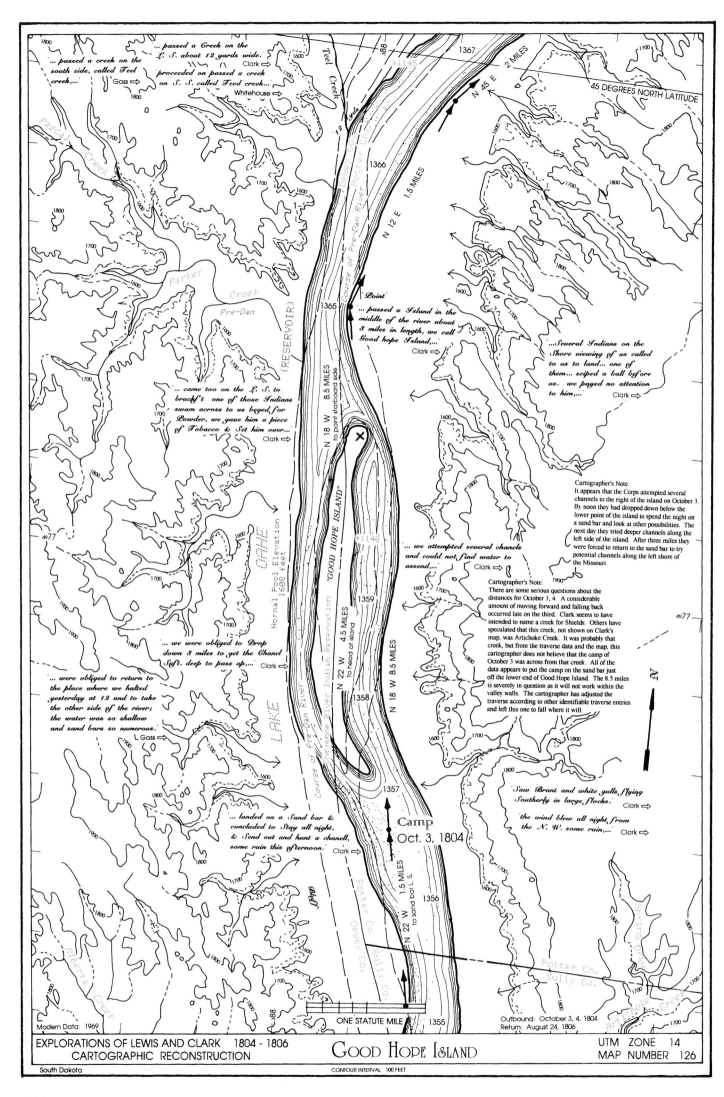

... passed a creek on the south side, called Teel creek,...   Gass ⇒

... passed a Creek on the L. S. about 12 yards wide.   Clark ⇒

proceeded on passed a creek on S. S. called Teel creek....   Whitehouse ⇒

Teel Creek

1800
1600
1700
1367
+1145
1366
N 12 E  1.5 MILES
1365

N 45 E  2 MILES

45 DEGREES NORTH LATITUDE

1700
1800

Pascal Creek
Pre-Dam

Parker    Creek
Pre-Dam

(RESERVOIR)

Course of Pre-Dam River  Potter Co.

Valley Creek

... came too on the L. S. to brackf't one of those Indians swam across to us beged for Powder, we gave him a piece of Tobacco & Set him over...   Clark ⇒

Point

... passed a Island in the middle of the river about 3 miles in length, we call Good hope Island,...   Clark ⇒

... Several Indians on the Shore viewing of us called to us to land... one of them... sciped a ball before us. we payed no attention to him,...   Clark ⇒

✗

Normal Pool Elevation 1600 feet

N 18 W  8.5 MILES to point starboard side

"GOOD HOPE ISLAND"

Cheyenne River Indian Reservation

LAKE

Course of Pre-Dam River

N 22 W  4.5 MILES to head of island

+1148

1359

1358

... we attempted several chanels and could not find water to assend,...   Clark ⇒

Cartographer's Note:
It appears that the Corps attempted several channels to the right of the island on October 3. By noon they had dropped down below the lower point of the island to spend the night on a sand bar and look at other possibilities. The next day they tried deeper channels along the left side of the island. After three miles they were forced to return to the sand bar to try potential channels along the left shore of the Missouri.

Cartographer's Note:
There are some serious questions about the distances for October 3, 4. A considerable amount of moving forward and falling back occurred late on the third. Clark seems to have intended to name a creek for Shields. Others have speculated that this creek, not shown on Clark's map, was Artichoke Creek. It was probably that creek, but from the traverse data and the map, this cartographer does not believe that the camp of October 3 was across from that creek. All of the data appears to put the camp on the sand bar just off the lower end of Good Hope Island. The 8.5 miles is severely in question as it will not work within the valley walls. The cartographer has adjusted the traverse according to other identifiable traverse entries and left this one to fall where it will.

4977

... we were obliged to Drop down 3 miles to get the Chanel Sift. deep to pass up,...   Clark ⇒

... were obliged to return to the place where we halted yesterday at 12 and to take the other side of the river; the water was so shallow and sand bars so numerous.   Gass

N 18 W  8.5 MILES

1357

1358

N 22 W  4.5 MILES

Saw Brant and white gulls flying Southerly in large flocks.   Clark ⇒

the wind blew all night from the N. W. some rain,...   Clark ⇒

... landed on a Sand bar & concluded to Stay all night, & Send out and hunt a chanell, some rain this afternoon.   Clark ⇒

Camp
Oct. 3, 1804

N 22 W  1.5 MILES to sand bar L.S.

1356

N

Bluff

Potter Co.
Dewey Co.

Potter Co.
Sully Co.

Artichoke Creek

Alberta Creek

Spring Creek

ONE STATUTE MILE

1355

Outbound: October 3, 4, 1804
Return:  August 24, 1806

Modern Data: 1969

EXPLORATIONS OF LEWIS AND CLARK   1804 - 1806
CARTOGRAPHIC RECONSTRUCTION

GOOD HOPE ISLAND

UTM ZONE   14
MAP NUMBER  126

South Dakota

CONTOUR INTERVAL  100 FEET

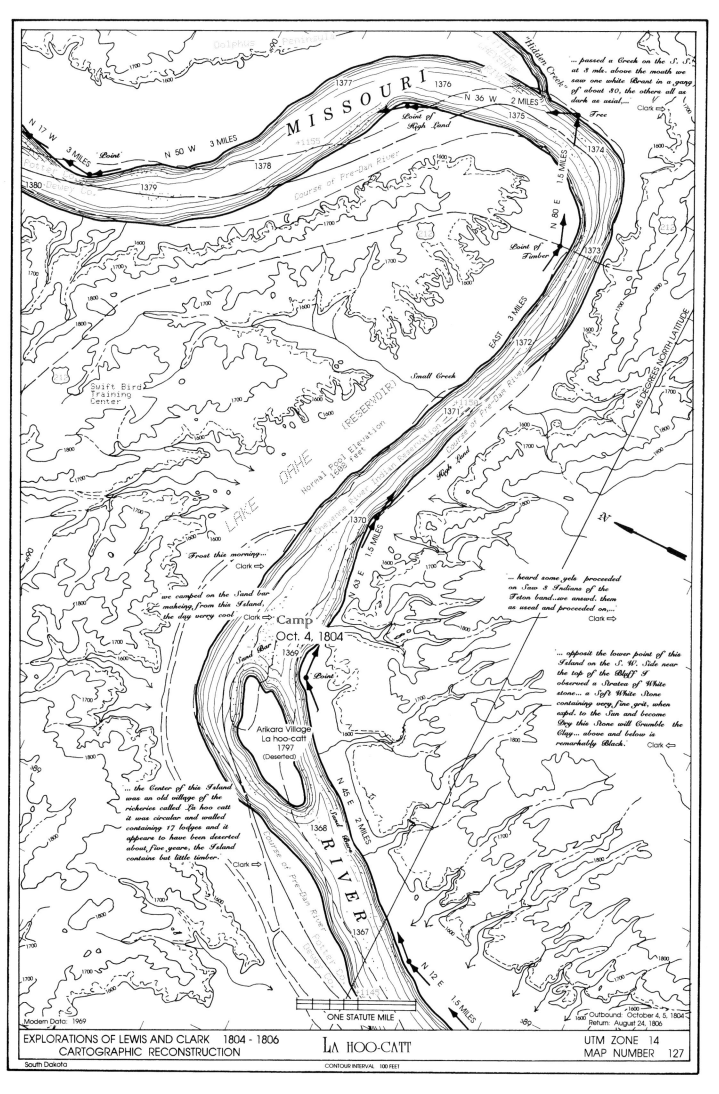

MISSOURI

1377    1376    N 36 W    2 MILES

... passed a Creek on the S. S.
at 3 mls. above the mouth we
saw one white Brant in a gang
of about 30, the others all as
dark as usial,...    Clark ⇨

N 17 W
3 MILES    Point    N 50 W    3 MILES    Point of
High Land    1375    Tree
+1155    1374
1380 Potter Co.    1379    1378    1377    1600

Dewey Co.

Course of Pre-Dam River    N 80 E    1.5 MILES    1373

Point of
Timber

211

1700    1600    EAST    3 MILES    1372

Swift Bird
Training
Center    1700    Small Creek    +1150    1371    High Land    Course of Pre-Dam River    45 DEGREES NORTH LATITUDE

LAKE    OAHE    (RESERVOIR)

Normal Pool Elevation
1608 feet

Cheyenne River Indian Reservation

1370    N 63 E    1.5 MILES

N

Frost this morning...
Clark ⇨

... heard some yels proceeded
on Saw 3 Indians of the
Teton band...we answd. them
as useal and proceeded on,...
Clark ⇨

we camped on the Sand bar
makeing from this Island,
the day verry cool    Clark ⇨    Camp
Oct. 4, 1804
1369
Point
Sand Bar

Arikara Village
La hoo-catt
1797
(Deserted)

... opposit the lower point of this
Island on the S. W. Side near
the top of the Bluff I
observed a Stratea of White
stone... a Soft White Stone
containing very fine grit, when
expd. to the Sun and become
Dry this Stone will Crumble the
Clay... above and below is
remarkably Black.    Clark ⇦

... the Center of this Island
was an old village of the
rickeries called La hoo catt
it was circular and walled
containing 17 lodges and it
appears to have been deserted
about five years, the Island
contains but little timber.
Clark ⇨

1368    Sand Bar    N 45 E    2 MILES

RIVER

1367

N 12 E

Course of Pre-Dam River

Potter Co.

Dewey Co.

1145

Modern Data: 1969

ONE STATUTE MILE

1.5 MILES

Outbound: October 4, 5, 1804
Return: August 24, 1806

EXPLORATIONS OF LEWIS AND CLARK    1804 - 1806
CARTOGRAPHIC RECONSTRUCTION    LA HOO-CATT

UTM ZONE    14
MAP NUMBER    127

South Dakota    CONTOUR INTERVAL    100 FEET

151

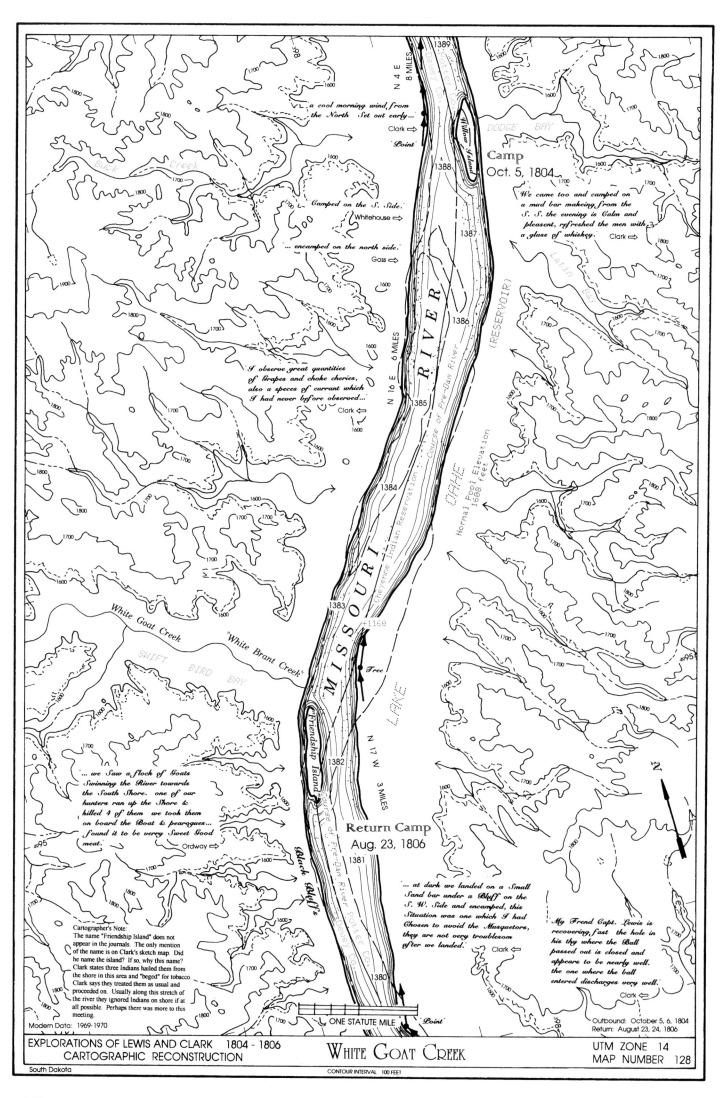

598

1800

1800

1700

1600

N 4 E
8 MILES

1389

... a cool morning wind from
the North Set out early...

Clark ⇨

*Point*

1800

DODGE BAY

1800

1388

Camp
Oct. 5, 1804

*We came too and camped on
a mud bar makeing from the
S. S. the evening is Calm and
pleasant, refreshed the men with
a glass of whiskey.*   Clark ⇨

*Willow Island*

Co. Carried Co.

1387

Camped on the S. Side.
Whitehouse ⇨

... encamped on the north side.
Gass ⇨

Latin BAY

1386

RIVER

(RESERVOIR)

*I observe great quantities
of Grapes and choke cheries,
also a speces of currant which
I had never before observed...*

N 16 E
6 MILES

1385

Clark ⇦

Course of Pre-Dam River

Cheyenne Indian Reservation

Normal Pool Elevation
1608 feet

1384

MISSOURI

+1160

1383

White Goat Creek

"White Brant Creek"

SWIFT BIRD BAY

Tree

LAKE

OAHE

"Friendship Island"

N 17 W
3 MILES

1382

*... we Saw a flock of Goats
Swinning the River towards
the South Shore. one of our
hunters ran up the Shore &
killed 4 of them  we took them
on board the Boat & pearogues...
found it to be very Sweet Good
meat.*

Return Camp
Aug. 23, 1806

1381

Ordway ⇨

4595

Course of Pre-Dam River

Black Bluffs

Potter Co.
Sully Co.

1380

*... at dark we landed on a Small
Sand bar under a Bluff on the
S. W. Side and encamped, this
Situation was one which I had
Chosen to avoid the Musquetors,
they are not very troublesom
after we landed.*   Clark ⇦

*My Frend Capt. Lewis is
recovering fast  the hole in
his thy where the Ball
passed out is closed and
appears to be nearly well.
the one where the ball
entered discharges very well.*

Clark ⇦

Cartographer's Note:
The name "Friendship Island" does not
appear in the journals. The only mention
of the name is on Clark's sketch map. Did
he name the island? If so, why this name?
Clark states three Indians hailed them from
the shore in this area and "beged" for tobacco.
Clark says they treated them as usual and
proceeded on. Usually along this stretch of
the river they ignored Indians on shore if at
all possible. Perhaps there was more to this
meeting.

Modern Data: 1969-1970

ONE STATUTE MILE

*Point*

Outbound: October 5, 6, 1804
Return: August 23, 24, 1806

EXPLORATIONS OF LEWIS AND CLARK   1804 - 1806
CARTOGRAPHIC RECONSTRUCTION

WHITE GOAT CREEK

UTM ZONE 14
MAP NUMBER 128

South Dakota

CONTOUR INTERVAL  100 FEET

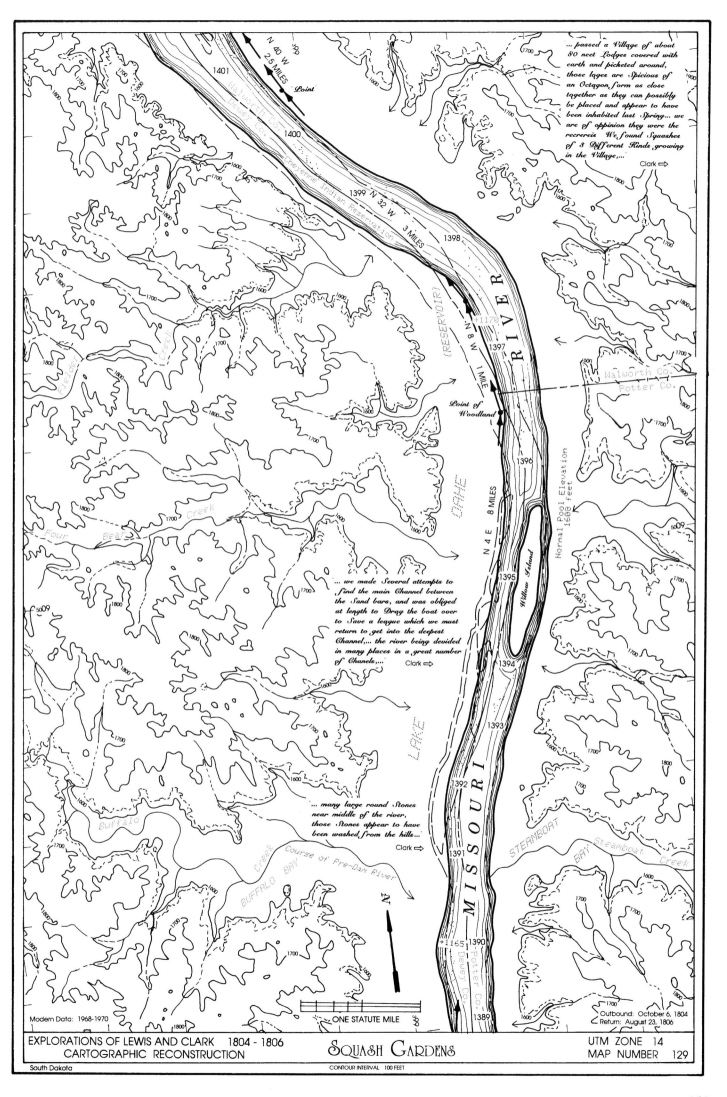

... passed a Village of about 80 neet Lodges covered with earth and picketed around, those loges are Spicious of an Octagon form as close together as they can possibly be placed and appear to have been inhabited last Spring... we are of oppinion they were the recrereis We found Squashes of 3 Different kinds growing in the Village,...
Clark ⇒

N 40 W 2.5 MILES
Point
399
1401
1400
N 32 W 3 MILES
1399
1398
1397
N 8 W 1 MILE
+1178
Point of Woodland
1396
Normal Pool Elevation 1608 feet
N 4 E 8 MILES
Willow Island
1395
1394
1393
1392
1391
1390
+1165
1389

Malworth Co. Dewey Co.
Cheyenne Indian Reservation
(RESERVOIR)
RIVER

Fletcher Creek
1700
1800
1600
Bear Creek
Four
Buffalo Creek
BUFFALO BAY
Course of Pre-Dam River

OAHE
LAKE

Malworth Co. Potter Co.

STEAMBOAT BAY
Steamboat Creek
5009
Potter Co. Dewey Co.
MISSOURI

... we made Several attempts to find the main Channel between the Sand bars, and was obliged at length to Drag the boat over to Save a league which we must return to get into the deepest Channel,... the river being devided in many places in a great number of Chanels,...
Clark ⇒

... many large round Stones near middle of the river, those Stones appear to have been washed from the hills...
Clark ⇒

N

Outbound: October 6, 1804
Return: August 23, 1806

Modern Data: 1968-1970
ONE STATUTE MILE

EXPLORATIONS OF LEWIS AND CLARK 1804 - 1806
CARTOGRAPHIC RECONSTRUCTION
South Dakota
SQUASH GARDENS
CONTOUR INTERVAL 100 FEET
UTM ZONE 14
MAP NUMBER 129

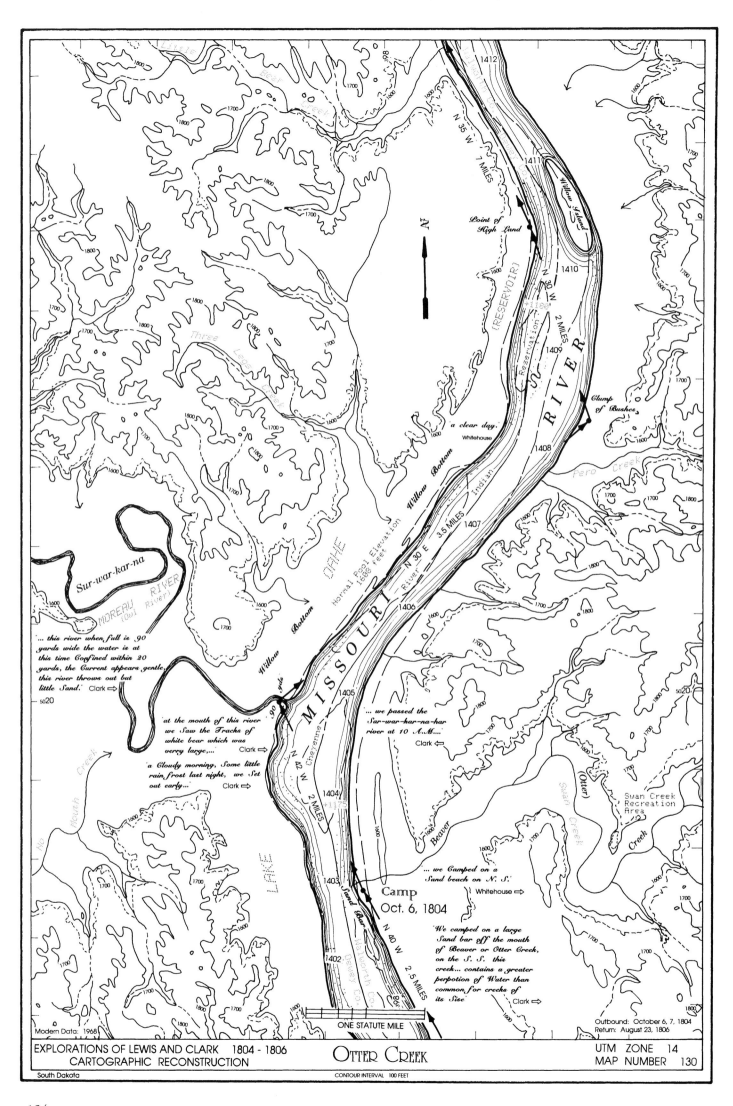

1412

1800
1700
1700

1800

1800

1700
1800
1700

1800

1700

1700

1700

1411

Point of
High Land

1410

N 35 W
7 MILES

N 30 W
2 MILES

Willow Island

*N*

1409

+1198

(RESERVOIR)

Reservation

RIVER

1700

1700

*a clear day.*
Whitehouse

1408

Clump
of Bushes

Pero Creek

1700    1800

1800

Willow Bottom

Indian

N 30 E
3.5 MILES

1407

1800

*Sur-war-kar-na*

1800

1700

1600

Three Legs Creek

Willow Bottom

1700

1600

MOREAU (OAHE) RIVER

1600

1700

*MISSOURI*

River

1406

1700

1800

1800

*... this river when full is 90
yards wide the water is at
this time Confined within 20
yards, the Current appears gentle,
this river throws out but
little Sand.'* Clark ⇨

—5020

90 yds

1405

*... we passed the
Sar-war-kar-na-har
river at 10 A.M....*
Clark ⇦

5020

*at the mouth of this river
we Saw the Tracks of
white bear which was
verry large,...* Clark ⇨

N 42 W
2 MILES

+1175

1404

*a Cloudy morning, Some little
rain, frost last night, we Set
out early...* Clark ⇨

No Heart Creek

LAKE

OAHE

1600

1700

1600

1600

Beaver

1600

Otter

1800

Swan Creek
Recreation
Area

Creek

1700

1800

1403

*... we Camped on a
Sand beach on N. S.'*
Whitehouse ⇨

Sand Bar

**Camp**
**Oct. 6, 1804**

*We camped on a large
Sand bar off the mouth
of Beaver or Otter Creek,
on the S. S. this
creek... contains a greater
perpotion of Water than
common for creks of
its Sise* Clark ⇨

N 40 W
2.5 MILES

1402

1700

1700

1700

1700

1600

1700

1800

Halworth Co.
Dewey Co.

ONE STATUTE MILE

Modern Data: 1968

Outbound: October 6, 7, 1804
Return: August 23, 1806

EXPLORATIONS OF LEWIS AND CLARK    1804 - 1806
CARTOGRAPHIC RECONSTRUCTION

OTTER CREEK

UTM ZONE    14
MAP NUMBER    130

South Dakota                    CONTOUR INTERVAL    100 FEET

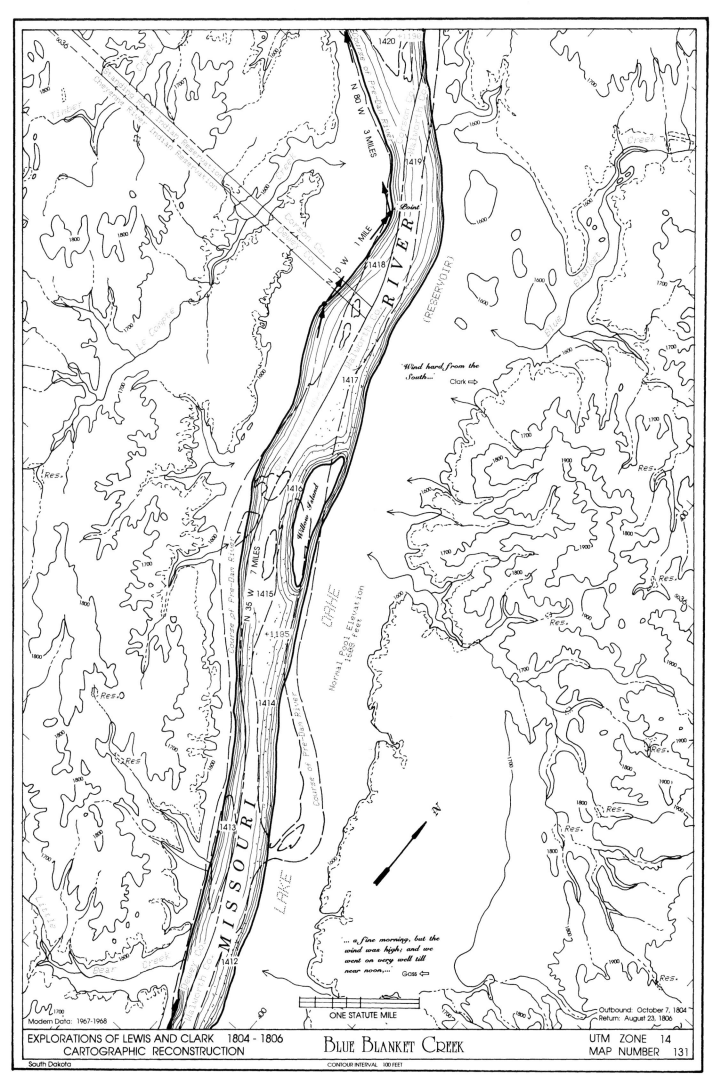

Wind hard from the South... Clark ⟹

Normal Pool Elevation 1600 feet

...a fine morning, but the wind was high; and we went on very well till near noon,... Gass ⟸

N

ONE STATUTE MILE

Modern Data: 1967-1968

Outbound: October 7, 1804
Return: August 23, 1806

EXPLORATIONS OF LEWIS AND CLARK   1804 - 1806
CARTOGRAPHIC RECONSTRUCTION

BLUE BLANKET CREEK

UTM ZONE   14
MAP NUMBER   131

South Dakota

CONTOUR INTERVAL   100 FEET

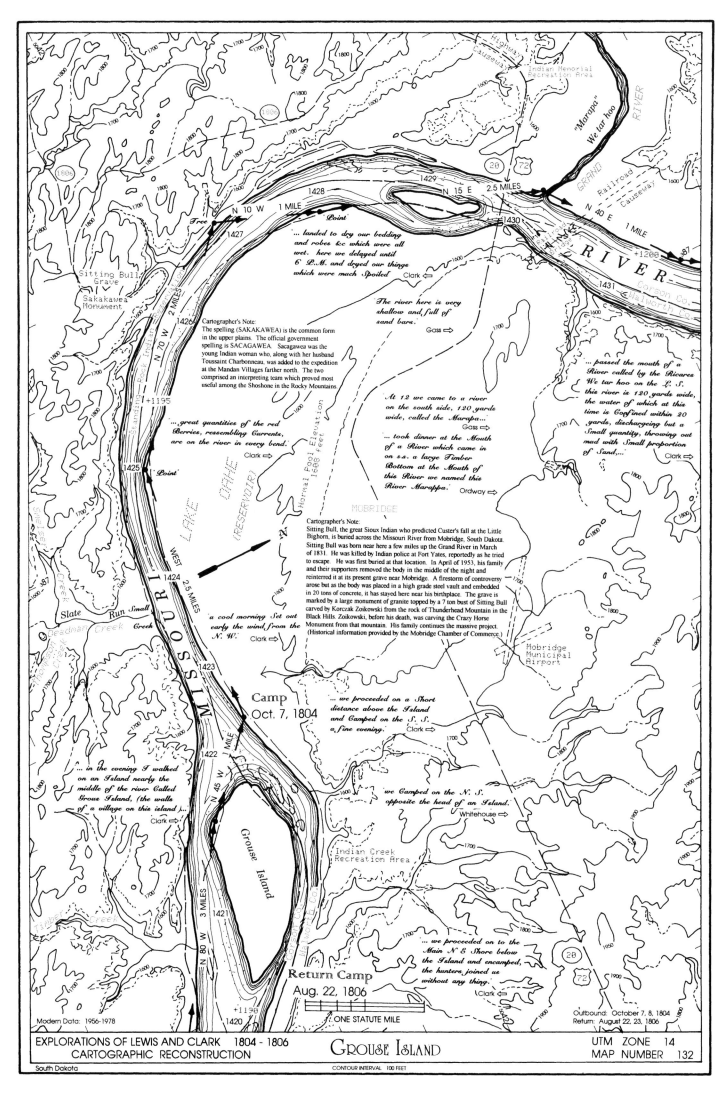

EXPLORATIONS OF LEWIS AND CLARK   1804 - 1806
CARTOGRAPHIC RECONSTRUCTION
GROUSE ISLAND
UTM ZONE 14
MAP NUMBER 132

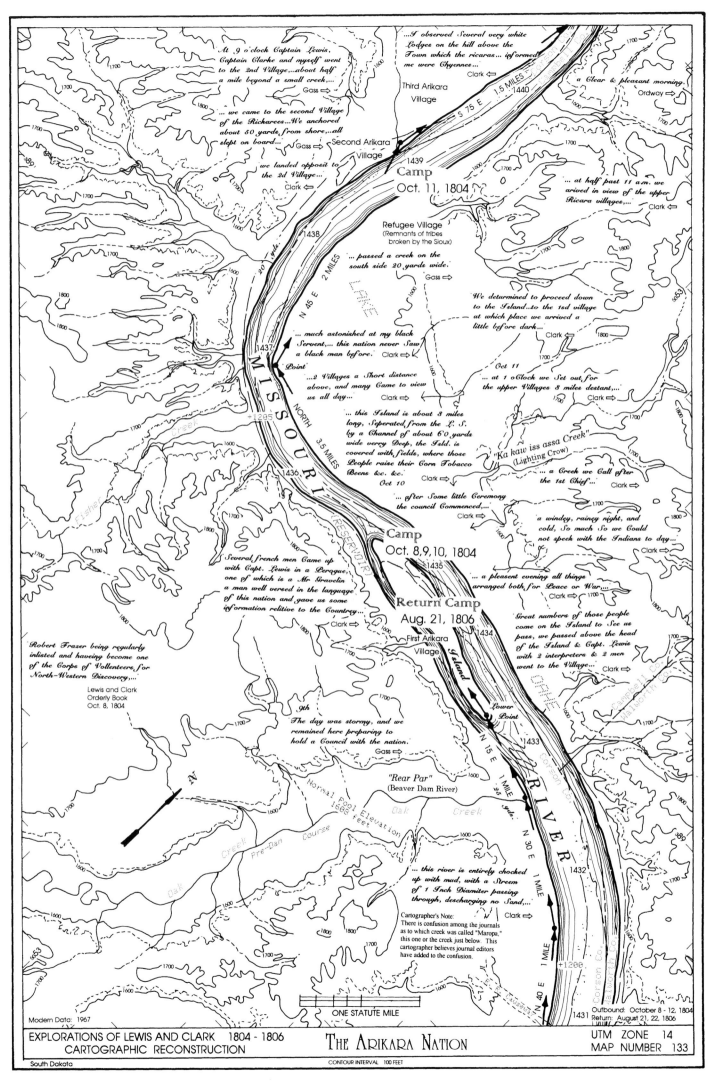

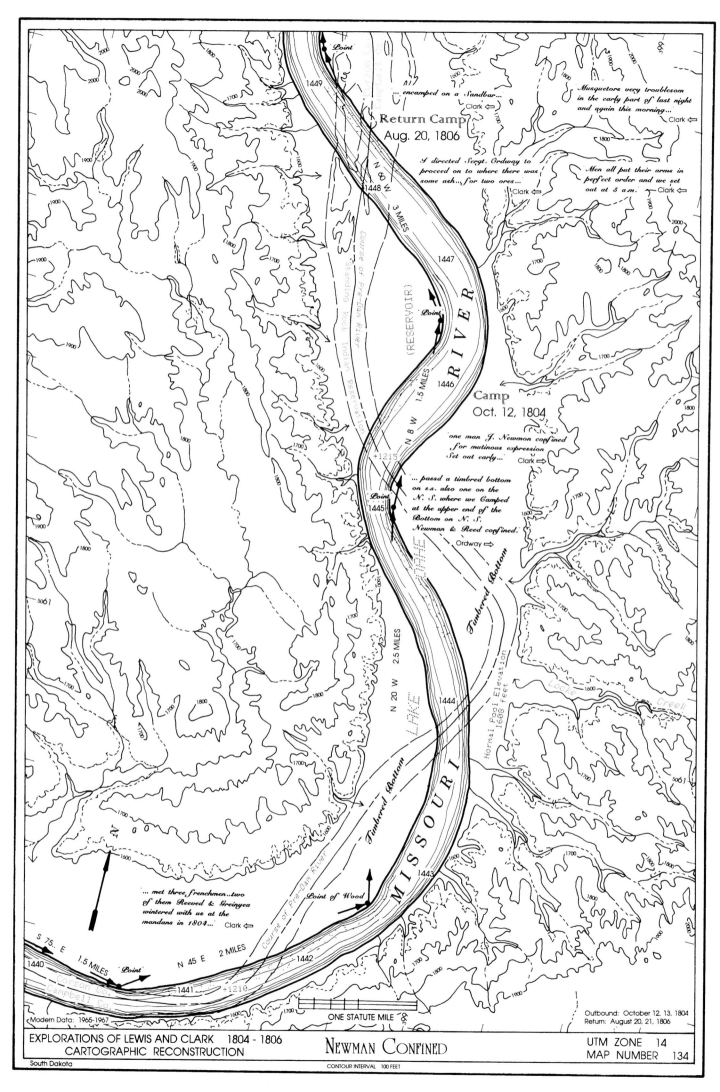

...encamped on a Sandbar...
Clark ⇐

Musquetors very troublesom
in the early part of last night
and again this morning...
Clark ⇐

Return Camp
Aug. 20, 1806

I directed Sergt. Ordway to
proceed on to where there was
some ash...for two ores...
Clark ⇐

Men all put their arms in
perfect order and we set
out at 5 a.m. ⌐Clark ⇐

Camp
Oct. 12, 1804

one man J. Newman confined
for mutinous expression
Set out early...
Clark ⇒

...passd a timbred bottom
on s.s. also one on the
N. S. where we Camped
at the upper end of the
Bottom on N. S.
Newman & Reed confined.
Ordway ⇒

...met three frenchmen...two
of them Reeved & Greinyea
wintered with us at the
mandans in 1804...
Clark ⇐

Point of Wood

ONE STATUTE MILE

Outbound: October 12, 13, 1804
Return: August 20, 21, 1806

EXPLORATIONS OF LEWIS AND CLARK  1804 - 1806
CARTOGRAPHIC RECONSTRUCTION

NEWMAN CONFINED

UTM ZONE  14
MAP NUMBER  134

South Dakota

CONTOUR INTERVAL  100 FEET

Modern Data: 1965-1967

158

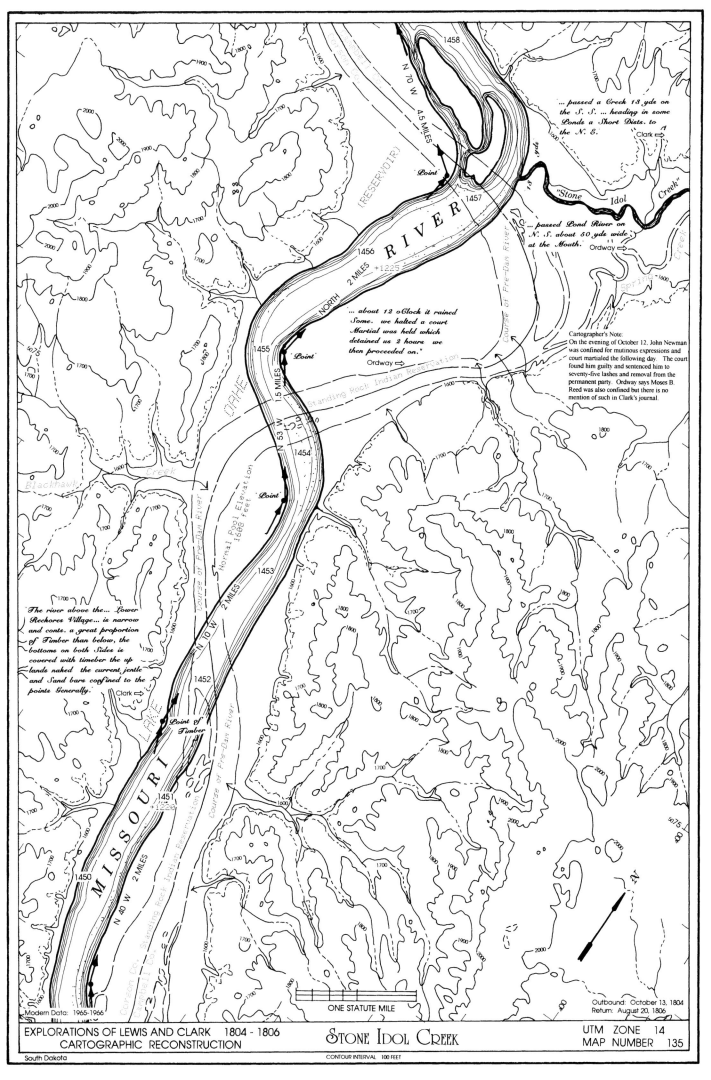

1458

... passed a Creek 18 yds on
the S. S. ... heading in some
Ponds a Short Dista. to
the N. E.

Clark ⇒

"Stone Idol Creek"

... passed Pond River on
N. S. about 50 yds wide
at the Mouth.

Ordway ⇒

Cartographer's Note:
On the evening of October 12, John Newman
was confined for mutinous expressions and
court martialed the following day. The court
found him guilty and sentenced him to
seventy-five lashes and removal from the
permanent party. Ordway says Moses B.
Reed was also confined but there is no
mention of such in Clark's journal.

Point

1457

1456

+1225

1455

Point

... about 12 oClock it rained
Some. we halted a court
Martial was held which
detained us 2 hours we
then proceeded on."

Ordway ⇒

1454

Point

1453

The river above the... Lower
Rechores Village... is narrow
and conts. a great proportion
of Timber than below, the
bottoms on both Sides is
covered with timeber the up
lands naked the current jentle
and Sand bars confined to the
points Generally.

Clark ⇒

1452

Point of
Timber

1451
+1226

1450

Normal Pool Elevation
1600 feet

ONE STATUTE MILE

Modern Data: 1965-1966

Outbound: October 13, 1804
Return: August 20, 1806

EXPLORATIONS OF LEWIS AND CLARK    1804 - 1806
CARTOGRAPHIC RECONSTRUCTION

STONE IDOL CREEK

UTM ZONE   14
MAP NUMBER   135

South Dakota

CONTOUR INTERVAL  100 FEET

159

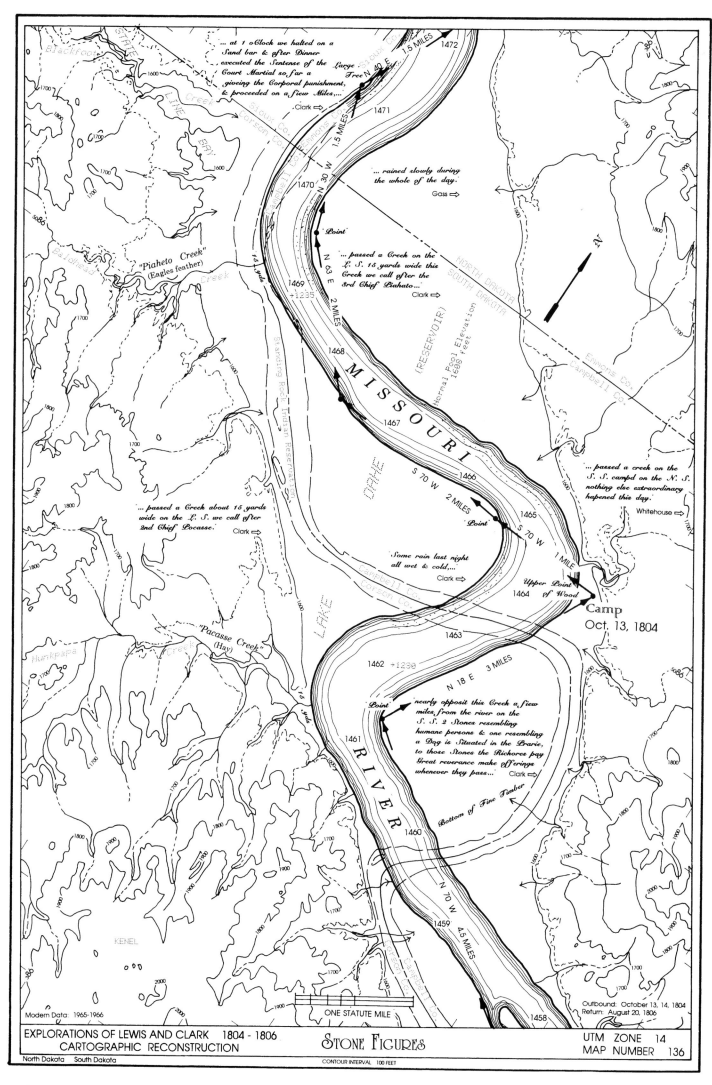

... at 1 oClock we halted on a
Sand bar & after Dinner
executed the Sentence of the
Court Martial so far a
giveing the Corporal punishment,
& proceeded on a fiew Miles,...

Clark ⇨

Large
Tree  N 40 E

1.5 MILES

1472

N 30 W
1.5 MILES

1471

1470

... rained slowly during
the whole of the day.

Gass ⇨

"Piaheto Creek"
(Eagles feather)

Point

N 63 E
2 MILES

1469
+1235

... passed a Creek on the
L. S. 15 yards wide this
Creek we call after the
3rd Chief Piahato...

Clark ⇨

1468

MISSOURI

(RESERVOIR)

Normal Pool Elevation
1608 feet

1467

... passed a Creek about 16 yards
wide on the L. S. we call after
2nd Chief Pocasse.

Clark ⇨

S 70 W
2 MILES

1466

1465

Point

S 70 W
1 MILE

... passed a creek on the
S. S. campd on the N. S.
nothing else extraordinary
hapened this day.

Whitehouse ⇨

Some rain last night
all wet & cold,...

Clark ⇨

Upper Point
1464  of Wood

Camp
Oct. 13, 1804

"Pacasse Creek"
(Hay)

1463

1462  +1230

N 18 E
3 MILES

Point

1461

nearly opposit this Creek a fiew
miles from the river on the
S. S. 2 Stones resembling
humane persons & one resembling
a Dog is Situated in the Prarie,
to those Stones the Rickores pay
Great reverance make offerings
whenever they pass...

Clark ⇨

Bottom of Fine Timber

1460

N 70 W
4.5 MILES

1459

1458

Modern Data: 1965-1966

Outbound: October 13, 14, 1804
Return: August 20, 1806

ONE STATUTE MILE

EXPLORATIONS OF LEWIS AND CLARK   1804 - 1806
CARTOGRAPHIC RECONSTRUCTION

North Dakota   South Dakota

STONE FIGURES

CONTOUR INTERVAL  100 FEET

UTM  ZONE  14
MAP  NUMBER  136

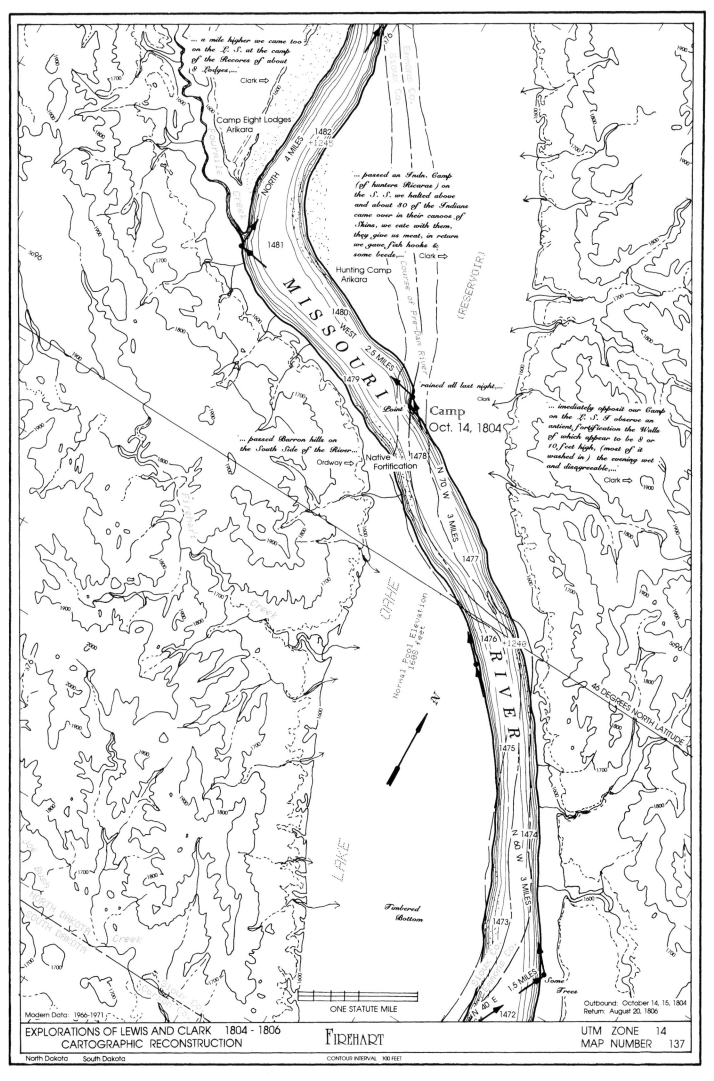

... a mile higher we came too
on the L. S. at the camp
of the Recores of about
8 Lodges,...

Clark ⇨

Camp Eight Lodges
Arikara

1482
+1245

NORTH 4 MILES

... passed an Indn. Camp
(of hunters Ricaras) on
the S. S. we halted above
and about 30 of the Indians
came over in their canoos of
Skins, we eate with them,
they give us meat, in return
we gave fish hooks &
some beeds,...

Clark ⇨

1481

Hunting Camp
Arikara

MISSOURI

1480

WEST 2.5 MILES

Course of Pre-Dam River

(RESERVOIR)

1479

WEST 2.5 MILES

rained all last night,...

Clark

Point

Camp
Oct. 14, 1804

... passed Barron hills on
the South Side of the River...

Ordway ⇨

Native
Fortification

1478

N 70 W 3 MILES

... imediately opposit our Camp
on the L. S. I observe an
antient fortification the Walls
of which appear to be 8 or
10 feet high, (most of it
washed in) the evening wet
and disagreeable,...

Clark ⇨

1477

Normal Pool Elevation 1661 feet

N

1476 +1248

46 DEGREES NORTH LATITUDE

RIVER

1475

LAKE

N 60 W 3 MILES

1474

Timbered
Bottom

1473

Some
Trees

1.5 MILES

N 40 E

1472

Modern Data: 1966-1971

ONE STATUTE MILE

Outbound: October 14, 15, 1804
Return: August 20, 1806

EXPLORATIONS OF LEWIS AND CLARK   1804 - 1806
CARTOGRAPHIC RECONSTRUCTION

FIREHART

UTM ZONE 14
MAP NUMBER 137

North Dakota     South Dakota

CONTOUR INTERVAL 100 FEET

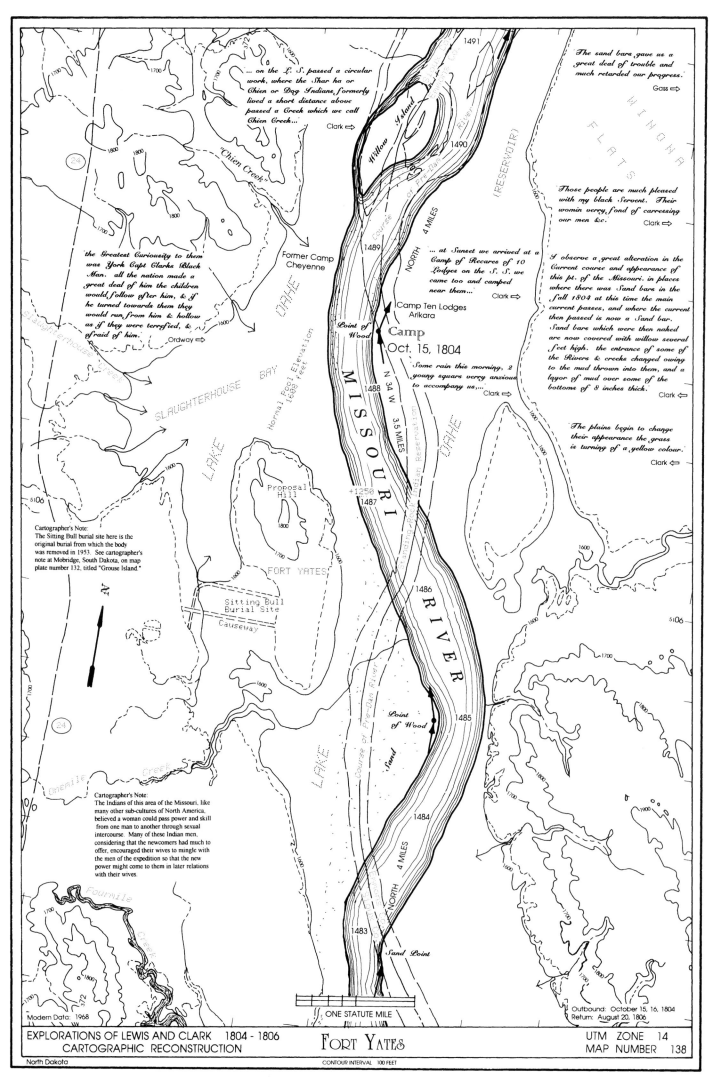

...on the L. S. passed a circular work, where the Shar ha or Chien or Dog Indians, formerly lived a short distance above passed a Creek which we call Chien Creek... Clark ⇒

The sand bars gave us a great deal of trouble and much retarded our progress. Gass ⇒

"Chien Creek"

Former Camp Cheyenne

the Greatest Curiosity to them was York Capt Clarks Black Man. all the nation made a great deal of him the children would follow after him, & if he turned towards them they would run from him & hollow as if they were terrified, & afraid of him. Ordway ⇒

Those people are much pleased with my black Servent. Their womin verry fond of carressing our men &c. Clark ⇒

...at Sunset we arrived at a Camp of Recares of 10 Lodges on the S. S. we came too and camped near them... Clark ⇒

I observe a great alteration in the Current course and appearance of this pt. of the Missouri. in places where there was Sand bars in the fall 1804 at this time the main current passes, and where the current then passed is now a Sand bar. Sand bars which were then naked are now covered with willow several feet high. the entrance of some of the Rivers & creeks changed owing to the mud thrown into them, and a layor of mud over some of the bottoms of 8 inches thick. Clark ⇐

Camp Ten Lodges Arikara

Point of Wood

Camp Oct. 15, 1804

Some rain this morning, 2 young squars verry anxious to accompany us,... Clark ⇒

The plains begin to change their appearance the grass is turning of a yellow colour. Clark ⇐

MISSOURI RIVER

Normal Pool Elevation 1602 + Feet

SLAUGHTERHOUSE BAY

LAKE

Cartographer's Note:
The Sitting Bull burial site here is the original burial from which the body was removed in 1953. See cartographer's note at Mobridge, South Dakota, on map plate number 132, titled "Grouse Island."

Proposal Hill

FORT YATES

Sitting Bull Burial Site

Causeway

Cartographer's Note:
The Indians of this area of the Missouri, like many other sub-cultures of North America, believed a woman could pass power and skill from one man to another through sexual intercourse. Many of these Indian men, considering that the newcomers had much to offer, encouraged their wives to mingle with the men of the expedition so that the new power might come to them in later relations with their wives.

Point of Wood

Sand

Sand Point

ONE STATUTE MILE

Outbound: October 15, 16, 1804
Return: August 20, 1806

EXPLORATIONS OF LEWIS AND CLARK   1804 - 1806
CARTOGRAPHIC RECONSTRUCTION

FORT YATES

UTM ZONE 14
MAP NUMBER 138

North Dakota

CONTOUR INTERVAL 100 FEET

Modern Data: 1968

162

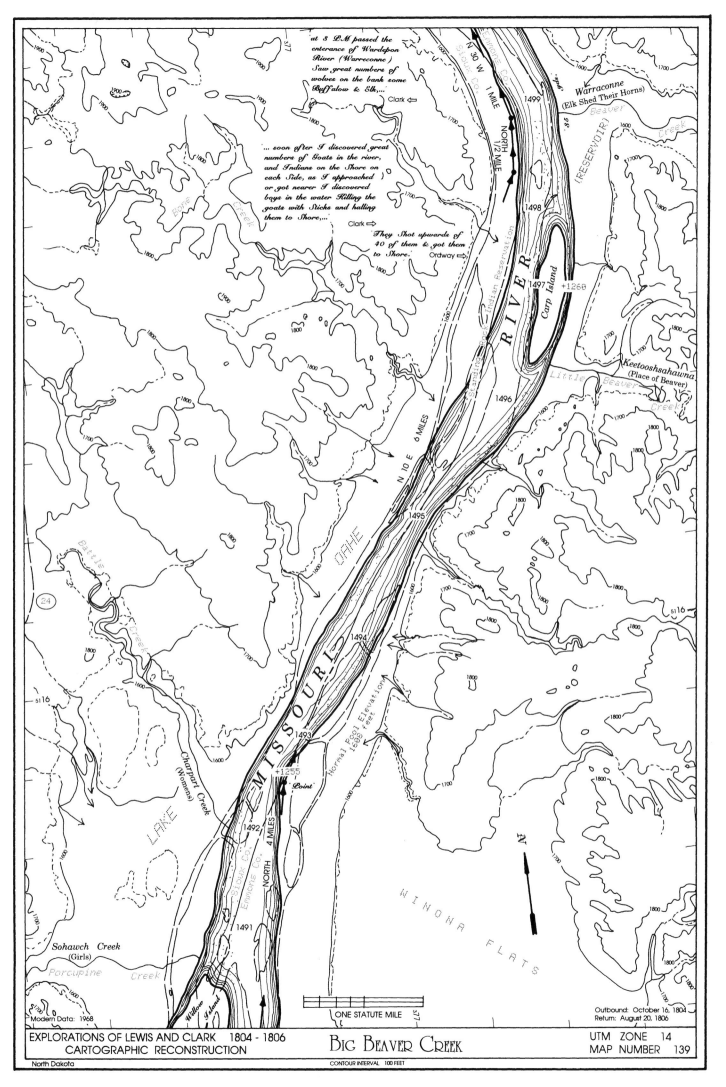

at 3 P.M passed the
enterance of Wardepon
River (Warreconne)
Saw great numbers of
wolves on the bank some
Buffalow & Elk,...
Clark ⇐

Warraconne
(Elk Shed Their Horns)

... soon after I discovered great
numbers of Goats in the river,
and Indians on the Shore on
each Side, as I approached
or got nearer I discovered
boys in the water Killing the
goats with Sticks and halling
them to Shore,...
Clark ⇒

They Shot upwards of
40 of them & got them
to Shore.
Ordway ⇒

Keetooshsahawna
(Place of Beaver)

RIVER

Carp Island
+1260
1497

1498

1499

1496

1495

1494

1493

+1255
Point

1492

1491

MISSOURI

LAKE

Charpart Creek
(Womens)

Sohawch Creek
(Girls)

Porcupine Creek

Willow Island

Modern Data: 1968

ONE STATUTE MILE

N

WINONA FLATS

Outbound: October 16, 1804
Return: August 20, 1806

EXPLORATIONS OF LEWIS AND CLARK   1804 - 1806
CARTOGRAPHIC RECONSTRUCTION

BIG BEAVER CREEK

UTM ZONE   14
MAP NUMBER   139

North Dakota

CONTOUR INTERVAL   100 FEET

163

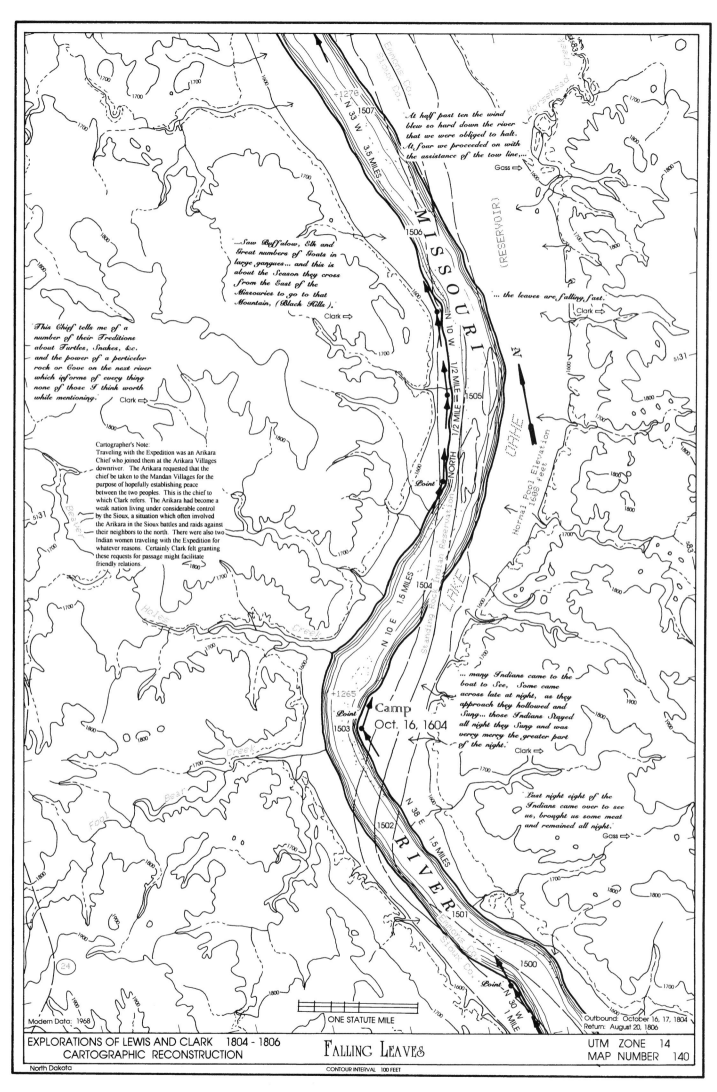

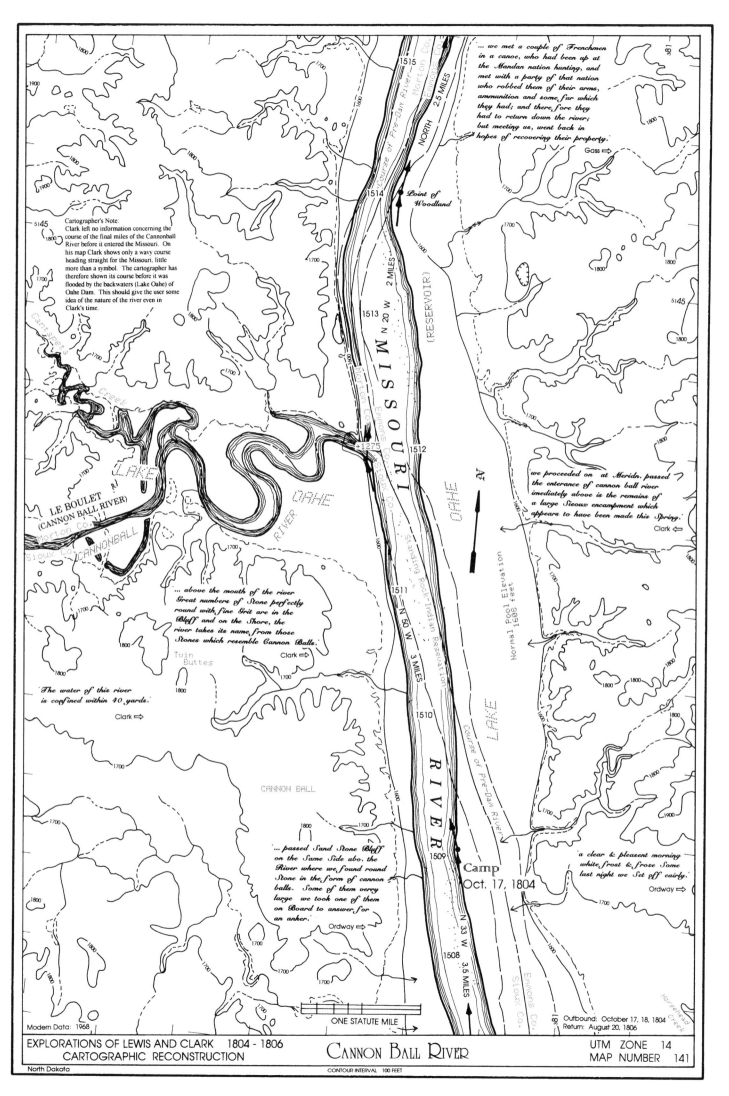

Cartographer's Note:
Clark left no information concerning the course of the final miles of the Cannonball River before it entered the Missouri. On his map Clark shows only a wavy course heading straight for the Missouri, little more than a symbol. The cartographer has therefore shown its course before it was flooded by the backwaters (Lake Oahe) of Oahe Dam. This should give the user some idea of the nature of the river even in Clark's time.

... we met a couple of Frenchmen in a canoe, who had been up at the Mandan nation hunting, and met with a party of that nation who robbed them of their arms, ammunition and some fur which they had; and there fore they had to return down the river; but meeting us, went back in hopes of recovering their property.
Gass ⇒

Point of Woodland

we proceeded on at Meridn. passed the enterance of cannon ball river imediately above is the remains of a large Sieoux encampment which appears to have been made this Spring.
Clark ⇐

LE BOULET (CANNON BALL RIVER)

... above the mouth of the river Great numbers of Stone perfectly round with fine Grit are in the Bluff and on the Shore, the river takes its name from those Stones which resemble Cannon Balls.
Clark ⇒

The water of this river is confined within 40 yards.
Clark ⇒

Twin Buttes

CANNON BALL

... passed Sand Stone Bluff on the Same Side abo. the River where we found round Stone in the form of cannon balls. Some of them verry large we took one of them on Board to answer for an anker.
Ordway ⇒

Camp Oct. 17, 1804

a clear & pleasant morning white frost & froze Some last night we Set off eairly.
Ordway ⇒

Normal Pool Elevation 1605 feet

Course of Pre-Dam River

ONE STATUTE MILE

Modern Data: 1968

Outbound: October 17, 18, 1804
Return: August 20, 1806

EXPLORATIONS OF LEWIS AND CLARK    1804 - 1806
CARTOGRAPHIC RECONSTRUCTION

North Dakota                CONTOUR INTERVAL  100 FEET

CANNON BALL RIVER

UTM  ZONE  14
MAP NUMBER  141

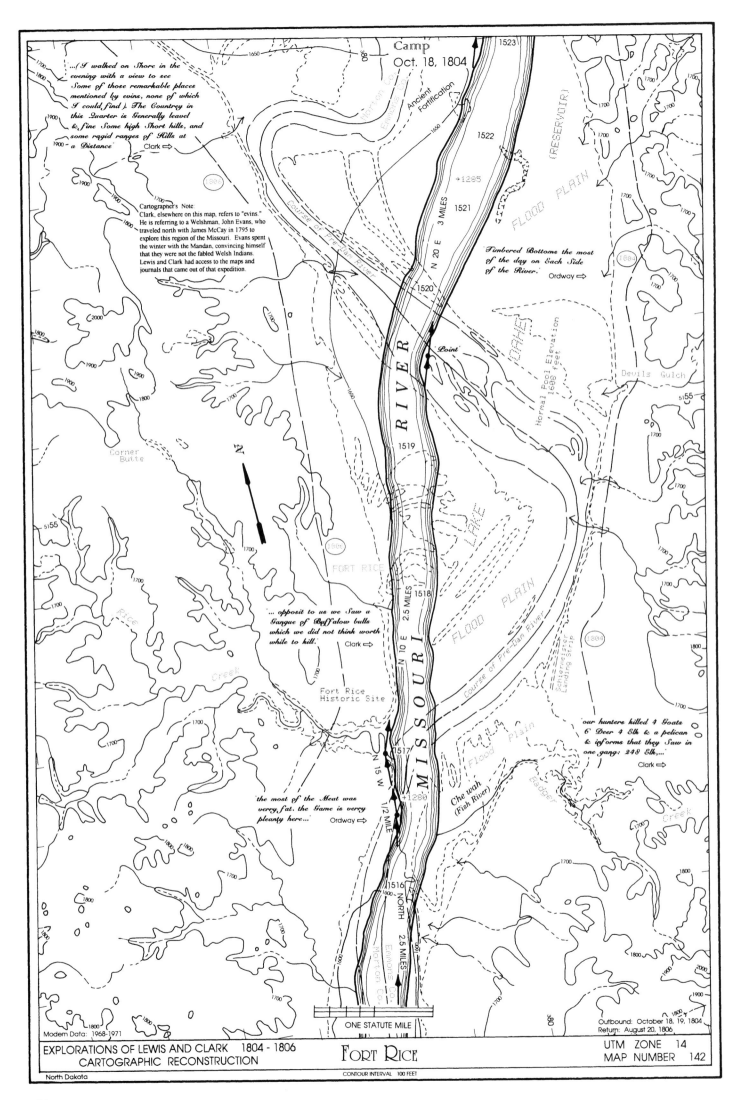

...I walked on Shore in the evening with a view to see Some of those remarkable places mentioned by evins, none of which I could find ). The Country in this Quarter is Generally leavel & fine Some high Short hills, and some ragid ranges of Hills at a Distance
Clark ⇨

Cartographer's Note:
Clark, elsewhere on this map, refers to "evins." He is referring to a Welshman, John Evans, who traveled north with James McCay in 1795 to explore this region of the Missouri. Evans spent the winter with the Mandan, convincing himself that they were not the fabled Welsh Indians. Lewis and Clark had access to the maps and journals that came out of that expedition.

Camp
Oct. 18, 1804

Ancient Fortification

1523
1522
1521
+1285
1520

Timbered Bottoms the most of the day on Each Side of the River.
Ordway ⇨

FLOOD PLAIN (RESERVOIR)

Course of Pre-Dam River

Point

Devils Gulch

5155

1519

N 20 E    3 MILES

Corner Butte

N

RIVER

LAKE

5155

1804

FORT RICE

1518

N 10 E    2.5 MILES

... opposit to us we Saw a Gangue of Buffalow bulls which we did not think worth while to kill.
Clark ⇨

FLOOD PLAIN

Course of Pre-Dam River

Schiermeister Landing Strip

MISSOURI

Fort Rice Historic Site

our hunters killed 4 Goats 6 Deer 4 Elk & a pelican & informs that they Saw in one gang: 248 Elk,...
Clark ⇨

1517

N 15 W    1/2 MILE

+1280

the most of the Meat was verry fat. the Game is verry pleanty here...
Ordway ⇨

Che-wah (Fish River)

FLOOD PLAIN

Badger

Creek

Rice

Creek

1516

NORTH    2.5 MILES

Emmons Co.
Morton Co.

Normal Pool Elevation 1600 feet

ONE STATUTE MILE

Outbound: October 18, 19, 1804
Return: August 20, 1806

Modern Data: 1968-1971

EXPLORATIONS OF LEWIS AND CLARK   1804 - 1806
CARTOGRAPHIC RECONSTRUCTION

FORT RICE

UTM   ZONE   14
MAP NUMBER   142

North Dakota

CONTOUR INTERVAL   100 FEET

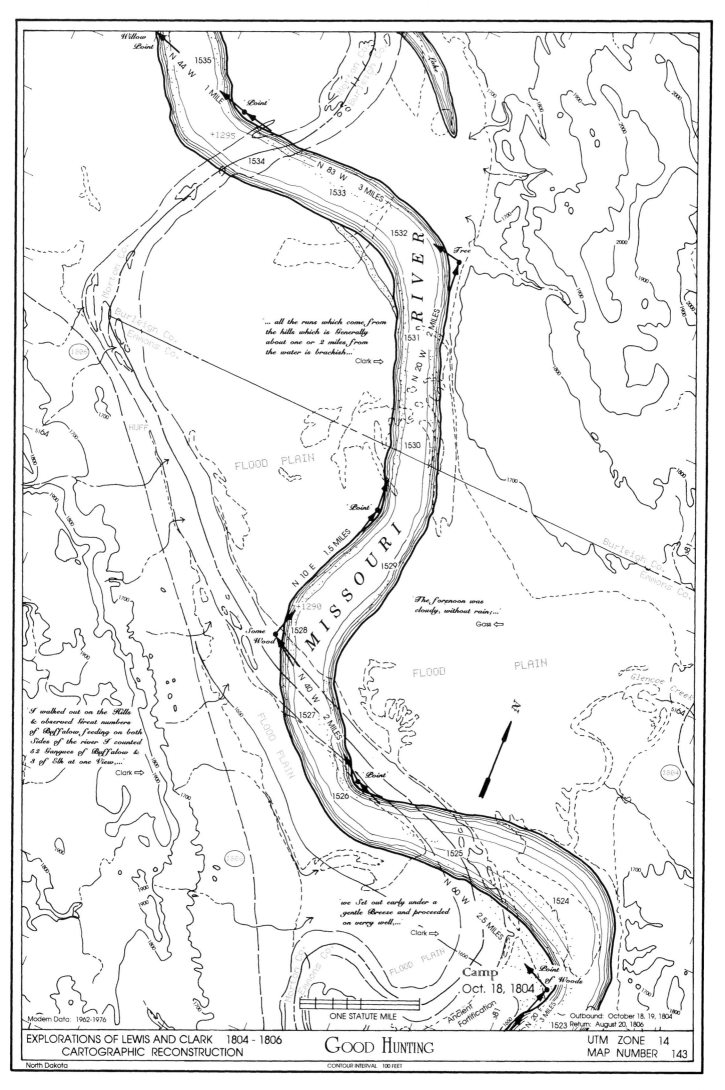

Willow
Point

N 44 W
1 MILE

1535

Point

+1295

1534

N 83 W    3 MILES

1533

1532

Tree

RIVER

2 MILES

... all the runs which come from
the hills which is Generally
about one or 2 miles from
the water is brackish...
Clark ⇒

1531

N 20 W

1530

FLOOD PLAIN

1700

MISSOURI

Point

N 10 E    1.5 MILES

1529

The forenoon was
cloudy, without rain;...
Gass ⇐

+1290

Some
Wood

1528

FLOOD       PLAIN

Glencoe Creek

N 40 W

N

I walked out on the Hills
& observed Great numbers
of Buffalow, feeding on both
Sides of the river I counted
52 Gangues of Buffalow &
3 of Elk at one View,...
Clark ⇒

1527    2 MILES

FLOOD    PLAIN

Point

1526

1525

1524

we Set out early under a
gentle Breeze and proceeded
on verry well,...
Clark ⇒

N 80 W    2.5 MILES

FLOOD PLAIN    1650

Camp
Oct. 18, 1804

Point
of Woods

Ancient
Fortification

N 20 W    3 MILES

1523

Modern Data: 1962-1976

ONE STATUTE MILE

Outbound: October 18, 19, 1804
Return: August 20, 1806

EXPLORATIONS OF LEWIS AND CLARK    1804 - 1806
CARTOGRAPHIC RECONSTRUCTION

North Dakota

Good Hunting

CONTOUR INTERVAL    100 FEET

UTM ZONE    14
MAP NUMBER    143

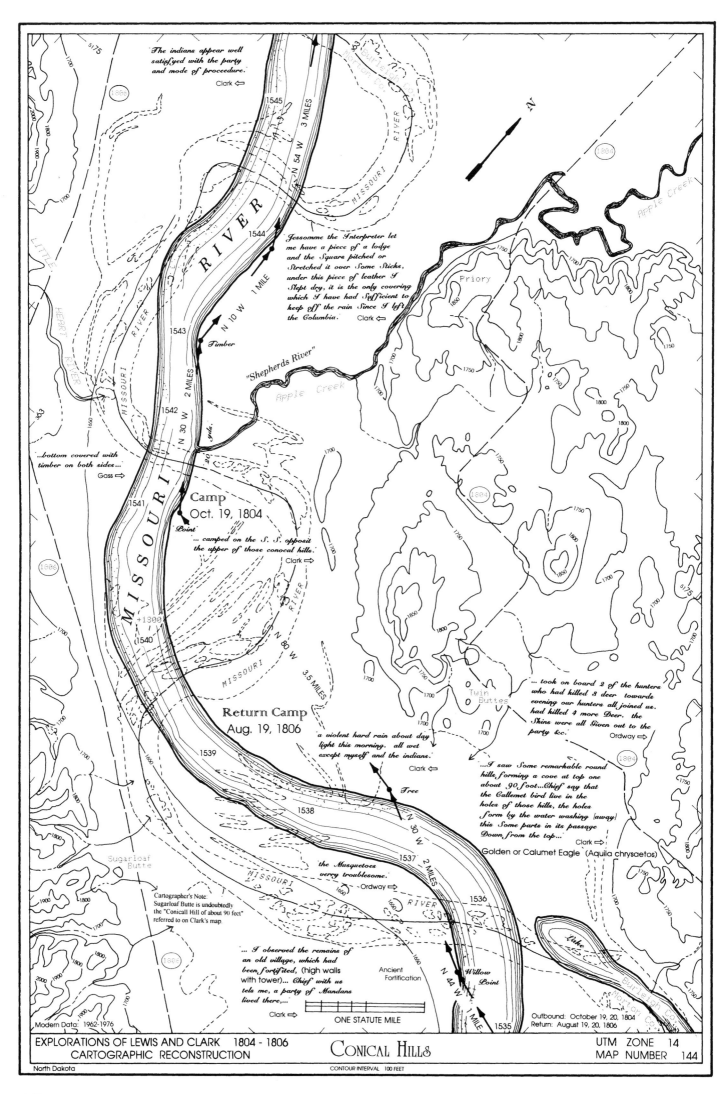

The indians appear well satisfyed with the party and mode of proceedure.
Clark ⇐

1545

3 MILES

N 54 W

Jessomme the Interpreter let me have a piece of a lodge and the Squars pitched or Stretched it over Some Sticks, under this piece of leather I Slept dry, it is the only covering which I have had Sufficient to keep off the rain Since I left the Columbia.
Clark ⇐

1544

N 10 W 1 MILE

1543

Timber

"Shepherds River"

Apple Creek

N 30 W 2 MILES

1542

Ids.

...bottom covered with timber on both sides...
Gass ⇒

1541

Camp
Oct. 19, 1804

Point

... camped on the S. S. opposit the upper of those conical hills.
Clark ⇒

N 80 W

MISSOURI

+1300

1540

3.5 MILES

Return Camp
Aug. 19, 1806

a violent hard rain about day light this morning. all wet except myself and the indians.
Clark ⇐

Tree

1539

1538

Sugarloaf Butte

the Musquetoes verry troublesome.
Ordway ⇒

Cartographer's Note:
Sugarloaf Butte is undoubtedly the "Conicall Hill of about 90 feet" referred to on Clark's map.

1537

N 30 W 2 MILES

1536

... I observed the remains of an old village, which had been fortifited, (high walls with tower)... Chief with us tels me, a party of Mandans lived there,...
Clark ⇒

Ancient Fortification

Willow Point

N 44 W 1 MILE

1535

ONE STATUTE MILE

Modern Data: 1962-1976

Missouri River

Little Heart River

Priory

Twin Buttes

... took on board 2 of the hunters who had killed 8 deer towards evening our hunters all joined us. had killed 4 more Deer. the Skins were all Given out to the party &c.
Ordway ⇒

...I saw Some remarkable round hills, forming a cove at top one about 90 foot...Chief say that the Callemet bird live in the holes of those hills, the holes form by the water washing [away] this Some parts in its passage Down, from the top...
Clark ⇒

Golden or Calumet Eagle (Aquila chrysaetos)

Apple Creek

Lake

Burleigh Co.
Morton Co.

Outbound: October 19, 20, 1804
Return: August 19, 20, 1806

EXPLORATIONS OF LEWIS AND CLARK   1804 - 1806
CARTOGRAPHIC RECONSTRUCTION

CONICAL HILLS

UTM ZONE   14
MAP NUMBER   144

North Dakota

CONTOUR INTERVAL   100 FEET

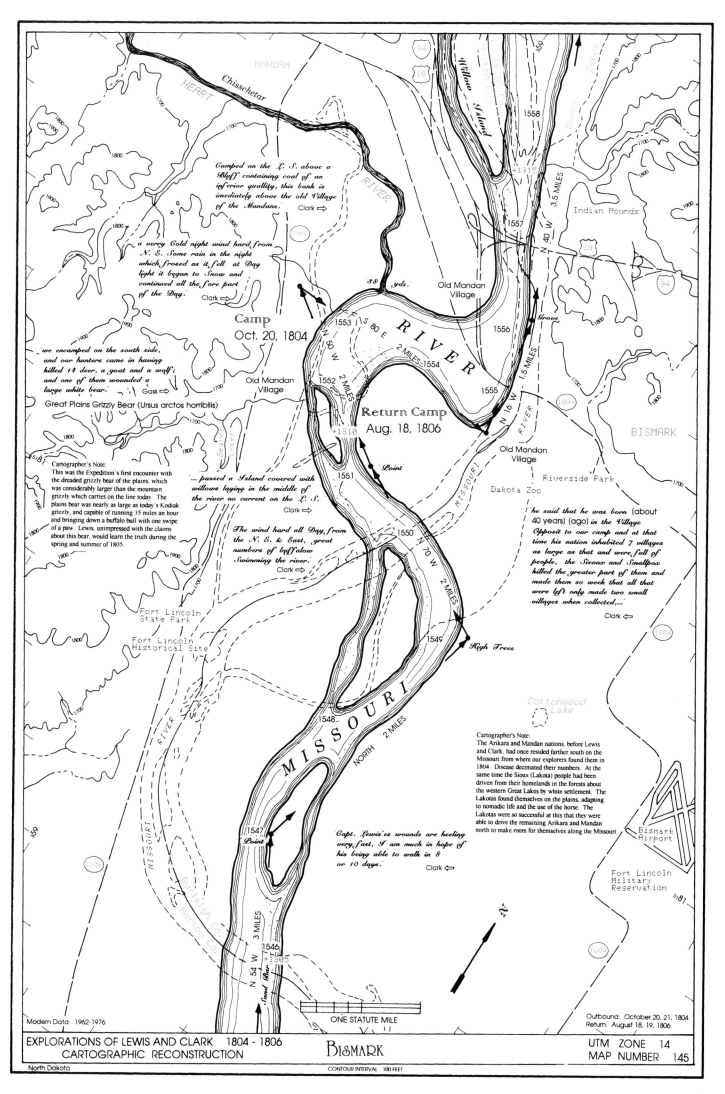

Camped on the L. S. above a Bluff containing coal of an inferior quallity, this bank is imediately above the old Village of the Mandans. Clark ⇒

a verry Cold night wind hard from N. E. Some rain in the night which frosed as it fell at Day light it began to Snow and continued all the fore part of the Day. Clark ⇒

**Camp**
**Oct. 20, 1804**

we encamped on the south side, and our hunters came in having killed 14 deer, a goat and a wolf; and one of them wounded a large white bear. Gass ⇒

Great Plains Grizzly Bear (Ursus arctos horribilis)

Cartographer's Note:
This was the Expedition's first encounter with the dreaded grizzly bear of the plains, which was considerably larger than the mountain grizzly which carries on the line today. The plains bear was nearly as large as today's Kodiak grizzly, and capable of running 35 miles an hour and bringing down a buffalo bull with one swipe of a paw. Lewis, unimpressed with the claims about this bear, would learn the truth during the spring and summer of 1805.

...passed a Island covered with willows laying in the middle of the river no current on the L. S. Clark ⇒

The wind hard all Day, from the N. E. & East, great numbers of buffalow Swimming the river. Clark ⇒

Old Mandan Village

Old Mandan Village

**Return Camp**
**Aug. 18, 1806**

Point

Old Mandan Village

Riverside Park

Dakota Zoo

he said that he was born (about 40 years) (ago) in the Village Opposit to our camp and at that time his nation inhabited 7 villages as large as that and were full of people, the Sieoux and Smallpox killed the greater part of them and made them so week that all that were left only made two small villages when collected,... Clark ⇐

Indian Mounds

BISMARK

High Trees

Cottonwood Lake

Cartographer's Note:
The Arikara and Mandan nations, before Lewis and Clark, had once resided farther south on the Missouri from where our explorers found them in 1804. Disease decimated their numbers. At the same time the Sioux (Lakota) people had been driven from their homelands in the forests about the western Great Lakes by white settlement. The Lakotas found themselves on the plains, adapting to nomadic life and the use of the horse. The Lakotas were so successful at this that they were able to drive the remaining Arikara and Mandan north to make room for themselves along the Missouri.

Point

Capt. Lewis'es wounds are heeling very fast, I am much in hope of his being able to walk in 8 or 10 days. Clark ⇐

Bismark Airport

Fort Lincoln Military Reservation

Fort Lincoln State Park

Fort Lincoln Historical Site

MISSOURI RIVER

Sand Bar

Modern Data: 1962-1976

ONE STATUTE MILE

Outbound: October 20, 21, 1804
Return: August 18, 19, 1806

EXPLORATIONS OF LEWIS AND CLARK   1804 - 1806
CARTOGRAPHIC RECONSTRUCTION

BISMARK

UTM ZONE   14
MAP NUMBER   145

North Dakota

CONTOUR INTERVAL   100 FEET

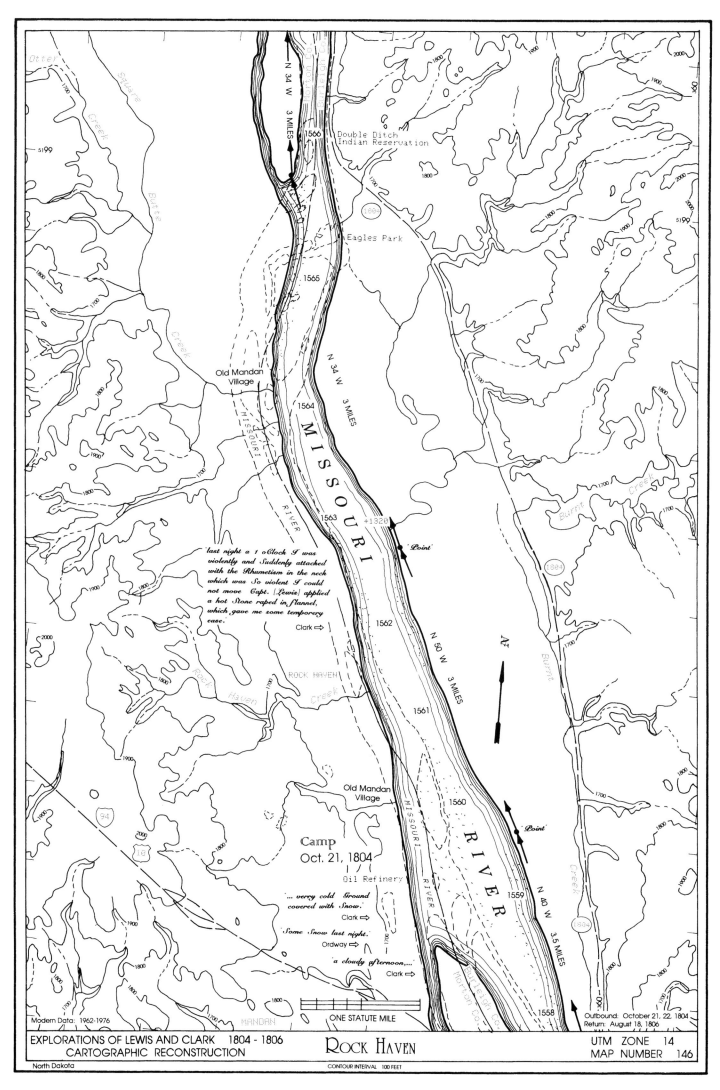

N 34 W
3 MILES

1566

Double Ditch
Indian Reservation

1804

Eagles Park

1565

Old Mandan
Village

N 34 W
3 MILES

1564

M I S S O U R I

1563        +1320

Point

last night a 1 oClock I was
violently and Suddenly attacked
with the Rhumetism in the neck
which was So violent I could
not move Capt. [Lewis] applied
a hot Stone raped in flannel,
which gave me some temporery
ease.

Clark ⇨

1562

1804

Burnt

N 50 W
3 MILES

ROCK HAVEN

1561

Old Mandan
Village

1560

Point

Camp
Oct. 21, 1804

Oil Refinery

N 40 W
3.5 MILES

...verry cold Ground
covered with Snow.

Clark ⇨

1559

Some Snow last night.

Ordway ⇨

a cloudy afternoon,....

Clark ⇨

1558

Outbound: October 21, 22, 1804
Return: August 18, 1806

Modern Data: 1962-1976

MANDAN

ONE STATUTE MILE

R I V E R

EXPLORATIONS OF LEWIS AND CLARK    1804 - 1806
CARTOGRAPHIC RECONSTRUCTION

ROCK HAVEN

UTM ZONE    14
MAP NUMBER    146

North Dakota

CONTOUR INTERVAL  100 FEET

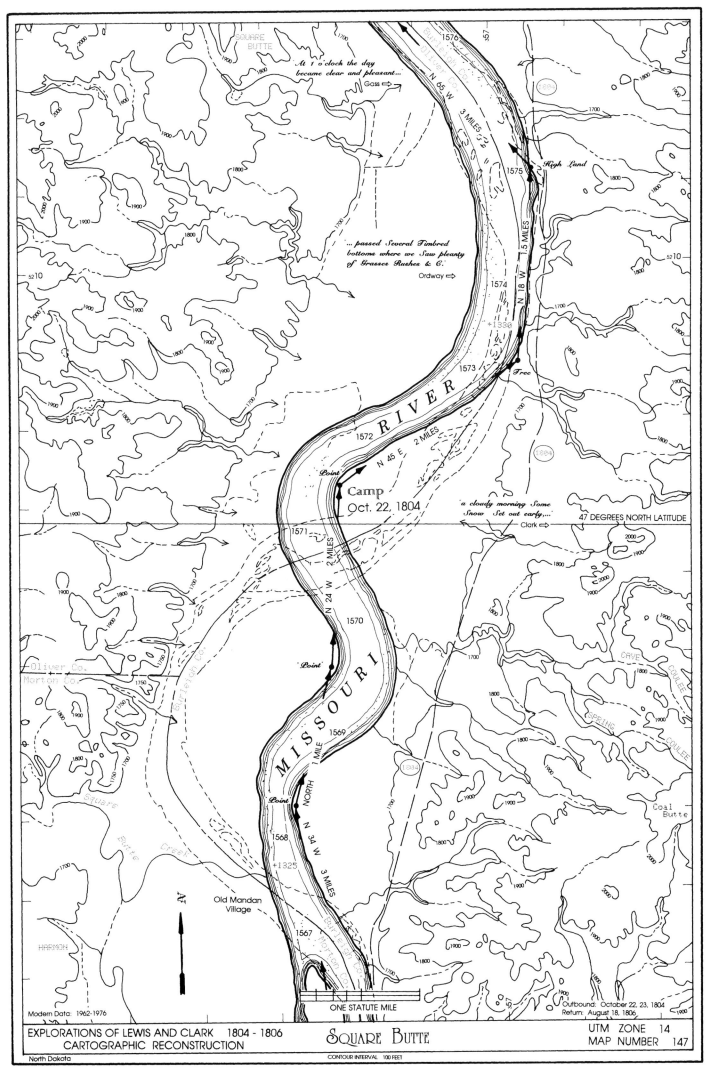

At 1 o'clock the day
became clear and pleasant...
Gass ⇨

... passed Several Timbred
bottoms where we Saw plenty
of Grasses Rushes & C.
Ordway ⇨

'a cloudy morning Some
Snow Set out early,...'
Clark ⇨

47 DEGREES NORTH LATITUDE

High Land

Tree

R I V E R

M I S S O U R I

Camp
Oct. 22, 1804

Point

Point

Point

Point

1576
1575
1574
1573
1572
1571
1570
1569
1568
1567

+1330
+1325

N 65 W 3 MILES
N 18 W 1.5 MILES
N 45 E 2 MILES
N 24 W 2 MILES
N NORTH 1 MILE
N 34 W 3 MILES

SQUARE BUTTE
Square Butte Creek
Burleigh Co.
Oliver Co.
Morton Co.
Old Mandan Village
HARMON
Coal Butte
CAVE COULEE
SPRING COULEE

1804

N

ONE STATUTE MILE

Modern Data: 1962-1976

Outbound: October 22, 23, 1804
Return: August 18, 1806

EXPLORATIONS OF LEWIS AND CLARK  1804 - 1806
CARTOGRAPHIC RECONSTRUCTION

SQUARE BUTTE

UTM ZONE  14
MAP NUMBER  147

North Dakota

CONTOUR INTERVAL  100 FEET

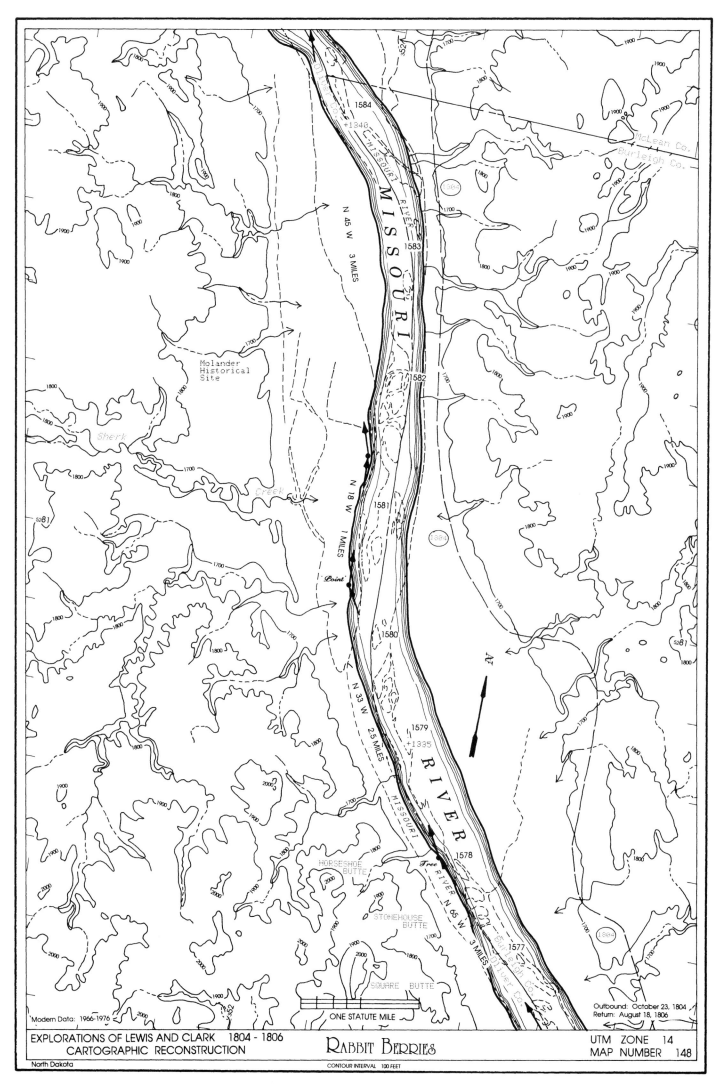

MISSOURI RIVER

1584
+1340

N 45 W
3 MILES

Molander
Historical
Site

1583

1582

N 18 W
1 MILES

1581

Point

1580

N 33 W

2.5 MILES

1579
+1335

N

HORSESHOE
BUTTE

Tree

1578

STONEHOUSE
BUTTE

N 65 W

3 MILES

1577

SQUARE BUTTE

Modern Data: 1966-1976

ONE STATUTE MILE

McLean Co.
Burleigh Co.

MISSOURI

RIVER

Outbound: October 23, 1804
Return: August 18, 1806

EXPLORATIONS OF LEWIS AND CLARK   1804 - 1806
CARTOGRAPHIC RECONSTRUCTION

North Dakota

RABBIT BERRIES

CONTOUR INTERVAL  100 FEET

UTM  ZONE   14
MAP  NUMBER   148

172

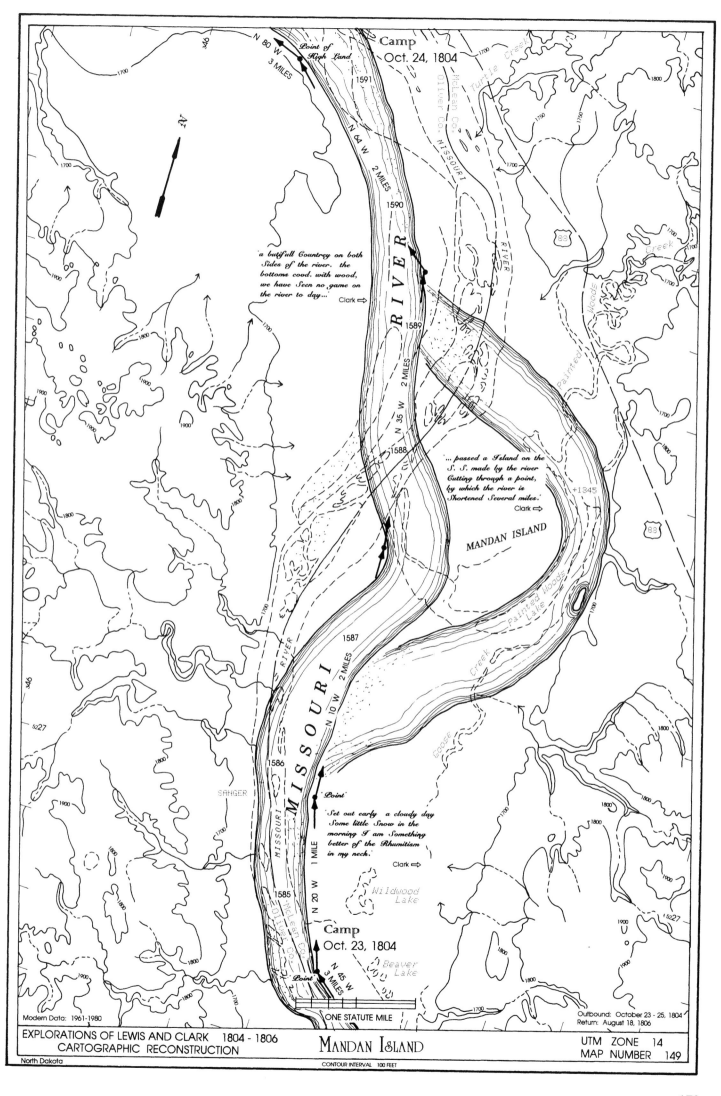

N 80 W
3 MILES

Point of
High Land

N

Camp
Oct. 24, 1804

1591

N 64 W
2 MILES

1590

*a butifull Countrey on both
Sides of the river. the
bottoms covd. with wood,
we have Seen no game on
the river to day...*
Clark ⇒

1589

N 35 W
2 MILES

1588

*... passed a Island on the
S. S. made by the river
Cutting through a point,
by which the river is
Shortened Several miles.*
Clark ⇒

+1345

MANDAN ISLAND

RIVER

1587

N 10 W
2 MILES

1586

SANGER

MISSOURI

*Point*

*Set out early a cloudy day
Some little Snow in the
morning I am Something
better of the Rhumitism
in my neck.*
Clark ⇒

Wildwood
Lake

N 20 W
1 MILE

1585

Camp
Oct. 23, 1804

Point

N 45 W
3 MILES

Beaver
Lake

ONE STATUTE MILE

Modern Data: 1961-1980

Outbound: October 23 - 25, 1804
Return: August 18, 1806

EXPLORATIONS OF LEWIS AND CLARK    1804 - 1806
CARTOGRAPHIC RECONSTRUCTION

North Dakota

MANDAN ISLAND

CONTOUR INTERVAL 100 FEET

UTM ZONE    14
MAP NUMBER    149

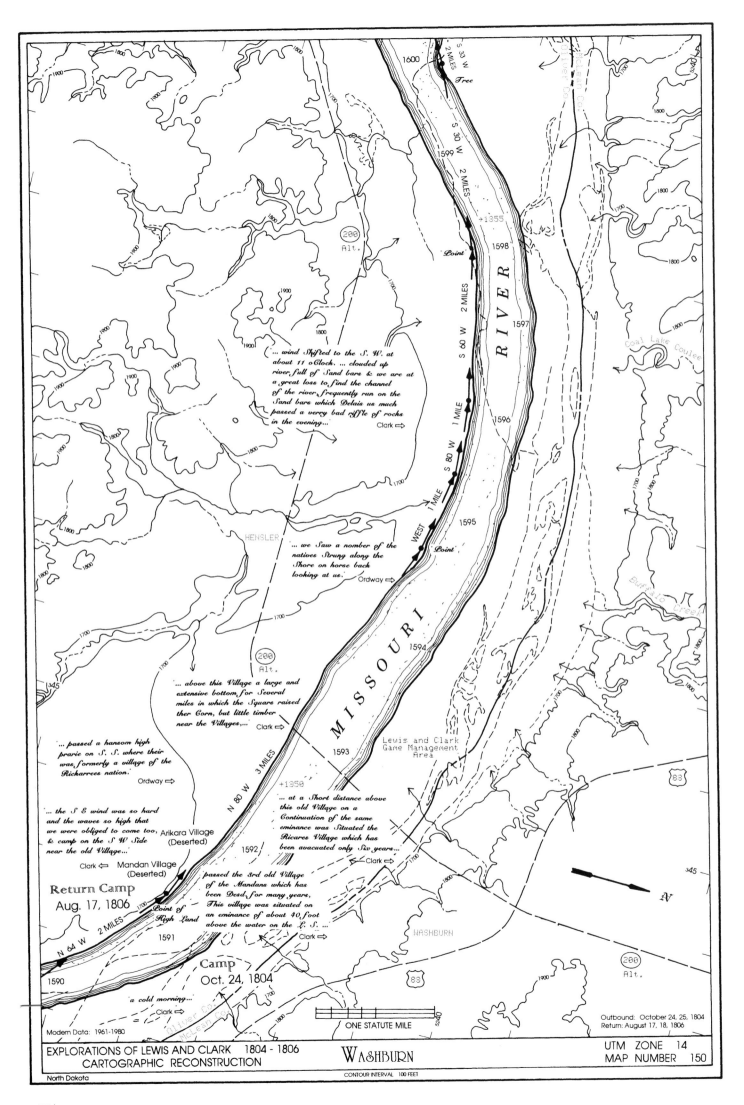

S 33 W
2 MILES
*Tree*
1600

S 30 W
2 MILES
1599

+1355
*Point*
1598

RIVER

1597

S 60 W
2 MILES

S 80 W 1 MILE

1596

*... wind Shifted to the S. W. at*
*about 11 o'Clock. ... clouded up*
*river, full of Sand bars & we are at*
*a great loss to find the channel*
*of the river, frequently run on the*
*Sand bars which Delais us much*
*passed a verry bad riffle of rocks*
*in the evening...*
Clark ⇨

1595

WEST 1 MILE

*... we Saw a number of the*
*natives Strung along the*
*Shore on horse back*
*looking at us.*
Ordway ⇨

*Point*

MISSOURI

1594

*... above this Village a large and*
*extensive bottom, for Several*
*miles in which the Squars raised*
*ther Corn, but little timber*
*near the Villages,....*
Clark ⇨

Lewis and Clark
Game Management
Area

1593

+1350

N 80 W 3 MILES

*... passed a hansom high*
*prarie on S. S. where their*
*was formerly a village of the*
*Richarrees nation.*
Ordway ⇨

*... at a Short distance above*
*this old Village on a*
*Continuation of the same*
*eminance was Situated the*
*Ricares Village which has*
*been avacuated only Six years...*
⇦ Clark

*... the S E wind was so hard*
*and the waves so high that*
*we were obliged to come too*
*& camp on the S W Side*
*near the old Village...*
Clark ⇦

Arikara Village
(Deserted)

1592

Mandan Village
(Deserted)

**Return Camp**
**Aug. 17, 1806**

*Point of*
*High Land*

N 64 W
2 MILES

1591

1590

*passed the 3rd old Village*
*of the Mandans which has*
*been Desd, for many years,*
*This village was situated on*
*an eminance of about 40 foot*
*above the water on the L. S. ....*
Clark ⇨

**Camp**
**Oct. 24, 1804**

*a cold morning...*
Clark ⇨

WASHBURN

N

Modern Data: 1961-1980

ONE STATUTE MILE

Outbound: October 24, 25, 1804
Return: August 17, 18, 1806

EXPLORATIONS OF LEWIS AND CLARK   1804 - 1806
CARTOGRAPHIC RECONSTRUCTION

WASHBURN

UTM ZONE 14
MAP NUMBER 150

North Dakota

CONTOUR INTERVAL 100 FEET

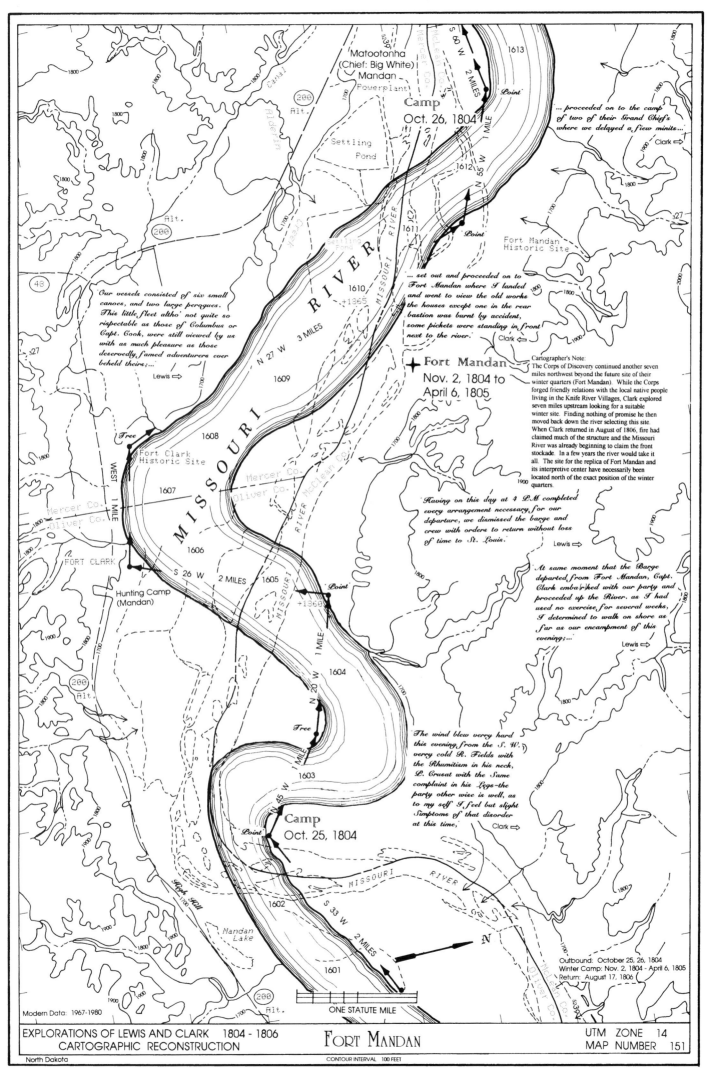

Matootonha
(Chief: Big White)
Mandan
Powerplant
Camp
Oct. 26, 1804

1613

2 MILES
N 80 W

1612
N 55 W

1611

Point

Point

...proceeded on to the camp
of two of their Grand Chiefs
where we delayed a few minits...

Clark ⇒

Fort Mandan
Historic Site

...set out and proceeded on to
Fort Mandan where I landed
and went to view the old works
the houses except one in the rear
bastion was burnt by accident,
some pickets were standing in front
next to the river.

Clark ⇐

Cartographer's Note:
The Corps of Discovery continued another seven
miles northwest beyond the future site of their
winter quarters (Fort Mandan). While the Corps
forged friendly relations with the local native people
living in the Knife River Villages, Clark explored
seven miles upstream looking for a suitable
winter site. Finding nothing of promise he then
moved back down the river selecting this site.
When Clark returned in August of 1806, fire had
claimed much of the structure and the Missouri
River was already beginning to claim the front
stockade. In a few years the river would take it
all. The site for the replica of Fort Mandan and
its interpretive center have necessarily been
located north of the exact position of the winter
quarters.

1900

Our vessels consisted of six small
canoes, and two large perogues.
This little fleet altho' not quite so
respectable as those of Columbus or
Capt. Cook, were still viewed by us
with as much pleasure as those
deservedly famed adventurers ever
beheld theirs;...

Lewis ⇒

MISSOURI    RIVER

1610

+1365

N 27 W    3 MILES

1609

Fort Mandan
Nov. 2, 1804 to
April 6, 1805

Having on this day at 4 P.M completed
every arrangement necessary for our
departure, we dismissed the barge and
crew with orders to return without loss
of time to St. Louis.

Lewis ⇒

Tree

Fort Clark
Historic Site

MISSOURI

1608

WEST    1 MILE

1607

Mercer Co.
Oliver Co.

River McClean Co.

Mercer Co.
Oliver Co.

FORT CLARK

1606

S 26 W    2 MILES

1605

MISSOURI

1 MILE

Point

+1360

At same moment that the Barge
departed from Fort Mandan, Capt.
Clark embarked with our party and
proceeded up the River. as I had
used no exercise for several weeks,
I determined to walk on shore as
far as our encampment of this
evening;...

Lewis ⇒

Hunting Camp
(Mandan)

1604

N 20 W

Tree

1 MILE

1603

N 45 W

Camp
Oct. 25, 1804

Point

The wind blew verry hard
this evening from the S. W.
verry cold R. Fields with
the Rhumitism in his neck,
P. Crusat with the Same
complaint in his Legs—the
party other wise is well, as
to my self I feel but slight
Simptoms of that disorder
at this time,

Clark ⇒

MISSOURI    RIVER

Ash Fall

1602

S 33 W

2 MILES

N

Mandan
Lake

1601

Outbound: October 25, 26, 1804
Winter Camp: Nov. 2, 1804 - April 6, 1805
Return: August 17, 1806

Modern Data: 1967-1980

ONE STATUTE MILE

EXPLORATIONS OF LEWIS AND CLARK    1804-1806
CARTOGRAPHIC RECONSTRUCTION

Fort Mandan

UTM ZONE    14
MAP NUMBER    151

North Dakota

CONTOUR INTERVAL    100 FEET

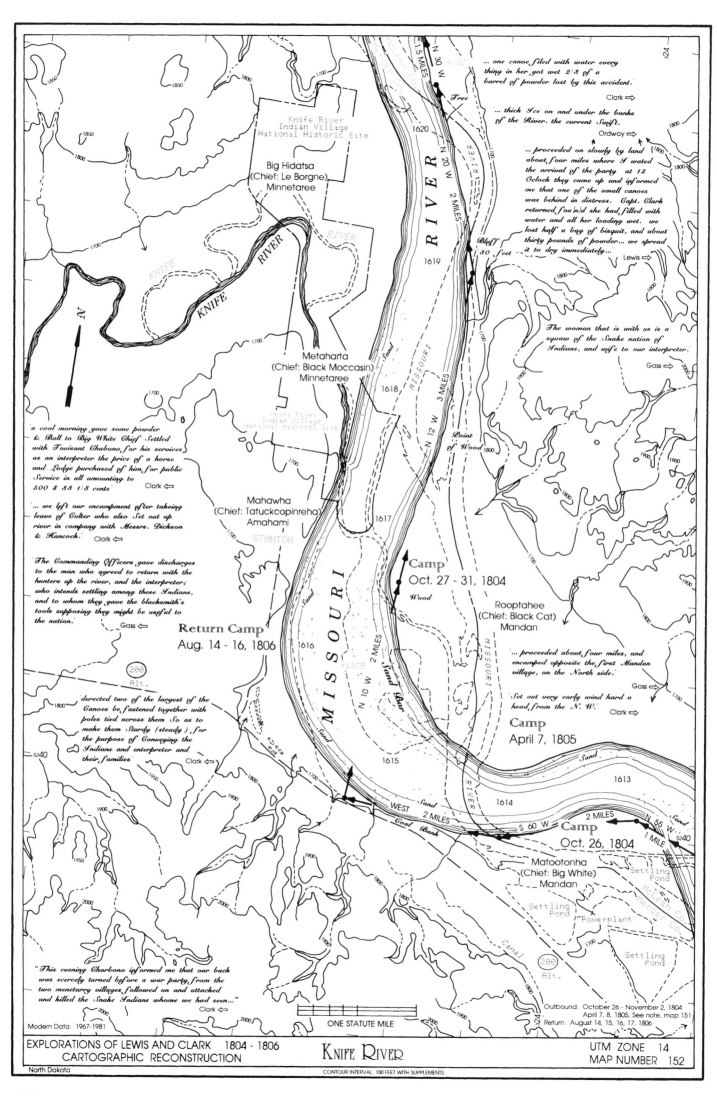

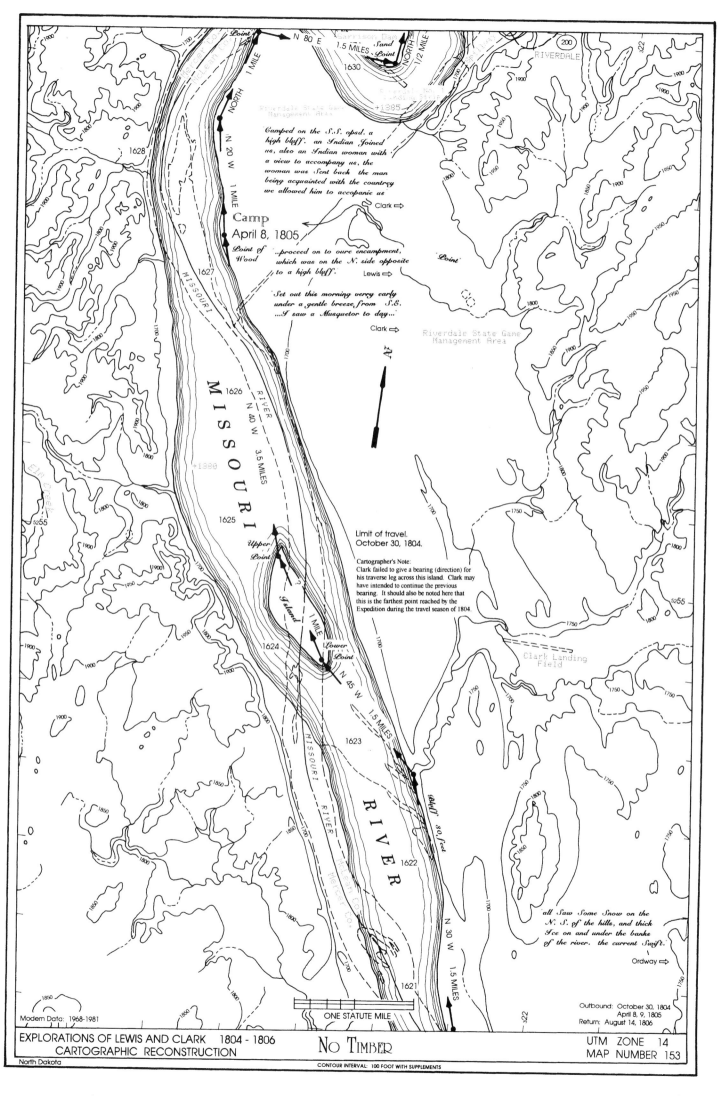

Point

N 80 E

Garrison Dam
1.5 MILES

Sand
Point

NORTH
1/2 MILE

200

RIVERDALE

1630

1 MILE

Riverdale No. 1
Landing Strip

NORTH

1628

1 MILE

N 20 W

+1585

Riverdale State Game
Management Area

*Camped on the S.S. opsd. a
high bluff. an Indian Joined
us, also an Indian woman with
a view to accompany us, the
woman was Sent back the man
being acquainted with the country
we allowed him to accopanie us*

Clark ⇒

Camp
April 8, 1805

1627

Point of
Wood

*..proceed on to oure encampment,
which was on the N. side opposite
to a high bluff.*

'Point'

Lewis ⇒

MISSOURI

*Set out this morning verey early
under a gentle breeze from S.E.
....I saw a Musquetor to day...*

Clark ⇒

Riverdale State Game
Management Area

N

1800

1626

RIVER

N 40 W
3.5 MILES

+1580

1625

Limit of travel.
October 30, 1804.

Upper
Point

**Cartographer's Note:**
Clark failed to give a bearing (direction) for
his traverse leg across this island. Clark may
have intended to continue the previous
bearing. It should also be noted here that
this is the farthest point reached by the
Expedition during the travel season of 1804.

5255

Island

1 MILE

1624

Lower
Point

N 45 W
1.5 MILES

1700

Clark Landing
Field

1623

Bluff 80 feet

MISSOURI RIVER

RIVER

1622

*all Saw Some Snow on the
N. S. of the hills, and thick
Ice on and under the banks
of the river. the current Swift.*

Ordway ⇒

1621

N 30 W
1.5 MILES

ONE STATUTE MILE

322

Outbound: October 30, 1804
April 8, 9, 1805
Return: August 14, 1806

Modern Data: 1968-1981

EXPLORATIONS OF LEWIS AND CLARK    1804 - 1806
CARTOGRAPHIC RECONSTRUCTION

North Dakota

No Timber

CONTOUR INTERVAL: 100 FOOT WITH SUPPLEMENTS

UTM ZONE    14
MAP NUMBER  153

# INDEXES TO THE
# LEWIS AND CLARK TRAIL MAPS,
# VOLUME I

Outbound and Return Camps

Outbound and Return Dates

Selected Locations and Events

Place Names

# Outbound and Return Camps

# Outbound and Return Dates

# Selected Locations and Events

# Place Names

185

191